D1162723

The Effects of World War I:
The Class War after the Great War:
The Rise of Communist Parties
in East Central Europe, 1918–1921

Edited by
Ivo Banac

832589

EAST EUROPEAN MONOGRAPHS NO. CXXXVII

Copyright © 1983 by Atlantic Research and Publications
Library of Congress Catalog Card Number 82-63191
ISBN 0-88033-028-7

Printed in the United States of America

ATLANTIC STUDIES

Brooklyn College Studies on Society in Change No. 32
Editor-in-Chief Béla K. Király

WAR AND SOCIETY IN EAST CENTRAL EUROPE
Vol. XIII

Contents

Acknowledgements

Brooklyn College Program on Society in Change conducts research, organizes conferences, and publishes scholarly books. The Program was commissioned by the President of Brooklyn College. It has been encouraged and supported by Dr. Robert L. Hess, the President of Brooklyn College. The National Endowment for the Humanities awarded the Program a research grant for the years of 1978–1981, which was renewed for another three-year term (1981–1984). Without these substantial and much-appreciated supports, the Program could not realize its goals, indeed could not exist. Additional financial contributions helped us in completing the research, holding conferences, and covering the costs of preparing the manuscript for publication. Among those institutions that aided our work are the International Research and Exchanges Board and the Joint Committee on Eastern Europe of the American Council of Learned Societies and the Social Science Research Council. Part of the production cost was borne by a Montclair State College Alumni Association Faculty Grant.

The copyediting was done by John G. Ackerman, and the preparation of the manuscript for publication by Mrs. Dorothy Meyerson, Assistant Director, and Mr. Jonathan A. Chanis, Assistant Editor of Brooklyn College Program on Society in Change.

For all these institutions and personalities, I wish to express my most sincere appreciation and thanks.

Highland Lakes, New Jersey
March 15, 1983

Béla K. Király
Professor Emeritus
Editor-in-Chief

Red Wave in East Central Europe: A Repercussion of a Total War

BÉLA K. KIRÁLY

The present volume is the thirteenth in a series that, when completed, will constitute a comprehensive survey of the many aspects of the interrelationship between warfare on the one hand, and economic, social, and political changes on the other in East Central Europe. These volumes deal with the peoples whose homelands lie between the Germans to the west, the Russians to the east and north, and the Mediterranean and Adriatic Seas to the south. They constitute a particular civilization, one that is an integral part of Europe yet substantially different from the West. Within the area there are intriguing variations in language, religion, and government; so, too, are there differences in concepts of national defense, of the characters of the armed forces, and of the ways of waging war. Study of this complex subject demands a multidisciplinary approach; therefore, the contributors to this volume — as is the case with all of the other books in this series — have been drawn from among scholars of various disciplines and universities of the United States, Canada, and Western Europe. We have also sought to include studies by scholars from the East Central European states in our volumes.

Our investigation focuses on comparative surveys of military behavior and the public's attitudes toward that behavior. We try to identify what these attitudes were under the pressure of war and revolution and to ascertain which of them were peculiar to East Central European societies, which, if any, were socially and culturally determined, and which were due to particular circumstances. Each of the essays in this volume, for example, considers the disintegrating effects of Communist movements on the armies of the old regimes during and immediately after World War I.

Our methodology takes into account that in the last three decades the study of war, revolution, and national defense systems has moved away from a narrow concern with battles, campaigns, and leaders and has come to concern itself with the evolution of the entire society. In fact, historians, political scientists, sociologists, philosophers, and other students of war and national defense now recognize the interdependence of changes in society and changes in warfare; they accept the proposition that military institutions closely reflect the character of the society of which they are a part. This recognition is one of the keystones of our approach to the subject.

Works in Western languages adequately cover the diplomatic, political, intellectual, social, and economic histories of these peoples and this area. In contrast, few substantial studies of their national defense systems have yet appeared in Western languages, and none have analyzed the effect of the postwar Communist wave on the armed forces of East Central Europe as a whole. Thus, taken together, this and the other volumes in the series are at once a pioneering effort and a comprehensive study of war and society in East Central Europe.

The present volume focuses on the period immediately after World War I in an attempt to analyze the euphoric wave of socialist revolution that swept through the lands of East Central Europe even as the monarchies collapsed, national boundaries were redrawn, and the Bolsheviks issued repeated calls to worldwide proletarian revolution. Each of the contributors attempts to answer the fundamental question — why did this Red Wave erupt simultaneously throughout East Central Europe at the end of World War I? There are very few historical events for which one can isolate a single overriding cause, though in the case of the Red Wave, World War I was, in fact, just such a pivotal cause. Let us consider why this was so.

War, if reason prevails, is waged to obtain a peace better than that which existed prior to the hostilities. During the nineteenth and early twentieth centuries — an era characterized by balance of power and limited wars — the victor usually attained its goals in full or at least in part through peace negotiations that often involved compromises. This was still the case during the last war cycle before World War I. Russia lost the Crimean War, and consequently had to give up the southern part of Bessarabia and demilitarize her Black Sea shores. In 1859, France and its Sardinian ally were victorious. As a result, Austria had to relinquish Lombardy, satisfying part of the victor's goal. In 1866 Prussia won, consequently expelling Austria from Germany and dissolving the German Confederation. In 1870 the Germans won, and France had to give up Alsace and Lorraine and reconcile itself to the unification of Germany. In 1905 Russia lost, enabling Japan to expand its possessions in the Pacific at Russia's expense. In the two Balkan Wars, the Balkan states won, the consequence being the virtual elimination of the Ottoman Empire from the Balkans. In all these wars the belligerents entered the war with a design for the postwar peace and the victors attained all or part of what they had intended. Thus the peace was, without exception, better for the victors than the situation they had enjoyed before the outbreak of hostilities.

This was not, however, the case in World War I. None of the great powers went to war in 1914 with a definitive design for the postwar peace.[1] In fact, not one of the belligerents — victors or vanquished — envisaged in 1914 anything that resembled the actual consequences of World War I. Except for a small band who followed Jozef Piłsudski into Russia even before the official declaration of war in 1914, no one went to war to restitute Poland or to create a Yugoslav state. Even the small group of political and military leaders in Belgrade, who wanted the war more than anyone else, envisaged only the enlargement of Serbia as the result of a possible victory. Nor did anyone enter the war to create Czechoslovakia. Even Thomas Masaryk went into exile in the fall of 1914 only to agitate for the transformation of the Habsburg monarchy from its dualistic into a trialistic form, that is, to achieve for the Czechs rights identical to those which the Hungarians had achieved in 1867. No one went to war to destroy the German, Russian, Ottoman, or Habsburg Empires, and most certainly no one sought to create the first socialistic state — the USSR. Not even Lenin had dreamed that it would emerge in the near future. No one planned or envisaged a Red Wave in postwar East Central Europe. Yet these were the wholly unexpected and profound results of World War I.

Surely the powers of Europe went to war without clearly defined war aims. In fact, until 1916, excepting a few peace feelers, no meaningful peace proposal was made by the responsible governments of the belligerents. In late 1916, however, a series of peace proposals were suddenly put foward, each of them without exception advocating a compromise. They contained no demands for unconditional surrender — a concept typical of a total war — or for a dictated peace. No one demanded the partition of the Habsburg Empire, the single political structure that so deeply affected each of the Communist movements in East Central Europe.

The most spectacular peace effort was, of course, the Sixtus Affair. In early August 1917, after a long and arduous negotiation in that process, the Entente powers' proposition to the Habsburg monarch was positive in the extreme. It made no mention of the empire's dissolution, but instead proposed the enlargement of the Dual Monarchy. In fact, prior to the Brest-Litovsk Treaty of February 9, 1918, all peace proposals advocated compromise. President Woodrow Wilson's Fourteen Points,

promulgated on January 19, 1918, held that the place of Austria-
Hungary should be safeguarded among the nations.[2]

Two facts are demonstrated here. First, it was the Entente's intention
that compromise be an integral part of peace negotiations. Second, and
more important, the dissolution of Austria-Hungary was not contem-
plated by the Western powers until early 1918. The question arises: why
did a multitude of peace proposals begin to emerge in late 1916, whereas
none had been put forward before? Also, why was the original spirit of
compromise replaced by a determination to fight to the bitter end and to
impose a treaty on the vanquished rather than to negotiate with them? It
is no oversimplification to state that one of the major causes of this
change of attitudes and purposes was the change in the nature of
warfare in 1916 and 1917 — the period during which World War I was
transformed into a total war.

Total war is an armed combat waged with all national resources —
human, as well as material. In total war, big battalions are neither more
nor less important than energy and financial resources, farms, factories,
mines, transportation systems, and research establishments. All become
elements in waging the war and, subsequently, legitimate targets of
hostile action. The unrestricted British blockade of the Central Powers
and the German reply — unrestricted submarine warfare — are cases
in point. Since all soldiers and civilians participate in the war effort in
total war, the maintenance of morale, the efforts to increase the population's will to fight and to destroy the enemy's, becomes pivotal. Thus,
psychological warfare is a basic ingredient of the war effort, no less
important than armed combat and economic warfare.[3]

Whether World War I was a total war is a question that can be
resolved by analyzing the events of 1916 and early 1917. Between
February 1916 and mid-May of 1917, three battles changed the face of
World War I. In the Battle of Verdun, 522,000 Frenchmen and 434,000
Germans died. In the Battle of the Somme, 615,000 Allied soldiers
(420,000 British and 195,000 French) and 650,000 Germans died. The
Nivelle offensive, which lasted from April 29 to May 20, 1917, and was
supposed to break through the German lines, resulted in the death of
120,000 Frenchmen in five days. Even so, the offensive did not produce
any mentionable advance in the position of the French front.[4] This
outcome precipitated widespread mutiny in the French army.[5] Only the
extraordinary discipline of the Entente media and the deficiency of the
German intelligence service prevented the German High Command
from learning that the French sectors of the Western front were virtually
denuded. These battles, with their unprecedented waste of human lives
and materiel, and their remarkable lack of success, revealed that the

war was hopelessly stalemated. Rapid industrial development and technological advances prior to and during the war created a formidable firepower. At the same time, they failed to produce equivalent means of mobility. (This happened only later, in the interwar decades.) The result was a deadlock in the trenches. Statesmen saw but two alternatives: either to start peace negotiations and accept compromises, or to push the war effort to its extreme limits and dictate peace to the vanquished. This situation explains the flurry of peace proposals, most of which date from late 1916.

Since all the efforts at compromise had failed for one reason or another, only the second alternative appeared to remain open. Subsequently, the world was dragged into the continuation of the first total war in modern times. As has already been indicated, psychological warfare is a basic ingredient of total war. Since propaganda is a major weapon in this kind of warfare, it is not surprising that its role grew by leaps and bounds, to the point of madness. In a life and death struggle, a nation's propaganda serves only to strengthen the morale of its own people and to undermine the enemy's will to fight. Truth plays no role in such efforts.[6] On both sides war propaganda fostered the belief that one's own cause was pure and just whereas the enemy's was the embodiment of evil. It created a state of mind which tolerated no compromise and which, once the war had ended, proved slow in yielding its distortions. This war propaganda poisoned European minds and created a cancer more harmful and more lasting than the physical losses caused by the war itself. The failure of compromise led to a constant intensification of combat which in the end resulted in total war. And total war shaped the notion of total victory, and led to a reflex action: dictated peace, a peace that knew no victors. Even though the victorious leaders foresaw that a dictated peace would sow the seeds of future wars, they seemed either unwilling or unable to overcome its momentum. The statesmen of the victors could have shaped history in harmony with their beliefs. Instead, they declined that august role. World War I, therefore, became what Raymond Aron has called a "hyperbolic war," one that created more problems than it resolved.[7]

Among the problems created was the partition of Hungary and the interrelated establishment of the Hungarian Soviet Republic, the most substantial success and failure of communism in East Central Europe. The Hungarian experience with communism was a direct consequence of World War I and the dissolution of the Dual Monarchy, as were all the other Communist movements discussed in this volume.

The material and even the human losses of World War I healed, some faster, others slower, but they healed. The psychological and emotional damages healed very slowly if at all. The changes in East Central Europe as well as the reverberations of the Red Wave left deep and lasting scars. The antagonisms, domestic, social, and international, did not diminish but rather increased. East Central Europe did not move closer to a fraternal community of nations; instead, further rifts developed. Communism failed as an alternative to the domestic and international ills that beset the region. This failure did not make the second Red Wave, which followed World War II, more successful or more popular than the first. And though communism remains an important force in East Central Europe today, it evokes none of the promise that galvanized its supporters during the Red Years.

This volume investigates one of the most profound effects of World War I on East Central European society. Other works in the series treat other aspects of this complex, multifaceted topic. Indeed, four volumes that are either already published or being published simultaneously with this book should be viewed as its companions. Together they offer a broad view of the impact that World War I, the first total war, had on East Central Europe. These companion volumes, all part of the series War and Society in East Central Europe, are:

Vol. V. *Essays on World War I: Origins and Prisoners of War.* Edited by Samuel R. Williamson, Jr. and Peter Pastor, 1983.

Vol. VI. *Essays on World War I: Total War and Peacemaking, A Case Study on Trianon.* Edited by Béla K. Király, Peter Pastor, and Ivan Sanders, 1983.

Vol. IX. Kálmán Janics. *Czechoslovak Policy and Hungarian Minority, 1945–1948,* 1982.

Vol. XII. István I. Mocsy. *The Effects of World War I: The Uprooted: Hungarian Refugees and Their Impact on Hungarian Domestic Politics: 1918–1921,* 1983.

NOTES

1. Kenneth J. Calder, *Britain and the Origins of New Europe, 1914–1918* (London, 1976), p. 8. Wilfried Fest, *Peace or Partition* (New York, 1978), pp. 7–9. For a brief but excellent summary of the war aims, see Gerhard Schulz, *Revolutions and the Peace Treaties.* This book also identifies peace feelers in 1915; first swallows that did not herald the arrival of the spring of peace. On war aims, see A. J. P. Taylor, "The War Aims of the Allies in the First World War," in R. Pares and A. J. P. Taylor, eds., *Essays Presented to Sir Lewis Namier.* For Hungary's position, see Norman Stone, "Hungary and

the Crisis of July, 1914," in Walter Laqueur and George L. Mosse, eds., *1914: The Coming of The First World War* (New York, 1966), pp. 147–164.

2. *Congressional Record,* vol. 56 (1918), pt. I., pp. 680–681. Richard B. Morris, ed., *Basic Documents in American History* (New York, 1956), pp. 153–157.

3. Charles Roetter, *The Art of Psychological Warfare, 1914–1945* (New York, 1974), pp. 27–94.

4. For the place of World War I in the framework of wars since the defeat of Napoleon, see J. David Singer and Melvin Small, *The Wages of War 1816–1965; A Statistical Handbook.*

5. Richard M. Watt, *Dare Call It Treason* (New York, 1963).

6. Arthur Ponsonby, M.P., *Falsehood in War Time. Containing an Assortment of Lies Circulated throughout the Nations during the Great War* (Torrance, Calif., 1980). First published in Britain in 1928.

7. Raymond Aron, *The Century of Total War* (Boston, 1955), pp. 24–31.

The Emergence of Communism in East Central Europe, 1918–1921

IVO BANAC

For the past several decades or so it has been more or less an accepted opinion that Communism is somehow a logical culmination of history in Eastern Europe, the only political solution possible for the problems of a vast area of the continent that has long lagged behind the West. The idea of East European apartness is itself a relatively recent one. To be sure, certain areas of Eastern Europe long had a spiritual distinction in that they clung to the Eastern church; and the domination of the Ottoman Empire also made for certain differences in the Balkans. But the notion that Warsaw, Prague, Budapest, and Dubrovnik were somehow less European than London, Paris, and Vienna became firmly fixed in the collective consciousness of the West only in the last two centuries. It was a natural accompaniment to the rise of capitalist production in the Atlantic states and the growing importance of the vernacular. As the unity of Europe became shattered, the countries of Western Europe began to think of the countries lying to the east as backward and impenetrable, and in the process the great diversity among the lands and peoples east of the imaginary dividing line from the mouth of the Elbe to the Adriatic basin was lost sight of. The whole area was lumped together as a strange and backward land.

Communism, therefore, appeared to be a second defining feature —a political system which issued simultaneously from the despotic traditions of the East as a response to the urgent need to modernize — that is, Europeanize. And the model was Soviet Communism, adopted with only minor variations. This idea, like the idea of the uniform foreignness of East Central Europe, is a vast simplification. As the essays in the present volume show, East European Communism is extremely diverse and has been so from the very beginning of its development. Half a century ago, there was almost no suggestion of the Stalinist metamorphosis of Communism. The various parties faithfully mirrored the peculiarities of their national and regional histories — even when, as in

Poland, where the Communists went out of their way to oppose the mass petition for national independence, it was in a reverse image.

The early Communists were frequently urban particularists and individualists who, even when they were not intellectuals, had a fine sense for political controversy. But they were mere dilettantes at the art of revolution. The extreme Left of the Second International may have elicited its strongest support in Eastern and East Central Europe (besides the Russian Bolsheviks it counted the SDKPiL and the PPS-Left in partitioned Poland, Blagoev's *Tesnyatsi* in Bulgaria, the followers of Tucović in Serbia, and of Dobrogeanu-Gherea in Romania), but it cannot be said that the orthodoxy of some of the ultra-leftist groups from the East complemented Lenin's revolutionary activism. The inability to turn the obstacles of nationalist aspirations and peasant land hunger into political advantages was not merely un-Bolshevik; it also demonstrated that the attractiveness of Bolshevism frequently had little to do with its dissembling features. Moreover, various "centrist" and "opportunist" tendencies also thrived in the East and in some cases (Bohemia) oddly proved as drawn to Moscow as any of the Left Socialists.

Thus the October Revolution did not crack open the Socialist movement, because it had never been one solid mass, and at least on the eve of the Great War was already very un-unified. The Bolsheviks made an attempt to fashion a militant front against "opportunism," but, the Twenty-One Points notwithstanding, the structure was much too sprawling. It was not even within the power of the Bolsheviks to bring all the warring leftist factions together. Yet, if Lenin had not been successful — or rather, had there not been the crisis of European civilization which culminated in the Russian Revolution — the cracks in the Social Democratic movement might not have been final.

The revolution in Russia engendered such optimism in Socialist ranks that even the levelheaded old Marxists, with their faith in the steady movement of mighty historical forces, suddenly assumed that the outbreak of worldwide proletarian revolution was imminent. Under the circumstances, ordinary coalition politics seemed unsuitable and unnecessary. Why court the peasants or the disaffected nationalities when all problems were shortly to be resolved in one grand turnabout? The very success of the Bolsheviks thus encouraged euphoric inertia which stamped the Red Wave of 1918–1920. The collapse of the monarchies, the reshaping of national borders, and, in some areas, the temporary inability of the middle classes to find appropriate political expression inspired revolutionary expectations where there was no real basis for them at all. At no point during the Red Wave were the new Communists of Eastern Europe capable of seizing power, notwithstanding Béla Kun's brief experiment in proletarian dictatorship. The Red Wave, with all its strikes, rebellions, peasant uprisings, and occasional bloodshed, demonstrated not only the weak spots of the established order but, even more, the weakness of Socialist Revolution.

The Russian Revolution, in other words, was a unique phenomenon. The conditions that produced it could not be duplicated anywhere else in Europe, even in those areas of the defeated Central Powers which most resembled Russia in social structure. As the Tsarist political edifice collapsed in ruins, the Bolsheviks came forward as an elementary force, organized, articulate, with an attractive program. They were doubly favored in having leaders of genius and originality and foes of remarkable ineptitude. Furthermore, despite their internationalist outlook, they had no intention of altering Russia's national integrity. In Eastern Europe, this Russianism of the Bolsheviks was exaggerated. The Russophobia was understandable in view of the history of Russian expansionism in the area, and although it did not operate everywhere or in the same way, the nationalism that was partly a consequence of it was the best barrier against the Revolutionary Left, especially in the countries that gained or consolidated their national independence after the war.

Inspired by the premise that there were no irreconcilable contradictions among peoples of the same lineage, Poles, and Romanians, dominant Czechs in Czechoslovakia, and Serbs in Yugoslavia experienced their own national apotheosis in 1918. To the French syndicalist Alfred Rosmer, who passed through Prague on the way to Moscow in 1920, the Czechs "spoke of the Russian Revolution unsympathetically, in an aloof manner; Czechoslovakia was going to show the world what a real democracy was."

The failure of the Red Wave permitted not only an opening to rightist dictatorship, which in one form or another gripped most of the area by the early 1930s, but also the slow "Bolshevization" of the Communist parties. For as long as they were incapable of effecting revolutionary change in their home countries, the Communists were reduced to bondage by Moscow. Only in Czechoslovakia, where the party continued to function legally, did the Communists retain significant political influence. The exciting years of the Red Wave were remembered as a period of independence, when numerous political directions seemed possible. A historicist redefining of the Communist movement glossed over this heritage to justify various later changes. But the full history of the Red Wave makes possible a new understanding of subsequent trends in East European Communism. It also shows that, compared with the 1918–1921 period, the Stalinist homogenization of Eastern

Europe was no more than a passing phenomenon. And it shows, too, that the phenomenon of Communism in Eastern Europe may also undergo transformation.

The Origins of the Communist Party in Poland, 1918–1921

TADEUSZ SZAFAR

The Communist takeover in Poland in 1944 was imposed on a reluctant nation by the sheer military force of the Soviet Army and with the explicit acquiescence of the Western powers. There was — at least in the preliminary stages — only token participation by Polish Communists in the Soviet emigration and inside Poland. These circumstances have unavoidably led politicians, and even scholars, to distort the origins and early development of the Polish Communist Party, all too often dismissing it as "a rather insignificant revolutionary movement of antistate opposition."[1] Though this sweeping statement contains a grain of truth, it ignores the fact that at one time the Communist movement was an indigenous, substantial force on the Polish political scene. In that part of the world now loosely defined as East-Central Europe, Polish communism for several decades — in the last quarter of the nineteenth and the first quarter of the twentieth centuries — was among the most influential components of the international revolutionary movement. Profoundly rooted in the native political culture, it left an unmistakable imprint on the Polish national liberation movement, on workers' organizations, and on several generations of Polish intellectuals. At times it was ideologically and politically creative and innovative. It strongly influenced similar movements in adjacent countries, especially in Germany and Russia, and supplied them with many of their best-known leaders. It was, in short, a force to be reckoned with.

In the months and years immediately after World War I, however, this proud movement fairly quickly degenerated into a small sect, increasingly preoccupied with its own internal squabbles, even then barely comprehensible to public opinion and at present virtually meaningless. Moreover, it was later transformed into an appendage of Soviet foreign policy, or even of Soviet secret services. This entire process took place in a relatively short period of time, between 1918 and 1923, with the 1920 Polish-Soviet war as its watershed. In this chapter I attempt to trace the early stage of this development, from the first "unity" congress

of the Communist Workers' Party of Poland (16 December 1918),[2] until
the party's reconstruction after its virtual demise during the battle of
Warsaw.

Even today, over six decades after these events, their scholarly
evaluation *sine era et studio* presents a difficult, if not an impossible task.
Historical data and most of the contemporary publications are fairly
well known,[3] but the most interesting primary sources, in particular
those on internal party organizational matters and ideological or political divergences, if extant at all, are deposited in central party archives in
Moscow and (on microfilms) in Warsaw. Accessible only to orthodox
party historians and researchers, these sources become generally known
only insofar as they are quoted in authorized publications. There is no
possibility of checking the accuracy of such quotations, much less of
tracing additional documents, many of which are conceivably ignored
because of their incompatibility with the current party line.

Even with such a limited souce-base, however, it seems possible,
indeed necessary, to sum up — at least in its general outline — the
convoluted development of Polish communism in the first years after
World War I. The picture that emerges does not support the simplistic
view that disparages the movement as a mere tool of foreign interests.
Still less does it conform to the obligatory Communist picture of a party
moving steadily forward according to the historical logic of Marxism-
Leninism, overcoming the legacy of "Luxemburgist errors" and eventually embracing the uniquely correct "Leninist line."

The Communist party in Poland (KPRP) was among the first organizations of its kind to emerge in postwar Europe. It held its founding
congress in Warsaw on 16 December 1918, more than a fortnight before
the numerically much smaller *Spartakusbund* proclaimed itself the
Communist Party of Germany.[4] Unlike virtually all other Communist
parties in and outside Europe, it was not the product of a split sparked
by a left-wing revolutionary minority in an existing social-democratic or
socialist party. In Poland, on the contrary, the "unity congress" was the
result of a merger between two long-established political parties. Both
of them had been weakened considerably by the war and subsequent
revolutionary upheavals, which scattered a large percentage of their
leaders throughout Central and Eastern Europe. These Polish socialists
were truly internationalist in spirit; they believed the world revolution
to be one and indivisible and acted on this belief, joining the local
battles without reservations. Some of them perished — Rosa Luxemburg and Jan Tyszka (Leon Jogiches) being the best-known examples.
Many others, especially those who were in Russia, stayed where they

were, convinced that by serving the new Soviet state as soldiers, diplomats, or policemen they were also promoting the cause of revolution in Poland. As a result, the leadership of the Communist Party in Poland consisted, at best, of people of the second, or even third, caliber.

Though the merger that led to the founding of the KPRP was arranged according to the principle of parity ("equal rights"), this principle did not extend to ideological matters. In the realm of ideology, the Social Democratic Party of the Kingdom of Poland and Lithuania (SDKPiL) was the unquestioned senior partner. This party traced its origins back to the first Polish Marxist party, *Proletariat* (1882–1886), and had been constituted formally in 1893. In the Second International the SDKPiL enjoyed enormous prestige, largely due to the exceptional intellectual and organiztional qualities of its leaders — Rosa Luxemburg, Jan Tyszka, Julian Marchlewski, Feliks Dzierżynski, and Adolf Warski (Warszawski). All of them spent most of their lives in political emigration and were active not only in the Polish but also in the Russian and German revolutionary movements, consistently standing on the extreme left of these parties.

The SDKPil has been characterized as "more of a pressure group in international Socialism than a political party," but this description must be qualified.[5] During the short periods when it was allowed to act more or less freely (e.g., during the 1905–1906 revolution in Russian Poland, and in Warsaw under the German occupation, 1916–1917), the SDKPiL managed to win the active support of all segments of the working class and of the intelligentsia. Such support also belies the claim, still made today in the name of orthodox Leninism, that the SDKPiL was guilty of the "sins of Luxemburgism": an alleged "national nihilism" and the underestimation of the revolutionary potential of peasantry. Indeed, on both those issues it was Luxemburg who remained loyal to Marxist doctrine and Lenin who attempted to revise it. Its contemporaries generally considered the SDKPiL part and parcel of mainstream European socialism, while the Bolsheviks were viewed as tainted with an alien ("Asian") streak of "putschism."

The differences of opinion between Lenin and Luxemburg on the national and agrarian questions bore, in any case, a rather tactical character. The problems of party organization were the most important stumbling block preventing wholehearted, long-term cooperation between them. Though confined to conspiratorial activities under tsarist rule, the SDKPiL wanted to become a mass party, modeled chiefly on the SPD. It rejected the Leninist concept of an avant-garde party that substitutes for the working class and aims at dictatorship over it. When, after the collapse of the 1905–1906 revolution, SDKPiL finally agreed to

join the Social-Democratic Workers' Party of Russia (RSDRP), unified
on a federative basis that had long been anathema to Lenin, it did so
only on its own terms, safeguarding its full political autonomy within the
newly created framework. In retaliation Lenin began his campaign,
which lasted many years, to split the SDKPiL, coupled with an "ideological" offensive against Rosa Luxemburg herself. He finally succeeded
in 1911, when the SDKPiL broke into two warring factions. Still, the
"splitters" (*rozłamowcy*) around the Warsaw committee did not deviate
at all from the official party line as represented by Rosa Luxemburg and
the rest of the Main Committee (*zarządowcy*) in the West European
emigration.[6]

Lenin had deliberately provoked the split because he resented the
criticism of Bolshevik organizational policies by the SDKPiL leadership,
and the authority the Polish party enjoyed in the Second International.[7]
The breakup proceeded along personal lines and it began to heal as soon
as the outbreak of war prevented Lenin from influencing the SDKPiL
organization inside Poland. The split was finally overcome by late 1916,
its only lasing result being that a number of Polish revolutionaries —
Czesław Hanecki (Jakub Fürstenberg) and Karol Radek (Sobelsohn)
in Western Europe, and many others in Russia — joined the Bolsheviks, serving Lenin in various capacities before, during, and after the
October Revolution.[8]

The other founder of the Communist party in Poland, the Polish
Socialist Party–Left Wing (*PPS–Lewica*), was itself a product of a split
that had occurred in 1906. The PPS, another component of the workers'
movement in Poland (in Russian Poland, to be precise), broke up when
its right wing, led by Józef Piłsudski, was exluded from the party for
putting the cause of Polish unification and independence — by armed
insurrection, if necessary — above the class struggle of a proleterian
revolution. During the prewar period the PPS–Lewica drew closer to
the SDKPiL, but it continued to object to the latter's commitment to
unconditional internationalism. The main obstacle on the road to unification was a tangle of personal prejudices unavoidable in political exile.
Lenin's intrigues, too, were a major factor in keeping the two parties
apart. Still, by 1914 the conditions for a merger seemed to be ripening.
The International Socialist Bureau urged unification as part of its effort
to reconcile all the warring factions in the all-Russian revolutionary
movement. Consequently, during the war years, the two SDKPiL
factions closely collaborated with PPS–Lewica, both in exile (in the
Zimmerwald antiwar movement and later in the Russian 1917 revolution) and in Poland, notwithstanding their unresolved personal and
political differences.

In the fall of 1918, the PPS–Lewica was the primary advocate of unification. It had finally assimilated the SDKPiL political and ideological platform *in toto,* and, back in 1916, part of its membership had voluntarily joined the sister party. The SDKPiL — especially the former "splitters" — held back from a reconciliation to the very end, however. Apparently its leaders feared that the newcomers were not yet sufficiently purged of their alleged "nationalism," which might compromise the party's ideological purity.

When unification was finally decided, however, not all of the PPS–Lewica joined the new Communist party. One faction — the "Workers' Opposition," based mainly in Łódź and led by Antoni Szczerkowski, backed out at the last moment. It later joined with the *PPS–Frakcja Rewolucyjna* (a product of the 1906 split in PPS) to form by early 1919 a unified Polish Socialist Party (PPS) which also included the Galician Social-Democratic Party (PPSD) and Polish socialist organizations in the Prussian partition. A considerable part of the party intelligentsia, including some very well known intellectuals prominent in interwar Poland, also refused to accept the merger with the SDKPiL, but did not join the PPS either. They retired from active politics, but contributed significantly to the creation of an atmosphere of sympathy for the extreme left, giving it a certain respectability even when the Communists put themselves beyond the pale by supporting the Soviet invasion in 1920.[9]

Although by 1917 virtually all the ethnically Polish lands either formed part of the German and Austro-Hungarian empires or were under the military occupation of the Central Powers, the revolutionary upheavals in Russia had strong repercussions in Poland. Their influence on public opinion, and specifically on the formation of a Communist party, have been greatly exaggerated by Communist historians, both Polish and Soviet, however. The Polish revolutionary movement had always been oriented toward the West. It shared the universal expectation that revolution was imminent in Germany and in Austria and continued to draw inspiration from the social-democratic parties (or, at least, their left wings) in those two countries. The Russian revolution was enthusiastically welcomed, but Bolshevik rule was critically assessed by Rosa Luxemburg[10] and other Polish Communist leaders, except those who early and unconditionally threw in their lot with Lenin. Wera Kostrzewa (Maria Koszutska), one of the leading ideologists of the PPS–Lewica and later of the KPRP and KPP, faithfully echoed Luxemburg's sentiments (then unknown to her): in summer 1918 she blamed the Bolsheviks who "in their system of rule had turned the terror and coercion not only against the bourgeoisie but often even there, where ideological force only should have overcome."[11] Even Warski, the model of orthodoxy, admitted a few years later: "In 1918 I had many doubts concerning the October Russia. Who did not have them? The Bolsheviks, maybe?"[12] In a German-language pamphlet published in Moscow in early 1919, Marchlewski wrote that "certainly there is no lack of mistakes and shortcomings in what the Bolsheviks have achieved up till now."[13] Uncritical adoration was still a thing of the future.

When the decision to found a unified Communist party was finally taken, the founders therefore sought acceptance not in Russia (where most of the SDKPiL and PPS–Lewica leaders were living) but in Berlin. In November 1918 Henryk Walecki (Maksymilian Horwitz) of the PPS–Lewica, on his way home from political exile in Switzerland, stopped in Berlin to discuss the merger with Luxemburg and Tyszka. A few weeks later, Józef Ciszewski (also from the PPS–Lewica) was illegally dispatched from Warsaw to Berlin to submit the unification program for approval, which he obtained with no reservations whatsoever.[14] The only message from abroad, read out at the unity congress of the KPRP, was from the German *Spartakusbund,* signed by Karl Liebknecht. The word "Workers'" was added to the new party's official name in order to emphasize that Poland — like other West European countries, but unlike peasant-dominated Russia — stood on the threshold of a proletarian revolution.

As a matter of fact, however, at the end of 1918 Poland was probably the least likely arena of a working-class revolution in all of Central and Eastern Europe. In the first place, Poland lacked the economic and demographic base for such a revolution. During enforced evacuation of the Kingdom of Poland in 1915, the tsarist armies had removed not only the locally recruited draftees but also many industrial plants and their workers. Thereafter, the German occupation authorities closed most of the remaining factories (except those working directly for the war effort), and forcibly shipped the unemployed to the Reich for work. Between two and three million people — a large proportion of them adult males and workers — were removed in all. As late as April–May 1919, the number of industrial workers in the former Kingdom of Poland hovered around 100 thousand — between one-quarter and one-fifth of the total prewar employment.[15]

Furthermore, in all the neighboring countries where revolution did occur, the revolutionary situation had been preceded by a military defeat, with subsequent disintegration of the state and general dissatisfaction among the disillusioned masses. In Poland, on the contrary, the end of the war brought the long-awaited unification of ethnically Polish lands and the resurrection of an independent, sovereign state. This new state was still very weak, and conditions bordered on anarchy, but the regaining of national independence after nearly a century and a half of partition and oppression gave rise to a powerful upsurge of patriotism — a virtually universal joy that touched even those who had long discounted such an eventuality. Social aspirations and demands were not excessive, and the first parliamentary elections in January 1919, boycotted by Communists who still expected an immediate revolution, brought a resounding defeat to the left as a whole. Of 394 deputies elected, there were only 35 socialists and 71 radical peasants, but 140 representatives of the right-wing *Endecja* and 131 of center-right parties.[16] The moderate left that dominated the first two governments of independent Poland introduced much socially progressive legislation, thereby defusing the potential dissatisfaction among the war-weary population. The claim, often advanced by Communist historians, that a revolutionary situation existed in postwar Poland, only to be squandered because of the party's weakness, its "Luxemburgist errors," or its deviation from Leninist precepts, is ahistorical wishful thinking, usually dictated by the political requirements of the moment.

Even A. Warski admitted at that time that for all the fiery rhetoric there was no genuine "revolutionary situation" in Poland. On the eve of the founding congress of the KPRP, he published an article that earned him the wrath of his SDKPiL comrades, who, despite his seniority and the authority derived from years of collaboration with Luxemburg, refused to elect him to the first Central Committee (he was coopted later). Warski described Poland as a "country that still breathes as much as it can at the mercy of foreign revolutions, of the Russian one [or] the German one." Poland "still cannot afford a Polish revolution of her own, not only a socialist one but even a Russian 'March' one, or a German 'November' one."[17]

Waiting for the European revolution, the young Communist party could not help but underestimate the impact on the popular mood of the newly regained independence. Ideologically and politically, the KPRP was the heir and successor of the SDKPiL, which for years had argued that an independent Polish state was impossible under capitalism and irrelevant under socialism; it tended, therefore, to ignore even the *fait accompli*. As late as February 1918, a SDKPiL conference had posited "a union of Poland with the proletarian Russian Republic." Its pamphlet "Revolution and War" explained that the party regarded "liberation from the shackles of national oppression and exploitation not in the construction of a class state, not in independence card-sharping, but in an international revolution which would topple the capitalist system"[18]

In accordance with these expectations, several SDKPiL leaders in Russia (Stanisław Pestkowski, Julian Leński [Leszczyński], and Stanisław Bobiński) in the fall of 1918 participated in the creation of the so-called Little International (Central Bureau of Communist Countries Occupied [by the German Army]). In addition to the Poles, it included Communists from Lithuania, Latvia, Estonia, Belorussia, the Ukraine, and Finland, that is, from those Western borderlands of the former Russian Empire which were "temporarily" under German military rule.[19] The crucial role played by Poles (Pestkowski was appointed chairman of the Central Bureau) showed they still considered their country part of Russia.

The PPS–Lewica, more responsive to popular sentiments, proposed the slogan "Long Live the Polish Soviet Republic!" But the SDKPiL still regarded any mention of a separate statehood, even if it were Soviet in form, as a "concession to nationalism," and the PPS–Lewica temporarily acquiesced. Only in early 1919 did the Communist party deign to include the concept of "Soviet Poland" in its program; some members continued to consider the slogan not internationalistic enough.

The ideological dominance of the SDKPiL in the KPRP was evident in the political platform accepted by the unity congress:

> In the epoch of international social revolution which destroys the foundations of capitalism, the Polish proletariat rejects all political slogans derived from the development of the capitalist period, such as autonomy, independence, self-determination. Aiming at dictatorship, at opposing all its enemies with its own revolutionary armed forces, the proletariat will fight against all attempts to create a bourgeois, counterrevolutionary Polish army, against all wars for national frontiers; the international camp of social revolution has no problem of national frontiers . . . because it embraces the principle of common interests of the international working class which excludes national oppression of all kinds, and cuts the ground from under all nationality- or language-based conflicts, both within the existing frontier areas and in relations to dispersed so-called national minorities.[20]

This credo was later used to charge Polish Communists not only with national nihilism but with outright treason. In fact, it conformed closely to the accepted Marxist tenets, then professed by most of the extreme leftist groups in Europe. It was the logical consequence of the conviction that Poland, like most of the West, had already entered the era of direct struggle for socialism. Marchlewski, for example, explained a few years later that "we had been firmly convinced that any frontier lines would lose their importance in the near future, because a revolutionary upheaval all over Europe, hence in Poland too, was a question of time only, a question of a few years."[21] To raise issues such as independence or national statehood under those circumstances would amount to distracting the revolutionary workers from their immediate tasks. The revolutionary optimism, which Polish Communists shared with their comrades throughout the continent, determined the subsequent tactical decisions — to boycott parliamentary elections, for instance, and to ignore the need for formal legalization of the party. Their doctrinaire "nonrecognition" of the independent Polish state, for which they were later scorned, played a secondary role, if indeed it influenced their actions at all.[22]

Almost nothing is known about the party's internal ideological discussions. Judging by its politics and — to a certain extent — by its contemporary pronouncements, one is apt to conclude that the leaders did not exaggerate their chances for seizing power and imposing a "proletarian dictatorship" on their own. The united party had at best 5,000 members,[23] concentrated almost exclusively in the three main industrial centers of the former Kingdom of Poland: the Dąbrowa coal basin (some 2,400 members), Łódź (1,700 — with an exceptionally large percentage of Jews and Germans), and Warsaw (1,000).[24] Given this circumstance and the widespread postindependence euphoria of the Polish people, the unity congress seemed most realistic when it resolved that "In its difficult struggle for the final victory the Polish proletariat will rely on social revolutions in other countries."[25] Yet soon after, in connection with the Polish-Soviet war, this reliance on revolution sparked and supported from abroad proved the undoing of the Communist movement in Poland. Polish Communists, however, were incredibly slow to learn: as many as five later, at the Second KPRP Congress, this tone still prevailed: "It seems . . . that our revolution will be made in spite of us. Our task is modest, we are but an auxiliary troop of the international revolution, not one of its mainstays."[26] "The conviction that our revolution will be made *only* by the Red Army of the USSR," or possibly of Soviet Germany, is still vivid among our comrades."[17] (One should remember that in December 1918 the Russian revolution was sorely embattled and separated from ethnic Poland by hundreds of miles of German-occupied territories and "White" armies; in its place the German revolution was the main source of hope for the Polish Communists.)

The Bolsheviks had, of course, no qualms about joining hands with the revolution in Western Europe, over the dead body of "bourgeois" Poland if necessary. Lenin still considered the slogan of "national self-determination" the best tactical weapon to win allies among the oppressed nationalities, and, as a result, he was at first much acclaimed by the noncommunist left in Poland. As early as January 1918 (at the Third All-Russian Congress of Soviets), however, Stalin frankly stated that the slogan was to be interpreted as "the right to self-determination not of the bourgeoisie but of the labouring masses of the given nation" — in practice, then, the right of its Communist party.[28] Despite all the evidence to the contrary, Lenin assumed an identical position: "If the concrete situation is such that the existence of the socialist republic [in Russia] is being imperilled at the present moment on account of the violation of the right to self-determination of several nations (Poland, Lifland, Courland, etc.), naturally the preservation of the socialist republic has the higher claim."[29] As soon as the revolution broke out in Germany and Austria-Hungary, Trotsky, as chairman of the Military-Revolutionary Council, openly stated Bolshevik objectives: "Through Kiev goes the direct way of linking up with the Austro-Hungarian revolution, just as the way through Pskov and Vilna leads to a direct contact with the revolution in Germany."[30]

It was probably in connection with Lenin's plans to assist the Soviet Republic in Hungary that Feliks Próchniak, a Polish Communist in Russia, was sent to Warsaw in January or February 1919. He was instructed to contact the Central Committee of the KPRP and to clarify the possibility of the Red Army's entry into the Lublin area, ostensibly en route to Eastern Galicia. The CC resolution, presumably voted in response to Próchniak's suggestion, acknowledged the principle of international revolutionary solidarity:

> If political and military considerations should demand the entrance of Soviet troops into the Lublin area, absolutely all measures should be avoided likely to substantiate the charges of an attempt to incorporate Poland or her part into the Soviet Republic. Soviet authorities should very clearly state that they do not aim at any restriction whatsoever of Poland's independence. Our comrades (incoming Polish ones — but in the first place the local ones) should proclaim a "Lublin Commissariat of the Polish Soviet Republic." Instructions to the Lublin organization should be given in this sense. The CC asks to be forewarned regarding the time and place of eventual entry, in order to be able to issue the necessary dispositions, to transfer appropriate activists, etc.[31]

The brother of the emissary, Edward Próchniak ("Sewer"), who reconstructed the resolution from memory over a year later, added however: "From conversations with the comrades in Warsaw and my familiarity with the conditions at that time, I know it was generally thought that the entry of the Soviet armies on Polish soil would be harmful for the cause of the revolution in Poland, and only consideration of the needs of the Russian revolution prompted the organization [in Poland to vote] the above-mentioned resolution."

This document, unknown until recently, deserves considerable attention. The principle of "international solidarity" had long been universally accepted by the left-wing revolutionary movement in Europe. Before 1914, for example, the SDKPiL had frequently provided money, printing facilities, and technical aid to the RSDRP, especially the Bolsheviks. Thus, the acceptance of Russian financial, or even military, support was not perceived as incompatible with the revolutionary ethos, since the whole problem was considered on an inter-party, not an inter-state level. The Próchniak account clearly shows that neither those who dispatched him to Poland nor his interlocutors in Warsaw regarded such support as a one way street. After all, Polish Communists were expected to help the young Soviet republic discharge its revolutionary obligation to the comrades in the West. Even more important, the whole exchange was on the basis of strict equality; the Russians were seeking Polish agreement, which implied the recognition of the Poles' sovereign right to shape the revolution in Poland and to decide if, and when, Russian help would be needed.

In mid-February 1919 the first conference of the KPRP met in Warsaw.[32] The sensitive problem of separate Polish statehood was still unresolved on the ideological level, but the state existed, and for reasons of practical politics the party was compelled to define its attitude. Hence, the draft resolution that the Communists submitted to the Warsaw Council of Workers' Delegates (4 March 1919) mentioned, for the first time, the goal of a "proletarian Poland . . . [a] Polish Republic of Councils of Workers' Delegates, linked in a fraternal alliance with workers' republics of other nations."[33] In April a draft resolution of the CC KPRP addressed to the national congress of the councils formulated the same position more precisely: "To win by revolutionary means a Polish Republic of Delegates' Councils of urban and rural workers."[34]

The concept of a "Polish Soviet Republic" had thus emerged, but the stress on "workers' delegates" underlined the purely proletarian character of the revolution in Poland, distinguishing it from the situation in backward Russia, where the soviets were to include delegates of peasants and soldiers ("peasants in uniform") as well.[35] By then Bolshevik and Comintern policy statements also provided for a "Soviet Poland."[36] Polish Communists were convinced that the existence of Soviet power in Russia and the imminent revolution in Germany would be decisive in shaping their country's future. Since there was no indigenous revolutionary situation in Poland, their own efforts would play at best a secondary role.

Accordingly, Polish Communists did little more than engage in propaganda and agitation, evidently hoping that the rising tide of European revolution would engulf Poland, giving them power without their having to struggle for it. Together with the PPS, some nonsocialist workers' parties, and Jewish workers' parties, the Communists did take part in the Councils of Workers' Delegates, but it is difficult to avoid the impression that they did so rather halfheartedly. The councils had, in fact, sprung up spontaneously in November–December 1918, in imitation of a similar movement in Germany, the experience of the Russian soviets playing a much more modest role.

Though it is now claimed that there were some 100 councils altogether, they were most successful in the Dąbrowa coal basin, Łódź, and Warsaw, and virtually nonexistent outside the former Kingdom of Poland. Not even the Communists, for all their revolutionary hyperbole, have ever maintained that the councils were alternative revolutionary organs of state power. With the benefit of hindsight, KPRR leaders themselves admitted that the councils "had not grown up out of a revolution."[37] Only in the Dąbrowa region were there attempts to arm proletarian Red Guards, but after offering only token resistance they capitulated to the weak government troops that were hastily dispatched from Galicia. By May–June 1919 the PPS decided to terminate collaboration with Communists in the councils, effectively ending the whole enterprise. The PPS maintained its own councils for a short time, but after a couple of months both Communist- and socialist-led councils quietly disappeared, leaving no lasting trace in the workers' tradition.

That the Communists were no more successful in the trade unions was only in part because of the numerical and organizational weakness of the labor movement as a whole. At first they did not pay much attention to the unions, convinced that in the face of imminent revolution the economic struggle to improve labor conditions and living standards would distract the workers from their immediate political tasks.[38] Even when the councils lost all their practical meaning, the Communists still tried to make the unification of the labor unions dependent on their acknowledgment of the councils' superior role.[39] The unification was achieved, nevertheless, in July 1919. The Communists had fought to the last against the plan that the labor unions should embrace "the entire proletariat, irrespective of nationality, political belief, and party membership" and remain "totally independent" in their "struggle for the workers' everyday needs."[40] Ironically, it was the unions' organization according to these principles that later allowed the Communists to try to extend their influence over a considerable part of the working class.[41]

Although the only major labor dispute in which the Communists managed to play a substantial role was, curiously enough, the farm workers' strike in October 1919, it would be erroneous to underrate their influence. Party membership was small and declining quickly,[42] but at least throughout 1919 they managed to compete with the PPS on more or less equal terms. In the short-lived workers' councils the Communists had an absolute majority in the Dąbrowa coal basin (of 405 delegates, 250 represented the KPRP, 120 the PPS), and substantial minorities in Warsaw (297 KPRP, 333 PPS), Łódź (153 KPRP, 213 PPS) and some other cities. According to contemporary Communist sources, in nineteen major councils representing some 221,000 organized workers, the Communists had 62,000 votes while the PPS had 70,000.[43]

Similar results were obtained in the trade unions. In July 1919, at the time of their unification, Communist-dominated labor unions claimed 78,669 members, the PPS-inspired ones, 93,256.[44] The Provisional Executive Council of the Trade Unions (KCZZ), elected at that time, consisted of 15 PPS and 11 KPRP members. At the first trade union congress — held in May 1920 when the war against Soviet Russia had already substantially reduced Communist influence — the KPRP still had 60 out of 161 delegates.[45]

At a time of widespread "revolutionary optimism," when a violent upheaval seemed to lurk just around the corner, at least part of the Communist rank-and-file lost all patience with the party's grueling effort to win influence in the unions. By mid-1919, after the workers' councils had been suppressed and a number of street demonstrations dispersed by newly reorganized police, a considerable part of the membership demanded the immediate institution of "fighting actions," the revival of the terrorist traditions that dated from the tsarist period, the right to "self-defense," and so on. Branding this tendency "putschism," the party leadership intervened forcefully, even expelling some of the hotheads, but shunned open discussion of the issue. The entire episode is studiously avoided by present-day Communist historiography.

Because of censorship, the Communists were unable to maintain a legal press of their own over an extended period of time. They frequently had to change the titles of their publications, and finally went over to clandestine printing only. The circulation of Communist newspapers fluctuated and was never very large, but then neither was press readership in general, particularly among workers. Significantly, news from Germany always took precedence over reports from Soviet Russia in these newspapers.[46]

Also indicative of Communist influence were a number of secessions from other left-wing parties, after which organized groups or individuals

joined the KPRP despite police reprisals. An extreme faction of the
socialist party, the *PPS–Opozycja,* was formed as early as January 1919
under the leadership of Tadeusz Żarski and Adam Landy. By mid–1920,
at the height of the Polish-Soviet war, this group merged with the
KPRP.[47] The formal merger was delayed because the PPS–Opozycja
insisted on the KPRP's "clear and firm commitment to the unification of
all lands inhabited by a majority of Polish population in a Polish
Socialist Republic as an independent member with equal rights in one
family of socialist nations of the world" — a position that the KPRP
described as "nationalist." PPS–Opozycja also categorically rejected the
"armed assistance of the Russian proletariat" for the revolution in
Poland — assistance that was axiomatic for the KPRP leadership.[48]
After the end of the Polish-Soviet war the ranks of the KPRP — seriously depleted as a result of its unconditional support for the Red
Army — were replenished by other socialist groups, including: the
PPS (Lewica), headed by the former secretary-general of the PPS, Jerzy
Czeszejko-Sochacki (who was promptly coopted to the Central Committee of the KRRP); Stanisław Łańcucki (PPS deputy to the *Sejm*)
and his followers in Galicia; the entire PPS district organization in
Poznań, headed by Czesław Porankiewicz (Communists up till then
had been without any influence whatsoever in the former Prussian
partition); a left-wing group of the Polish Peasant Party (*PSL–Lewica*)
in Galicia with its Sejm deputy, Tomasz Dąbal; and relatively strong
splinter groups from various Jewish socialist parties — Bund, Poaley-
Zion Left, and Feraynigte.[49] The incorporation of the former Communist Party of Upper Silesia and Communist Party of Eastern Galicia
(later renamed the Communist Party of Western Ukraine) had a somewhat different character.[50]

Virtually all these splits were the result of sincere ideological and
political evolution, and not — as often happened in later years — the
work of Communist "plants" ordered to join other parties in order to
split them. It is thus an impressive list, one that shows that the attempts
to isolate the Communist party were (at least in those years) not entirely
successful. Thanks to these "late-comers" the KPRP, which had boycotted the 1919 elections, emerged with a parliamentary faction of its
own in 1921: two deputies to the first legislative *Sejm* (Łańcucki and
Dąbal). A large number of top Communist leaders emerged from the
ranks of the late-comers. Moscow never trusted them entirely, however,
and many were "liquidated" on Stalin's orders long before the same fate
befell all the leading KPP cadres.[51]

During this same period, however, the Polish Communist movement was beginning to lose its organizational, and consequently its political and ideological, independence, not — as would have been natural under the circumstances — to the Communist International, but rather to the Russian Bolsheviks, and subsequently to the Soviet state. We have already seen that the founders of the SDKPiL attached fundamental value to this independence, an attitude that provoked their long-standing dispute with Lenin and the Bolsheviks. The SDKPiL cadres who were in Russia at the time of the 1917 revolution, and their comrades from the PPS–Lewica as well,[52] at first consistently tried to maintain the autonomy standards established by their leaders imprisoned in Germany. Although they joined the Bolshevik party[53] and assumed many responsible and dangerous posts, they did it as an independent political group. The First All-Russian Conference of the SDKPiL Groups in Russia was held in Petrograd in January 1918. The conference elected its Central Executive Committee and began publication of the daily paper *Trybuna*.[54] Most important, it defined its relationship with the Bolshevik party by forming autonomous "Polish sections" that were affiliated with local Russian or Ukrainian organizations and sent their own representatives to city and regional committees. The conference bluntly emphasized the organizational and political autonomy of the SDKPiL Groups in Russia[55] — a "declaration of independence" which allowed Polish Communists in Russia to defend their positions against the Bolsheviks even when such issues as the Brest-Litovsk Treaty[56] and, later, the advisability of the Red Army's advance into Poland were being debated. In practice, however, it was becoming more and more difficult to maintain this principled position. For example, even though the SDKPiL in Russia opposed the Brest treaty, two of its leading members, Karol Radek and Stanisław Bobiński, appeared as official members of the Soviet delegation, claiming to be "representatives of the laboring masses of Poland."[57]

Soviet authorities soon ceased to treat "the Polish comrades" on the basis of equality, instead preferring to deal with them through their own party and state organs, even though these posts were at first occupied primarily by Poles.[58] When Poland regained her independence, the Soviet government for a considerable time refused to extend diplomatic recognition. It dealt with Warsaw as if Poland continued to be part of the former Russian Empire, even using Polish Communists as emissaries.[59] Increasingly, sensitive questions that bore directly on Polish affairs were resolved not by Polish Communists and their organizations, but by Soviet bodies, in particular by the Commissariats for Nationalities Affairs and for Polish Affairs. The merger between the SDKPiL and PPS–Lewica groups in Russia and the formation of the Central Executive Committee of the KPRP in Russia (January 1919) changed nothing in this respect.[60]

At first some Polish Communists in Russia may sincerely have believed that "we consider the conception of purely military conquest of Poland for the Soviet idea, i.e., of military invasion of Poland, unsocialistic, harmful for the revolutionary development there, and utopian."[61] But, as the two armies jockeyed for position in the vast borderlands of Lithuania, Belorussia, and the Ukraine, a head-on clash between Poland and Soviet Russia became a distinct possibility. This prospect demanded from Polish Communists in Russia, as from the KPRP leadership in Poland, an unambiguous stand. Because of their "internationalistic" commitment, and even more because of their double membership (in the KPRP and in the Russian — later also in the Ukrainian — Communist parties), the Polish Communists in Russia found it progressively more difficult to question the political and military decisions taken by the Bolsheviks and by Soviet auhorities. They could, at best, express their hope that the Red Army would stop at Poland's ethnic borders (never exactly defined), and that farther advance would be undertaken only by Polish Communist military formations, such as the Western Rifle Division —raised by and formally subordinated to a hastily proclaimed (January 1919), and as quickly forgotten, "Military Revolutionary Council of Poland."[62]

As for the KPRP's official attitude toward the question of Soviet aid for the Polish revolution, the party council in Warsaw (in mid-February 1919) passed a resolution that stated: "Armed assistance by the Russian proletariat, if needed by the maturing Polish revolution, would constitute no invasion or expression of imperialistic tendencies incompatible with the essence of socialist government; it would have nothing in common with designs for conquest or with the slogan of national wars, but would simply be the fulfillment of slogans of international solidarity of the revolutionary proletariat."[63] The problem was as yet of no practical importance, since the hostilities consisted of skirmishes along an ill-defined line, far away from Poland proper. But it was as a direct consequence of this stand that the KPRP, throughout 1919, consistently abstained from raising the question of a formal peace treaty between Poland and Soviet Russia.

During this period, then, the Polish left manifested two quite different attitudes toward the war. On the one hand, the PPS, other left-wing noncommunist parties, and even some right-wing parties wanted peace. *Endecja,* for example, opposed Piłsudski's aspiration to extend the frontiers of the Polish state as far as possible to the East in order to lay the foundations for a multinational federation in the Jagiellonian tradition. The KPRP, on the other hand, was not interested in a speedy peace, knowing that the termination of hostilities would leave the party to its own devices, thus for all practical purposes ruling out revolution in Poland. Moreover, the KPRP entertained no doubts that the military victory of the Red Army would necessarily result in the breakdown of the Polish state: the party "figured that in this hopeless war of ravaged Poland against the entire, by now unfettered might of workers' Russia, the Polish state and military machine would tumble down."[64] While denouncing the PPS peace campaign as a pacifistic sham, the Communists pointed out that a "war of capital against revolution cannot end with a 'peace' of understanding. To desire the end of the war means to desire the victory of one of the belligerents."[65]

This "ultra-leftist" attitude conformed to the doctrine of "permanent revolution," then represented not only by Trotsky but also by Lenin and most of the other Bolshevik leaders. Still, it did not take into account the immediate needs of embattled Soviet Russia, whose very existence was imperilled by the civil war, especially when Denikin's army came within striking distance of Moscow in 1919. The available documents do not reveal to what extent the Polish Communist leadership was unanimous in its approach to the issue of war and peace. A year later one of the party's founding fathers, Henryk Walecki (who later represented the "right-wing tendency"), was exceptionally outspoken in his criticism. In his pamphlet "On the Tactics and on Attitude to Parliamentarism," he characterized as a "typical tactical error" the Communist denunciation (in early 1920) of the PPS peace campaign, claiming that it represented the Communists' "fear of the pacifistic peace slogans, fear of spreading pacifistic illusions in the masses."[66]

Ostensibly, the party's official position (inside Poland) can best be described as unqualified support for Soviet Russia and an all-out effort to undermine the "bourgeois" Polish state and its armed forces. No clear answer, however, was apparently given to another set of questions: Was Soviet military "assistance," while theoretically and ideologically admissible, indeed desirable? Would it advance the cause of the revolution in Poland, or on the contrary, would it rally the people in defense of their newly won state independence? And — probably the most important question — who was supposed to resolve those problems? In this respect the February 1919 resolution of the party council was deliberately vague. It stated in general terms that "our duty consists of preparing the revolution *by our own forces.*" At the same time, however, it affirmed that "the international revolution and its needs should determine the direction of the proletarian parties' policies in various countries. It is from this point of view that the assistance of our

Russian brethren should be considered. We have the *right* to demand this assistance from them; *they have the duty* to render it to us." Once the revolution breaks out in Poland, "the Bolsheviks marching in would be welcomed not by Communists alone but by the masses themselves . . . *as allies arriving to the aid of the Polish revolution* against the Polish bourgeoisie and the Coalition that stands behind it."[67]

By early 1920, when it became clear that Piłsudski's military preparations, and in particular his alliance with Ukrainian nationalists under Petliura, presaged an imminent Polish offensive against the Soviets, the KPRP suddenly changed its line and clamored for an immediate peace. This turnabout, however, did not result from internal party discussions (of which we know, it is true, next to nothing), or even from prodding by Polish comrades in Russia.

The Polish Communists in Russia had been grappling with problems similar to those that preoccupied their comrades in Poland and — as a rule — they had been giving similar answers: they were ideologically "correct" in their commitment to "internationalism" and to the admissibility of a revolution imposed from outside, but manifested only a vague concern for the current problems and needs of the Soviet state.

In June–July 1919, when the fate of the Soviet power in Russia was at stake, the Soviet government again sent Julian Marchlewski to negotiate with Piłsudski's emissaries a definite peace treaty between Poland and Russia. Apparently, neither the KPRP in Poland nor Polish Communists in Russia were consulted about this mission.[68] When the secret negotiations failed, Marchlewski was severely criticized at specially convened meetings of the Central Executive Committee of the KPRP in Russia (Minsk, 2 and 9 July 1919). The majority, which included Leński, Pestkowski, Unszlicht, Dolecki, *et al*, disavowed him, and by implication the Soviet government and Lenin personally, for making too far-reaching concessions to "bourgeois Poland." They rejected the principle of secret peace negotiations in general, but were especially piqued by the violation of their party's political autonomy: Marchlewski's mission had been "undertaken without the consent and knowledge of the Central [Executive] Committee and [was] inadmissible, bearing in mind that Marchlewski as a member of the Party [i.e., of the KPRP in Russia] was subject to the decisions and directives of its leading organs."[69] If talks with Poland were to go on, the conference demanded that they proceed openly and under KPRP supervision. Marchlewski and Konstanty Brodzki were appointed its plenipotentiaries.

The Bolshevik leadership, which assessed the military situation of Soviet Russia in a much more realistic way, totally ignored those demands. G. V. Chicherin agreed to inform the KPRP representative attached to the Peoples' Commissariat for Foreign Affairs of the talks, but only on the condition that no details of the secret negotiations with Poland be revealed to the Central Executive Committee of the KPRP in Russia.[70]

During the Minsk conference Marchlewski quoted Lenin's authority in support of his mission, claiming that the Russian leader "by now believed that a Communist regime cannot be introduced in contravention of popular aspirations." Marchlewski argued that "at this moment the entry of the Red Army into Poland would be fatal for communism in Poland." Most of those present disagreed with him. They regarded secret negotiatons as prejudicial to the cause of Polish revolution. Leński put the matter bluntly: "Either the Red Army would support it, or the Polish army would squash it."[71] Obviously, Polish Communists, both in Russia and in Poland, were of two minds on this question, but no justification can be found for a later historian's categorical claim that "followers of revolutionary war constituted a minority in the Polish party."[72] Neither is it true that it was the Polish Communists who urged the Soviets to extend the war with Poland; the reality was much more complex.

There is no way to determine to what extent this open rebellion against the Bolshevik leadership influenced the already initiated "reorganization" that deprived the Polish Communists in Russia of their political independence and, in the words of a Soviet historian, transformed their supreme body into "an organ of the Russian Communist Party (bolshevik) for work among the Polish population."[73] In any case, the "dissidents" were quickly brought to heel and the interests of the Soviet state remained paramount. On 2 February 1920, the Council of Peoples' Commissars, knowing all about Piłsudski's military preparations, issued an appeal for peace with Poland. The same day, when the appeal was submitted for ratification to the All-Russian Executive Committee of the Soviets (VTsIK) in Moscow, Marchlewski read out a declaration in support of the peace negotiations, signed by forty-two prominent Polish Communists in Russia. The signatories, denying their own record, now claimed that Communists had always "rejected the thought of conquest of Poland by Soviet Russia," because communism in Poland "cannot be introduced by forces coming from the outside, by a foreign army. On the contrary, any invasion of Poland by a foreign army would give the bourgeoisie the chance to provoke in the masses, which for 150 years had experienced all the pleasures of national oppression, extreme chauvinism with its fatal consequences."[74]

Whatever its misgivings, the KPRP leadership in Poland immediately rallied to the new Soviet line. The very next day the Warsaw party committee issued a leaflet "Down With the Massacre!" in which it demanded immediate, open peace negotiations between Poland and Soviet Russia, even though it continued to censure the PPS peace campaign as "hypocritical."[75] The KPRP even tried to proclaim a general strike throughout the country (8 February) to thwart the war preparations. Since it refused to cooperate with the PPS and other left-wing parties in their mass campaign against aggression against Soviet Russia, however, the Communists' initiative elicited a response commensurate with their waning influence. There was no strike movement outside the Dąbrowa coal mines, and even there it fizzled out after a day or two.[76]

Such uncritical acceptance of Soviet policies by Polish Communists in both Russia and Poland, without even an attempt to adapt them to specific local conditions, was in a way typical of developments then occurring in other non-Russian parties affiliated with the Comintern. In the case of the KPRP, it is especially difficult to reconstruct this process without access to the archives; the published accounts present much too simplistic a picture.

On the original invitation to the First Congress of the Third International (*Pravda* on 24 January 1919) the name "Karski," representative of "the foreign bureau of the Communist Workers' Party of Poland," appeared immediately after signatures of Lenin and Trotsky.[77] "Jan Karski" was the party alias of Julian Marchlewski, and when his signature appeared in *Pravda* he was on assignment in Germany. In any case, just like all the other non-Russian signatories, he had no formal mandate whatsoever, although a Soviet historian claims that Marchlewski had taken part (before leaving for Germany) in a meeting chaired by Lenin and devoted to preparations for the founding congress of the Communist International; apparently it was impossible to pinpoint the exact date of this meeting.[78]

In its resolution, "The Founding of the International," the KPRP unification congress in Warsaw had endorsed the idea of a new International in general terms only, appealing to various left-wing groups to join forces.[79] Apparently Polish Communists "participated in private conversations held at the time in Berlin"[80] — a phrase that certainly signifies contacts with Rosa Luxemburg, who considered the move to found a new International premature. One can assume that at least some of the leaders shared her reservations about the hasty convocation of a new International dominated by the Leninist conceptions she had consistently rejected. There is no trace of a resolution that would have empowered the Central Executive Committee of KPRP in Russia to act at that time as a "Foreign Bureau" of KPRP. No one was sent to Russia to take part in the First Congress, and the Comintern Manifesto was signed "for Poland" by Józef Unszlicht ("Jurowski"), a former SDKPiL activist who by then was a higher Red Army commissar.[81] Officially, the CC KPRP decided to join the International only in June 1919,[82] but it is not possible to determine whether there was any opposition to that decision.

In March 1919, shortly after the founding congress of the International, the Eighth Congress of the Russian Communist Party (bolshevik) (RKP[b]) decided to dissolve all the national groups and sections, including the KPRP groups in Russia and their supreme body, the Central Executive Committee. Most Polish Communists in Russia openly opposed this move. They objected to the liquidation of their political autonomy, which Luxemburg and Tyszka had defended against Lenin for so many years. The Central Executive Committee, however, had no option but to accept the verdict. Dzierżynski in particular was active in the liquidation of the KPRP groups in Russia. Most of them, despite their members' reluctance, were therefore incorporated in local RKP (b) organizations as "Polish sections," not more autonomous than the "Jewish sections" (Yevsektsiia), for example.

The "Polish sections" were subordinated to a newly created Central Bureau for Agitation and Propaganda among Poles in Russia, an organ of the Central Committee of the RKP (b) which was headed by the former SDKPiL member Samuel Lazowert. The "Polish Bureau," as it was called, and the "Polish sections" were Polish in the purely linguistic sense; in all other respects they were part of the all-Russian party, with no special relationship to Poland and the KPRP. Distinct Polish military units were also dissolved and incorporated into the Red Army. Since in July 1919 the CC KRPR — apparently ill informed about the "reorganization" then in progress — officially empowered the already defunct Central Executive Committee to represent it in the Communist International, it was decided to form a special KPRP Executive Bureau in Russia, which would act as a foreign representation of the KPRP but have no network of local organizations.[83] The KPRP sent no delegation to the Second Comintern Congress (July 1920) either, ostensibly because of the Polish-Soviet war, which was then approaching its climax. It was represented by J. Marchlewski (member of the Executive Bureau), but did not play any significant role in the debates.[84]

Gradual changes were already undermining the character of the Communist movement in Poland as well. It was probably unavoidable that since the end of 1918 the center of gravity of the party leadership had been shifting from Warsaw to Moscow. This imbalance was increased by the generous support in cadres and money that Moscow rendered through the KPRP Central Executive Committee, and later through the Polish Bureau, to the party in Poland, which in those early stages was restricted by the personnel requirements of the young Soviet state and by its own limited financial capabilities. But there were other factors at work, too. As the short period of semilegal activity in Poland drew to an end, and the approaching war with Soviet Russia gave rise to intensified police repression, a growing number of Central Committee members were arrested or interned. Others left the country "for the good of the party," and established formal centers in Berlin, where the Comintern maintained its West European secretariat, and in Gdansk (Danzig) which as a free city was immune from interference by Polish secret police but allowed for easy communication with clandestine party organizations inside Poland.

In the Polish (and Russian) revolutionary movement, there was, in fact, a long tradition of moving the political decision-making centers abroad, an action that could always be justified by security considerations. But, whether in Russia or in Germany, leaders in the emigration were much more susceptible to outside pressure, much less able to resist it by appeal to the rank-and-file. By mid-1920 the exodus of leaders in conjunction with the mass arrests of local cadres had virtually paralyzed all party activities inside Poland. Thus, on the vital matters, in particular those connected with the changing character of the Polish-Soviet war, Polish Communist leaders had to accept decisions that no longer originated with them. The membership itself had no say on such matters.

In fact, the crucial controversy over "revolutionary war" — personified by the clash at the July 1919 Minsk conferences between Marchlewski, on the one hand, and Lenski, Unszlicht *et al,* on the other — was only superficially resolved by the February 1920 declaration of the forty-two Polish Communist leaders in Russia. By then the real decision-making body was the Bolshevik Politburo, where Lenin apparently espoused a point of view roughly like that of Marchlewski. But even though the whole question was of paramount importance for the Polish party — and indirectly for the future of Poland too — Polish Communists in Russia, in the meantime deprived of their autonomous organizations, were no longer consulted as a body. It is not clear from the text of the declaration of the forty-two whether they signed it in their individual capacity as Polish-speaking members of the Russian party, or as exiled leaders of the KPRP in Russia.[85]

In April 1920, shortly before the Polish offensive in the Ukraine, an exchange of political prisoners allowed three leading Polish Communist cadres to reach Moscow.[86] The emissaries, who included Stanisław Budzynski ("Tradycja") and Edward Próchniak ("Sewer"), conveyed to the

Polish Bureau the views of the Communists in the Polish underground (it is not clear whether there had been a formal CC resolution): the Red Army should not advance beyond Polish ethnic borders, for such an action would consolidate the masses, including the working class, under banners of national defense, and would undoubtedly strike a heavy blow against communism in Poland. The Polish Bureau transmitted this assessment to the Central Committee of the RKP (b) without adding any recommendation of its own.[87]

During Piłsudski's Kiev campaign and the early stages of the Red Army's counteroffensive, Polish Communists in Russia probably kept as low a profile as possible.[88] But as soon as Soviet armed forces regained the strategic initiative and began their march to the West, the Politburo had to decide whether these forces should halt at the Bug river or go on, in hope of reaching the German frontier and triggering a revolution in the heart of Europe.[89] The result is well known: against the advice of Trotsky and many others, Lenin, dizzy with victory, changed his mind. In early summer 1920 he decided to accept Tukhachevskii's plans to carry the revolution to Central Europe on the bayonets of the Red Army, over the corpse of "bourgeois Poland."[90] This was a unilateral decision: no representative and authoritative body of Polish Communists had been consulted and no such body proferred advice on its own.[91]

But Lenin did, as a matter of fact, consult one of the leading Polish communists — not, as would have been natural, Marchlewski or Dzierżynski, who ranked among his closest collaborators, or even Karol Radek, who was member of the Executive Committee of the Communist International.[92] Their opinions were apparently known, and unwelcomed. Radek, for instance, did not conceal his conviction that any attempt "to export" revolution to Poland would provoke national resistance: he explicitly warned Lenin and, for his pains, was dubbed a "defeatist."

Instead, Lenin chose to question Józef Unszlicht, a veteran SDKPiL member, who was then a prominent official in the political apparatus of the Red Army on the western front. He asked Unszlicht: "Do you consider a Soviet revolution [in Poland] likely, and how soon?" Lenin probably anticipated Unszlicht's answer: While it would be preferrable to stop the Red Army on the Polish frontiers, the advance should continue if no peace can be imposed by then, since the prospects for an internal upheaval were propitious. "We consider a Soviet revolution in Poland, with the advance of our troops toward her borders, most likely within a short time."[93]

This totally misleading answer distorted the real situation in Poland.

Several months earlier the noncommunist left, especially the PPS, had fought actively for peace with Soviet Russia and opposed any offensive campaign in the Ukraine. In March the PPS answered the Soviet peace appeal by stressing that: "We agree with the opinion expressed by the Soviet government that there are at present no economic or territorial problems between Poland and Russia which could not be resolved by a peaceful agreement," and even added a "fraternal message" from Polish workers for the Russian proletariat.[94] But initial successes, and especially the occupation of Kiev (8 May 1920), brought about a change of heart. The same party now welcomed the Polish feats of arms in Kiev, and its deputies enthusiastically participated in the festive reception prepared by the *Sejm* for the victorious commander-in-chief, while continuing to urge Piłsudski to conclude a speedy peace that would sanction the newly won independence of the Ukraine.

The mood changed even more radically when the Red Army mounted its counteroffensive and began to approach the ethnic borders of Poland. All the left-wing parties supported the new government "of National Defense," formed on 24 July 1920, with the peasants' leader, Wincenty Witos, as prime minister, and Galician socialist leader, Ignacy Daszyński, as his deputy. Faced with military defeat and diplomatic pressure from Poland's Western allies, the right wing was now more susceptible to pressures for peace, but the left mounted a great propaganda campaign, skillfully manipulating the fact that the Bolsheviks, for the first time, were exploiting the Great-Russian nationalism of the population.[95] The PPS called for volunteers to join the army, organized its own recruiting offices, armed a militia to defend Warsaw in case of further retreat of the regular army, and even started preparations for underground sabotage and guerrilla activities under Soviet occupation.[96] The response was staggering. Never before had Poland witnessed such a quasi-unanimous upsurge of patriotism. The Communists were isolated politically: hundreds were rounded up by police and put in internment camps;[97] those who evaded arrest and did not escape to Germany lay low waiting for the imminent entry of the Red Army — unavoidable in their opinion.[98] They were universally regarded as traitors to the national cause, active supporters of an armed invasion of their own country.

There were excellent reasons for such an attitude. The overconfident Soviets had given up any pretense of recognizing Poland's right to independent statehood. The armistice conditions, presented through the good offices of British Prime Minister Lloyd-George at the height of the Red Army's advance on Warsaw, provided for a Polish-Soviet border along the so-called Curzon line, demobilization of the Polish army to 50,000 men, the transfer to Russia of all surplus weapons and the arming of a "workers' militia," the dismantling of Polish war industries, the establishment of exclusive Soviet control over a railroad line to East Prussia, and so on.[99] A veteran Polish Communist described this ultimatum as "blatant interference — even though in the interest of the development of the Polish revolution — in internal Polish affairs"; complying with its terms would be tantamount to the transformation of Poland into a "rump mini-state, almost deprived of armed forces and, in fact, doomed to remain dependent on Soviet Russia."[100] The Soviet government was, at the same time, preparing another partition of ethnic Poland: in return for Germany's benevolent neutrality, the high command of the Reichswehr was promised the restoration of the pre-1914 eastern frontier of the Reich, that is, reincorporation of Upper Silesia, Greater Poland (Posnania), and Pomerania ("the Polish Corridor").[101]

Polish Communists in Russia, who had not been consulted about the Red Army's crossing of the Bug river, were now told nothing about the Soviet intentions toward Poland, except that a Soviet Republic would be installed. In mid-July 1920, when the Red Army was approaching the ethnic borders of Poland (the final decision to cross them was taken by Lenin on July 17), the Bolshevik leadership decided to mobilize all Polish Communists in Russia and the Ukraine. A conference was called in Moscow on July 18 under the chairmanship of Feliks Dzierżyński; a new "Polish Bureau" was apppointed, without any prior clarification of its double affiliation with the KPRP (by then to all intents and purposes defunct) and with the RKP (b).[102] It seems that there was no discussion on the merits of the case: even those who, like Marchlewski and Radek, had warned that any attempt to impose Soviet rule would be fatal to the cause of communism in Poland did not raise any objections this time. They were ordered to join the advancing Red Army, and, as soon as the first major Polish town was seized, to form a Provisional Polish Revolutionary Committee (to be headed by Marchlewski) and to proclaim a Polish Soviet Republic. It was — to use the formulation of a Polish Communist historian — a "plan to install a provisional revolutionary power [in Poland] by using Communist émigrés, participants of the revolution and civil war in Russia, based on armed forces of the Red Army."[103]

On 28 July 1920, Soviet troops entered Białystok. Two days later members of the Polish Bureau appeared in the town, bringing previously printed copies of a "Manifesto to the Polish Working People in Cities and Countryside,"[104] as well as a communiqué proclaiming the Provisional Polish Revolutionary Committee (*Polrevkom*) composed of Marchlewski, Dzierżyński, Kon, Unszlicht, and Próchniak.[105] Similar *revkoms* were formed by the Red Army in other small towns in north-eastern Poland, but they received no support from the local population and played a minimal role. Lenin later tried to explain this away by pointing out that the Red Army had failed to capture any large industrial centers.[106] But Polish Communists knew better. In private letters even Dzierżyński admitted that in Białystok "one felt no power, there were no active revolutionary developments," and expressed fear that even Warsaw would "not greet us as we would wish it," blaming the weakness of the Communist party.[107] Marchlewski, too — ex post facto — shared this opinion: he complained that among the Polish population "the sentiment of joy caused by having got rid of a foreign yoke had overcome, for the time being, the class consciousness," and workers had "easily succumbed to nationalistic agitation."[108]

Not only did the revolution in Poland fail to materialize, but there were no major attempts to support the Red Army's advance by strikes or sabotage; there was not even an intensified propaganda effort on the part of the Communist party. According to internal party accounts, the number of leaflets published by the KPRP amounted to 156,000 copies in June 1920 and 250,000 copies in July, but fell to 43,000 in August, 35,000 in September, 21,000 in October, 28,000 in November, and 37,000 in December 1920.[109]

The liberation of Białystok by Polish troops on 25 August put an end to the ephemeral *Polrevkom* and its four-week rule on Polish soil. Although Polish Communist historians tend at present to describe it as "an embryo of revolutionary state power of the Polish laboring masses,"[110] the *Polrevkom* did little more than issue a stream of noisy propaganda and a series of decrees: on nationalizing industry that virtually did not exist, on confiscating landowners' estates that peasants refused to accept and parcel out, on forming a "Polish Red Army" and creating security police and "revolutionary tribunals" (both, most appropriately, under Dzierżyński's direction), on reforming the school system, and so on.[111] It was in fact, an appendage to the military administration of the Red Army, and could neither protect the population against the ravages of war nor even impose the use of Polish in local administration (Russian, and sometimes Yiddish, were preferred). Local Soviet commanders and commissars were fully aware of its weakness, and refused to be bothered.[112]

This isolated episode did not even serve as the starting point for a principled discussion of future Communist strategy and tactics in Poland. Such a discussion was nipped in the bud as soon as it started with Marchlewski's pamphlet. Though the claim that "there were no winners in the 1920 war" appears as doubtful today as the exaggerated descrip-

tion of the Soviet failure at the gates of Warsaw by the British ambassa-
dor to Poland,[113] it seems indeed true that the "indisputably losing side
in this war was Polish Communists."[114]

Polish Communists in Russia had been prevented from freely expressing
their attitude to the war — in any way other than as individual members
of the RKP (b) — by the 1919 "reorganization." But, incredible as it
seems, the KPRP leadership in Poland and abroad never took a clear
stand on this vital question either. The de facto leader of the KPRP in
Poland (there was as yet no post of secretary-general or chairman) was
Adolf Warski, who in mid-1920 had left the country and set up the
KPRP Foreign Bureau in Berlin and later in Danzig. In the previously
mentioned letter of October 1920 to Zofia Dzierżyńska, he wrote:

> Until June 28 [1920], i.e., until the moment I left for Danzig and there fell
> ill for several months, the party's Central Committee voted no official
> resolution in the specific question whether we should have aimed at
> crossing the Polish ethnic border, at seizing Warsaw and Sovietizing the
> country. No CC member had even thought to move a resolution in this
> matter. First of all because (1) cut off from the world, *we had been not at
> all capable of realizing* the international situation. Second, because (2) all
> of us in the CC were of the opinion that this specific question should have
> been, and must be, *resolved by Russia,* not from the point of view of our
> party or political interests in Poland, but from the point of view of the
> interests of the Russian revolution and of the global situation.[115]

Warski was even more outspoken in a letter sent a month later from
Berlin to the Polish Bureau of the CC RKP (b) in Moscow:

> Two prominent representatives of the CC KPRP with whom we held a
> meeting stated most emphatically that from the very beginning of the Red
> Army counteroffensive until its total retreat across the borders of Poland,
> the CC had never discussed, and took no decision, whether and how far
> the counteroffensive should have advanced, whether or not we should
> have aimed at Sovietization of Poland with the assistance of the Red
> Army. They have never posed such a question, simply because it would
> not have mattered at all in their practical policies. They were cut off from
> the world, and did not know all of the motivations and aims of the
> counteroffensive. Privately, however, a CC member, after the crossing of
> the Polish frontier by the Red troops, more than once expressed the
> opinion that the counteroffensive was harmful, and that it was in the
> interest of Russia to conclude peace. Only after the defeat of the Red
> troops, a difference of opinion emerged among the CC members, but
> even then there was no official pronouncement on behalf of the CC.[116]

Thus, not only did the KPRP voluntarily abdicate its right to

influence the course of events, but its leader, even after the defeat, saw
no reason to regret it. But his was by no means the only point of view,
though information on dissenters is sketchy. The CC member mentioned in Warski's letter, the one who had objected to the Red Army
advance, was almost certainly Henryk Stein-Kamienski (alias Domski,
"Krakus"), a veteran SDKPiL activist who also lived in Berlin at that
time. On 22 July he published an article entitled "Sowjetrussland und
der Frieden" in *Rote Fahne,* the German Communist newspaper.
Domski argued that in every country the working class should make its
revolution on its own, without foreign armed assistance.

> Only those masses who, like the Russian ones, had made their own
> revolution, would willingly suffer and survive the shortcomings and strifes
> caused by the upheaval. Whereas a Soviet system, imposed from outside
> by foreign troops, would have encountered much stronger resistance of
> the owning classes, and would have commanded weaker support in the
> laboring masses.[117]

Not content with a public statement of his dissenting view, Domski
repeated his misgivings in a letter to the Polish Bureau in Moscow on
31 August 1920. He asked to convey to the CC of the RKP (b) that he
was opposed to the Red Army's advance on Warsaw: not only had it
ended with a military defeat, but it also had provoked an upsurge of
chauvinism and morally compromised the Communist cause. The letter
was read at the Ninth Conference of RKP (b) in September 1920, and
soundly condemned for "left-wing deviation" by both Zinoviev and
Bukharin. Only Radek attempted to defend his one-time comrade in the
SDKPiL–"splitters," though he did not subscribe to his point of view.
The conference, having listened to an optimistic report by a KPRP
emissary from Warsaw, happily voted its appreciation that "Polish
Communist workers had fully approved the armed support for the
Sovietization of Poland, and had made no concession either to national-
ism nor to pacifism." The *Rote Fahne* article and similar pronounce-
ments "were not the voice of the Polish Communist party."[118]

Most Polish Communists obediently approved this position, without
even discussing in depth Domski's "heretical" views. When at the
Second Congress of KPRP (1923) Tadeusz Żarski in a most cautious
way tried to raise doubts about "revolution imposed from outside,"[119] he
was sharply rebuked by Marchlewski himself, then a Soviet dignitary
without any direct links to the Polish party. Marchlewski, who once
opposed the Soviet armed invasion of Poland, by then had approved the
Stalinist line without, apparently, any mental reservations.[120]

Warski rejected Domski's arguments, together with the previously mentioned objections of the PPS–Opozycja leaders (including T. Żarski) which had delayed their merger with the KPRP. He did not mention that similar rejection of intervention of foreign armies had been included in the declaration of the forty-two leading Polish Communists in Russia in February 1920. A few years later Warski was even more outspoken, recalling "a Polish Communist for whom a counterrevolutionary commandment of social-chauvinists had appeared sacred, and had provoked him to address to RKP (b) a passionate protest against Red Soviet imperialism and to a public announcement [in the Berlin *Rote Fahne*] against 'foreign troops' [the Red Army] imposing Soviet power from outside."[121] It is most significant that the whole incident remains taboo to this very day, and is barely mentioned by Communist historians, even though the sources are easily available in party archives.[122]

According to the authorized version, during the 1920 war Polish Communists "not only performed their class and international duty towards Polish laboring masses and the whole world, but also their duty as genuine defenders of the interests of the nation and of the country."[123]

Contemporary Polish opinion, even that of the workers, certainly did not share this view. When, in mid-October 1920, the Polish-Soviet negotiations in Riga (Latvia) brought about the signing of peace preliminaries and a cease-fire all along the front, the CC KPRP issued an appeal, surprisingly out of tune with Soviet policies. Titled "Peace with Open Annexation and Concealed Contribution," it denounced the "imperialist triumph of the Polish bourgeoisie in Riga" and warned that it was *not a lasting and genuine peace.*"[124] Marchlewski's pamphlet, published simultaneously in Moscow, was free of such doubts: to the question, will the peace be lasting, he answered crisply: "It depends on the laboring people in Poland."[125]

"The laboring people in Poland" were by that time thoroughly tired of the war that had moved to far-away places, and interested mainly in their immediate social and economic problems. The PPS, which returned to opposition once the danger was over, considerably increased its influence among workers, advocating their demands for improved labor and living standards. Though the number of strikes in Polish industry dropped to a minimum in the third quarter of 1920, that is, at the height of the war, it peaked as soon as hostilities ceased. The labor disputes continued well into 1921, in most cases bringing the workers substantial wage rises — but without any visible participation of Communists who by then began to reappear from internment camps and from their hiding places.[126] They were absent during several strikes on the railroads in October 1920, content to critize *post factum* the trade

union and socialist leaders for their allegedly conciliatory policies.
Communists managed, however, to play some role in the nationwide
strike of railwaymen in February 1921, supported by the short general
strike of solidarity led by the PPS, which ended military administration
of the railways.[127]

When Communists, in accordance with new Comintern guidelines,
tried to rebuild their influence in the unions, they were blackballed
because of their attitude during the 1920 war. Their political isolation
increased when they denounced as "nationalistic" the Polish efforts to
regain Upper Silesia first by plebiscite (March 1921), and later by
armed insurrection (3 May 1921).[128]

There was, therefore, no outcry even among the working class when
the Central Commission of Trade Unions (KCZZ), dominated by the
PPS, formally voted (26 April 1921) to sever relations with the KPRP
and to resist Communist infiltration of the labor movement, thus
revoking the July 1919 unity agreement that sanctioned the independence of the trade unions vis-à-vis political parties. Local PPS organizations and committees were forbidden to join hands with Communists. Even though KPRP activists were being excluded from the
unions and local branches dominated by them dissolved, the Communists proved unexpectedly resilient, in particular in such traditional
fiefs as the mining industry. But even in Warsaw the Communist-
dominated "Red faction" won a clear majority of votes in July 1921.
The socialists objected that the election had been rigged, provoking a
split in the Warsaw Trade Union Commission.[129] Subsequently, Communist influence in the unions was drastically reduced.

The reconstruction of the KPRP clandestine organization after its
1920 nadir proceeded very slowly and with difficulty. Despite a percep-
tible relaxation of police repression after the end of hostilities, when
the state of emergency and martial law were lifted, and an even greater
tolerance after the signing of the Riga peace treaty, only the hard core
of party membership returned to the fold. By the end of 1921 even in
the party's main stronghold, the Dąbrowa coal basin, there were only
500 members — one-fifth the 1919 membership; the Warsaw organization reported 600 members, but admitted they had virtually no foothold in the factories.[130] The intelligentsia formed a disproportionately
large part of the defectors. In many parts of the country local committees reemerged only after the influx of new members, following the
splits in various left-wing parties. The party's disproportionate share of
national minorities, as compared to ethnic Poles, originated at that
time, as a direct result of the role the Communists had played during
the war; the open hostility displayed by the Soviets toward the Polish

state until the mid-1930s conspicuously exacerbated this unnatural state of affairs.

Profound divergences of opinion among the leading *aktif*, both inside the country and in the emigration, only increased the KPRP's disarray. The crucial question of assessing the party's acceptance of a revolution brought from outside was not openly discussed, despite the fact that Domski was by no means alone in his criticism.[131] In a camouflaged way it surfaced even in a previously mentioned pamphlet by Henryk Walecki; the Central Committee immediately discussed its contents, condemned it, and decided to destroy all the existing copies, ostensibly because of its criticism of the 1919 boycott of parliamentary election.[132]

The new line of the Communist International, expressed in Lenin's book on "infantile disorder"[133] and in the resolutions of the Second Congress, met with considerable resistance among KPRP leaders and rank-and-file, both in Poland and among the émigrés. Particularly outspoken in the opposition to the new "rightist" and "opportunist" line — alongside with Domski, Leński, and several other prominent émigré leaders in Germany and in Russia — was Władysław Kowalski ("Grzech", Ślusarski), a veteran of the PPS–Lewica who had joined the SDKPiL after the split in 1916. Their views, especially on the rejection of the "united front" tactics in relations with the socialists, and on the so-called revolutionary parliamentarism, were in many respects similar to those of the KAPD in Germany and of the "Left" Communists in Soviet Russia and in other European parties. These views also had many followers in the middle-level *aktif* of the KPRP in Poland — a majority, for example, in the Warsaw organization, which opposed any form of participation in the next election to the *Sejm*.[134] In terms reminiscent of the earlier polemics of Rosa Luxemburg against Lenin and the Bolsheviks, the "Grzechists" emphasized the purely working-class character of the KPRP. They were reluctant to regard as allies of the proletarian revolution either the peasants, who were demanding an agrarian reform, or the separatist movements of oppressed national minorities. They also questioned the relevance of the Russian experience for more advanced European countries, including Poland.

In order to refute those views, it was decided — probably in early 1921 — to publish (outside Poland) a Communist theoretical monthly. In fact *Nowy Przegląd* appeared only in mid-1922: the delay was caused by the party *aktif*, which to a large extent supported "Grzech." In a series of articles written for the new journal, Warski "proved" that the Grzechists represented a "standpoint hostile to Soviet Russia and her ruling party."[135] For several years the "leftists" were unable to prevail over the KPRP leadership, which was supported by Moscow and known as "the three W's" — Warski, Walecki, and Wera Kostrzewa (Maria Koszutska).[136]

The various political and tactical problems were first raised at an informal meeting of the KPRP leadership, held in Berlin (10 January 1921), and then at the second party conference (Warsaw, February 1921) and the third party council (Warsaw, May 1921).[137] All three meetings confirmed the ascendancy of "the three W's" and aligned the party with the Comintern guidelines. Among the policies emphasized were: leading the workers' struggle for better living standards in the hope that intensified class conflicts would lead to a revolutionary situation; supporting nonproletarian strata (including, for the first time, poor peasants as well); participating in elections to the parliament, municipal councils, and similar bodies (eighteen voted in favor of this policy; eleven Grzechists opposed); accepting the Comintern's "Twenty-one Conditions" (to the party's name was added: "Section of the Communist International"); and remaining in the united trade unions (a sizable minority preferred separate "Red unions").

It is significant that for the last time Communist conferences were held in Poland.[138] The newly elected members of the Central Committee and Secretariat were supposed to remain in the country, but in fact most of them soon emigrated (Warski settled in Danzig), leaving behind only a small operative body that resolved organizational questions but was not supposed to determine policy. Discussion was still relatively unfettered, and the membership was apprised not only of the resolutions voted by the majority, but also of the minority's dissident views. Very soon, however, the process of "Bolshevization" would begin to take its toll, stamping out the traditions of the revolutionary movement in Poland and molding the party in a uniform Stalinist spirit.

The shape of things to come was clearly discernible at the Third Congress of the Communist International (22 June–12 July 1921), the first in which a genuine delegation of Polish Communists took part. The delegation was about twenty men strong, most of them from the German and Soviet emigration, including people totally committed to Soviet party and state work: Marchlewski, Bobiński, Konstanty Brodzki, etc. In addition, Dzierżyński, Unszlicht, and Feliks Kon attended some meetings of the delegation.[139] The Grzechists were to be found mainly among the delegates who came directly from Poland. Polish affairs did not play a conspicuous role in the debates, even though Lenin took part in a meeting with some European delegations, including that from Poland.[140] Subsequently (on 19 October 1921) he addressed a "Letter to Polish Communists" which betrayed almost total ignorance of the situation in Poland, but at the same time indirectly threw overboard a few of the previously binding dogmas.[141]

Not less fateful for the future of the Communist movement in Poland were those resolutions of the Third Congress of the Comintern which dealt with tactical matters and with the organizational structure of Communist parties. They were received by the Polish delegation with — to say the least — mixed feelings.[142] The slogan "To the masses," which laid the groundwork for the "united front" tactics, was quite inapplicable in Poland since the PPS staunchly refused any cooperation with Communists, whom they charged with high treason. The "united front" was opposed not only by the "Grzechists" but also by a large part of the membership, bitterly aware that it could never be achieved in an atmosphere poisoned by memories of 1920. It was finally imposed, but thanks only to severe curtailment of free discussion within the party. Its implementation, however, proved a total failure. The organizational resolution, severely criticized by Lenin just one year later,[143] went against the grain of Polish revolutionary traditions. If the Comintern guidelines failed to encounter the resistance one might have expected from the party of Rosa Luxemburg, the 1920 debacle and the reconstruction of the party ranks under conditions of total lack of grass-roots support and strict illegality were among the contributing factors. Equally ominous were the Comintern-imposed principles, demanding "unconditional support of Soviet Russia [as] the cardinal duty of the communists of all countries" and "a categorical imperative for every communist," and affirming that "The Comintern is no loose structure of affiliated sections, but the unified party of communist workers of the entire world."[144]

By 1921, then, the basic foundations for intensive "Bolshevization" of the Communist party, in Poland as throughout Europe, have already been laid. The extent to which this process has developed can best be gauged by an event that, though insignificant by itself, is fairly typical. By 1922 a group of Polish Communists in Russia, ex-members of the SDKPiL, started to prepare for their thirtieth anniversary. In the Polish-language "Communist Calendar for 1922," issued in Moscow, Stanisław Bobiński wrote: "The Communist Party of Poland, founded a full ten years earlier than the Russian Bolshevik party (1903) — since its origin should be considered 1893, that is to say the year the Social-Democracy of the Kingdom of Poland had been founded — is perhaps the oldest party in the Third International."[145] This claim might have seemed innocuous enough, especially since five years earlier when the SDKPiL in Russia had celebrated its twenty-fifth jubilee it had received greetings from Yakov Sverdlov, the nominal head of Soviet Russia, as well as the representatives of the "fraternal parties" of Lithuania, Latvia, England, France, and Switzerland.[146] Five years later, however, the Soviet leadership had decided to celebrate its own party's jubilee and, in spite of the historical record, it was determined that no other party should claim seniority over the Bolsheviks. The task of teaching the upstarts a lesson was assigned to Adolf Warski, himself one of the founders of the SDKPiL. Warski obediently wrote an article under the title, "The Lessons of the Bolshevik Jubilee: A KPRP Jubilee?" In it he decimated Bobiński, denounced all errors and sins, real and imaginary, of the SDKPiL, and gave short shrift to Rosa Luxemburg, his one-time ideological teacher and preceptor, for having held views different from those of Lenin. Warski put his comrades on notice: "The Russian jubilee is the jubilee of the international revolutionary proletariat, the jubilee of all sections of the Communist International." A rival celebration would therefore be nothing but "ridiculous coxcombry, intended to show the world that we are the oldest Communist party, older than the Bolshevik one!"[147]

A straight path led from this repudiation of the party's own tradition to the subsequent identification — by Stalin — of "Luxemburgism" with all the worst crimes of Menshevism and Trotskyism, and its corollary, the wholesale massacre of Polish Communists in the 1930s, in which Warski (despite his abject "self-criticism") perished together with followers and opponents alike. Though most other Communist parties, in particular those which acted under conditions of illegality and were forced to maintain a considerable part of their leadership in the Soviet exile, also fell victim to the Stalinist purges, none of them shared the tragic fate of the KPP.

NOTES

1. Jan B. de Weydenthal, *The Communists of Poland: An Historical Outline* (Stanford, 1978), p. xv.

2. KPRP = *Komunistyczna Partia Robotnicza Polski*; hereafter I shall use either the Polish initials or the less precise designation "the Communist party" or "the Communist party of Poland." The official change of name to KPP = *Komunistyczna Partia Polski* occurred in 1925.

3. In English almost exclusively from M. K. Dziewanowski, *The Communist Party of Poland: An Outline of History* (Cambridge, Mass., 1959), written in the early 1950s, before most of the sources became available; the second edition (1976) is an unrevised reprint, with several chapters added. It can serve, at best, as a very general introduction to the subject, and should be used with extreme

caution. In Polish, in addition to an interwar pamphlet written by a police informer (Jan Alfred Reguła [pseud.], *Historia Komunistycznej Partii Polski,* 2d ed. [Warsaw, 1934]), there are several collections of documents, which are not always comprehensive; e.g., *KPP: Uchwały i Rezolucje,* vol. 1 (Warsaw, 1953), hereafter cited as *KPP; Dokumenty i materiały do historii stosunków polsko-radzieckich,* vols. 1–4 (Warsaw-Moscow, 1962–), hereafter cited as *DiM; Materiały archiwalne do stosunków polsko-radzieckich,* vols. 1–3 (Warsaw, 1954–67); *Tymczasowy Komitet Rewolucyjny Polski* (Warsaw, 1955); *Rady Delegatów Robotniczych 1918–1919,* vols. 1–2 (Warsaw, 1962–65). Selections of writings of some prominent Communist leaders include: Maria Koszutska, *Pisma i przemówienia,* vols. 1–3 (Warsaw, 1961–63), Julian Marchlewski, *Pisma Wybrane,* vols. 1–2 (Warsaw, 1956); Adolf Warski, *Wybór pism i przemówien,* vols. 1–2 (Warsaw, 1958); Henryk Lauer-Brand, *Pisma i przemówienia* (Warsaw, 1970); Henryk Walecki, *Wybór pism,* vols. 1–2 (Warsaw, 1967). The textbooks include: Józef Kowalski, *Zarys historii polskiego ruchu robotniczego w latach 1918–1939,* vol. 1 (Warsaw, 1962), hereafter cited as *Zarys; Historia polskiego ruchu robotniczego 1864–1964,* vol. 1 (Warsaw, 1967); Antoni Czubinski, ed., *Polski ruch robotniczy: Zarys historii,* 2d ed. (Warsaw, 1974). A growing number of monographs have been published by, or written under the aegis of, the Institute of History of the Polish Workers' Movement of the Central Committee of the Polish United Workers' Party in Warsaw. They include: Franciszka Świetlikowa, *Komunistyczna Partia Robotnicza Polski 1918–1923* (Warsaw, 1968), hereafter cited as *KPRP*; Henryk Malinowski, *Program i polityka rolna Komunistycznej Partii Robotniczej Polski 1918–1923* (Warsaw, 1964); Maria Meglicka, *Prasa Komunistycznej Partii Robotniczej Polski 1918–1923* (Warsaw, 1968); Ignacy Pawłowski, *Polityka i działalność wojskowa KPP 1918–1929* (Warsaw, 1964); Edward Kołodziej, *Komunistyczna Partia Robotnicza Polski w ruchu zawodowyn 1918–1923* (Warsaw, 1978).

4. According to one of the founding fathers of the KPRP, the party came into being as "second among the Communist parties in general, a quarter of a year before the foundation of the Communist International"; cf. "Komunistyczna Partia Polski" (1922) in H. Walecki, *Wybór pism,* vol. 2, p. 132.

5. J. P. Nettl, *Rosa Luxemburg,* 2 vols. (London, 1966), vol. 1, p. 261.

6. In the 1960s some Polish Communist historians, hoping to supply plausible antecedents to legitimize their party's current nationalistic line, tried to discover some special ideological affinity on the national and agrarian questions between the SDKPiL–"splitters" and the Bolsheviks. The most extreme example of outright falsification of history can be found in Marian Żychowski, *Polska myśl socjalistyczna XIX i XX wieku (do 1918 r.)* (Warsaw, 1976). In the spirit of those years, Żychowski tried to draw the dividing line between Feliks Dzierżyński and Julian Marchlewski, both ethnic Poles of noble descent, and "the Jews," Luxemburg, Tyszka and Warski. Such zealous efforts were remarkably unsuccessful, and more conscientious scholars have refuted them easily.

7. "Behind the 'splitters' stood Lenin"; Georg W. Strobel, *Die Partei Rosa Luxemburgs, Lenin und die SPD: Der polnische "europäische" Internationalis-*

mus in der russischen Sozialdemokratie (Wiesbaden, 1974), p. 438. This is by
far the best and most detailed work on the history of the SDKPiL.

8. It is significant that in Poland the only serious scholarly attempt to deal
with the relations between SDKPiL and the RSDRP steered clear of this
most important period; Walentyna Najdus, *SDKPiL a SDPRR: 1893–1907*
(Warsaw, 1973). See also, Jan Sobczak, "Udział SDKPiL w życiu wew-
nętrznym SDPRR w latach 1909–1910," *Z pola walki* (Warsaw), (1963),
no. 4, pp. 46 ff.; idem; "Współpraca SDKPiL z SDPRR i bolszewikami w
latach 1906–1911," in *Polska-ZSRR: Internacjonalistyczna współpraca-
historia i współczesność* (Warsaw, 1977), vol. 1, pp. 257–289.

9. Roman Jabłonowski, *Wspomnienia 1905–1928* (Warsaw, 1962),
pp. 231 ff. Although heavily edited, these memoirs of a prominent member
of PPS–Lewica (later KPP) are a valuable eyewitness account for many
events usually omitted by party historians.

10. In her famous book, *Die Russische Revolution: Eine kritische Würdi-
gung* (Berlin, 1922), written in a German prison and published posthumously
(English translation: The Russian Revolution and Leninism or Marxism [Ann
Arbor, 1961]). A Polish translation was in preparation in 1956, but its
publication was prevented by censorship; it appeared in Paris (Adam
Ciołkosz, *Róża Luksemburg a rewolucja rosyjska* [Paris, 1961]). In an
unpublished letter to Stefan Brodowski (Bratman), a member of the SDKPiL
and then a Soviet diplomat (Berlin, 3 Nov. 1918), Luxemburg very critically
assessed the Cheka terror, deploring the role played by Dzierżyński and
many other Polish Communists, and added: "There is no way to keep
completely silent" about their abuses; quoted in, Feliks Tych, "Stosunek
SDKPiL, PPS–Lewicy i KPRP do Rewolucji Październikowej," in *Rewolucja Październikowa a Polska,* Tadeusz Cieślak and Leon Grosfeld, eds.
(Warsaw, 1967), pp. 133–184.

11. M. Z. [Maria Koszutska], "Rewolucja rosyjska a proletariat między-
narodowy," *Głos robotniczy* (Warsaw) no. 55, 15 Aug. 1918, quoted in *Ruch
robotniczy i ludowy w Polsce (1914–1923)* (Warsaw, 1960), pp. 238–239. In
later years this outspoken criticism supplied one of the pretexts for removing
Kostrzewa from the KPP leadership.

12. Warski, *Wybór pism,* vol. 2, pp. 1–9.

13. Marchlewski, *Pisma Wybrane,* vol. 2, p. 701.

14. J. Cieszewski, "Wspomnienia z roku 1918," *Z pola walki* (Moscow,
1929), no. 7–8, p. 286, quoted in *KPRP,* pp. 28 and 41.

15. Kołodziej, *KPRP w ruchu zawodowym,* pp. 11–12; cf. also Z. Landau
and J. Tomaszewski, *Gospodarka Polski międzywojennej* (Warsaw, 1967),
vol. 1 (1918–1923); idem, *Robotnicy przemysłowi w Polsce 1918–1923:
Materialne warunki bytu* (Warsaw, 1971).

16. Adam Próchnik, *Pierwsze piętnastolecie Polski niepodległej,* 2d ed.
(Warsaw, 1957), pp. 47 ff.

17. A. Warski, "Niech żyje zjednoczenie!" (Dec. 1918), in *Wybór pism,*
vol. 1, pp. 9–10. Five years later, in his report to the Second Congress of the
KPRP, Warski still recalled the then widespread conviction that "the

neighbors would make the revolution for us" ("Pięć lat KPRP," in ibid., vol. 2, p. 209.

18. Quoted in Żychowski, *Polska myśl socjalistyczna*, pp. 490–491.

19. Wiesława Toporowicz, "Początki Międzynarodówki Komunistycznej (w 50 rocznicę utworzenia)," *Z pola walki* (Warsaw), (1969), no. 1, pp. 14–19; Maria Meglicka and Wiesława Toporowicz, "Lenin a Polacy w III Międzynarodówce," ibid., (1970), no. 1, pp. 61–87.

20. *Sprawozdanie ze zjazdu organizacyjnego KPRP* (Warsaw, 1919), p. 9 (reprinted in *KPP*, vol. 1, pp. 33–58); the English translation in Dziewanowski, *Communist Party of Poland*, p. 78, leaves much to be desired.

21. J. Marchlewski, "Rosja proletariacka a Polska burżuazyjna" (1921), in *Pisma Wybrane*, vol. 2, p. 755.

22. This gratuitous charge reappears, however, even now in communist historiography as an example of "Luxemburgist errors." In fact, a parliamentary boycott was observed by all the European Communist parties, including Germany, until Lenin decided by 1921 that the revolutionary wave had ebbed, and from then on "bourgeois parliamentarism" should be exploited in order to unmask the sham of democracy. The failure of the KPRP to register with the authorities did not matter one way or another: the party was tacitly tolerated for nearly a year, and then repressed under martial law, introduced because of the approaching all-out war against Soviet Russia. Besides, no Polish law required advance licensing of political parties, and in later years this legal loophole was used to form several Communist-front organizations.

23. The figure of ten thousand party members by mid-1919 (*KPRP*, p. 73) seems grossly inflated, and is not justified by membership figures for local and regional party organizations which the same author quotes from contemporary internal reports.

24. For a revealing discussion of this point, see "Zasięg wpływów KPP w II Rzeczypospolitej," *Z pola walki* (Warsaw), (1978), no. 4, pp. 85–126. To the very end of its existence, the Communist Party of Poland was unable to overcome its largely regional character, derived from the limited area of operations of its antecedents, the SDKPiL and the PPS–Lewica, otherwise than through absorption of splitter groups from socialist and peasant parties (in Western Galicia and Posnania), or by merger with national minorities' parties (in Eastern Galicia, Upper Silesia, etc.).

25. *Sprawozdanie*, p. 6.

26. Edward Orłowski-Sokołowski in, "Protokóły II Zjazdu KPRP," *Z pola walki* (Warsaw), (1958), no. 4, p. 161.

27. Roman Jabłonowski, ibid., p. 171 (emphasis in original).

28. J. V. Stalin, *Works* (Moscow, 1953), vol. 4, p. 33.

29. V. I. Lenin, "On the History of the Question of the Unfortunate Peace" (7 Jan. 1918), *Collected Works* (Moscow, 1964), vol. 26, p. 449.

30. Leon Trotsky, *Kak vooruzhalas revoliutsia* (Moscow, 1923), vol. 1, p. 394.

31. The letter of Edward Próchniak to the Polish Bureau of the Central Committee of the RKP (b) dated Moscow, 15 July 1920, survived in the Soviet party archives, and was published for the first time in Artur Leinwand, *Polska*

Partia Socjalistyczna wobec wojny polsko-radzieckiej 1919–1920 (Warsaw, 1964), pp. 37–38. This is the first time that the formulation "Polish Soviet Republic" appears in a party document.

32. *KPP,* vol. 1, pp. 86–103; *DiM,* vol. 2, pp. 30–31.

33. H. Bicz [Henryk Bitner], *Rady Delegatów Robotniczych w Polsce w 1918–1919 r.* (Moscow, 1934), p. 115; quoted in *Zarys,* p. 125.

34. *Zasady i taktyka partii komunistycznej* (Warsaw, 1920), p. 32; quoted in ibid., p. 125.

35. J. Kowalski, "Z zagadnień rozwoju ideologicznego KPRP w latach 1918–1923," in *Ruch robotniczy i ludowy,* pp. 294–300.

36. The Manifesto of the Second World Congress of the Communist International (Moscow, August 1920) called for a "World Federation of Soviet Republics." The appeal "To the Proletarians of All Countries," issued by the Congress in connection with the Polish-Soviet war, also concluded with the slogan: "Long Live Soviet Poland!" Cf. Jane Degras, ed., *The Communist International 1919–1943: Documents,* 3 vols. (London, 1956), vol. 1, pp. 113, 177.

37. Brand and Walecki, "Kommunizm w Polsce" (1921), in Lauer-Brand, *Pisma,* p. 38.

38. This attitude later gave rise to internal discussion in the party: "Although we had participated in organizing labor unions [and] we had used them as points of support for agitation, we dealt with them rather from the point of view of the future, as organs of future proletarian power, subordinated to the councils as representatives of that power. For the time being, we assigned them, as their main task, the fight for the councils' power" (ibid., pp. 43–44).

39. Walecki, "O taktyce, etc.," *Wybór pism,* p. 9.

40. Quoted in Kołodziej, *KPRP w ruchu zawodowym,* p. 83.

41. For a detailed, though one-sided and often exaggerated account of the Polish labor movement in those years, see Henryk Malinowski, "Charakter i formy walki polskiej klasy robotniczej w latach 1918–1919," in *Rewolucja Październikowa a Polska,* Tadeusz Cieślak and Leon Grosfeld, eds. (Warsaw, 1967), pp. 71–131.

42. This decline was admitted in the report submitted to the first party conference in May 1920, and explained away by a wave of arrests which accompanied the intensification of the Polish-Soviet war; cf. *KPRP,* p. 157.

43. Bicz, *Rady Delegatów,* quoted in *KPRP,* pp. 116–120.

44. Kołodziej, *KPRP w ruchu zawodowym,* p. 84. The figures cover the former Kingdom of Poland only; the PPS-led unions in Galicia and former Austrian Silesia had some 71,000 members.

45. *KPRP,* pp. 130–144; according to Brand and Walecki (Lauer-Brand, *Pisma,* p. 48) there were 60 Communist delegates out of 155, and Communist drafts were rejected by 86 vs. 68 votes.

46. Meglicka, *Prasa KPRP, passim* (esp. pp. 137, 148, 161).

47. Krystyna Kawecka, "PPS-Opozycja (1919–1920)," *Z pola walki* (Warsaw), (1961), no. 3, pp. 38–60.

48. Kowalski, "Z zagadnień," pp. 299–300, who quotes unpublished documents from Polish party archives.

49. Most of those mergers took place after 1921, but the process which resulted in

splits in the noncommunist left-wing parties had already begun by 1919. The first group of former Poaley-Zion members, for instance, joined the KPRP in December 1918. In April 1919, at the Third Bund Conference, the majority voted for the dictatorship of the proletariat and transfer of state power to the workers' councils. The splinter group, called the Communist Bund (*Kombund*), emerged as a separate party in the second half of 1921, and the formal merger with the KPRP took place in 1923 (Larysa Gamska, "Lewica żydowskich partii socjalistycznych wobec III Międzynarodówki i KPRP [1918–1923])," *Biuletyn Żydowskiego Instytutu Historycznego w Polsce* [Warsaw, Jan.–March 1976], no. 1/97, pp. 61–77; Gereon Iwański, "Żydowski Komunistyczny Związek Robotniczy Kombund w Polsce [1921–1923]," *Z pola walki* [Warsaw], (1974), no. 4, pp. 43–76; cf. Moisei G. Rafes, *Ocherki po istorii Bunda* [Moscow, 1923]).

50. Franciszek Hawranek, *Ruch komunistyczny na Górnym Śląsku w latach 1918–1921* (Wrocław, 1966); Janusz Radziejowski, *Komunistyczna Partia Zachodniej Ukrainy 1919–1929: Węzłowe problemy ideologiczne* (Cracow, 1976). Cf. also Roman Solchanyk, "The Foundation of the Communist Movement in Eastern Galicia, 1919–1921," *Slavic Review* vol. 30, no. 4, (Dec. 1971), pp. 774–794.

51. Sochacki, Żarski, and his wife, Zofia Maciejewska-Żarska, together with the former Pilsudskite intelligence officer Sylwester Wojewódzki (who joined the Communists after a split in the left-wing peasant party *PSL–Wyzwolenie*), were the first to be "unmasked" in 1934 as agents-provocateurs. Allegedly, they had joined the party on the orders of the Polish counter-intelligence (*defensywa*) to undermine it by propagating "nationalism." The KPP leadership of that period applauded their execution without even a parody of trial. The turn of Łańcucki, Dąbal, and others, came next. Cf. Józef Kowalski, *Trudne lata: Problemy rozwoju polskiego ruchu robotniczego 1929–1935* (Warsaw, 1966), pp. 628–633.

52. According to a reliable historian, at the turn of 1917/18 there were in Russia some 5,000 SDKPiL and at least 3,000 PPS–Lewica members, i.e., considerably more than in Poland proper; Walentyna Najdus, *Lewica polska w Kraju Rad 1918–1920* (Warsaw, 1971), p. 424 (hereafter cited as *Lewica*). Some 2,000 became members of the Bolshevik party by 1919.

53. According to incomplete sources, at least 7,700 Poles actively participated in the Russian revolution and civil war; cf. *Księga Polaków-uczestników Rewolucji Październikowej 1917–1920: Biografie* (Warsaw, 1967). The total number of Polish refugees and evacuees in Russia is roughly estimated at about 2.5 million.

54. The best known among its members were Feliks Dzierżyński, Julian Leński (Leszczyński), Józef Unszlicht, Stanisław Bobiński, Edward Próchniak ("Sewer"), and others. Julian Marchlewski, Karol Radek, Czesław Hanecki, and many others joined them after regaining Russia.

55. Clause one of the by-laws of the SDKPiL groups in Russia defined its members as those "who belong to the SDWDR [RSDRP] (bolshevik), *in the Polish problem support the SDKPiL position,* acknowledge the present statutes,

and pay membership dues" (emphasis added); *Lewica,* pp. 61–62. After the merger with the PPS–Lewica in Russia, this clause was transferred *verbatim* into the statute of the KPRP goups in Russia (ibid., p. 175).

56. Dzierżyński, as member of the CC of the Bolshevik party, defied Lenin by voting against the treaty. When it was finally signed, members of the SDKPiL, together with the so-called Left-Communists (Bukharin, Piatakov, Uritskii, etc.) abstained (ibid, pp. 69–70).

57. *Zarys,* pp. 42–43.

58. Stanisław Pestkowski, member of the SDKPil, became the acting head of the Peoples' Commissariat for Nationalities Affairs immediately after the Bolshevik seizure of power (Stalin, his nominal superior, devoted most of his time to the Military-Revolutionary Committee); Julian Leński (Leszczyński) was appointed Commissar for Polish Affairs shortly afterwards; Kazimierz Cichowski and Stanisław Bobiński were his deputies.

59. Julian Marchlewski was first appointed the Soviet envoy to Warsaw. When Polish authorities refused to recognize his status, Bronisław Wesołowski ("Smutny"), member of the CC of the SDKPiL in Petrograd, was sent to Warsaw in December 1918, ostensibly on behalf of the Russian Red Cross —more probably, on behalf of the Central College for Affairs of Prisoners and Refugees (*Tsentroplenbezh*), headed by another SDKPiL leader Józef Unszlicht — without even prior notification of the Polish government; he was murdered on his way back to Russia. Confidential diplomatic missions undertaken in the subsequent months by J. Marchlewski belonged to the same category.

60. *Lewica,* pp. 77, 123, 170–175.

61. Ibid., p. 171n. This statement originated with the secretariat of the PPS–Lewica in Russia shortly before the formal merger, but was followed by a rider: "As far as we know, the Central Executive Committee of the SDKPiL shares this view."

62. Ibid., pp. 190–191, 206–219. The entire complex of problems arising from the involvement of Polish Communists in the affairs of the shortlived Lithuanian-Belorussian Soviet Republic (*Litbel*) and her armed forces is omitted here. Many regarded it, rightly, as a dress rehearsal for the Sovietization of Poland proper.

63. *Sprawozdanie z Rady Partyjnej zwołanej w połowie lutego 1919 r.* (Warsaw, 1919); quoted in Pawłowski, *Polityka,* pp. 26–27.

64. Brand and Walecki, in Lauer-Brand, *Pisma,* p. 58.

65. *Czerwony Sztandar* (Warsaw, October 1919); reprinted in *DiM,* vol. 2, p. 798.

66. H. Walecki, "O taktyce i o stosunku do parlamentaryzmu" (February 1921); reprinted in *Wybór pism,* vol. 2, pp. 10–12. For the PPS peace campaign, see also Kazimierz Więch, *Polska Partia Socjalistyczna 1918–1919* (Warsaw, 1978), esp. pp. 149–215.

67. Full text in *KPP,* vol. 1, pp. 63–69 (emphasis added).

68. Cf. Weronika Gostynska, "Rola Juliana Marchlewskiego w tajnych rokowaniach polsko-radzieckich (czerwiec–lipiec 1919 r.)," *Z pola walki* (Warsaw), (1966), no. 2, pp. 23–40.

69. Quoted in Norman Davies, *White Eagle, Red Star* (London, 1972), p. 71.

70. *Lewica,* pp. 252–255. The KPRP representative was Czesław Hanecki

(Jakub Fürstenberg), who during World War I was Lenin's intimate aide in secret dealings with the German military headquarters.

71. *DiM,* vol. 2, p. 313; *Lewica,* pp. 252–255; Gostynska, *Rola Juliana Marchlewskiego,* p. 35.

72. Feliks Tych, "Stosunek SDKPiL," p. 183.

73. R. Ermolaeva, "K istorii polskikh kommunisticheskikh organizatsii i organov RKP (b) dlia raboty sredi polskogo naseleniia na territorii sovetskoi respubliki v 1917–1921 gg.," in A. Ia. Manusevich, ed., *Oktiabrskaia revolutsiia i zarubezhnye slavianskie narody* (Moscow, 1957), p. 36.

74. Full text in *DiM,* vol. 2, pp. 575–576; in 1955 the same document had been reprinted in *Tymczasowy Komitet Rewolucyjny Polski,* pp. 33–34, with all but five of the signatories' names omitted. In translation, I have substituted "chauvinism" for the Polish *nacjonalizm,* as closer to the meaning of the original.

75. Full text of the leaflet in *DiM,* vol. 2, pp. 809–810.

76. Ibid., pp. 576–578; Brand and Walecki, "Komunizm w Polsce," in Lauer-Brand, *Pisma,* p. 57.

77. Degras, *Communist International,* vol. 1, p. 5.

78. Wielmira Niewolina, "Miedzynarodówka Komunistyczna i rewolucyjna współpraca RKP (b) z Komunistyczną Partią Robotniczą Polski (1918–1923)," in *Polska-ZSRR,* vol. 1, p. 393.

79. Full text in *DiM,* vol. 2, pp. 31–33.

80. Brand and Walecki in Lauer-Brand, *Pisma,* p. 87.

81. Degras, *Communist Internaional,* vol. 1, p. 47; Unszlicht was a member of the Peoples' Commissariat for Internal Affairs, later Dzierżynski's deputy in the *Cheka,* and deputy commissar for war.

82. *KPRP,* p. 112; Niewolina, "Miedzynarodówka Komunistyczna," p. 396.

83. I have followed here the detailed account in *Lewica,* pp. 261–272.

84. For unknown reasons, the official representative of the KPRP in the Bureau of the Comintern, Henryk Stein-Kamienski (Domski), who then lived in Berlin, did not participate in the Second Congress; it is possible that he was prevented from coming to Moscow because he was considered "leftist," and the instructions for Polish delegates, prepared by another "ultra-leftist," Władysław Kowalski ("Grzech"), were very critical of the turn to the right prepared by the Russian party leadership and imposed on the Congress (cf. Niewolina, "Miedzynarodówka Komunistyczna," p. 399; I. S. Iazhborovskaia, *Idieinoe razvitie polskogo rabochego dvizheniia* [Moscow, 1973], p. 388). For oppositional views of Domski and "Grzech," see below.

85. The declaration was apparently written in Russian, since two Polish-language newspapers (in Moscow and Kiev) published two slightly different translations; *Lewica,* p. 287n.

86. Exchange of prisoners between Poland and Soviet Russia was always a sensitive issue. Those most concerned, Communist activists inside Poland, as a rule opposed it because it could jusify the charge that KPRP was an agency of a foreign government, and it would weaken the local cadres (but R. Jabłonowski noted a probably typical reaction of a party member stopped by a policeman in Warsaw: don't bother, if the worst comes to the worst, we can go for exchange;

Wspomnienia, p. 273). The idea apparently originated in Moscow, since the first wholesale exchange had been arranged by Marchlewski during his 1919 secret negotiations. In later years it became instrumental in making the Communist movement in Poland even more dependent on the Soviets (cf. *KPRP*, pp. 169–173).

87. *Lewica*, p. 295. The author concludes that this reticence meant full agreement with the assessment, especially since it was also shared by Marchlewski, then head of the Secretariat of the Polish Bureau. Not necessarily; the Polish Bureau, despite its name, was an organ of the CC RKP (b), and as such was not entitled to formulate policy.

88. The Polish Bureau of the CC RKP (b) apparently called only one conference in Moscow, on 3–5 May 1920. It decided to mobilize all Polish Communists in Russia for "front-line duties," but did not discuss any specific issues connected with the changing character of the Soviet-Polish war; cf. Rozalia Jermo-łajewa, "Polacy-Internacjonalisci w Rewolucji Październikowej i wojnie domowej w Rosji w latach 1917–1920," in *Polska–ZSRR*, p. 384.

89. There is also abundant literature on the military and diplomatic history of the Polish-Soviet war in English. See, e.g., E. H. Carr, *The Bolshevik Revolution, 1917–1923* (New York, 1953), vol. 3, pp. 148–228; Titus Komarnicki, *Rebirth of the Polish Republic: A Study in the Diplomatic History of Europe 1914–1920* (London, 1957), pp. 397–748; Josef Korbel, *Poland between East and West: Soviet and Germany Diplomacy toward Poland 1919–1933* (Princeton, 1963); Piotr S. Wandycz, *Soviet-Polish Relations, 1917–1921* (Cambridge, Mass., 1969); Norman Davies, *White Eagle, Red Star: The Polish-Soviet War 1919–1920* (London, 1972).

90. For those arguments see: Mikhail Toukhatchevskii, "La révolution introduite de l'extérieur," *Partisans* (Paris), no. 61, Sept.–Oct. 1971.

91. The Second Congress of the Comintern, meeting in Moscow in July 1920, was not consulted either, even though the Red Army offensive was the main subject of conversations in the lobbies. According to G. Zinoviev's later account, "In the hall of the congress hung a large map. Every day we marked on it the advance of our forces, and every day with breathless interest the delegates examined the map. . . . All of them understood that if the military objectives of our troops were reached, it would mean an immense acceleration of the international proletarian revolution. All of them understood that on every step forward of our Red Army depended, in the literal sense of the word, the fate of the international proletarian revolution. . . . We had to discuss as a practical matter whether a victorious workers' republic could carry socialism into other countries at the point of bayonets. There were differences of opinion." Quoted in Degras, *Communist Internaional*, vol. 1, pp. 110–111. In fact, no such discussion took place at the Comintern Congress either.

92. Klara Zetkin, *Erinnerungen an Lenin* (Vienna, 1929), pp. 20–21. In January 1920, on his way back from Germany to Russia, Radek passed through Poland and addressed an open letter to the leaders of the PPS. He argued that "if the Polish working class would prove unable to seize power by its own means, it would not be capable of maintaining it, had it been handed by foreign

bayonets." The letter was published in *Robotnik* (Warsaw) on 10 March 1920, and reprinted in translation in *Soviet Russia* (New York), 1 May 1920 (quoted by Carr, *Bolshevik Revolution,* p. 159); full text in Leinwand, *PPS,* pp. 251–256.

93. The exchange of messages, in the original Russian, was reprinted in Leinwand, *PPS,* p. 184. Since no dates were given (probably June 1920), it is difficult to conclude whether Lenin had already made a decision and needed Unszlicht's opinion only to confirm it. Nor is it clear in whose name the answer was given, as Unszlicht throughout used the form "we"; probably more Polish Communists in Russia shared his view.

94. *Robotnik* (Warsaw), no. 68, 9 March 1920; quoted in ibid., pp. 133–134.

95. The fall of Kiev, the capital city of the Ukraine, was presented as a danger to Russia; the Red Army's daily *Krasnaia Zvezda* called for fighting for "one and indivisible Red Russia," and even *Pravda* stressed the national character of the war.

96. For details see, Leinwand, *PPS,* pp. 187 ff., and Więch, *PPS,* pp. 216–269. Cf. also *DiM,* vol. 3, p. 147.

97. The usually quoted figure is 2,000 (*KPRP,* p. 159), though some contemporary sources mentioned 7,000 detained (H. Walecki, *Wybór pism,* vol. 2, p. 134). All of them seem exaggerated: police reports speak about 569 people detained between 1 April and 31 December 1920 on charges of communist activity; 165 among them were arraigned for trial (Józef Ławnik, "Represje policyjne wobec ruchu komunistycznego w Polsce 1918–1939," *Z pola walki* (Warsaw) (1978), no. 3, p. 35). The discrepancy is difficult to account for, even assuming that the internees included all those politically unreliable, army deserters, etc.

98. A. Warski, in a letter written a few months later to Zofia Dzierżyńska in Moscow (Feliks' wife and a Polish Communist leader in her own right) admitted that "for a long time our comrades in Warsaw were virtually unable to show their faces in the streets." He tried to justify the party's helplessness and avoidance of any revolutionary actions, as well as the lack of response among the workers, by the fact that "*among the working masses the will to live to see liberation through foreign aid was general*" (reprinted in full in *DiM,* vol. 3, pp. 495–499; emphasis in the original). Other Communist witnesses corroborate this: "The working class in its mass remained passive" (Brand and Walecki, in Lauer-Brand, *Pisma,* p. 59); Jabłonowski, (*Wspomnienia,* p. 259) recalled that Warsaw Communists in the underground "had already discussed the makeup of the future government of peoples' commissars," but admitted that "our influence was quite negligible."

99. *DiM,* vol. 3, pp. 340–342.

100. Roman Zambrowski, "Uwagi o wojnie polsko-radzieckiej 1920 roku," *Zeszyty historyczne* (Paris, 1976), no. 38, p. 11. This is an arbitrary abridged and sloppily edited reprint of a Polish *samizdat* publication; unfortunately the original was not available. The author, a lifelong official of the Communist Party of Poland and of the Communist International, was in the years 1945–1963 member of the Politburo and secretary of the CC of the Polish United Workers' Party.

101. The Soviets officially promised their German interlocutors to honor the old (i.e. pre-1914) frontier of the Reich. They were unable to keep their word because of military necessities, but in the only major locality in the former Prussian partition temporarily occupied by the Red Army, Działdowo (Soldau), they installed a "revolutionary municipal council" composed solely of representatives of the German minority. See Gerhard Wagner, *Deutschland und der polnisch-sowjetische Krieg 1920* (Wiesbaden, 1979), pp. 87, 100, 126–135, 151–153. Cf. also Robert Himmer, "Soviet Policy toward Germany during the Russo-Polish War, 1920," *Slavic Review*, vol. 35, no. 4 (Dec. 1976); Korbel, *Poland between East and West,* p. 85 ff.

102. The minutes of the conference (*DiM,* vol. 3, p. 177) state: "Comrade Dzierżyński announced to the audience the resolution of the Central Committee of the RKP (b) concerning the total mobilization of Polish Communists in light of the possible entry of the Red Army into Polish territories." Elected then and there the Polish Bureau (the election was not formal, since the Polish Bureau was supposed to be appointed by the CC RKP (b), not elected) consisted of Dzierżyński as chairman, Dolecki (replaced the next day by Feliks Kon — it is not clear who decided on the change), Marchlewski, Próchniak, and Unszlicht; Pestkowski was appointed secretary. The next month Radek was coopted; cf. *Lewica,* pp. 297 ff.

103. Ibid., p. 299.

104. Full text of the manifesto and appeals (to the Red Army soldiers, to Polish legionaires, to proletarians all over the world, etc.) in *Tymczasowy Komitet Rewolucyjny Polski,* pp. 70–94.

105. Próchniak, the only member with recent Polish experience (he had spent about one year in underground party activities and several months in prison, before being exchanged), stayed behind in Moscow to supervise the mobilization of Polish cadres; Unszlicht, too, took no part in the *Polrevkom* work, ostensibly because of illness, probably because of his more important assignment in the political apparatus of the Red Army. I. T. Smilga, head of the Red Army Political Administration at the Western Front, was a "consulting member" of the *Polrevkom.*

106. In a speech delivered at the Ninth Conference of RKP (b) (22 Sept. 1920), Lenin said: "We have not been able to affect the industrial proletariat of Poland beyond the Vistula and in Warsaw (this being one of the main reasons for our defeat)," and then added, ostensibly quoting Polish sources: "It was the upsurge of patriotism that saved [Poland]." Lenin, *Collected Works,* vol. 31, pp. 275–278.

107. Quoted by Wandycz, *Soviet-Polish Relations,* p. 230.

108. Marchlewski, "Rosja proletariacka a Polska burżuazyjna," p. 747.

109. *KPRP,* p. 164n.

110. Maria Grinberg, "Z zagadnień wojny polsko-radzieckiej," in *Ruch robotniczy i ludowy,* p. 509.

111. A detailed, if biased, account of *Polrevkom* rule appears in *Lewica,* pp. 302–347. It follows closely a contemporary account by Julian Marchlewski ("Rosja proletariacka a Polska burżuazyjna," pp. 745–786) — best proof that no independent research has been allowed up till now.

112. The well-known Russian scholar Ivan Skvortsov (Stepanov), assigned to the Polish Bureau and then to the Polrevkom by the CC RKP (b), remarked that even at the gates of Warsaw all were beset by doubts whether the storming of the Polish capital would be profitable for the Polish revolutionary movement, whether it would not make it easier for the Polish government to consolidate its forces based on patriotic sentiments of the people, whether a revolutionary movement in Polish environment should not have been rather allowed to ripen more slowly. *S krasnoi armii na panskuiu Polshu* (Moscow, 1920), pp. 41–42, quoted in *Lewica,* p. 341.

113. E. d'Abernon, *The Eighteenth Decisive Battle of the World: Warsaw 1920* (London, 1931).

114. Zambrowski, "Uwagi o wojnie," pp. 13–14. He admits that Polish Communists "stood in solidarity with Soviet Russia when the majority of the Polish society considered the advance of the Red Army a menace to the independence of Poland, and all of the opprobrium fell on them."

115. *DiM,* vol. 3, p. 495 (emphasis in the original).

116. Full text in Adolf Warski, "Korespondencja polityczna z lat 1920–1926," *Z pola walki* (Warsaw), (1970), no. 4, p. 154. The letter also contains a most revealing description of the moods that prevailed among the Polish Communists during the battle of Warsaw: "The CC and all the party still at liberty were making unheard-of efforts to provoke some kind of mass movement in order to welcome the Red Army appropriately. But the entire country was under martial law. Warsaw was directly on the front line, civilian authorities ceased to operate, replaced by military authorities and courts-martial. Workers would not risk anything, convinced, or rather certain, that the Red Army would be in Warsaw any day. . . . Our party in Warsaw was certain of the entry of the Red Army to such an extent that it had made detailed preparations and issued specific instruction to district [committees]. It appointed a commander for Warsaw, and picked up people for various posts. It decided, *inter alia,* to reactivate the Executive Committee of the former Council of Workers' Delegates, after purging it of uncertain elements. The Executive Committee was supposed to act simultaneously as a provisional government, and at the same time to prepare new elections to the council. Because of this, the news of the formation of a Polish Soviet government in Białystok was received with certain dissatisfaction. They thought it would have been better if the first provisional government were constituted by Warsaw workers." Ibid., p. 151.

117. Quoted by Pawłowski, *Polityka i działalność,* pp. 30–31.

118. *Deviataia konferentsiia RKP (b): Protokoly* (Moscow, 1972), pp. 4–10, 51, 219 ff., 232, 273. The issue was raised again at the Fourth Congress of the Communist International in 1923.

119. "In technical preparations the emigration in Russia can render us enormous service, but here it should be stressed that *revkoms* made ready by them which would arrive in Poland all set, would be a mistake. Such *revkoms,* composed of people for a long time cut off from the country, not only could frequently appear to be in conflict with the native population, but would create

an impression that we strive not for a revolution in Poland but for incorporation of Poland by Russia." Cf. "Protokóły II Zjazdu KPRP," p. 186.

120. "We are preparing [the *revkoms*] to have administrative organs ready after the [Red] Army enters Poland. They are necessary, just as they were necessary in 1920. Then it was done too late. That was bad. If we could expect to achieve a speedy upheaval by Polish forces, the entry of the Red Army to Poland would be superfluous. We cannot expect that. After an outbreak of a revolution in Germany and Bohemia the [Red] Army's passage through Poland might become necessary. To argue against it is superfluous" (ibid., pp. 184–185).

121. Warski, *Wybór pism,* vol. 2, p. 506.

122. Cf. Pawłowski, *Polityka i działalność,* p. 131n. The "Domski affair" was discussed, however, by Reguła, *Historia KPP,* pp. 43–44.

123. *Historia polskiego ruchu robotniczego,* vol. 1, p. 321.

124. Full text in *DiM,* vol. 3, pp. 500–504 (emphasis in the original). Since by mid-1920 the KPRP virtually ceased to exist, it is not clear who and where did in fact issue this leaflet (most probably the émigré leaders in Berlin) or how it was circulated. But the same can be said about other publications signed by the CC KPRP which appeared throughout the summer; nonetheless they are most instructive. In July, for instance, before the Red Army had crossed the Bug River, the CC still called for termination of the war and signing of peace (ibid., pp. 259–260). On August 1, when Soviet victory appeared assured, a leaflet instructed workers to intensify revolutionary activities, to rebuild the almost forgotten Councils of Workers' Delegates, and to arm workers and form detachments of the "Polish Red Army" "to collaborate with the Red Army of Soviet Russia in order to overthrow capitalist power all over Poland." The appeal ended with slogans previously not used: "Death to Capitalist Poland! Long Live the Polish Soviet Republic!" (ibid., pp. 261–263). Another leaflet issued by the Warsaw Committee of the KPRP, titled "The Fatherland Is In Danger!" similarly ended with "Long Live the Polish Soviet Republic! Long Live the International Workers' Revolution!" (ibid., pp. 299–300). As soon as the retreat of the Red Army from Warsaw began, the tone changed: a CC KPRP leaflet, dated August 25, ended with "Long Live Soviet Russia! Long Live the International Proletarian Solidarity! Long Live the World Social Revolution!" (ibid., pp. 366–368). In September, the CC KPRP still maintained, all the evidence to the contrary notwithstanding, that Polish workers had treated the Red Army not as an enemy and invader, but as an ally and defender of the Polish proletariat, whether it had fought on the Berezina or the Vistula, but reproached them for "not having nerved themselves for any revolutionary mass action," allegedly because of the "extreme terror" (ibid., pp. 445–450). Finally, the leaflet protesting against the Riga peace preliminaries confined itself to generalities: "Long Live the Dictatorship of the Proletariat! Long Live Socialism!" The slogan "Long Live the Polish Soviet Republic!" returned in subsequent publications.

125. Marchlewski, "Rosja proletariacka a Polska burżuazyjna," p. 785.

126. According to an eyewitness account, there were mass escapes from the camps because the authorities turned a blind eye; most of the leaders, nevertheless, preferred to go abroad (Jabłonowski, *Wspomnienia,* p. 264).

127. Even the Central Strike Committee, brought into being by Communists to counterbalance the existing trade unions, remained largely isolated despite the militancy of its members; see Kołodziej, *KPRP w ruchu zawodowym*, pp. 111–117; Janusz Żarnowski, "Strajk kolejarzy i strajk powszechny w lutym–marcu 1921 r.," *Kwartalnik historyczny* (Warsaw), (1956), no. 1, pp. 55–58.

128. *DiM*, vol. 2, p. 313; *Lewica*, p. 253. Here again KPRP was insensitive to the repercussions in Polish public opinion. Its pro-German bias resulted from toeing the Comintern line: the Soviets aimed at blowing up the Versailles treaty system in Europe and still expected an imminent revolution in Germany. Polish Communists therefore ignored the fact that in Upper Silesia the industrial workers were mainly Polish, while the bourgeoisie was German; at one time Marchlewski had expressed the hope that the coal basin "would become a land bridge linking Polish and German Communists."

129. *KPRP*, pp. 186–199.

130. Ibid., pp. 210, 214.

131. "In the same manner the problem was formulated by many other leading comrades as well," Jabłonowski, *Wspomnienia*, p. 260.

132. Walecki, *Wybór pism*, vol. 2, pp. 5–46; A. Warski, *Wybór pism*, vol. 2, p. 215. At the Second Congress of the KPRP (September 1923), Warski admitted that "the party's Central Committee dealt with the pamphlet in March 1921 in order to denounce it and order its destruction"; most of the party members "did not even get acquainted with it" (*Z pola walki* [Warsaw] (1958), no. 4, p. 146). In his letter of 11 May 1921 (probably to the CC KPRP) Walecki protested against such —then still rather unusual —high-handed suppression of discussion in the party. He claimed that his criticism was "restrained" and accorded with party and Comintern principles, and that discussion on tactical issues was necessary. Since the KPRP was then in any event preparing to revise its stand on the boycott question and to take part in the next parliamentary election, Warski's indignation does not appear justified. It seems more probable that Walecki's sin consisted of violating the taboos connected with the 1920 war.

133. Lenin, "'Left-Wing' Communism — An Infantile Disorder," *Collected Works*, vol. 31, pp. 21–118. The book was written in April–May 1920 and published in June. Communist cadres in Poland were acquainted with it as soon as the war ended.

134. *KPRP*, pp. 174–175.

135. A. Warski, "W sprawach partyjnych," *Nowy Przegląd* (Gliwice), nos. 3–4, 5, 6–7 (Aug.–Sept., Oct., Nov.–Dec., 1922); re-edition (Warsaw, 1957), pp. 190–200, 312–321, 447–461.

136. Walecki and Kostrzewa had been leaders of the PPS–Lewica; Warski, who came from the SDKPiL, had moved closer to their point of view before the 1918 merger. During the post-1924 factional struggle in the Soviet Communist party, "the three W's" had the misfortune to take the losing side, that of Trotsky. Stalin unceremoniously removed them from the KPRP leadership, and to the "leftists," most of them one-time SDKPiL "splitters,"

assigned the thankless task of "Bolshevization" — subsequently renamed Stalinization — of the Polish party. This was only one of the paradoxes that marked the troubled history of communism in Poland.

137. In spite of the impressive appellation, those were very small gatherings; the second conference, for instance, was held in a worker's apartment in an industrial suburb of Warsaw (cf. Jabłonowski, *Wspomnienia,* p. 265). According to an official account, it consisted of 38 members, of whom 29 were voting members. The third party council was attended by 23 members (17 with voting rights). The reports, either contemporarily published or preserved in the party archives ("Sprawozdanie z narady z towarzyszami z kraju": *W sprawach partyjnych. Druga konferencja KPRP* [Warsaw, 1921]; *Sprawozdanie z rady partyjnej* [Warsaw, 1921]) were not available to me. They are quoted (very selectively!) in *KPRP,* pp. 174–186 and *Zarys,* pp. 202–208.

138. The third conference (1921) was convened in Sopot (Free City of Danzig); all subsequent congresses and conferences were held in the USSR.

139. Niewolina, "Miedzynarodówka komunistyczna," p. 410. The Polish delegation decided to exclude, or rather to transfer to the RKP (b), all the members of the KPRP who were living and active in Russia, and defined the relations between the KPRP representation at the Executive Committee of the Comintern and the Polish Bureau of the CC RKP (b). In practice, this delimination was hardly ever observed.

140. Lenin, *Collected Works,* vol. 42, pp. 324–328.

141. Ibid., pp. 354–355. Lenin began by stating that "the revolution in Poland is coming to a head" — at a time when the party was in total disarray — and went on to warn against *"premature* uprising." The only one who dared to question Lenin's wildly exaggerated optimism was E. Brand (Henryk Lauer); in a letter to Edward Próchniak, the KPRP representative to the Comintern in Moscow, he wrote that Lenin overrated the momentum of the workers' movement in Poland and complained about "great apathy among the proletariat" (quoted in: H. Lauer-Brand, *Pisma,* p. 11). Still, Lenin's claim that "the victory of Soviet power *from within* Poland will be a gigantic internaional victory" (emphasis in the original) could be construed as a modest departure from the doctrine that had provided for imposing a revolution from outside, by the Red Army.

142. Two participants of the congress placed the Polish delegation, alongside the German, Czech, Italian, and some others, on the "so-called left wing," the one that stressed "the danger from the right." See H. Lauer-Brand, *Pisma,* p. 86.

143. See Lenin, *Collected Works,* vol. 33, p. 436.

144. Degras, *Communist International,* vol. 1, pp. 255, 282, 300.

145. "Od 'Proletariatu' do Komunistycznej Partii Polski," *Kalendarz Komunistyczny na rok 1922* (Moscow).

146. *Lewica,* p. 77; Jermolajewa, "Polacy-Internacjonalisci," p. 371.

147. Adolf Warski, "Nauki jubileuszu bolszewickiego. Jubileusz KPRP?" *Nowy Przegląd* (Gliwice), no. 8 (June 1923); re-edition (Warsaw, 1957), pp. 70–88.

The Origins of Czechoslovak Communism

F. B. M. FOWKES

The Communist parties of the interwar years, when "polycentric communism" was neither a phrase nor a reality, inevitably possessed a dual character. On the one hand, they were directly subject to the Comintern, an institution with its headquarters in Moscow which was in effect dominated by the Russian Communist party; on the other hand, they were rooted in the particular conditions of their own countries, to which they had to adapt themselves, and which could not fail to have an impact on their policies.

This apparently obvious point is in fact ignored in the majority of the accounts of the Communist party of Czechoslovakia (CPC). For a long time studies written from within the party merely reflected the Prague/Moscow duality, without grasping it.[1] Admittedly things have changed in this respect in the last few years. Western accounts, which are so far few in number,[2] tend to follow Franz Borkenau's pioneering but journalistic study of the whole Communist movement in overemphasizing the nonindigenous side of the CPC's history.[3] Since they have tended to see the CPC as a mere reflection of Kremlin policy, Western historians have presented a picture of unwilling Czechoslovak Social Democrats forced by the Russians to form a Communist party that then proceeded to adopt policies slavishly copied from the Soviet Union and entirely unsuited to Czechoslovak conditions.

The Communist historiography of the CPC, on the contrary, has passed through a variety of phases. The first full-scale work on the subject was written in 1931 by Paul Reimann, an important member of the CPC Central Committee. He emphasized the danger posed by social-democratic survivals, which needed purging before a genuinely Bolshevik Communist party could be created.[4] This view corresponded to the Comintern's ultra-left phase (1929–1933), when attacks on Social Democrats were de rigueur. In the same way, the personality cult of the early 1950s produced the hero worship of Lenin and Zápotocký, to the exclusion of less orthodox figures, which is found in the work of

Jindřich Veselý,[5] and to a lesser extent in that of Koloman Gajan.[6] Then, in the second half of the 1960s, there at last developed a tendency toward a more objective approach, an emphasis on establishing the true facts about Czechoslovak political history of the early 1920s. This tendency toward greater objectivity did not mean, however, that the authors failed to draw very definite conclusions. The lesson of the 1920s was presumably that precipitate revolutionary action was dangerous, and that the broad masses must be involved in the party's activities — views entirely commensurate with the policy of the CPC at that time. For example, Zdeněk Kárník's article on the foundation of the CPC and the Comintern, published in 1969, concludes with the suggestion that the "democratic communism" represented by Šmeral in 1921 prefigured the "short but intensive period of the destalinizing socialist renaissance"[7] — in other words, the Dubček era of 1968. And finally, after 1969, the historiographic line has changed again. In a recent article, Jurij Křížek criticizes Kárník for using Šmeral's 1921 tactics as "an alleged proof of the incorrectness of 'dogmatic and conservative' Communist policies."[8]

The present article seeks to avoid the common practice of distributing blame or praise among individuals and factions, and instead attempts to grasp the dual nature of the CPC in the 1920s and the role individuals played in the context of their time. This approach should make it easier to analyze the relative strength of internal and external factors in the history of the party.

The CPC grew directly out of the labor movement that existed in the Czech lands before 1917. It was in no sense an alien, external force, but rather a continuation of the prewar Czechoslav Social Democratic Workers' Party (CSDWP), as regards both its leaders and its membership. A glance at the list of top leaders in 1921 gives us such names as Bohumír Šmeral, Edmund Burian, Miloš Vaněk, Karl Kreibich, Václav Houser, Antonín Zapotocký, Alois Muna, and Alois Neurath. These men were all prominent in the social-democratic movement before the war, and in effect formed a personal guarantee of continuity. There was considerable continuity among lesser functionaries as well, as indicated by the fact that 338 out of the 527 delegates elected to an ordinary party congress of the CSDWP were prepared to attend the September 1920 congress that set up a new party (CSDWP[Left]), which represented a transitional stage between social democracy and communism, and accepted the principles of the Comintern. Moreover, only seven out of the 569 delegates to the next congress of the CSDWP(Left) wanted to remain in this transitional stage and refused to vote for the conversion of the party into a Communist one.[9] In 1924, 73 percent of the CPC membership were former Social Democrats. There was, then, a high degree of continuity, but we must make an important qualification: this continuity was personal rather than ideological. Before the First World War, there was nothing to suggest that the third largest Communist party in Europe would emerge from the CSDWP. Prewar Czech social democracy was divided into a right and a center, and no one has ever suggested that it contained a left. Before 1914 the European "extreme left" comprised the Bolsheviks (plus a number of non-Bolshevik Russian Social Democrats such as Trotsky), the SDKPiL, and the PPS-Left in Poland, the Bulgarian "Narrows" (*Tesnyatsi*), and various groups in Holland, Serbia, and Romania. The Czechs were securely attached to the center, dominated by Kautsky and the German Social Democrats.[10] In their case, then, we confront a sharp ideological break, not a continuing tradition of revolutionary Marxism.

The subject of the origins of the CPC naturally falls into two divisions. First, we must analyze the nature of the various indigenous groups of the Czechoslovak left which later coalesced to form the CPC. Second, we must examine the process by which the CPC was constructed out of the disparate elements of the Czechoslovak left as a centralized and multinational organization.

The portmanteau term "Czechoslovak left" covers four main groups: the German social-democratic left, the Czech anarchists, the Czech social-democratic left, and the Slovak social-democratic left. Given that each of these groups developed separately until 1920, it will be convenient to deal with them individually, in the above order.

Unlike the Czech left, the German social-democratic left in 1918 inherited a tradition of struggle against its own party leadership. Since at least 1910 there had existed a definite group within the Austrian Social Democratic party, centered on the city of Liberec[11] in the German-speaking area of Bohemia, which opposed what it regarded as the nationalism and revisionism of the main body of the party, and which figured as part of the prewar "extreme left."[12] When the First World War broke out, and the main body of the Austrian Social Democratic party failed to oppose it, the local party paper, the Liberec *Vorwärts,* adopted an attitude of uncompromising opposition which led to its suppression by the Austrian authorities. In 1917 we find Alois Neurath, one of the local party leaders, agitating in favor of the Zimmerwald movement.[13] After the war, Liberec was the main center for the left-wing movement within German social democracy, which culminated in the founding of the German section of the Communist party.

We should not overrate the consistency of the Liberec left, however. Here, as elsewhere in Central Europe where the nationalities were mixed, the national question played some strange tricks. In the confusion of 1918, Kreibich,[14] Neurath, and their comrades abandoned their previous internationalism. At this time all German Social Democrats in Czechoslovakia, whether of the right or the left, were faced with the problem of their relationship to the new state. The right-wing majority of the party placed itself behind the attempt of the German nationalists to set up an independent "German Bohemia" on the basis of the principle of national self-determination. The Liberec left went along with this scheme, advancing the rather specious argument that since the newly formed state of Czechoslovakia was a counterrevolutionary creation of the Entente, the German-speaking area should be attached to Germany or Austria, where the prospects for revolution looked very bright in 1918 and 1919.

The process of enlightenment which took place after the failure of this attempt to establish *Deutschböhmen* was gradual. Only in June 1919 did the Liberec *Vorwärts* cease to propagate the idea that the "German Bohemian" working class was engaged, side by side with the nationalist bourgeoisie, in a struggle for self-determination. Later in 1919, the Liberec left took up a "centrist" position close to that of Friedrich Adler and Otto Bauer in Austria, and of the Independent Social Democrats in Germany: Soviet Russia was to be supported against intervention by the capitalist world, but the methods applied by the Bolsheviks in Russia were not valid in Central Europe with its democratic traditions and mass parties. Thus, at the Teplice Congress of the German Social Democratic party in Czechoslovakia, held in September 1919, Kreibich opposed the idea of adhering to the Third International.[15] The slow evolution of the Liberec left toward communism in the years 1920 and 1921 occurred under the impact of events in Czechoslovakia as a whole, and we shall deal with this subject later.

Nevertheless, there *were* German Communists in Bohemia in 1919: the members of an Association of Communist Groups, active in the area of the town of Děčin. They had close connections with Dresden, just across the border in Germany, and took their political line from the ultra-leftist wing of the Communist party of Germany, which was very strong in that city.[16] During May and June 1919, a newspaper entitled *Die Rote Fahne* was published in Děčin, with a program of adhesion to the Third International, rejection of reformism, and seizure of power by workers', peasants', and soldiers' councils on the Bolshevik model. The newspaper was immediately suppressed by the Czech authorities, and the Liberec left itself denounced this agitation as an attempt to split the German working class in Czechoslovakia.[17] Despite this, the Association of Communist Groups continued to exist, and continued to quarrel with the Liberec left, until both groups were merged into the unified CPC in 1921.

As we have seen, the German components of the CPC demonstrate a certain continuity, but it would be hard to say the same of the Czech left. Until 1918 a left-wing section of the CSDWP did not exist because the preponderance of the national problem prevented left-right divisions from arising. The party was divided during the war over the policy to be adopted toward the Habsburg state, and in particular toward the Czech nationalists' objective of destroying that state and setting up their own state of Czechoslovakia.[18] National radicalism implied cooperation with Czech bourgeois politicians, and to that extent was not likely to be advocated by left-wingers[19]; but the opposite stance implied collaboration with the Habsburg state, and certainly excluded opposition to the war effort. It is not surprising, then, that the revolutionary opposition constituted along the lines advocated by Lenin and the Zimmerwald Left[20] comprised two groups that were entirely outside the field of Czech social-democratic politics: the anarchists, who were ideologically separate from the CSDWP; and the Czech and Slovak prisoners of war in Russia, who were separated temporarily from the mother party by distance.

A minority among the Czech working class in Bohemia had long inclined toward anarchism. In the 1880s the anarchists played an important role in the working-class movement throughout Austria, although by the end of that decade their strength had been almost crushed — directly through the severe repression imposed by Habsburg authorities and indirectly as a result of the penetration of Marxist ideas into the country. Nevertheless, the anarchists retained a foothold among the miners of Northern Bohemia and the textile workers of the Northeast, and because of their independence of the CSDWP they were able to present the only revolutionary opposition in Czech Bohemia during the First World War. They were taken very seriously by the Habsburg authorities, who always ascribed the more militant actions of the Bohemian miners to anarchist rather than social-democratic influence.[21]

In 1918 there emerged two conflicting tendencies in the anarchist movement in the Czech lands. On the one hand, there were those who accepted the offer of the Czech National Socialists to join hands in a purely nationalist struggle against the Habsburg Monarchy to achieve Czech self-determination. Led by Bohuslav Vrbenský, this group spent four difficult years in the Czech Socialist Party, formed in March 1918 as a result of the fusion between the National Socialists and the anarchists, and eventually joined the CPC when it became clear that the Czech Socialists were a right-wing party closely identified with the Czech state.[22] On the other hand, there were those anarchists who preferred to maintain their independence of all parties, and instead set up a number of anarcho-communist groups, the activities of which for a long time remained obscure, owing to a certain unwillingness on the part of the historians of the 1950s to discuss this aspect of Communist history.[23]

The anarchist groups of the North Bohemian mining district coalesced into the Federation of Czechoslovak Communists at the time of the First Comintern Congress, and on March 1919 began to bring out the paper *Komuna,* which was intended to act as a focus for a Czechoslovak Communist party. Like all the other leftist groups that had this idea at the time, they soon had to give up because of lack of support. The Federation of Czechoslovak Communists was joined in its endeavors by the anarchist intellectuals grouped around the journal *Červen,* founded by S. K. Neumann, who at first tried to work within the Czech Socialist Party, but left it in April 1920 in order to found a Communist organization. This junction between the federation and *Červen* was the origin of the Union of Communist Groups, set up in May 1920 at Lom u Mostu, in the mining region of Northwest Bohemia. The union sent Hugo Sonnenstein and Helena Malířová as delegates to the Second Congress of the Comintern, held in Moscow in July and August 1920, with the demand that the Union of Communist Groups be recognized as the Czech section of the Third International, and that left-wing members of the CSDWP be instructed to join it. The Comintern did not accept Sonnenstein's version of the situation, and instead instructed the anarcho-communists to act jointly with the developing opposition within the CSDWP.[24] Despite this setback, the Union of Communist Groups issued a declaration at the conference held in Prague on 15 August 1920 which stated that it was necessary to proceed without delay to the foundation of a Communist party for the whole Czechoslovak republic. The anarchists' eagerness to found a Communist party stands in striking contrast both to the history of anarchism and to their role at this time in other countries. Elsewhere, the anarchists looked closely at developments in Russia after 1917 and decided that, although they supported the revolution, they must oppose Bolshevism. The anarchists of the Czech lands, on the contrary, thought it their first duty to respond to the appeal of the Third International and to found a Communist Party in Czechoslovakia.

The Czech and Slovak prisoners of war in Russia, who were gradually released in the course of 1917, were naturally highly responsive to the revolutionary turmoil that surrounded them, and their ranks were soon deeply divided between nationalists and Socialists. Some saw their salvation in the Entente, others in world revolution. Since this latter goal involved the defense of the Bolshevik revolution, the Bolsheviks had every reason to encourage the Czech revolutionaries, and in May 1918 they therefore helped them to found the first Czechoslovak Communist party. The Bolsheviks also had a pressing practical motive, however. A few weeks earlier, a dangerous conflict had arisen between the Czechoslovak Legion (an army formed of nationalist Czechs) and the Soviet authorities over the question of the former's transfer out of Russia to fight on the western front. The Bolsheviks thus saw the new party's task as persuading Czech and Slovak ex-prisoners to join the Red Army, or at least to desert from the Czechoslovak Legion.[25] It cannot be said that they were tremendously successful; the Czechoslovak Legion retained control of several key cities of Siberia throughout 1918, and when it left it did so as a body and voluntarily.[26]

With the collapse of the Central Powers in October 1918, the Czechoslovak Communists in Russia saw the possibility of fomenting a revolution in the Habsburg lands, and agents were sent out with the aim of founding a Communist party within Czechoslovakia itself to lead the revolution. When the leader of the CPC in Russia, Alois Muna,[27] returned to Czechoslovakia in November 1918, however, he was confronted with an insuperable difficulty: there was no pro-Communist left wing within the CSDWP. None of the party's leaders supported Bolshevism, and the workers themselves were full of enthusiasm for the new Czechoslovak state, and not inclined to take part in attempts to overthrow it. There was plenty of platonic sympathy for the Russian revolution, of course, but the only issue on which the left could be mobilized was that of keeping Muna himself in the party when the right made an attempt in January 1919 to expel him for being a Communist rather than a Social Democrat. Muna had to bow to necessity and place his hopes on patient work within the CSDWP. Those Czechoslovak Communists who remained in Russia were still enthusiastically in favor of the formation of a small party on German or Hungarian lines, but conditions were against them. The first CPC took on a more and more shadowy existence in the years 1919 and 1920. A conference held in Moscow in March 1919 decided to close down the party's paper *Průkopník Svobody* and transfer all activities to the Ukraine.[28] In due course the members all drifted back to Czechoslovakia and were absorbed into the CSDWP. The CPC itself was progressively demoted in status, becoming first "The Czechoslovak section under the CC of the RKP (b)" and finally "the Cultural and Propaganda Section for Czechoslovakia."[29] The only element of continuity between the first and the second Czechoslovak Communist party was personal: the original leaders of the first party, Alois Muna, Břetislav Hůla,[30] and Jaroslav Handlíř, all returned to Czechoslovakia and worked actively to promote the founding of the second party.[31]

We have now to consider the most important component of the later CPC, the old majority of the CSDWP, led by Bohumír Šmeral.[32] Šmeral was a contradictory character, who has been much misunderstood by historians. Julius Braunthal, for instance, states that Šmeral "was on the extreme right wing of the Czech Social Democratic party during the war," and that he was a "loyal Habsburg patriot" who did not take over the leadership of the left wing of the CSDWP "until the war was over."[33] In fact, both before and during the war Šmeral was an adherent of the Austro-Marxist trend of thought, to be placed alongside such people as Otto Bauer in Austria and Karl Kautsky in Germany. Braunthal's mistake can be explained quite simply: Šmeral had a very moderate position on the question of Czech self-determination. Austria-Hungary was for him "the given framework of our agitation" and he believed that on economic grounds it would be madness to break up this large state.[34] (Rosa Luxemburg said much the same thing about the Russian Empire, at the same time.) Until 1917 Šmeral saw to it that the Brno Program of 1899, with its emphasis on the maintenance of Austria-Hungary and the establishment within it of national autonomy for the Czechs, was retained in the program of the CSDWP. This policy came under fierce attack from those who wanted a more radical anti-Habsburg line to be taken in cooperation with the Czech bourgeois parties and with those Czech politicians, such as Thomas Masaryk and Eduard Beneš, who had placed their faith in the Entente and gone into voluntary exile for the duration of the war. As a result, the Brno Program was abandoned and in 1917 three representatives of the CSDWP went to the international socialist conference at Stockholm with a demand for the transformation of Austria-Hungary into a federation of national states with all the attributes of sovereignty. Šmeral and his supporters lost ground to the "radical-socialist" advocates of union with the National Socialists in the Socialist Council, although they were able in February 1918 to defeat an attempt to merge the two parties. During 1918 he stayed in the background, while the nationalist right wing effected that cooperation with other Czech parties which culminated in the peaceful transfer of power and the establishment of the republic of Czechoslovakia in October 1918.[35]

The Twelfth Congress of the CSDWP met in December 1918 in an atmosphere of national unity and concord. Old disputes were smoothed over, Šmeral was absolved from blame for his wartime *rakušanství*,[36] and a resolution in favor of entering the Czechoslovak government was carried unanimously. The dominant tendency of the congress was clearly toward the right, as represented by Antonín Němec, Vlastimil Tusar, and František Soukup, who favored continuing the alliance with the Czech bourgeois parties. Certain local organizations were, however, already identifiably left wing, in particular those of Kladno, Hodonín, and Ostrava. A delegate from Hodonín, Tomáš Koutný, claimed there was 90 percent support for bolshevism in his region, but went on to describe it in such a way as to make it sound like moderate social democracy: "We want to gain political power in our National Assembly, to make a coalition with other parties, so as to defeat the bourgeoisie and capitalists and dictate our demands in a legislative way." And Antonín Zápotocký[37] from Kladno — "red Kladno" as communist historians describe it — demanded that the Social Democrats "break with the all-national tendency and adopt proletarian socialist policies."[38] Still, he did not carry his opposition so far as to vote against the final resolution on entering the government, and the context of his speech must be borne in mind if we are to evaluate it properly. He was pleading for a more independent policy, and opposing the renewed demands for a merger with the National Socialists (now renamed the Czech Socialist Party). "The comrades who helped to overthrow the old Austrian state," Zápotocký said, "have got into too close a relationship with the bourgeoisie." There was nothing particularly Communist or Bolshevik about his remarks.[39]

In this situation, there was little Šmeral could do. His pro-Austrian policy had collapsed with the fall of Austria itself, and he realized that this was not the moment to attack the apparent national unity centered around the figures of Masaryk and Beneš, the victorious heroes of the wartime anti-Habsburg emigration and the founders of the Czechoslovak state. Soon afterward, however, for reasons that will become clear, this mood of unity evaporated.

As far as the Czechs were concerned, the nationality question had been settled with the establishment of their state, but once that state had proved its viability, which it did in the course of 1919, there was no longer any overriding reason for the maintenance of national unity on every issue. The leaders of the CSDWP showed their keenness to cooperate with the bourgeois parties in placing Czechoslovakia on a firm and of course capitalist foundation. They took part in the Kramář cabinet that ruled from November 1918 to July 1919, when the Social Democrat Tusar formed his own cabinet with the support of the Agrarians and the Czech Socialists. By this time there was something of a revolutionary ferment in Czechoslovakia, disturbances having begun in

the spring of 1919 under the impulse of events in Germany, the establishment of the Hungarian Soviet Republic, and the return of many
Czech Communists from Russia. Workers' councils were formed in the
Kladno area, a number of left-wing social-democratic newspapers
emerged (including the Kladno *Svoboda,* the Prague *Sociální Demo-
krat,* and the Brno *Rovnost*), and in May 1919 a short-lived Slovak
Soviet Republic was formed under the protection of Hungarian troops.[40]

This new atmosphere witnessed the very gradual development of a
left opposition within the CSDWP, which emerged as a definite and
identifiable group, the "Marxist Left," at an October 1919 party conference that adopted a joint platform containing the following demands:
the CSDWP must act independently of the other parties in the government; it must put forward socialist proposals in the Assembly; and it
must leave the cabinet if these proposals are rejected.[41] It should be
noted that these were not specifically Bolshevik demands. Rather, they
reflected disillusionment with the policy of coalition and with the
CSDWP's failure to achieve any far-reaching reforms now that it was
actually in power. The aim of the Marxist Left, the name that the
Šmeralite opposition chose to describe itself, was to convert the party
to the position that Communist history terms "Centrist," and that
Kárník summed up as "different both from the reformism of the
Second International and from the Central European Communists'
plans for world revolution."[42]

In the next two years the Marxist Left, led by Šmeral, proceeded
gradually toward the formation of a Communist party. There were two
reasons for the slow pace of this development. First, the members of
the Marxist Left themselves were not clear about their future course.
Very few of them envisaged anything more than a refurbished and
purified Social Democratic party. They were in agreement, therefore,
with Giacinto Serrati in Italy and Kautsky in Germany in rejecting
coalition with other political parties, while placing their faith in the
gradual conversion of the majority of Socialists to their point of view
and ignoring Bolshevik appeals for an attempt to seize power and
overthrow capitalism by violence. Given these views it is hardly surprising that the members of the Marxist Left were in no hurry to become
Communists.

The second reason for the drawn-out nature of the process — the
reason given far greater weight by present-day Czech historians — was
tactical. After the Marxist Left had rejected the idea of founding a party
outside the existing Social Democratic party, on the Austrian or German model, gradual permeation of the CSDWP was the only method
that remained available to them. In 1919, no matter how close the

members of the Marxist Left were to bolshevism in their own attitudes, they could not hope to carry the majority of the party on any but a moderate centrist program — one that was closely tailored to the Czechoslovak workers' immediate discontent with the Tusar government. The platform of October 1919 was itself rejected by 62 votes to 35 when it was put to a meeting of party representatives in Prague (5 October 1919). This vote gives some indication of the level of support for the Marxist Left among party functionaries: it was a minority, but a powerful one.

The program of 7 December 1919, adopted at the conference that formally founded the Marxist Left, was somewhat closer to communism than the earlier declaration, though still essentially centrist.[43] It called for the socialization of the means of production, the establishment of workers' councils as organs of proletarian rule, and a break with the Second International. Only an international opposed to compromise with the bourgeoisie could be accepted, and the Marxist Left claimed to discern "the promising beginnings of such an organization" in the Third International. Despite this, the Marxist Left concluded that salvation lay in a return to the past, to the Hainfeld Program of 1888 which the CSDWP had never officially repudiated: all that was needed was to return to its spirit, which the right-wingers had betrayed.

Having constituted itself as an independent group, the Marxist Left went from strength to strength in numerical terms: with the Social Democrat Vlastimil Tusar in charge of a coalition government of Agrarians, Czech Socialists, and Social Democrats, the right wing of Czech socialism found itself saddled with responsibility for the high level of unemployment, the continuous rise in prices, and the anti-Soviet foreign policy of the government. Though they could claim that they had inherited the postwar crisis of adjustment to Czechoslovakia's new independence, this argument did not convince the workers. By March 1920 thirteen out of the twenty-six district party organizations of Bohemia and Moravia had declared their acceptance of the December 1919 statement of principles. Šmeral hoped that at the next party congress he would be able to bring the whole of the CSDWP over to the Comintern. He therefore pursued a policy of "loyal opposition," in order not to give the right an excuse for expulsions. This policy was carried very far, involving as it did cooperation with the right at the elections of April 1920 and a series of votes in favor of the Tusar government in the Assembly. Šmeral's tactics were in one sense successful, in that the Marxist Left provided the numbers to make the CPC a mass party; but in the year 1920, when the Comintern had high hopes for revolution, Moscow regarded the Marxist Left with some suspicion for its resolute avoidance of any decisive action. As we have seen, the Czech anarchists tried to bypass the Marxist Left and obtain recognition as the official Communist party at the Second Comintern Congress. The Comintern rejected their claim, but still implicitly rebuked the Marxist Left by urging it to create a Communist party "in the shortest possible time."[44]

Thus far we have considered developments in the Czech lands proper — Bohemia, Moravia, and Silesia. In the more backward provinces of eastern Czechoslovakia, namely Slovakia and Ruthenia, different problems presented themselves. Both provinces had been dominated by Hungary rather than by Austria and their separation from Hungary in 1918 proved a serious economic blow. What Slovak industry there was (14.9 percent of the labor force was employed in industry in 1921) looked to Hungary for its markets and, for various geographical and technical reasons, was unable to compete with Czech industry. Moreover, it was impossible to draw a clear line of demarcation between Slovakia, Ruthenia, and Hungary on ethnic grounds, and as a result there was a considerable Hungarian minority in the new state. From the first the attitude of the Slovak Social Democrats was confused by these problems. Czechoslovakism (or the idea that the Slovaks formed a part of a single Czechoslovak nation) and Slovak autonomism were rival tendencies of roughly equal strength. The right-wing leader of the Slovak Social Democrats, Ivan Dérer, was strongly in favor of Czechoslovakism, whereas the Social Democrats of the Hungarian minority saw themselves as part of the Social Democratic party in Hungary proper. In addition, the Jews, the Poles, the Ruthenes, and the Germans all had their own parties with aspirations to function as part of a larger national whole.

The left wing in Slovakia and Ruthenia therefore had to adopt a position on the nationality question as well as on the Comintern. The standpoint they took was the Bolshevik one: support for national self-determination, combined with "the full and unconditional unity of the workers of the oppressed nation and those of the oppressor nation."[45] Hence the opposition to the right-wing leadership of the Slovak branch of the CSDWP developed conjointly with a movement to merge the Slovak, German, and Hungarian organizations. A conference of German and Hungarian Social Democrats held at Žilina on 14 March 1920 demanded both the unification of the German and Hungarian trade union organizations and adherence to the Third International. At the Košice Conference of 27–30 June 1920, the Slovak Social Democrats who supported the Marxist Left met Hungarian and Slovak representatives from Ruthenia and decided to set up an "International Socialist Party of Czechoslovakia," and apply as such to join the Third International.[46] They criticized the Marxist Left of the Czech lands for its hesitations, but took no further action as they were unwilling to get out of step with the much larger Czech group.

We have seen, then, that there was nothing homogeneous about the main components of the future CPC.[47] The potentially Communist groups were in fact divided three ways: in political origin — some were in the course of emerging from anarchism, most from social democracy; in national origin — most came from the ruling Czech nation, but all the other nationalities had their own left-wing Social Democrats; and in their attitude to political tactics — some favored the immediate formation of a Communist party, others the gradual permeation and transformation of the CSDWP. It is hardly surprising that the Comintern found it difficult to push through its policy of creating a centralized, internationally-unified, and revolutionary party for the whole of the country.

Up to 1920, the Comintern had played little part in developments in Czechoslovakia, attempting to do no more than set an example that left-wingers were free to follow if they wished. But in the second stage of the development of the CPC, the creation of a unified, centralized, and disciplined party, the Comintern took a more active and effective interest in Czech affairs. Nevertheless, it would be wrong to treat internal factors as of secondary importance, even for the year 1921. Though the Comintern wished its decisions to be binding, they were not, because submission to them was in the last resort voluntary. The Comintern could reject applications for admission, but parties could refuse to apply if they found the Comintern's directives unacceptable. In the case of Czechoslovakia, the basic conflict was between the Marxist Left's own judgment, based as it was on local conditions, and the Comintern's insistence that certain general rules be applied to every situation.

Throughout 1920, Šmeral made tremendous efforts to maintain the unity of the CSDWP, for he wanted to bring the entire party over to the Comintern. Since the party leaders (apart from Šmeral) were in the government, he was forced to perform the most extraordinary contortions in order simultaneously to take advantage of the mass discontent that was building up against that government and to remain in the party. The Marxist Left publicly opposed Tusar's government proclamation of 1 June 1920, stigmatizing it as an act of cooperation with the bourgeoisie in its attack on the working class, but voted in favor of it in the National Assembly, in order not to break party discipline.[48] At this point the Executive Committee of the Comintern (ECCI) began to intervene. The Second Comintern Congress had just accepted its list of twenty-one stringent conditions for membership of the Comintern, which included a total break with the right as well as with a large number of explicitly named "centrists" (fortunately there were no Czechs on the list).[49] Yet here was the Czech Marxist Left still operating within a party whose leadership was actively involved in maintaining bourgeois rule over Czechoslovakia!

In August 1920 the ECCI sent a sharp message "to the Czechoslovak proletariat," reprimanding both the Marxist Left and the anarcho-communist groups:

> The vote of the Marxist Left for the coalition government's proclamation was too dear a price to pay for their remaining in the Social-Democratic party. Concern for tactics within the political party should never lead to political acts that might appear to the workers as serving the governmental needs of the bourgeois regime . . . . The Executive Committee expects from the Communist groups that they will bear in mind the creation of a united Communist party and energetically combat survivals of sectarianism in their ranks. The Marxist Left and the Communist groups must unite their endeavors to create a united Communist front throughout the whole of Czechoslovakia. They must take the initiative of setting up a united and centralized Communist party, comprising the revolutionary workers of all the nationalities of Czechoslovakia.[50]

This message gives a clear idea of ECCI's conception of the future Communist party in Czechoslovakia. Their tactical advice, if not their conception of the party, met with much resistance from the Marxist Left. Šmeral and his closest associates (in particular Edmund Burian, Václav Houser, and Antonín Zápotocký) were still in no hurry. They expected that events would develop automatically in their favor. They did not want to break with Tusar, Němec, and the other right-wing leaders, but instead preferred to swamp them with votes at party meetings. Moreover, the leaders of the Marxist Left did not want to weld all the nationalities together in a single organization, but rather to maintain the existing divisions, in particular that between German and Czechoslovak Social Democrats. Unity could best be achieved, thought Šmeral, within a federal structure, like that which had held together the old Austrian Social Democratic party for so long. Not surprisingly, there was a minority opinion within the Marxist Left which favored creating a Communist party immediately. Bohuš Jílek and Jan Doležal, who made their views known through the Hodonín district organization's organ, *Slovacko,* were the leading spokesmen of this view.[51] In some respects, as we shall see, these disputed questions were resolved by events. In other respects, it required considerable pressure from the Comintern, and from the leftist groups of each nationality to bring the majority of the Marxist Left into line.

The question of Šmeral's refusal to break with Tusar was settled neither by the Comintern nor by the Marxist Left, but by the right itself, which was anxious to isolate and stamp out the Bolshevik threat. On 12 July 1920, a meeting of the right-wing faction of the CSDWP decided to throw out the leftists and to postpone the party congress, scheduled to take place in September, in order that the expulsion could be accomplished before the congress convened. A month later, at a meeting of the parliamentary fraction of the CSDWP, Rudolf Bechyně (a rightist who was chairman of the CSDWP fraction) spoke of the inevitable split in the party. Šmeral kept quiet during these remarks and, when confronted with the charge of fomenting revolution, replied, on Kautskyan rather than Leninist lines, " Revolution grows out of objective conditions independently of our own wishes." To this Bechyně replied in the name of the right: "Revolutions too are made. Objective conditions are not sufficient. There must be revolutionaries to make revolutions."[52] The party leaders were not inclined to wait until they were defeated by Šmeral's quiet, gradualist tactics, and resolved that, in order to save social democracy, they had to split the party. The Marxist Left, on the contrary, were confident that a majority of the party now supported them and they therefore thought only in terms of the forthcoming party congress. On 5 September 1920 a conference of representatives of the Marxist Left accepted the basic principles of communism and demanded that the leaders of the party either accept them at the next party congress or resign.[53]

The next few months, from September to December 1920, were a period of crisis in Czechoslovak social democracy, indeed in the whole Czechoslovak state, and everything that followed this crisis, including the foundation of the CPC in 1921, was in the nature of an epilogue to it. The right's long-planned attack followed hard on the heels of the conference of 5 September. Masaryk himself, who held strong views about communism, had spent the summer traveling around the country speaking out against the Marxist Left and writing articles to influence intellectuals. Now he held meetings with the government coalition, at which it was agreed that the Tusar government should resign in order to give the social-democratic leaders a free hand for the coming political battle.[54] The revolutionary threat was to be dealt with by installing a cabinet of officials under Jan Černý, hitherto the provincial president of Moravia.

In accordance with this plan Tusar resigned on 14 September and the Executive Committee of the CSDWP, on which the right had a majority, resolved by thirty-eight votes to eighteen to postpone the party congress and proceed with the necessary expulsions. Support for the Comintern was declared to be incompatible with membership of the CSDWP and it was said that the leftists had to be expelled "to ensure that decisions will be made only by social-democratic delegates at the coming congress."[55] The workers of Prague, who were overwhelmingly in favor of Šmeral, replied on 15 September by resolving to ignore the leadership's decision and hold the party congress as planned.[56] At the same time, they occupied the "Lidový Dům" (People's House) and took over the editorial offices of *Právo Lidu,* the party' central organ — both of which were situated in the same building. All these acts were illegal, in addition to constituting a breach of party discipline, but they were in fact a spontaneous popular reaction to the government's measures — a reaction far in advance of the position taken by the leaders of the Left Social Democrats.

When the Thirteenth Party Congress assembled on 25 September 1920, it became clear that 64 percent of the delegates elected to the legal and postponed congress had decided to attend the congress of the left, which, formally speaking, was illegal. According to Hůla, perhaps a biased witness, this 64 percent represented 80 percent of the members of the CSDWP.[57] And the proportion would certainly have been higher but for the refusal of the Marxist Left to admit fifty-one of the eighty Slovak delegates to the congress (the Slovaks claimed they had not been given enough representation when they affiliated with the CSDWP in 1918; the Marxist Left accepted the claim but wanted to stay within the party statutes).[58] On this level, then, Šmeral's tactics had been success-ful. He had brought the majority of the CSDWP with him in his journey toward the Third International, against the wishes of the party leader-ship.

Yet even at this stage, after the split in the party, he continued to follow a cautious and gradualist policy. In the name of the newly elected left leadership, he accepted the principles of communism. But he did not propose immediate entry into the Comintern or the acceptance of all the Twenty-one Conditions, some of which were in his view not appropri-ate to Czechoslovakia, and he specifically rejected "the advice of the Russians." Instead of renaming the party the Communist party of Czechoslovakia (as the conditions required), he called it the CSDWP (Left). Indignantly, he defended his party against the charge of foment-ing revolution: "The uninformed public regards us not as the analysts of the revolution but as its instigators." Instead of revolution he offered a perspective of parliamentary work: "The workers' parties of all nation-alities will be able to get a majority of socialist votes. We need not dispute about what happens afterward, but up to this point we can all go forward jointly." [59]

The Comintern could only regard Šmeral's parliamentary road to socialism as a serious deviation — a deviation that consisted first and foremost in the refusal to contemplate a revolutionary seizure of power. Šmeral's speech to the Thirteenth Congress also contained a number of minor deviations on the nationality question and the Czechoslovak state. Lenin's attitude on the nationality question in general was that national minorities had an absolute right to self-determination, if necessary involving the division of a state into its national components, but certainly implying some form of national autonomy. Šmeral, however, believed that Czechoslovakia must be preserved as an undivided state. Hence, he asserted that it was "necessary to overcome the previous intensity of the national idea and replace it with the higher ideal of humanity, socialism." [60] This attempt to, as it were, transcend existing problems in a higher synthesis meant in practice that the CSDWP (Left) recognized the existing boundaries of the state and rejected the German, Hungarian, Ruthene, and Slovak claims to autonomy.

Turning to the German left within Czechoslovakia, we see that, if anything, they were hanging behind the development of the Czech left. Their attitude was partly a result of the German Social Democrats' opposition to the Czechoslovak state; the party's right-wing leaders could not be charged with responsibility for the measures taken by the Czechoslovak government, since they were in fact boycotting it. Later, the German left was held back by a feeling of weakness, a sense that its influence was limited to the Liberec area. As a result, they concluded a number of compromises that parallel those engaged in by the Czech Marxist Left. Admittedly, a conference at Liberec on 9 May 1920 pronounced in favor of applying to join the Comintern and accepted the dictatorship of the proletariat as the aim toward which they would work, but the German left remained part of a party that explicitly rejected such ideas. In October 1920 the differences in the German Social Democratic party were fought over at the Karlový Varý Party Congress. Here the left presented an Action Program, worked out on 11 September in consultation with the Czech left, and it was rejected by 295 votes to 147. The program itself was criticized by Paul Frölich, a leader of the KPD who was then close to Radek, as "Menshevism of the purest water." [61] But in any case it was replaced by a compromise formula that the right could accept: party members could continue to discuss the problems of socialism according to their own convictions, both within the party and with the Czech Social Democrats. [62] Here, just as in the case of the Czech left, tactical considerations led to the rejection of the advice given by the Second Congress of the Comintern, that there should be an immediate split with the right, on the basis of the Twenty-one Conditions.

Indeed, it required a further jolt, provided again by the right rather than the Comintern, before the various left groups could make up their minds to advance any further toward the formation of a Communist party. Since September the left had used the "People's House" as their headquarters, thus precipitating the final stage in the legal conflict between the right and the left of the CSDWP over the party's property. From a strictly legal standpoint, the Executive Committee of the CSDWP was still the party's supreme authority, for the decision to postpone the September 1920 congress had been made by a majority of that Executive Committee. The only legal Thirteenth Congress of the CSDWP had been the right's congress, held between 27 and 29 November; hence the courts could only decide the issue of party property in favor of Němec and Tusar and against Šmeral. Accordingly, on 9 December 1920, the police and gendarmerie were sent to seize the "People's House" and the printing press that printed the newspaper *Rudé právo*, the left wing's replacement for the old *Právo lidu*.

This action had powerful symbolic meaning and the CSDWP (Left) responded by calling a general strike. When one million workers responded, the conflict was immediately broadened from the petty question of the possession of a building in Prague to issues of political power. In a number of places — notably in Kladno, Hodonín, and some parts of Slovakia — workers' councils were set up and for a short time exercized power at a local level.[63] The strike as a whole did not succeed, however, either in its broader aims, or in achieving the immediate practical goal of regaining control of the "People's House," one reason being that the railway workers refused to join in and thus allowed the armed forces to be transported quickly to the appropriate places.[64]

These dramatic events pushed the Czechoslovak and German lefts further toward the Comintern and communism. A meeting of representatives of the CSDWP (Left), held in January 1921, accepted the Comintern's principles and called for the creation of a unified Communist party of Czechoslovakia, but strangely decided to call yet another meeting for March 1921 before making a final decision. As for the Twenty-one Conditions, the Czechs at this stage took exception to two of them. Number three, on the construction of an illegal party organization parallel to the legal one, entirely contradicted the peaceful, law-abiding traditions of the Czech labor movement. Number seventeen, on the adoption of the name "Communist Party" in order to signal the decisive nature of the break with social democracy, clashed with the

Czechs' sentimental attachment to their old party, and with Šmeral's wish to preserve a link with its best traditions. The leaders of the German left were similarly hesitant, but for entirely different reasons. Kreibich was fully in agreement with the ECCI and with the leftists within the CSDWP (Left) who were trying to push Šmeral into action, but realized that to found a German Communist party in Czechoslovakia would be to make nonsense of his own internationalist position: a unified, multinational party must be founded, not a separate German one. Hence, on 9 January 1921, a conference of the German left at Liberec called merely for an extraordinary congress of the German Social Democratic party, which would be presented with the task of accepting the Twenty-one Conditions, adhering to the Comintern, and expelling those who disagreed.[65] The right in the German party replied by expelling the whole of the 16,000-member Liberec district organization (17 January 1921). Having now lost their footing in social democracy, Kreibich and his comrades had no reason to hesitate any longer: on 30 January a further conference of the Liberec district issued the call for a party congress in March in order to found "the German section of the Communist party of Czechoslovakia."[66] This action was in part an attempt to force Šmeral's hand.

The Slovaks too were now impatient with Šmeral's hesitations. In the crisis of September 1920 the Slovak Social Democrats had supported the Marxist Left almost to a man. At their party congress, held in Turčiansky Säty Martin on 19 September 1920, 117 out of the 132 delegates (89 percent) had sided with the left. Moreover, they had gone on record in favor of complete organizational unity, along Leninist lines, with the Czech left: "The Slovak proletariat must attach itself to the Marxist Left without regard to linguistic differences."[67] Hence, it is hardly surprising that, at a conference held on 16 and 17 January 1921, at Ľubochna, the Slovak left became the first group to accept the Twenty-one Conditions and organize a Communist party. The Slovaks not only accepted the Comintern's Conditions but immediately acted on them: their conference comprised delegates from every national group in Czechoslovakia (88 Slovaks, 36 Hungarians, 15 Germans, 6 Ruthenes, and 4 representatives of Poale Zion). This success, though gratifying, was also embarrassing in view of the slow pace of developments elsewhere. The Slovaks decided that although they themselves accepted Condition Seventeen, on the change of name, they did not wish to prejudge the issue for the whole party and would therefore postpone the decision until the forthcoming congress of the Czechoslovak left.[68]

But the forthcoming congress was somewhat in the distance: Germans and Czechs in the Czech lands continued to act separately. The German left, at their congress of 12 March 1921, accepted the Twenty-one Conditions, and immediately founded the Communist party of Czechoslovakia (German Section). They were encouraged in this by letters of greeting from three members of the Marxist Left, held in prison by the Czech authorities since the December strike — Zápotocký, Muna, and Hůla. Despite the Germans' decisiveness, Šmeral and the majority of the Marxist Left continued to delay. Šmeral was determined to avoid a repetition of the Italian disaster, the congress of the PSI (Socialist party of Italy) at which the Comintern had failed to obtain the majority as the result of an overly hasty attempt to enforce the Twenty-one Conditions (January 1921).[69] The left's answer to the centrists' attempt to split the CSDWP (Left) into pro-Comintern and anti-Comintern factions was to proceed with deliberation. Thus, on 6 March 1921, the Executive Committee, overriding the opposition of the left-wing leaders Doležal and Vajtauer, accepted a proposal from the Brno district (one of the strongest sections of the Marxist Left, with 203 of the 640 organizations represented at the May Congress) that the founding congress of the CPC, scheduled for March, be postponed until May "to give us time to create a huge Communist party."[70] All other interested groups naturally made attempts to speed up the process. Pressure came from the ECCI, from the German Section of the CPC, and from the leftist current in the Marxist Left. The ECCI called a meeting at Dresden in April 1921, at which Béla Kun and Gyula Alpári represented the Comintern, Karl Kreibich the Germans, and Karel Gorovský, Václav Houser, and Jan Doležal the Czechs. This meeting's decision to proceed immediately to establish a unified party for the whole of Czechoslovakia remained a dead letter, because Šmeral simply ignored it.[71]

When the founding congress finally met (14 to 16 May 1921) it received complaints and exhortations from all sides. The ECCI, the 'three martyrs of Pankrac' (Zápotocký, Muna, and Hůla), and S. K. Neumann's group of ex-anarchists all sent messages, the burden of which was the same in each case, namely, that a clear decision on the question of Comintern membership must be made immediately.

It might be thought that in May 1921, with the transformation of the CSDWP (Left) into the CPC, the long road from social democracy to communism had been negotiated successfully. It was not so. Šmeral's speech, accepted by the vast majority of the congress delegates, was highly ambiguous. While recommending unconditional entry into the Comintern and acceptance of the Twenty-one Conditions, he explicitly rejected a number of the Comintern's basic tenets. He refused to break with the centrists in the party, claiming that centrism was a "socialist tendency," and that "it would be madness if anyone were to be excluded from the party for deviationist opinions."[72] He opposed a merger with the CPC (German Section), even though this step was explicitly requested by the German Communists. He condemned "putschism," the "theory of the offensive," and the March 1921 uprising in Germany, but left uncertain his attitude to reformism.

Clearly, a great deal more remained to be done before the CPC became an obedient section of the Third International. The gap between Šmeral's opinions and the "orthodox" communism of the Comintern did not go unnoticed in Moscow.[73] The Third Congress of the Comintern (June and July 1921) devoted much of its time to discussing the affairs of the Czechoslovak party, and its intervention was for the first time decisive. It was only in 1921 that the impact of the Comintern's directives became an important factor in the development of the CPC; once a party had decided definitely to enter the Comintern it naturally tended to obey the decisions of that body.

The situation would have been difficult for Šmeral and his party had the Comintern not just changed its tactical line. In the course of that constant endeavor to steer between the Scylla of left sectarianism and the Charybdis of right opportunism which is a characteristic feature of Comintern tactics during the 1920s, the pendulum had swung by mid-1921 toward the right. The real danger, Moscow now proclaimed, was the threat of left sectarianism, in particular the "theory of the offensive" put forward by the left of the German Communist party in order to justify the disastrous attempted rising of March 1921. Communists still had to be on their guard against right opportunism and centrism, but the emphasis was now on the drawing together of forces rather than a direct assault on bourgeois rule. The main task of the Communist parties, as Grigorii Zinoviev said in introducing the sessions of the Third Congress, was to gain a majority of the workers to their side by patient organizational work.[74] Judged against this standard, of course, the CPC passed with flying colors.

Šmeral's general tactical line was therefore quite acceptable, but the ECCI was still concerned about his "centrist" tendencies, his lack of fighting spirit, and his errors on the nationality question. Zinoviev began the attack in a speech made on 13 June. On the question of centrism, he said, there could be no compromise. The Czechoslovak party, precisely because it was a mass party and not a sect, was very open to centrist influences, and must be transformed into a genuine Communist party through the removal of these influences. The party's lack of fighting spirit was made clear by a comparison between the Czech December and the German March. Whereas the KPD had conducted a hopeless but heroic struggle against the forces of order, the leaders of the Czech party had stood uncertainly aside in the face of events and had failed to conduct a revolutionary agitation in order to prepare the Czech workers to meet the onslaught of the right. Zinoviev then turned to the nationality question. "Our view," he said, "is that the boundaries of states are entirely provisional and will be transcended quickly by history. The Czechoslovaks must settle all nationality questions in an international sense. In particular they must form an internationally-led and internationally-composed Communist party."[75]

He finally raised the question of Šmeral himself. Zinoviev was inclined to accept the CPC into the Comintern, but to ask for the removal of Šmeral on the grounds of his errors in leadership. He ended his report by anticipating and endeavoring to answer an obvious objection: "There is much talk about dictation from Moscow. In fact the only complaint that can be made against us is this: that we are not sufficiently centralist, not organized together sufficiently."[76] The mood of the whole congress was certainly unfavorable to Šmeral. Indeed, the entire Comintern, not just Moscow, was dictating to the Czechs, and the Russian delegation had to defend its own position on the Czechoslovak question against attacks from the "left" (i.e., the advocates of greater severity).[77] Zápotocký and Muna had written to the ECCI from prison, criticizing Šmeral; Kreibich attacked him in the name of the CPC (German section) for refusing to merge the two parties; and the Italian delegation wanted to start a regular witch hunt against centrism in Czechoslovakia. Egidio Gennari proposed that (1) the Comintern forbid Šmeral from ever again taking up a leading position in the CPC, (2) a declaration be made to the Czechoslovak proletariat giving a list of opportunist deviations by Šmeral and his friends, and (3) the Comintern heighten its struggle against centrists and opportunists in general.[78]

Fortunately for Šmeral, the Italians were a year out of date. They still thought in terms of the situation in Italy in 1920, when Serrati was in control of their party and had adopted an ecumenical attitude similar to Šmeral's.[79] At that time the Comintern had been with them, but now it was against them. Lenin himself delivered a fierce speech condemning the "leftism" of the Italian delegates and insisting that "not an iota of the Theses on Tactics"[80] be altered.[81] "The Italians," he said, "make a game out of the struggle against the Right. We have driven off the Right, but we must say now: no more. People say Šmeral is cautious. There is nothing wrong with that. We too were cautious, and precisely in a revolutionary situation."[82]

The question was finally settled at a special session of the Commission on Tactics, at which both Šmeral and Kreibich spoke. "We were of the opinion," said Radek at this session, "that the leading group of the Czechoslovak party should take two or three steps to the left, while we gave the German-Bohemian organizations,[83] under the leadership of Kreibich, the advice that they should take a step nearer to the great masses of the Czechoslovak party."[84] Šmeral himself, having submitted to the criticisms of the Executive, and having declared himself ready to follow its line completely, could be retained as leader. The fight against centrist tendencies in the party would go on, but it would not be a fight against Šmeral in person.

This harmonious compromise found expression in the theses on the tasks of the Czechoslovak party which were adopted on 12 July. The theses fell into two parts: the one recommending a continuation of Šmeral's tactics, the other recommending certain changes. Part 1 read: "The Czechoslovak party must through a really Communist agitation draw in still more masses of workers, educate the old and new members through clear Communist propaganda, and form a solid front of proletarians against nationalism by uniting workers of all nations in Czechoslovakia." Part 2 stated that "all centrist traditions must be overcome. The Czechoslovak and German-Bohemian Communist parties are to urge their organizations into a united party, within a time limit to be laid down by the Executive."[85]

The ease with which the dispute between Šmeral and Kreibich was settled contrasted with the fierce factional struggles that the congress set off in the German and French parties. In 1921 the attack on "leftism" clearly had priority, and it soon became clear that the Czechs' only mistake had been to apply the Comintern's new line in advance of the Comintern's own decisions on the subject. Even if it were true, as Radek asserted, that "the December 1920 strike showed that the Czechoslovak party was incapable of leading a big, spontaneous proletarian movement, because it was not sufficiently Communist, because it still had in its blood the poison of opportunism,"[86] this was not a circumstance of vital importance in the context of 1921, since the Comintern had officially recognized that the tide of revolution had receded. As Lenin put it: "What is essential now is a fundamental preparation of the revolution, and a profound study of its concrete development."[87]

After the Third Comintern Congress, the only urgent task remaining for the Czechoslovak left was the unification of the various national parties into an international Communist party, a complicated process involving the entry of Poale-Zion (Left), the Polish Social Democratic party (Left), the Union of Communist Groups, and, most important, the CPC (German section) into the Communist party of Czechoslovakia. The unification comgress of the CPC took place from 30 October to 4 November, and produced an international and centralized Communist party in accordance with the decisions of the Comintern and the Twenty-one Conditions.[88] The new Communist party was the third largest in existence, only the Russian and German parties being larger. There is some doubt about its precise size, however. At the May 1921 congress, which did not of course represent the German section, Šmeral claimed 300,000 members.[89] The Third Congress of the Comintern was given estimates of 350,000 members for the Czechoslovak section and 60,000 members for the German section.[90] At the Unification Congress the membership was asserted to be 400,000.[91] A year later, however, at the Fourth Congress of the Comintern, the CPC only claimed 170,000 members.[92] Though this number appears to represent a catastrophic decline, it is possible that the earlier claims referred to registered members of the CSDWP (Left), who, it was assumed, would all enter the CPC. Evidently many of them did not.

Taking into account the prolonged birth pangs of the CPC, it should be possible to evaluate the respective importance that internal and external factors played in its formation. In the period from 1918 to 1920, the Comintern acted more as an observer than as an agent in the formation of the party. In 1921, on the other hand, the prodding of the Comintern and its Executive Committee had an important effect at certain crucial points. Yet it must not be forgotten that even in 1921 the Comintern was not acting only as an external force, but was taking sides in a continuing domestic dispute that pitted the Liberec left, the Kladno district organization, and the ex-anarchists against the Šmeral leadership, the Brno district, and most of the rest of the CSDWP (Left). The Comintern was powerless to impose its will without local support. The failure to implement the Dresden decisions of April 1921 is sufficient proof of this. Still, it possessed great moral authority, and local Communist factions got into the habit of appealing to the Comintern for support at a very early stage in its history, as when Zápotocký and Hůla sent one report, and Hugo Sonnenstein another, to the Second Comintern Congress.[93]

In 1920 it could not be asserted that the Czechoslovak labor movement had a strong revolutionary tradition behind it. Before the First World War the Czech Socialists had universally been considered a revisionist wing within Austrian social democracy, owing to their strong emphasis on national demands. If the CSDWP of the 1910s were less inclined than the German Austrian party to place its faith in the emperor Franz Josef it was because it had more faith in the Czech bourgeoisie. During the war, there was no manifestation of support either for the Zimmerwald Left or for the Bolsheviks. In 1918 it was only with great difficulty that the left-leaning elements in the CSDWP defeated the right's proposal to merge with the National Socialists, a clearly middle-class party. How then was it possible to create a mass Communist party, the third largest in Europe and the second largest in proportion to the total population of the country? A number of tentative answers may be suggested, but, first, the *direct* influence of the Bolshevik revolution can certainly be ruled out as a factor. The slogan of national self-determination worked in favor of Czech national unity, but the socialist content of the Bolshevik message was largely missed. The time gap between 1918, the year of the first CPC, and 1920, which saw the beginning of a mass movement in favor of the formation of the final CPC, was too great for there to be any real continuity between the two. The overwhelming majority of the CPC consisted of local Social Democrats who had never left Czechoslovakia, and who had only moved toward communism after December 1919, when the Marxist Left was formed as a faction within the CSDWP.

Of far greater importance than the direct impact of the Bolshevik revolution were (1) the personal role of Šmeral, an astute political tactician who knew how to bend the Comintern's line to suite local conditions; (2) the permanent advantage presented to the Marxist Left of the CSDWP by the right wing's participation in successive Czechoslovak governments; and (3) the economic position of the Czechoslovak working class, adversely affected as it was by the crisis of adjustment to the breakup of the Austro-Hungarian Monarchy, followed by the economic crisis of 1920–1921 and the accompanying decline in industrial production and the rise in unemployment. In addition, there were factors affecting specific regions, such as the discontent of the Slovaks with Czech rule, and the harsh policy of the Czechoslovak government toward unrest in Slovakia, or the irredentist tendencies of the Ruthenians in the easternmost part of the country. None of these factors can alone explain the existence of a mass Communist party, and they must remain tentative suggestions in the absence of any regional or occupational analysis of party membership.

The fact that the CPC was a very large party, on the surface very gratifying to the Comintern, presented difficulties as well as advantages. Since the process by which the CPC had been formed was one of agglutination rather than fragmentation, the party contained many different ideological trends. Emanuel Vajtauer, for instance, represented a direct link with the semi-anarchist inclinations of the Union of Communist Groups, and it was therefore no surprise that he became the chief theoretician of the Left (Jílekite) Opposition of the years 1921–1922, which put up a considerable resistance to the moderate line of the Šmeral leadership until most of its members were expelled (September 1922). The leftists opposed the defense of Czechoslovakia against the threat of a Habsburg restoration in Hungary, opposed the tactic of the united front and any kind of cooperation with the Social Democrats, and demanded that independent, Communist trade unions be founded. They were always a minority in the Executive Committee of the CPC (seven out of twenty-four in the years 1921–1922) but they had considerable local support, both among the ex-anarchists of northwestern Bohemia and in the nationally mixed coal-mining area of Moravská-Ostrava.[94]

If there was a left, there was also a center, which many people saw as a right: in fact the ECCI was inclined to view the 1922 outbreak of ultra-leftism as a historic punishment for the Šmeral-Kreibich leadership's tendency to lean toward the right.[95] This was the other side of the coin. Šmeral and Kreibich had managed to bring many old Social Democrats of both nationalities into the CPC; but even after the unification congress it was doubtful whether most of them could be regarded as orthodox Communists in Moscow's sense of the term. "Social-democratic survivals" was a leitmotif of the ECCI's complaints throughout the period up to 1929. Considerable care is needed, though, in evaluating this evidence, owing to the Comintern's habit of retrospectively rewriting its own history. Statements made by the ECCI in 1924 about "social-democratic survivals" are evidence of the political line adopted in 1924, not of anything else. Nevertheless, if we look carefully we can find evidence from the period before the "left turn" of 1924. At the Fourth Comintern Congress, held in November and December of 1922, Karl Radek, a man closely identified with the "united front" policy and therefore likely to be sympathetic to "Šmeralism," presented a long list of shortcomings in the Czechoslovak section, including lack of agitation in the army, lack of discipline and centralization, failure to fight effectively on behalf of the unemployed, and failure to link parliamentary activities with struggles in the streets, which arose from the fact that "the majority of the old Social-Democratic party had developed toward communism."[96] And the final resolution of the Comintern's committee on the Czechoslovak question included the assertion that "the deficiencies of the CPC were to be explained through its transition from a Social Democratic to a Communist party."[97]

But on the more general issue of the interpretation of the tactic of the united front and the slogan of a "workers' government," the Fourth Congress found that the CPC had performed adequately and that Šmeral's exceedingly moderate tactical line conformed to the Comintern's own. Hence, the criticisms of the opposition within the CPC were in part rejected, and their fears that Šmeral was quietly preparing a coalition with the Czech bourgeoisie were described by Radek as "groundless" — as indeed they were.

Inner-party conflicts continued in the CPC (as in most other Communist parties) throughout the 1920s.[98] The process of "bolshevization" inaugurated in 1924, and the various tactical turns of the international Communist movement that followed — culminating in the "class against class" line of 1929–1933 — took their toll in terms of members expelled for one deviation or another. By 1929 the original leading group had lost all influence in the CPC: at the Fifth Party Congress, held in February 1929, an entirely new Politburo and a largely new Central Committee were elected,[99] consisting of people who were ready to carry out whatever the Comintern might decree with the rigid obedience required in the years of Stalin's ascendancy. It was largely this new leadership — Klement Gottwald, Jan Šverma, Rudolf Slánský, and Evžen Fried — which presided, along with Antonín Zápotocký, a survivor from the previous era, over the triumph and tragedy of the party's seizure of power in 1948.

NOTES

This article is a considerably revised and expanded version of an essay originally published in *European Studies Review*, 1 (1974), no. 3: 249–274, the copyright of which is held by the publisher of that journal, Sage Publications, London and Beverly Hills.

1. This tendency is particularly evident in the discussions of the 1950s, when it was necessary simultaneously to overrate Lenin's contribution to the formation of the party, and to emphasize the elemental and overpowering mass enthusiasm for that step, without making the politically dangerous attempt to establish the relative importance of those elements.

2. Apart from the relevant sections of wide-ranging works such as G. D. H. Cole's *History of Socialist Thought* (London, 1953–60), J. Braunthal's *History of the International, 1914–43* (London, 1967), P. E. Zinner's *Communist Strategy and Tactics in Czechoslovakia, 1918–48* (London, 1963), G. D. Jackson's *Comintern and Peasant in East Europe* (New York, 1966), and Z. L. Suda,

Zealots and Rebels: A History of the CPC (Stanford, 1980), there is one article on the subject in English, by H. G. Skilling: "The Formation of a Communist Party in Czechoslovakia," *American Slavic and East European Review*, 14, no. 3 (1955): 346–358. Cf. also J. Rupnik, *Histoire du Parti Communiste Tchécoslovaque* (Paris, 1981).

3. F. Borkenau, *The Communist International* (London, 1938).

4. P. Reimann, *Geschichte der kommunistischen Partei der Tschechoslowakei* (Hamburg, 1931).

5. J. Veselý, *O vzniku a založení KSČ* (Prague, 1953).

6. K. Gajan, *Příspěvek ke vzniku KSČ* (Prague, 1954).

7. Z. Kárník, "Založení KSČ a Kominterna," *Revue dějin socialismu*, 9, no. 2 (1969): 200.

8. He pointedly ignores Kárník's work in the main body of his article, which is in fact largely a summary of the proceedings of the Twelfth Congress of the CSDWP. (J. Křížek, "České proletářské hnutí v letech 1918–1919," *K 50. Výročí Vzniku KSČ* [Prague, 1971], pp. 45–92.)

9. Kárník, "Založení KSČ," p. 193.

10. M. Hübl, *Z dějin II. Internacionalý* (Prague, 1961), p. 73. The whole question of factional divisions in prewar social democracy is highly problemical. A detailed discussion of the changing relationship between the "Kautskyan center" and the "left radicals" would be out of place here, however.

11. I have adopted the convention of using Czech or Slovak names for places within the boundaries of Czechoslovakia.

12. Hübl, *Z dějin II. Internacionalý*, p. 81.

13. Z. Kárník, *Socialisté na rozcestí: Habsburk, Masaryk či Šmeral?* (Prague, 1968), p. 147.

14. Karl Kreibich (1883–1966), editor of the Liberec *Vorwärts* 1911–1914; Social Democratic (1920–1921) and then Communist deputy (1921–1925) to the Czechoslovak National Assembly.

15. Z. Kárník, *První pokusy o založení komunistické strany v Čechách* (Prague, 1966), p. 41.

16. O. K. Flechtheim, *Die KDP in der Weimarer Republik* (Frankfurt-am-Main, 1969), p. 34 of H. Weber's introduction.

17. Z. Kárník, "O poměru levice německé sociální demokracie ke komunistickým skupinám v severnich Čechách v roce 1919," *Zpravy kateder dějin KSČ a dějin SSSR a KSSS*, 1958, pt. 1, pp. 48–56.

18. The attitude of the various factions of Czech social democracy during the war has been thoroughly analyzed by Z. Kárník in *Socialisté na rozcestí*.

19. It should be added that the position of Gustav Habrman and the Plzeň district organization of the CSDWP was somewhat more complex than this would suggest. Although a leader of the "nationally radical" opposition to Šmeral, he sympathized with the Bolshevik revolution, expecting that it would bring victory to the cause of national self-determination in Austria-Hungary. After Brest-Litovsk he decided that help for the Czech national cause would not be forthcoming from the Russians and, together with the Plzeň organization, he moved to the right of the party, advocating closer

collaboration with the National Socialists. Cf. Kárník, *Socialisté na rozcestí*, pp. 169–170.

20. The Zimmerwald Left were the supporters, at the September 1915 Zimmerwald Conference, of Lenin's program of "turning the imperialist war into a civil war."

21. See the reports sent to the Austrian Ministry of the Interior on strikes and demonstrations in the mining districts of Bohemia, in 1917 and 1918, in PMV/R 17/5 101, *Ustřední Statní Archiv,* Prague.

22. R. Wohlgemuthová, "Cesta anarchokomunistické skupiny B. Vrbenského ke KSČ," *Československý Časopis Historický* 9, no. 4, (1961): 495–514.

23. P. Reimann, writing in 1931, ignored the anarchist groups; so did J. Veselý in 1953. The official party history, *Dějiny KSČ* (Prague, 1961), devoted five lines to the subject. This omission has now been remedied to some extent. See Z. Kárník, *První pokusy* (1966) and R. Wohlgemuthová, *Příspěvek k dějinám českého anarchistického hnutí v letech 1900–1914* (Prague, 1971).

24. *Vtoroi Kongress Kominterna* (Moscow, 1934), p. 604.

25. J. Veselý, *Češi a slováci v revolučním rusku 1917–20* (Prague, 1954), p. 105.

26. Cf. J. F. N. Bradley, *La Legion tchécoslovaque en Russie, 1914–20* (Paris, 1965).

27. Alois Muna (1886–1943): pre-1914 member of the CSDWP, representative of the district of Králove Vinohrady at the 1909 congress, prisoner of war in Russia (where he edited *Svoboda* [Kiev]), founder-member of the first CPC. Central Committee member of the CPC 1921–1929, expelled from the party in 1929 for liquidationism.

28. J. Veselý, *Češi a slováci v . . . rusku,* p. 147.

29. *Příruční Slovník KSČ* (Prague, 1964), p. 94.

30. Brětislav Hůla (1894–19   ), founder-member of the first CPC, returned to Czechoslovakia in 1919 and became editor of the Kladno *Svoboda*. Sent to Moscow in 1920 to represent the Marxist Left of the CSDWP at the Second Comintern Congress. Expelled from the CPC in 1925.

31. A brief guide to the sources of the rather obscure history of the first CPC is given by A. Kriegel and G. Haupt, "Les groupes communistes étrangers en Russie et la révolution mondiale 1917–1921: état des travaux," *Revue d'histoire moderne et contemporaine,* 10 (Oct.–Dec. 1963): 293.

32. Bohumír Šmeral (1880–1941): chairman of the CSDWP 1914–September 1917, leading member of the Marxist Left 1919–1921, member of the CC of the CPC 1921–1925. Cf. M. Klír, "Úloha B. Šmerala při vypracování strategicko-taktické orientace KSČ," *Příspěvky k dějinám KSČ,* 4, no. 5 (October 1964): 651–684, and 5, no. 1 (February 1965): 3–35.

33. Braunthal, *History of the International,* p. 309.

34. *Protokol IX. Sjezdu ČSDSD ve dnech 4. až 8. září 1909 v Praze-Smíchově* (Prague, 1909), p. 101.

35. Kárník, "Založení KSČ," pp. 168–170.

36. "Austrianism"; not an attitude to be proud of in 1918.

37. Antonín Zápotocký (1884–1957): secretary of the Kladno district organization 1907–1911, Marxist Left delegate to the Second Congress of the Comintern, July 1920, in prison from December 1920 to August 1921. A member of the CC of the CPC 1922–1929, he became President of Czechoslovakia in 1953.

38. *Protokol XII řádného Sjezdu ČSDSD, konaného ve dnech 27, 28, 29 a 30, pros. 1918* (Prague, 1919), p. 98.

39. F. Peroutka, *Budování státu* (Prague, 1933), vol. 1, p. 481.

40. Cf. P. A. Toma, "The Slovak Soviet Republic of 1919," *American Slavic and East European Review*, 17, no. 2 (1958): 203–215.

41. *Založení KSČ: Sborník Dokumentů* (Prague, 1954), pp. 34–38.

42. Kárník, "Založení KSČ," p. 177.

43. *Založení KSČ: Sborník Dokumentů*, p. 41.

44. *Vtoroi Kongress Kominterna*, p. 604.

45. V. I. Lenin, "The Socialist Revolution and the Right of Nations to Self-Determination" (1916), in *Questions of National Policy and Proletarian Internationalism* (Moscow, 1970), p. 115.

46. J. Mlynárik, "Robotnícke hnutie na Slovensku roku 1920," *Historický Časopis*, 8, no. 1 (1960): 45.

47. One group we have deliberately omitted, in order to avoid a long discussion of the nationality problem under the Habsburg Monarchy is the Brno Centralists, led by Edmund Burian, later a leading member of the CPC. Their curious trajectory from Austrian social democracy via a small local splinter group to Czechoslovak communism has never been studied in detail, but some indications are provided in J. Kolejka, "Rozkol sociální demokracie na autonomisty a centralisty v roce 1910 a činnost centralistické sociální demokracie v letech 1911–1919," *Slezský Sborník* (Opava), 54, no. 1 (1956): 1–28. This article says nothing, however, about their significant role as a ginger group in the CSDWP after the reunification of March 1919.

48. Gajan, *Příspěvek*, p. 27.

49. *The Communist International 1919–43. Documents*, ed. J. Degras (London, 1956), vol. 1, pp. 168–172.

50. Message from the ECCI to the Czechoslovak proletariat, 26 August 1920, in *Kommunisticheskii Internatsional*, no. 13, 1920, cols. 2621–2624.

51. V. Šplíchal, "K historii závěrečného procesu vytvaření KSČ a jejího přijetí do komunistické internacionály," *Příspěvky k dějinám KSČ*, (Prague), 6, no. 6 (December 1966): 858.

52. Reimann, *Geschichte*, p. 91.

53. Z. Kárník, "Revoluční hnutí v českých zemích v období frontálního útoku české buržoazie (září–prosinec 1920)," *O revoluční jednotu československého dělnického hnutí*, Acta Universitatis Carolinae 1961, Philosophica et Historica (Prague, 1961), p. 22.

54. F. Nečásek, J. Pachta and E. Raisová, eds., *Dokumenty o protilidové a protinarodní politice T. G. Masaryka* (Prague, 1953), pp. 65–70; notes taken by Masaryk of his meetings of 8 and 12 September with members of the government coalition.

55. J. Veselý, *Osnovanie kommunisticheskoi partii chekhoslovakii* (Moscow, 1956), p. 145.

56. *Založení KSČ: Sborník Dokumentů,* pp. 67–70. Resolution by 291 representatives of Prague factories.

57. *Kommunisticheskii Internatsional,* no. 15 (Moscow, 1920), col. 3205.

58. Kárník, "Revoluční hnutí v českých zemích," p. 28.

59. *Protokol XIII sjezdu ČSDSD (Levice)* (Prague, 1920), p. 112.

60. Ibid., p. 116.

61. *Kommunismus* (Vienna) 1, no. 40 (16 October 1920): 1410.

62. Reimann, *Geschichte,* p. 108.

63. For detailed accounts of the various forms of strike action adopted at this time, see I. Malá and F. Štěpán, eds., *Prosincová generální stávka 1920* (Prague, 1961), section C, nos. 143–204.

64. There are clear correlations between occupation and the degree of support for revolutionary actions, with the railwaymen at one end of the spectrum and the lignite miners at the other. This subject has not yet received the detailed study it deserves.

65. As reported in *Kommunisticheskii Internatsional,* 1920, cols. 3915–3922.

66. Reimann, *Geschichte,* p. 124.

67. Mlynárík, "Robotnicke hnutie," p. 68.

68. Cf. L. Holotík, "Sjazd sociálnodemokratickej strany (ľavice) na Slovensku v januári 1921," *Historický Časopis,* 11, no. 3 (1963): 337–365.

69. *Rudé Právo* (Prague), 27 February 1921; an article by Šmeral.

70. Šplíchal, "K historii . . . vytvaření KSČ," p. 860.

71. K. Gorovský, "O založení KSČ: drázďanská konference v dubnu 1921," *Revue dějin socialismu,* 8, no. 3 (1868): 436.

72. *Protokol XIV sjezdu ČSDSD (Levice)* (Prague, 1921), p. 76.

73. This interpretation goes against the trend of recent Czechoslovak historiography, which attempts to establish (1) the lack of any real disagreement between Šmeral and the responsible leaders of the Comintern, and (2) the "ultra-leftism" of those who opposed Šmeral's policy. Z. Kárník, for instance, states ("Založení KSČ a Kominterna," p. 193) that "[At the congress of May 1921] Šmeral was admittedly attacked from leftist positions." These "leftist" positions were at that time the ECCI's own positions.

74. *Protokoll des III. Kongresses der kommunistischen Internationale* (Hamburg, 1921), p. 8.

75. Ibid., p. 215.

76. Ibid.

77. Šplíchal, "K historii . . . vytvaření KSČ," p. 871: "At the congress there was one-sided criticism from "left" positions by Kun, Alpári, and Rákosi, actively supported by Kreibich and Doležal."

78. *Protokoll des III. Kongresses,* pp. 240–242.

79. P. Spriano, *Storia del Partito comunista italiano,* vol. 1 (Turin, 1967), p. 157.

80. *Thesen und Resolutionen des III. Weltkongresses der kommunistischen Internationale* (Hamburg, 1921), p. 42; the theses on tactics adopted at the 24th session, 12 July 1921.

81. *Protokoll des III. Kongresses,* p. 511.

82. Ibid., p. 512.

83. This description of the CPC (German section) was incorrect, since the German section represented Germans in other parts of Czechoslovakia as well.

84. *Protokoll des III. Kongresses,* pp. 935–936.

85. *Thesen und Resolutionen des III. Kongresses,* p. 41. The time limit was to be three months.

86. *Protokoll des III. Kongresses,* p. 452.

87. Ibid., p. 749.

88. Gajan, *Příspěvek,* p. 258.

89. Ibid., p. 196.

90. *Protokoll des III. Kongresses,* p. 503.

91. Gajan, *Příspěvek,* p. 260.

92. *Protokoll des IV. Kongresses der kommunistischen Internationale,* p. 363.

93. *Berichte zum zweiten Kongress der kommunistischen Internationale* (Hamburg, 1921), pp. 63–76.

94. Cf. V. Dubský, *Ultraleve tendence v komunistické straně československa v letech 1921–1922 a boj za jejich překonání,* Acta Universitatis Carolinae, Philosophica et Historica, 1 (Prague, 1960), pp. 39–61.

95. *Bericht über die Tätigkeit des Präsidiums und der Exekutive der kommunistischen Internationale für die Zeit vom 6. März bis 11. Juni 1922* (Hamburg, 1922), p. 120; resolution of 11 June 1922: "Insufficient activity directed at conquering the trade unions has strengthened tendencies that . . . advocate splitting the trade unions."

96. *Protokoll des IV. Kongresses der kommunistischen Internationale,* pp. 925–929.

97. Ibid., p. 931.

98. This is not the place to discuss these conflicts in detail. For a brief summary, see H. G. Skilling, "The Comintern and Czechoslovak Communism 1921–29," *American Slavic and East European Review,* 19, no. 2 (1960): 234–247. On the period 1921–1923, see V. Mencl, *Na Cestě k Jednotě* (Prague, 1964). The books published in Czechoslovakia in the 1950s on bolshevization are perhaps best ignored.

99. In 1965 the Czechs issued a list of members of the highest party organs between 1920 and 1945 (*Příspevky k dějinám KSČ,* vol. 5 [Prague, 1965], pp. 757–784). Thanks to this list, we can follow the changing composition of the party leadership. The Politburo of 1929 contained no one who had been a member of the corresponding body in 1921; the 52-member Central Committee of 1929 contained only one survivor from the 24-member Executive Committee of 1921, the Pole Karel Sliwka, and he was expelled from the party in 1938 for a Polish nationalist deviation.

One Step Forward, Two Steps Back:
The Rise and Fall of the
First Hungarian Communist Party, 1918–1922

PETER PASTOR

Nowhere among the successor states did communism achieve a more spectacular success or failure than it did in Hungary during the three years following the end of the war. During this period the country made a transition from a multinational state to an ethnically almost homogeneous entity. It also experienced the rise and fall of a Communist Soviet Republic which, during its 133-day existence in the spring of 1919, seemed to fulfill in part the predictions of the Bolsheviks on the spread of communism to the West.

The policies of the Soviet Republic, however, alienated most people in Hungary. Following its collapse, the counterrevolutionary White Terror persecuted the outlawed Communists, and the Hungarian Communist party became the first illegal Communist party in Eastern Europe. The party virtually ceased to exist between August 1919 and the end of 1921, for its leaders were unable to develop an underground organization. Having experienced the glories of Soviet power, these men were now forced to seek haven in the West, mostly in Austria, or in the East, in Soviet Russia. The party they resuscitated in exile fell victim to the personal intrigues and factionalism of its small membership — an inglorious fate that further tarnished the party's reputation and diminished the appeal of the Marxist-Leninist ideology in Hungary.

Scholars who have examined the spread of communism have reached different conclusions as to the reasons for its rise in Hungary. In one of the earliest scholarly treatments of the subject, the exiled Hungarian sociologist Oszkár Jászi concluded that the war and Hungary's harsh treatment at the hands of the victors were the major causes for communism's emergence.[1] During the interwar era, conservative historians of Hungarian communism were greatly influenced by the prevailing anti-communist sentiments. They attributed the rise of the Communist movement to non-Hungarian elements, mainly Jews who, as former prisoners of war, had returned from Russia with Lenin's blessing to introduce communism in Hungary.[2] Both Jászi's "reformist" interpretation and the "counterrevolutionary" interpretations of historians such as Elemér Mályusz and Gyula Szekfű shared the view that communism had few, if any roots in prewar Hungary.

Official Marxist historiography, which has gone through two phases in its interpretation and reinterpretation of the immediate postwar period, takes a different position. It assails both the "reformist" and "counterrevolutionary" schools and claims that communism had historic roots in the Hungarian labor movement. These official works also argue that the war served only as a catalyst for communism in Hungary.[3] They pay no attention to the Jewish background of many of the chief protagonists of communism in post-armistice Hungary.[4] Thus, the late Aladár Mód, the Marxist historian of both the Rákosi and the Kádár regimes, identified the Jews only as intellectuals who had been the whipping boys of "counterrevolutionary" historians. Another party historian and bibliographer of the events of 1918–1919, András Siklós, also fails to note the Jewish connection. In his annotated bibliography, he, however, alludes to this fact with the comment that "counterrevolutionary" interpretations were welcomed by race-defense journals and by the so-called Christian nationalists.[5]

Unconstrained by official taboos, Western scholarship has been able to offer explanations for the disproportionate Jewish participation in the Communist ranks.[6] Thus, the prominent Sovietologist Richard Löwenthal attributes this to Hungary's having treated the Jews not as a class, but rather as a caste, from which they now sought emancipation with Moscow's blessings.[7] Löwenthal's thesis seems to be based on Robert Michels' 1915 argument that the almost exclusively Jewish leadership of Austro-Hungarian socialism stemmed from the failure of "social and moral emancipation" in that area.[8] Other explanations have also been suggested. One proposed that the Jews' inherent messianic impulse was translated into Communist activities by 1918. The hotbed of communism in Hungary was the industrial center and capital, Budapest, where the Jewish community made up twenty-five percent of the city's population. Another theory suggests that the "Jewishness" of the urban Marxist revolutionaries is less significant than their middle-class background. The "fathers" of these activists had also been interested in changing the system by working for modernization, an aim that they had tried to accomplish by serving the governments of the *ancien régime*. Since they had failed to hasten the process of modernization through existing institutions, their less patient sons chose more radical means to achieve the same end.[9]

Some scholars engaged in the comparative history of Communist movements pay little attention to the religious background in their discussions of the Hungarian case, instead emphasizing the direct role of Russia.[10]

Others claim that the Hungarians embraced "national communism" as a consequence of the desperate post-armistice situation, little related to ideological utopias.[11] This explanation is similar to those offered by Westerners who witnessed the Hungarian revolutions of 1918–1919.[12]

Regardless of this broad spectrum of interpretations on the social and economic causes of communism, all of these publications indicate that the actual organization of the Hungarian Communist party was Russian-inspired. They point out that it was not until a group of former prisoners of war returned to Hungary from Russia after the armistice that the Party of the Communists in Hungary was formed in Budapest. Many of the Hungarian prisoners of war in Russia came to sympathize with the Bolsheviks and their cause, primarily as a result of the harsh treatment they had received at the hands of the tsarist and later the provincial government. After the fall of Nicholas II, the Bolsheviks, convinced that better treatment of the prisoners of war could make the Austro-Hungarians more willing to negotiate peace, had directed attention to their plight. In addition, the pro-Bolshevik prisoners of war were looked upon as agents who, once repatriated, would spread the "bacilli of bolshevism."[13] The prisoners, in turn, hoped to see a Bolshevik government, expecting that with Russia out of the war their return to Hungary would be assured.[14] Although most Hungarian prisoners of war favored the Bolsheviks for these pragmatic reasons, a few were sincerely attracted to their cause.[15] These were the prisoners already acquainted with Marxism through their previous activities in the Hungarian Social Democratic party, or as a result of participation in Marxist discussion groups in the Russian camps.[16]

Most of the Bolshevik sympathizers among Hungarian prisoners of war joined the ranks in Russia only after the October Revolution. Among the few notable exceptions was Béla Kun, who had begun to work for the Bolsheviks in the summer of 1917.[17] His decision does not appear to have been motivated by an understanding of the ideological underpinnings of Lenin's road to socialism, but rather by the ambitions of an "adventurer-revolutionary."[18] Formerly a minor labor union official, Kun seemed to intuit the outcome of the Russian power struggle and promptly committed himself to the Bolshevik cause.

As we have seen, the pro-Bolsheviks among the Hungarian prisoners of war were expected to become the shock troops for the revolution that Lenin counted on to spread to the West.[19] It is with this revolution in mind that the Hungarian section of the Bolshevik Party was established

on 24 March 1918. Whether this action was Lenin's brainchild or that of
his Hungarian disciples is a question on which Hungarian party historians remain divided.[20] Since other national sections were established in
addition to the Hungarian, however, it would seem that the initiative
came from Lenin and the other Bolshevik leaders. The Hungarian
section had four founding members: Béla Kun, Ernő Pór, Endre
Rudnyánszky, and Tibor Szamuely.[21] Its umbrella organization, the
Federation of Foreign Sections of the Russian Communist (bolshevik)
party, came under the leadership of Béla Kun.[22]

Though the organization of foreign sections clearly contradicted the
terms of the recently signed Treaty of Brest-Litovsk,[23] the party's
absorption of pro-Bolshevik prisoners of war was desirable for immediate gains. Lenin, expecting the imminent outbreak of a civil war,
considered his party comrades among the prisoners of war as leaders
who could mobilize their conationals against Russian counterrevolutionaries.[24] As many historians have noted,[25] the Hungarian Communist
leaders, whose responsibility included recruitment into the section,
were all young men: Béla Kun, its president, was thirty-one, while
Szamuely was twenty-eight. None of these men — all of petit-bourgeois
background — had had any serious leadership experience in the social-
democratic movement before the war. Their youth suggests that historians err by approaching the Hungarian Communists only through the
paradigm of the alienated Jew or intellectual; they should consider them
also as participants in the youth revolution that gripped Europe during
the interwar period. The class background and the wartime experiences
of the youthful revolutionaries were similar to those of their peers
throughout Europe; everywhere European youth championed extremist
causes that sought to destroy an old world that they all loathed.[26]

Once organized, the Hungarian section in Russia swung into feverish
activity. Under the editorial guidance of Rudnyánszky, the Hungarian
Bolsheviks began to publish for the Hungarians in Russia *Szociális
Forradalom* (Social Revolution), a semiweekly tabloid with a distribution of between 15 and 20 thousand copies. Agitprop schools were set
up and several hundred prisoners of war went through their courses
during 1918.[27] In addition to the classic works of Marxism and Leninism,
the seminars studied Kun's *What Do the Communists Want,* a simplistic
summary of Leninism which forecast the spread of revolution to Hungary and the West.[28]

The outbreak of a full-scale civil war and the anti-Bolshevik intervention of the Czechoslovak Legion led to the organization of international
formations within the Red Army. Many of the Hungarian Communists,
including Kun, took an active part in leading Hungarian volunteers.

Kun and Szamuely played a commanding and bloody role when they participated in the crushing of the Left SR revolution in Moscow.[29] In Siberia, the Hungarian internationalists were pitted against the Czechoslovaks in a confrontation that became a civil war reflecting the animosities of the peoples of the Austro-Hungarian Monarchy[30] — the same animosities that sparked the revolutions in the monarchy during the closing days of the war in October 1918.

By the time the Austro-Hungarian representatives signed the Armistice of Padua on 3 November 1918, national councils were everywhere claiming authority as successors to the Dual Monarchy. In Hungary, the revolution of 30 October brought the Hungarian National Council to power. Some members of this council then became the officials of a new revolutionary government under Count Mihály Károlyi.

The new regime included the Social Democratic party, which, through its association with the labor unions, was the only mass party in Hungary. Although Socialist ministers were at first in a minority, they represented the real force behind the government.[31] The Socialists also were able to control the soldiers' and workers' councils, organizations that were modeled on the Russian example, but which never competed with the government for power.[32]

The government's program included the introduction of universal suffrage, as well as land and tax reforms. The Socialists hoped that monopoly industries would also be nationalized, though they cautioned against large-scale socialization. They argued that they did not want to take over industries that as a result of wartime dislocations were considered as mere "scrap metal."[33]

The Western orientation of the Károlyi regime was designed to secure a fair treatment for Hungary at the approaching peace conference. Károlyi was well known in Entente circles as being pro-Western, and the government was optimistic about its major objective — winning Allied support for Hungary's integrity. The Military Convention of Belgrade of 13 November 1918, which was signed by the representatives of the Allied forces commanded by General Louis Franchet d'Esperey, seemed to indicate that the Hungarians would be successful.[34] Consequently, the government aimed to solve the disruptive nationality problem by giving autonomous rights to the non-Hungarians. This policy, however, found little support among the nationalities who wanted to secede from Hungary and join their brethren in their own nation-states.

The national revolutions throughout the Habsburg Monarchy did not escape the attention of Lenin and the Bolsheviks. Developments in East-Central Europe seemed to bear out their deterministic views.

Lenin equated the fall of Emperor-King Charles with the fall of Tsar Nicholas and considered Károlyi another Kerensky.[35] On 3 November an open letter to the peoples of the defunct Dual Monarchy was sent by Lenin and Iakov Mikhailovich Sverdlov. It expressed the hope that the "Hungarian workers and peasants will rid themselves of the capitalists and the new government will be the government of workers and peasants."[36]

On the following day the Hungarian Section of the Bolshevik party, intent on transferring its operation to Hungary, met in Moscow to establish the Party of the Communists in Hungary. The notion of forming a party outside the bounds of the Bolshevik party had first been raised on 25 October, at the meeting of the Hungarian Communists. Kun declared that since the Hungarian Social Democrats had betrayed the proletariat, a revolutionary Communist party had to be organized. He proposed that the party structure imitate the Russian model and include all the nationalities of Hungary.[37] The Party Conference, representing the three-hundred Hungarian Communists in Russia,[38] met on 4 November and accepted Kun's proposals. The newly established Central Committee declared that the rules of the Russian party would be binding until the meeting of Lenin's brainchild, the Communist International, which was expected to issue instructions on party organization.[39]

The newly established party's leaders immediately ordered its members to return to Hungary, their repatriation being coordinated by the party's Foreign Bureau, headed by Rudnyánszky.[40] It is significant that the formation of the Hungarian party did not entail the disbanding of the Hungarian Section within the Russian party. Indeed, Rudnyánszky, who was expected to stay in Moscow to head the bureau, was now appointed president of the Hungarian Section of the Bolshevik Party.[41] This interlocking arrangement may have been unintentional, a consequence of organizational chaos. The Hungarian party's recognition of the supervisory role of the Russian Central Committee, however, may indicate that the overlap was intentional.

The so-called counterrevolutionary historians of the interwar era emphasized Moscow's role in fathering the Hungarian Communist party. In the thirties, the Hungarian Communist exiles in Moscow made similar claims. References to their earlier activities in Russia gave them legitimacy as revolutionaries, while also assuaging Stalin's needs to have the Soviet Union represented as the leader of the Communist International. Post-World War II official interpretations do not differ much on this point; the USSR must still be identified as first among equals in the Communist camp.[42] This emphasis on the Russian role, however, presents a problem for some historians in that it clearly contradicts the claim that communism had its roots in Hungarian soil. For this reason, the authoritative *Magyar forradalmi munkásmozgalom története,* which comes closest to being the Hungarian version of the *History of the Communist Party of the Soviet Union,* fails to indicate that the Party of the Communists in Hungary was first formed in Moscow with Lenin's blessing. It simply states that "On November 4, the leaders of the Hungarian Communist organization decided to return to Hungary in order to start a new party."[43]

About two hundred Communists returned to Hungary in November, including: Béla Kun, Ferenc Münnich, József Rabinovits, and Mátyás Rákosi. By the time they reached the frontiers, two radical groups in Budapest were already considering the organization of a Communist party in Hungary. The first group comprised some left-wing dissidents from the Social Democratic party who objected to their party's support of the Károlyi regime and favored secession. A second group, calling itself the Revolutionary Socialists, also toyed with the idea of a new party. This small group of young men, mostly college educated, was influenced by socialist and syndicalist thought. It was led by the twenty-five-year-old Otto Korvin, whom György Lukács would later characterize as the Hungarian Saint-Just.[44] Despite their dissatisfaction with the Social Democratic party's platform and with the Hungarian government, these dissidents concluded that their cause would be better served through an intraparty struggle, which would lead to the desired changes in Socialist policies.

Meeting with the dissidents, the Communists from Russia equated the Hungarian Social Democrats with the Mensheviks. Béla Kun announced bluntly that, regardless of the dissidents' intentions, a Communist party would be formed. At this juncture, Kun refrained from informing those at the meeting that the party had, in fact, been founded in Moscow. He probably intended to keep this fact secret so that no resentment would be aroused against foreign meddling. Since he offered no alternatives, the radicals went along with Kun and on 24 November the Communist party of Hungary was formed again, for the second time in a month. Béla Kun dominated the new Central Committee, although it did not have a Muscovite majority. In addition to the Central Committee, a Propaganda Committee and an Agitation Committee were established at this time.[45]

The new Hungarian party differed from those organized in the other successor states and in the West. Most of these were built around organized socialist splinter groups, whereas the Hungarian party gathered disgruntled individuals around a well-organized, Moscow-trained core.[46]

Despite its intention to copy Bolshevik party organization, the Hungarian party had no party program — a situation that has led party historians to identify either Kun's *What Do the Communists Want,* or the party paper's lead article, "We Want Class Struggle," as the program.[47] The "Temporary Party Rules" also differed from rigid Russian rules concerning membership. The Hungarians, in dire need of supporters, invited all wage earners to join the party, stipulating that only the nonsalaried need have the support of two party members for their application.[48] Despite these loose membership requirements, the party failed to gain many new adherents. In January 1919, its leaders initiated a "snowball recruitment" program, requiring each member to enlist ten new members.[49] Though this kind of recruitment has been judged successful by party historians and by some in the West,[50] others argue that it led to an erosion of party discipline, which had been the key element of Bolshevik success in 1917.[51] The final membership tally is still controversial. Party historians estimate that by March 1919 the party had between 30 and 40 thousand adherents. Western historians place the number between 4 and 7 thousand.[52]

The greatest failure of the recruitment drive was the party's inability to enlist the returning prisoners of war and use them as its shock troops. Although the Hungarian-language paper in Russia and the party paper in Hungary exhorted the returnees, many of them former Internationalists in the Red Army, to report to party headquarters upon their return, only a few of them did so.[53] Their apathy was proof that the support they gave to the Reds in Russia was prompted by their need for self-preservation rather than any ideological commitment to the Bolshevik cause. Once they had returned safely to their families, they no longer saw a need to pay lip service to the Communist cause. This lack of revolutionary zeal should have been a warning to the Hungarian Communists, who were still caught up in the euphoria of their Russian experience.

Whereas the fruits of the party's recruitment drive are much debated, there is little disagreement concerning the success of the party's propaganda through its organ, *Vörös Újság* [Red News], a tabloid that was first published on 7 December 1918. Tibor Szamuely was editor-in-chief, and Béla Kun, Béla Vágó, László Rudas, and Jenő László assisted him. The 40 thousand issues of the paper were printed semiweekly in December and three times a week from January on.[54] This quantity and frequency of publication at a time when newsprint was rationed in Hungary were a testimony to the financial support the Communists received from Soviet Russia, a fact that has never been denied.[55] In addition to printing ideological treatises and news about Communist movements, *Vörös Újság* served as a vehicle to attack the Social Democrats, the government, and the Entente. Although the party was not strictly modeled on the Russian example, the party paper closely copied *Pravda,* agitating for the transfer of power from the government to the workers' and soldiers' councils in a clear attempt to create a conflict of authority.[56]

Despite the scathing communist attacks on the Socialists, the socialist-controlled labor unions, with a membership of 700 thousand, did not object to the participation of their rank and file in the Communist movement. The right wing of the Social Democratic party mistrusted the Communists, but the more influential center, led by Zsigmond Kunfi, proved more tolerant. In general, the Socialist leaders believed that the Communists differed only in tactics and sought to avoid an open clash between the two proletarian parties.[57] Thus, the Communists were allowed to participate in the deliberations of the Workers' Council of Budapest. The needed public platform for their cause, therefore, was assured.

The Communists also sought to profit from Károlyi's handling of the nationalities problem. By January 1919 the government had lost large chunks of Hungarian territory to its neighbors. Despite the government's efforts to obtain Allied support for its territorial integrity, these exactions were taking place with apparent Allied acquiescence, and the government was forced to recognize that it was unable to preserve Hungary's integrity. In order to limit territorial losses, the government appealed to the principle of self-determination in the contested areas. The Communists argued that such a policy could not be achieved within a capitalist system. Capitalism, they maintained, created an international proletariat for whom the nation had no meaning. National self-determination was therefore but a ploy to strengthen the national bourgeoisie in its losing struggle against international monopoly capitalism. The imperialist era, which was the highest stage of capitalism, would see a further weakening of national consciousness, and once imperialism was destroyed by the proletariat, the nation state would cease to exist.

Denouncing the government's policy, *Vörös Újság* declared:

> There are no Frenchmen, Englishmen, Hungarians, or Romanians, only French proletarians and French bourgeois, Hungarian, Romanian, and English proletarians and Hungarian, Romanian, and English bourgeois. Our slogan can only be a call for the self-determination of the proletariat, regardless of language — which means the dictatorship of the proletariat.[58]

The Hungarian communist view of the nationality question has been faulted by historians both in the East and in the West. They claim that

Kun and his partisans followed N. Bukharin's position rather than that of Lenin, who, according to their argument, accepted the principle of national self-determination.[59] Richard Pipes, however, has convincingly demonstrated that, by the spring of 1919, Lenin had compromised with Bukharin and tied the question of self-determination to stages of historical development. This conclusion led to another compromise favoring the transitory federation of nations at different stages of historical development — a federation that would then evolve into a unified proletarian state.[60] In this respect, the Hungarian position was not very different from that of the Russian leaders.

Having offered solutions to all the problems the Károlyi regime was unable to resolve, the Hungarian Communists appeared confident in their quest for power. The increasing economic difficulties resulting from the territorial issue and the Czechoslovak coal blockade created a cabinet crisis in the middle of January. When some of the cabinet ministers resigned, the Communists demanded the transfer of power to the Workers' Council. At the same time, they accused the council of being a social-democratic institution and demanded that it change to a "class organization of the proletariat." Taking a cue from the Russian experience, they called for a congress of workers' councils.[61] When the Budapest Workers' Council instead gave its vote of confidence to the new government, the Communists launched a venomous propaganda attack on the Socialists.[62] The council reacted by censuring and expelling the Communists on 28 January.[63] As the thirteen Communist representatives were being ejected physically from the council chambers, the popular labor leader Sándor Garbai declared: "We must turn our guns against them! No one should be allowed to break the unity of the workers except at his own peril!"[64]

The Leninist attempt to undermine the government thus backfired, leading to a decline in Communist fortunes and an open break between the two Marxist parties. The Communists now acused the Socialists of being the lackeys of the capitalists who "made a bordello out of the Workers' Council." They called on their supporters to prepare for reprisals: "Terror for terror! This is the message to the government's socialist mafia."[65] The Communists were reciprocated for their threats when the Socialists expelled them from the labor unions.[66] Faced with increasing isolation, the Communists decided to modify their tactics by abandoning their threat of violence. The lessons of the bloody repression of the Spartacists by the socialist government in Germany may also have contributed to the cooling of Communist tempers in Hungary, even though party historians argue that it was the Hungarian Socialists who became more bellicose after the Berlin events.[67]

The Communist-Socialist rift did not become violent until 20 February 1919. By then the Communists had gained influence over the unemployed and on that date led them in a demonstration that terminated at the headquarters of the socialist paper *Népszava* [People's Voice]. The demonstration was intended to put pressure on the Socialists in the cabinet, to embarrass them because they had proven powerless to lift the coal blockade which had caused the factories to remain idle and brought transportation to a virtual standstill. Once the demonstration had begun, the mob in front of the building soon became unruly, and four policemen were shot in the ensuing melee. The assailants were not known, and whether they were Communist hirelings or not remains a mystery. The government reacted swiftly, however, holding the organizers of the meeting responsible for the bloodshed. The next day, the party press was temporarily seized and forty-eight Communist leaders were arrested, including Kun, Rabinovits, and Korvin. Sympathy for the dead policemen was such that the arrests at first met with popular acclaim.[68] This attitude was soon dramatically reversed, however, when some insubordinate policemen, including the brother of one of the victims, decided to take justice into their own hands by severely beating the imprisoned Béla Kun. An eyewitness news report led to a public uproar in support of Kun and his comrades.[69] The embarrassed cabinet responded by ordering that the Communist be treated with the deference accorded to political prisoners but did not order their release. This approach reflected the government's determination to reduce both left and right extremism. House arrests of some one hundred notables identified with right-wing counterrevolutionary activities followed the imprisonment of the Communists.[70]

In Moscow, Lenin was kept abreast of the Hungarian events and seemed highly satisfied, perhaps because he equated the Hungarian February with the Russian July Days.[71] To discourage the further abuse of Kun and the other prisoners, the Soviet leaders ordered that some Hungarian officers still in prisoner-of-war camps be held as hostages.[72] Lenin's perception of the Hungarian situation from afar, however, differed from that generally held in Budapest. With the Communists out of the picture, the Socialists saw their position further strengthened. They were convinced that the coming elections would bring a socialist victory, after which the new government would be able to socialize heavy industry, mines, and all public utilities, as well as continue land reforms. The Budapest Workers' Council, however, opposed the elections, fearing that the Socialists would not receive an absolute majority.[73]

When on 5 March the Workers' Council finally accepted the government's proposal to hold elections on 13 April, it also announced that if the vote were not in favor of the Socialists, the council would use force to break up the elected assembly. In effect, then, the Workers' Council was demanding a dictatorship of the Social Democratic party. This position, adopted by the representatives of the proletariat, later led some Socialist leaders to claim exaggeratedly that the workers associated with the Social Democratic party through the labor unions were Communists in all but name.[74] In turn, Communist party historians subsequently used this Socialist claim to justify *their* view that communism in Hungary had its roots among the masses.[75]

The council's deliberations on a socialist government in Hungary occurred at a time when increasing territorial exactions by Hungary's neighbors seemed to call in question the state's very viability. Driven to despair by Entente and successor state policies, Hungarian public opinion began to pay increasing attention to the propaganda of the Bolsheviks and their Hungarian surrogates. Their consistent denunciation of "Entente imperialism" seemed to ring true, and reports of Red Army troops in nearby Galicia raised hopes for an alliance with revolutionary Russia. As a result, the Hungarian Communists came to be seen as an asset capable of establishing new links between Hungary and Soviet Russia. With this in mind, early in March, the Workers' Council called for the readmission of the expelled Communists. This action also reflected the growing Hungarian opinion that the Bolsheviks' struggle against foreign intervention was akin to Hungary's resistance to the territorial demands of the successor states. A Hungarian General Staff officer, Lieutenant-Colonel Jenő Tombor, crystallized this sentiment when, in a public memorandum, he praised the patriotism of the Russian Bolsheviks in fighting against the "predatory imperialism of the Entente."[76]

The council's call for reconciliation between the two Marxist parties led to the dispatch of Ignác Bogár of the Metalworkers' Union to Béla Kun's prison cell. The result of these negotiations was a memorandum drawn up by Kun, outlining the conditions for a rapprochement. Kun reiterated his demands — power for the councils and socialization of land and industry. He called on the Socialists to adhere to the recently organized Third International. Turning to the nationality issue, he demanded that the Socialists abandon the "bourgeois concept of national sovereignty." Kun's stance did not, however, challenge the popular desire for national integrity, even though it claimed that Hungary was witnessing a shift from a national to a proletarian revolution.[77] Evidently, this shift meant the end of the transfer of territories to Hungary's bourgeois neighbors. Beneath the Marxist jargon, then, Kun was telling Hungarians what most of them wanted to hear, that communism stood for the preservation of Hungary's millennial territory. The later socialist charge that the Hungarian Communist were national Bolsheviks is difficult to dispute.

On 20 March the discussion of Marxist unity became an issue of burning immediacy. Colonel Fernand Vix, the head of the French Military Mission in Budapest, upon orders originating from Premier Georges Clemenceau in Paris, transmitted the decision of the Paris Peace Conference. The Hungarian government was given thirty-six hours to withdraw its troops to a demarcation line, the contours of which were strongly reminiscent of the unrealistic frontiers that the Entente had promised to the Romanians in the secret Treaty of Bucharest in 1916. President Károlyi claimed that any government that signed such a document could not survive one more day. The socialist minister of war Vilmos Böhm added that the Communist party would instantly swell to 200 thousand in protest against the Allied demand.

Böhm's military specialists proposed that the government appeal for Soviet support. They also favored the formation of a socialist government that could mobilize the masses for resistance and a compromise with the Communists to help secure the support of the Russians. For these reasons, at the emergency meeting of the Social Democratic party leadership, Böhm proposed that the Socialists should arrange for a *modus vivendi* with the Communists so that the latter would not undermine their authority in the emergency. A delegation led by Jenő Landler was dispatched to Kun's prison cell to ascertain the Communist reaction to this proposal.[78]

At the cabinet meeting, Károlyi proposed that the Vix Ultimatum be rejected and that the cabinet resign in favor of a socialist government. He hoped that the Socialists would be able to gain the support of the Socialist International, which had, at its February Congress in Berne, denounced the peace dictated by the victors and had called for self-determination based on plebiscite or referendum.[79] At the same time, he advised the Socialists to seek the passive support of the Communists, so that Hungary would not be attacked by the Red Army.[80]

The masses received the new of the Vix Ultimatum with defiance. On the morning of 21 March, soldiers, with the approval of the Soldiers' Council, started preparations for the defense of Budapest. The workers of the metallurgical union fulfilled Böhm's stark warning of the previous day: all 30 thousand of them joined the Communist party.

That same morning, following Landler's report of a positive response from the Communists, the Central Committee of the Social Democratic party decided to attempt the fusion of the two parties. A delegation consisting of Zsigmond Kunfi, József Pogány, Jakab Weltner, and József Haubrich was sent back to prison to negotiate with Béla Kun, Béla Vágó, Károly Vántus, Ernő Seidler, Ede Chlepko, and Ferenc Jancsik.[81] During this brief meeting, the Socialists accepted the conditions Kun had first offered to Ignác Bogár. The proposed election was called off, in return for which the Communists promised to deliver Bolshevik support to the new government.[82] Temporarily called the Socialist party of Hungary, the new fusion party declared its intention to join the Comintern, in whose councils the party's final name would be decided.[83] The swift capitulation of the Socialists was later defended by Zsigmond Kunfi on the grounds that they saw it as essential to preserve the accomplishments of the revolution and to provide the people with leaders whom they would trust.[84]

Kun's justification of the decision to accept the reunification of the Marxist movement went through several phases. Ten years after the events, he explained that revolutionary conditions in Hungary had to be exploited, regardless of the party's weakness.[85] Closer to the truth was the analysis he offered on 23 March 1919: fusion was accomplished because the Socialists had capitulated to his demands.[86] The possibility that a mature mass party would dominate a young party with an insignificant number of adherents and without national party organization did not seem to perturb Kun. A few days later, on 27 March, he tried to allay Lenin's misgivings in a message in which he drew parallels between the victory of the workers in Russia and in Hungary. He assured his teacher that his personal domination of the situation was decisive and that the masses were following him.[87]

Kun's report to Lenin indicates that he was acting on the basis of his experiences in Russia; indeed, that he probably saw himself as a Hungarian Lenin. Moreover, he may have assumed that if the Hungarians had been willing to fight among the Internationalists in Russia, they would now fight for Hungary's integrity with Communist slogans. In Russia, however, most of the Hungarian prisoners of war had fought for the sake of survival, which was not necessarily at stake in Hungary.[88]

Once the terms of the Communist-Socialist fusion were accepted by both sides, Károlyi's continued presidency, originally favored by the Socialists, had to be terminated. No doubt the fact that Lenin had compared him to Kerensky had considerable influence on this decision.[89] On the afternoon of 21 March, Prime Minister Dénes Berinkey and his cabinet rejected the Vix Ultimatum and resigned. The government's last act before its resignation was the liberation of the imprisoned Communists.[90]

With no government in power, the Workers' Council claimed executive authority and accepted the fusion party's right to form a government. The council assumed that this step would enable Hungary to form an alliance with Soviet Russia. Although the council had ejected the Communists from its midst a few weeks earlier, it now applauded the newly found Marxist unity. With the authority it gained through the Socialist-Communist agreement, which supposedly gave all power to the councils, the council called for the establishment of the Hungarian Soviet Republic. National indignation had transformed the delegates into supporters of Communist internationalism.

That same evening Kun met with the other Communist leaders and with those top Socialists who had accepted the fusion to form the provisional Revolutionary Governing Council. The new cabinet had only two Communist commissars, but to counterbalance the socialist majority each Socialist commissar had a Communist partner as vice-commissar. Béla Kun's presence as commissar of foreign affairs indicated the direction Hungary's policy would take.[91] The new president of the Council of Commissars was the Socialist Sándor Garbai.

On the morning of 22 March the Revolutionary Governing Council issued a communiqué informing the Hungarians of the changes. It stated that socialism and communism would prevent the economic collapse that further territorial concessions would have precipitated. A huge proletarian army, formed to protect the dictatorship of the proletariat against the Hungarian capitalists, the Romanian boyars, and the Czech bourgeoisie, was proposed. The council identified itself with the ideology of the Soviet Russian government, and offered it a military alliance.[92]

Since the new party was dominated by the Socialist center, the victory of communism appeared, paradoxically, to be the accomplishment of the Socialists rather than the Communists. This unique development was symbolized by the fact that the former Social Democratic party building served as headquarters for the new party. Fifteen years later, in his Moscow exile, József Rabinovits noted that the fusion was a major flaw of the Commune.[93] In March 1919, however, the Communists had hailed this same union. The Marxist philosopher and self-appointed theoretician of the merger,[94] György Lukács, claimed that there was no need for a transitory party dictatorship in Hungary, because the proletariat acted as a class through the councils.

Less than a year later, Lukács, now in exile in Vienna, practiced self-criticism by admitting that there had been no party organization before 21 March. Now working from the Leninist position that a revolution must be run by a party organization, he went on to fault the Communist leadership for not establishing one during the Commune.[95] Lukács's post-mortem for the Commune's failure was a confession that in Hungary communism had been propagated by a small group of agitators who rose to authority on a wave of national indignation. The socialist charge that the Communists came to power because they were national Bolsheviks is correct, then, but the countercharge that the Socialists were the nationalists[96] is equally true. For both parties the fusion had seemed a means to reverse the process of national humiliation by enlisting Soviet aid.

Aside from this common goal, a unified Socialist-Communist position did not emerge during the life of the Soviet Republic. Even after 21 March, the socialist *Népszava* and the communist *Vörös Újság* were printed separately. Guest articles by former opponents did appear in each paper, but content continued to be differentiated by party. For example, it was only in *Vörös Újság* that the Communists called for party purges and for the separation of the unions from the party — both Russian practices.

The separation of the unions was intended to limit the influence that the socialist union leadership exerted on the party leaders,[97] an influence that was an important obstacle to the Communist attempt to foist rules of the Bolshevik kind on the unified party.[98] On 12 and 13 June, when the congress met to adopt new rules, the Communists were unable to force their will on the 327 delegates, only sixty to ninety of whom were Communists. The Socialists dominated the newly formed executive committee and when the congress did adopt the party rules, they did not reflect Bolshevik principles. Membership was open to all and no mention was made of democratic centralism or of the separation of the unions from the party.[99] The congress also refused to heed the Comintern's dictate to call the party the Party of the Communists of Hungary. After bitter bargaining, it was decided to name the organization the Party of the Socialist-Communist Workers of Hungary.

Of the measures put forward by the Communists, only the party program was carried by the congress. This was considered a victory for Kun and his partisans, but the program was extremely vague, without any of the specifics that had characterized the Bolshevik program adopted at the Eighth Congress in March 1919. It followed Lenin's line on war, capitalism, and imperialism, but omitted his attack on the Socialists.

News of Kun's regime provoked temporary elation in Moscow,[100] for it seemed to indicate that communism was marching westward. Lenin, however, was dissatisfied with the Hungarian Communists. The decisions of the congress indicated that they were ineffectual and unable to influence party business in Hungary. Worried about the union of the two Marxist parties, Lenin demanded guarantees from Kun that the new government was not in the hands of the Socialist traitors.[101] Kun tried to allay Lenin's fears, insisting that the party had accepted the program drawn up by Bukharin and had adopted Lenin's thesis on the dictatorship of the proletariat.[102] Kun, who was now firmly in power, was irked by Lenin's testings and claimed that, as a good student of Marx and Lenin, he knew what he was doing.[103] The relationship between Lenin and Kun awaits its psychohistorian, but it has been suggested that a father and son relationship existed between them, and that Kun was far from receptive to Lenin's advice.[104] Party historians, not seeking psychological motives, have faulted Kun on ideological grounds. During the Stalinist Rákosi era, the purged Kun was accused of following Bukharinite and Trotskyite tendencies. After his rehabilitation in 1964, he was labeled a Leninist and his mistakes were attributed to youthful inexperience.[105]

Lenin tried to influence Kun directly, while the Comintern attempted to sway the fusion party. The Comintern advised that the party name be changed, later issuing this message in the form of an order.[106] Realizing that he could not dominate the Hungarians, Lenin began to praise them for their insubordination. By the end of May 1919, he termed the Hungarian experiment superior to the Russian in that it united all Socialists,[107] a statement typical of Lenin's *ex post facto* theorizing when events did not follow his earlier predictions.[108] But his praise had a distinctly hollow ring, for Lenin's actions indicated that he was not interested in saving the "superior" revolution by sacrificing the gains of the Russian revolution. The decision to support a full-scale Red Army push to unite with the Hungarians — the strategy favored by Trotsky — did not come. Instead, Lenin chose Stalin's strategy, to divide the army and make simultaneous pushes in the Ukraine and Siberia.[109] Another indication of Lenin's distrust was his failure to summon the Russian prisoners of war still in Hungary to join the Socialist party of Hungary. The thousand or so Russians fighting on the side of the Hungarians instead formed their own section of the Russian Communist party.[110]

Historians maintain that Lenin's failure to marshal Soviet forces to aid the Commune is understandable because an "advance of the Red Army into Hungary had to be subordinated to the general strategic requirements for the defense of Russia."[111] The same authorities con-

sider Lenin an internationalist, a view that provokes one to ask why
Siberia was more important to the cause of the world revolution than
Hungary. Lenin, too, might well have be termed a national Bolshevik.
Contrary to his propaganda, he seemed more intent on spreading
communism in the lands of the former Russian Empire than in the West.

In Hungary the invitation to share power had been extended to the
Communists in order to guarantee Soviet aid. When it was not forthcoming, the Communists nevertheless continued to press for the other
terms of their bargain with the Socialists. Total socialization was undertaken in earnest. The Communist Youth Organization, made up of
fourteen- to twenty-four-year olds, enthusiastically assisted in the socialization of the factories. Their excessive and highly dictatorial zeal
provoked hostile reactions from the older workers;[112] many seemed to
share Kunfi's view that the Soviet Republic of Workers was becoming
the Soviet Republic of Apprentices (*Tanoncköztársaság* instead of
Tanácsköztársaság).[113]

More serious resistance developed to the socialization of land.
Whereas the Károlyi regime had initiated land redistribution, the
Communists proceeded to socialize landed property, going far beyond
the Leninist practice in Russia. Most historians agree that the Communist Republic alienated the peasantry with this policy.[114] The lone
dissenting voice comes from the American scholar Andrew János, who
argues that peasant opposition did not spring from proprietary instincts,
but from anarchistic drives "common among rebels of primitive society."[115] He sees the peasants as habitual opponents of any type of
modernizing government, regardless of its specific rural policy.
Strangely enough, this view is substantiated through an article written
by Jenő Varga in 1929. This architect of socialization denied the charges
that the Soviet Republic collapsed because of peasant resistance to
collectivization. He argued that in most of Hungary the edicts of
socialization were never put into practice and, therefore, could not have
weakened the republic.[116] Considering that the Soviet power existed for
only 133 days, Varga's argument has validity and leads one to propose
other explanations for peasant hostility. Peasant resistance to the Soviet
Republic may therefore be attributed to centralization and to Communist attacks on traditional culture, which took the form of militant
atheism and anticlericalism.

Their nationality policy had also been instrumental in bringing the
Communists to power and the events in Hungary reinforced their theory
of the spread of anti-imperialist revolution. On 16 April *Vörös
Újság* declared that the Hungarian Soviet Republic did not recognize
the existence of a nationality question. It did not consider the non-

Magyar speaking citizens of Hungary to be nationalities and stated that the language problem would be solved by transforming the republic into a federal state.[117] This intent was reflected in the Commune's constitution promulgated on 29 June 1919, which proclaimed that the Hungarian state was now the Federated Socialist Soviet Republic of Hungary.[118] Kun clarified the constitution, indicating that the federation was formed out of autonomous republics and regions. The right of secession was not mentioned, he said, because it was deemed unnatural in a proletarian state.[119] The formation of the Ruthenian and German autonomous regions and of the Slovak Soviet Republic were examples of the policy's practical application.[120]

Clearly, the Hungarians did make use of Communist theory in their attempt to preserve Hungary's integrity. The charge that the Communists betrayed Marxist internationalism and were motivated primarily by nationalistic sentiments camouflaged by Communist slogans[121] has been rejected not only by party historians but also by some historians in the United States, including Eva S. Balogh and Rudolf L. Tőkés. They claim that the Communists were ideologues fixated by Bukharin's theories. For this reason, Tőkés faults the Communists for not going far enough in exploiting nationalist sentiments.[122] Hungarian historians see strength in the internationalism of the Kun regime. They emphasize that although the slogans of the regime may have been Bukharinite, the federalization of Hungary was correct and followed the internationalist position set forth by Lenin.[123] Clearly, this argument stands or falls on one's opinion of whether Lenin was a true internationalist or a national Bolshevik who put Russia's interest ahead of revolutions elsewhere.

Marxist historians in Czechoslovakia have also challenged their Hungarian counterparts on the issue of the Hungarian soviets' attitudes toward nationalism. During the "Prague Spring" the old "bourgeois" view, stressing the nationalistic character of the policies of the Hungarian Communists, was revived. For example, the Slovak historian, Martin Vietor, who in the 1950s praised the Hungarian Soviet Republic's effort to create the Slovak Soviet Republic, revised his position and argued that the Czechoslovaks were not ready for communism in 1919.[124] The East European debate on the Kun regime's nationality policy reflects the kinds of divisions that existed in 1919. While the Hungarian Marxists considered the Communist republic internationalist, the majority of the Romanian and Czechoslovak Marxists opted to practice communism in their own nation-states, parts of which were to be formed with lands ceded by Hungary.[125]

The Hungarian Soviet Republic's nationalistic tendencies have been detected even in such a seemingly internationalist action as the ill-fated

Bettelheim Putsch of June 1919. Ernő Bettelheim, a Hungarian envoy, led his Viennese comrades in a poorly organized uprising. Although on the surface it appeared that the Hungarians attempted to export revolution to the West, Franz Borkenau's scholarly analysis suggests that the Bettelheim putsch was Kun's diversionary attempt to save the Hungarian revolution.[126] Hungarian party historians, in effect, admit this charge but defend Kun's tactic. It is reasoned that the fate of Hungarian communism was important for the future of communism everywhere. Much as the Hungarian revolution weakened the intervention in Russia, they argued that a revolution in Austria could have weakened Hungary's enemies.[127] This thesis gives an ironic twist to proletarian internationalism, however, for it proposes that the proletariat of one country could be sacrificed for the proletariat of another.

On 2 August 1919 the Hungarian Communist experiment came to an end. In his farewell speech to the Budapest Workers' Council, Kun claimed that the Soviet Republic had failed militarily, economically, and politically. The proletariat had betrayed its leaders and itself. The workers who had been dissatisfied with the dictatorship of the proletariat, he warned, would soon learn about the brutalities of the dictatorship of the bourgeoisie and then they would become revolutionaries.[128] A similar message was sent to Lenin.

Lenin's post-mortem, delivered on 5 August, differed from Kun's. Although he had praised the fusion of the Hungarian Marxist parties only a few weeks ago, he now accused the Socialists of betraying the Communists. This view was reiterated by Grigorii Zinoviev in the Comintern's official statement.[129] Kun and the other "fugitive Bolsheviks" soon parroted Lenin's thesis, claiming that the Hungarian proletariat, lacking experience, had been misled and betrayed by the Socialists.[130]

After the collapse of the communist regime the new People's Republic of Hungary attempted to recapture the days of the Károlyi regime. It returned socialized property to private ownership and abolished all socializing organizations.[131] The new government, headed by Gyula Peidl, expected to be accepted by the Allied peacemakers, but four days later, on 6 August, it was overthrown. In the shadow of the Romanian occupiers, István Friedrich formed a government with the backing of Archduke Joseph. On 14 November, the Romanians withdrew from Budapest and a few days later, the counterrevolutionary national army, organized in French and Romanian-occupied Szeged, entered Budapest with Admiral Miklós Horthy leading the troops. That same month Friedrich was replaced with the clerical Károly Huszár, who was backed by Horthy's forces. In January 1920, corrupt parliamentary elections were held under the watchful eyes of the National Army. In March Admiral Horthy was "elected" Regent of the Kingdom of Hungary by Parliament.

The period between August 1919 and the end of 1921 has been called the "white terror." People identified with the Soviet Republic were persecuted and at times, prosecuted. There were 5 thousand victims of the terror and 70 thousand others were interned or imprisoned; about 100 thousand Hungarians were forced to emigrate.[132] The Social Democratic party was allowed to reconstruct itself. Its leaders came from second-rank officials, mostly union men untainted by charges of collaboration with the Communists.[133] The Communists were not so lucky. On 19 August 1919, the Friedrich government called for a judicial attack on them. A law had been passed in 1912 and amended during the war which called for the treatment of wartime political prisoners as common criminals. This law was now used to persecute the Communists. The fact that a peace treaty had not yet been signed justified the application of the law. A government decree called for the internment of suspected Communists "so that their rule could never be revived,"[134] and on 16 March 1921, the Communist party was officially outlawed.[135] The Hungarian Communist party thus became the first Communist party in Eastern Europe to be outlawed by the authorities. Unlike other illegal Communist parties, however, it was not able to build an underground organization — yet another indication of its shallow support among the Hungarian masses.

Communist exiles and later party historians blamed the white terror and government *agents provocateurs* for the party's disappearance from Hungary.[136] Granted, the magnitude of the terror was then unparalleled in Hungarian history, but dedicated Communists could have organized as they did in other countries when confronted with similar hardships. It was not the terror that deprived Hungarian communism of its followers, however; the root of the problem was that the party was led by discredited and incompetent men who continued to embrace discredited policies. This contention is proven by the developments in a unique "control" area where communism gained few champions despite the absence of terror.

The county of Baranya and its seat, Pécs, had been under Serbian occupation since November 1918 and thus was excluded from the experience of the Soviet Republic. The coal-mining region enjoyed freedom to organize, yet a Communist organization failed to develop. Instead, the Communist sympathizers remained a small faction in the Socialist party. After the collapse of the Kun regime, the Baranya

Socialist split off from the reorganized Hungarian Social Democratic party, now led by the moderate labor leader, Károly Peyer. Instead, they looked to Vienna for guidance. There, Kunfi and Böhm lead the exiled Social Democratic center, which refused to accept Peyer's compromise with the Horthy regime. Indicating their disassociation from the Social Democratic party in Budapest, the Pécs Socialists renamed their party the "Socialist Party of Pécs." Unlike the center in Vienna, which joined the short-lived Two and One-Half International, the Pécs Socialists applied to join the Comintern, where they were given only consultative, rather than full membership.[137]

The actions of the Pécs Socialists and of the Comintern indicated some confusion about Comintern rules — the Twenty-one Conditions that were passed in 1920 on Lenin's urgings. These terms, reflecting the lessons ostensibly learned from the Hungarian experience with Communism, barred Communist-Socialist collaboration as well as factionalism. Furthermore, Comintern-affiliated parties had to be called "Communist." None of these conditions were satisfied by the Pécs Marxists. Calling itself a Socialist party, the Pécs group had partisans of both communism and social democracy. Moreover, the Pécs party should have been charged with factionalism, since the Communist party of Hungary had jurisdiction over all of Hungary. For these reasons, the presence of both parties in the Comintern was an anomaly.

The Pécs party program called for a governmental system similar to that which had existed during the Károlyi regime. Clearly, the Socialist party wanted to play the same role in Pécs which the Social Democratic party had played in Hungary between November 1918 and March 1919. The dominance of the Socialists in Baranya politics seemed assured through the affiliation of 14 thousand union men with the party.[138] The party favored temporary autonomy for Baranya under Serbian protection until the expected collapse of the Horthy regime. The Serbs supported this position even though it contradicted the Allied decision for the return of the county to Hungary. Though the Serbs regarded their own Communists with suspicion, they gave free reign to the Hungarian Communists as long as they championed Serbian protection.[139] Regardless of this policy, the Communists made no headway in the Socialist party or among the miners and other workers of Baranya.

Pécs had been under socialist control since August 1920, following the elections to the National Council of the city. The Council President was Béla Linder, who for a few days had been minister of war in the Károlyi cabinet. As the leader of the council he claimed that the "Communists among the workers recognized that all divisive party agitation and Bolshevik propaganda among the workers must cease."[140]

Linder hoped that, through unity, the Socialists would be able to keep Baranya out of Horthy's Hungary.

Following the collapse of the Hungarian Soviet *Vörös Újság* was printed in Moscow as the journal of the Hungarian Section of the Russian Communist party. The newspaper praised the Socialists of Pécs for being fighters against Horthy's nationalist regime, and concluded that the proletariat of Pécs supported the Hungarian Communists.[141] In fact, the proletariat supported the Socialists, who were attempting to make Baranya into an Eastern Saarland. The Moscow Hungarians apparently had assumed that the Socialist party was Communist because Gyula Hajdu, the leader of the Communist faction in Pécs, had been instrumental in convincing the party to seek Comintern membership.

The Communist exiles in Vienna, however, able to view the Baranya developments from closer range, denounced Hajdu and his followers. They castigated them for supporting the Socialists and for regarding the Baranya question as a territorial issue between Yugoslavia and Hungary. The Vienna Communists wanted Baranya to serve as a nucleus for revolution in Eastern Europe,[142] believing that it would rekindle revolution in Hungary.[143] In May 1921, when the return of Baranya to Hungary was imminent, the Vienna Communists mounted a new attack on the Pécs faction, claiming that its members were bureaucratic servants of Serbian imperialism parading as Communists.[144] The exiled Communist organization in Vienna therefore issued a call to the Pécs workers to reject the Socialist party's leadership through mass meetings and a general strike.[145] Although Pécs did not respond to this call, the days of the Socialists in Pécs were numbered. According to the Treaty of Trianon, the Serbian Army had to evacuate Baranya, which remained under Hungarian sovereignty. On 14 August, in a desperate last-minute attempt, Linder and the Socialists invoked the right of self-determination and proclaimed the Autonomous Serbian-Hungarian Republic of Baranya-Baja. Encouraged by some officials in Belgrade, Linder and his partisans expected to have Serbian protection for the mini-state. Four days later, however, in response to Allied pressure, the occupying troops withdrew from the county. The republic collapsed and its leaders sought asylum in Yugoslavia and Austria.[146]

The Communist movement's failure to flourish under favorable conditions in Serbian-occupied Baranya contradicts the thesis that the concurrent white terror in Hungary was the major cause for the disappearance of the Communist movement in Hungary.[147] The conclusion that could be drawn is that the Communist brand of Marxism was not sufficiently popular, despite the political situation in the country. This uncomfortable historical fact, however, is not reflected in the official party history that deals with that period. The Pécs Socialist party is identified as being Communist, thereby attributing to the Communist movement a popularity that did not in fact exist.

Though party historians are reluctant to admit how things really were in 1921, the exiled Communist were brutally frank about the situation. Thus, Rudnyánszky in Moscow noted with gloom that the party, which had enjoyed power during the Soviet interlude, left no trace in Hungary and that there had been no underground. The Vienna exiles concurred, noting that their compatriots living under the Horthy regime were lethargic.[149]

The few enthusiasts who attempted to revive the movement in Hungary met with failure. They were quickly arrested, having found no supporters whom they could trust or who could shield them from the eyes of the authorities. Former Internationalists, acting as informers, sometimes contributed to the imprisonment of the organizers.[150] In other cases, the bungling of the exiled leaders led to the arrest of the Communist operatives.[151]

The absence of a Communist organization in Hungary after August 1919 of course meant that Communists outside the country again directed the movement. On 6 August, less than a week after the collapse of the Soviet Republic, the Hungarian Section of the Russian Communist party regained its position as a representative organization of the Hungarian Communists. On that day the Revolutionary Committee of Hungary was established for the purpose of continuing the revolutionary activities that had been cut short by the collapse of the Kun regime. The nine-member committee included Kun and other Communists who were seeking asylum in Vienna, as well as Rudnyánszky and his comrades who had not had the chance to return to Hungary during the Commune.[152] The committee, which proclaimed itself a government in exile, was open to all who had been governing members of the Commune and to members of the Central Committee of the party. Although membership requirements implied the Socialists' right to join, Lenin's attack on the Hungarian Socialists a day earlier indicated that the second Hungarian Soviet Republic would be a purely Communist affair. The quick organization of the Revolutionary Committee also demonstrated that both the Russian and the Hungarian Communists in Moscow believed that a revolution in Hungary, as well as in the West, was imminent.[153]

The Central Committee was not formed until a few months later, when the exiles in Vienna reestablished the Party of the Communists in Hungary. The new committee included Béla Kun, György Lukács,

Jenő Hamburger, Jenő Landler, Ernő Pór and János Hirossik. Its basic purpose was to help organize an underground in Hungary and to print propaganda literature for home consumption.[154]

The absence of Communist activity at home left the party organizers with little to do but analyze the reasons for the Soviet Republic's failure. They charged the Socialists with betrayal, thereby provoking a press war between the Communist paper *Proletár* and the journal of the Socialist exiles, *Világosság* [Enlightenment]. The Communists maintained that the first Soviet Republic had provided them with a "dress rehearsal"; it had taught them how to handle the Socialists in the coming revolution. They even claimed that the white terror was a policy that would make the Communists popular in Hungary.[155]

Meanwhile, the Socialists, whose spokesmen included Kunfi, Böhm, and Garbai, criticized the Communists for drawing false analogies to the Russian situation. The Socialists claimed that, unlike the Russian masses, the Hungarians had been unprepared to sustain sacrifices and that there was thus no need to accuse the Socialists of betrayal. (This analysis was quite similar to Kun's original post-portem, the one he had changed so quickly upon Lenin's cue.) The *Világosság* group, representing the views of the Socialist center, also refuted Kun's belief that the defeated revolution had had a useful purpose. The Communist-dominated policies of the Commune, they argued, had led to the white terror, which in turn, had thrown social development back a hundred years. The Socialists declared that the Communists had destroyed the first true parliamentary democracy in Hungary. The Károlyi regime had introduced revolutionary changes much like the ones introduced in Russia, including the redistribution of land. Pursuing this line of argument, the Socialists concluded that the Communists in Hungary were in fact counterrevolutionaries.[156] Socialist criticism of Communist agrarian policy proved especially painful, and the Communists were hard-pressed to come up with a reasonable defense. Jenő Varga referred back to Trotsky's view that the dictatorship's collapse was due to the military superiority of the interventionists,[157] and even those party historians who fault Kun's agrarian policy attribute the Communist debacle to external factors.[158] Such arguments may be true, but they skirt the fact that the unpopular domestic policies of the Kun regime were the major reason why communism found few partisans and countless enemies in Hungary after the Soviet Republic's demise.

The process of accounting for mistakes led not only to Communist-Socialist backbiting, but also spawned an intra-party rift that led to the emergence of two hostile groups, one around Béla Kun and the other around Jenő Landler. This split remains one of the unanalyzed, grey areas in the history of the Hungarian party. Noncommunist émigrés in Vienna and "counterrevolutionary" historians have portrayed it as a conflict among the opportunistic Communist exiles over the distribution of Moscow's dole.[159] On the other hand, most party historians describe it as a disagreement over tactics which ultimately degenerated into a conflict of personalities.[160] A recent exception to this official interpretation is György Borsányi's biography of Kun, which comes close to the traditional view. Not surprisingly, the book was withdrawn from circulation soon after its publication.[161] Yet another view is advanced by Tőkés, who sees the rift as the culmination of the disagreements that were already simmering during the Kun regime.[162]

Kun's departure for Russia in August 1920 led to the emergence of two geographical centers of Hungarian communism: Moscow and Vienna. His proximity to the Russian Bolsheviks strengthened Kun's hand. There were 3 thousand members in the Hungarian Section of the Communist party in Russia,[163] and they greeted him as their teacher and the leader of the Hungarian revolutionary proletariat.

On 27 September, the Hungarian Section of the Russian party held its "extraordinary conference." Jenő Varga, József Pogány, and Mátyás Rákosi also had taken refuge in Moscow, and the first two, along with Kun, represented the Hungarian party's Central Committee. The conference elected Kun to the new Central Bureau of the Hungarian Section.[164] His presence on both the Central Committee of the Hungarian party and the Central Bureau of the Hungarian Section of the Russian party seemed to indicate that an interlocking directorate had been set up and that direct ties between the Russian and Hungarian Communist movement had been reestablished. The Hungarians in Russia claimed that, while the Vienna faction was shrinking in size, their activities were the major beam supporting the Communist party of Hungary.[165]

The theses issued by the conference outlined the responsibilities of the Hungarian Communists. Their promulgation through an organization that was associated with the Russian Communist party indicated that Kun, who led the organization, intended to resume the direction of the Communist movement and had the support of his Russian mentors in these efforts. The Hungarian Section of the Russian party was charged with conducting *agitprop* work among the Hungarian prisoners of war still in Russia. This propaganda was to support the policies of the Hungarian and other Communist parties of the successor states. The theses indicate that contrary to what had happened in 1919, revolution in Hungary could now take place only in conjunction with Communist revolutions in neighboring states. Therefore, attention to the policies of the sister parties in Hungary's periphery was deemed necessary.

This view caused instructions to be given to Hungarian Communist propagandists to denounce the rampant irredentism of the more than 3 million Hungarians in the successor states. Clearly, continued support for irredentism, which had previously been seen as the consequence of "imperialist peace," would have precluded collaboration between the Communists of the dominant nationality and the Hungarian minority. This new opposition to irredentism implied that the very popular aspect of the 1919 Soviet Republic — its multinational federal system within historical frontiers — had been jettisoned and would not apply to the second revolution. Without this nationalist component, however, Communism was even less likely to gain adherents among the Hungarians.

The indoctrinated prisoners of war were expected to contact the Communist party when they returned to Hungary and to make use of any revolutionary experience they had gained in Russia. They were also instructed to join Hungarian labor unions "to fight against union bureaucracy" and to organize strikes. Peasant Communists were to conduct propaganda campaigns to show that the Communists were not against small rural holdings. Turning to the potential draftees of the Hungarian army, the theses urged the organization of secret cells in the military and the smuggling of arms to the workers. Finally, the Hungarian Communists were expected to convince the Hungarian population that there was no difference between the Social Democrats and the Horthyites.[166]

These theses indicated that the Hungarian Communists were out of touch with reality. The Hungarian population was not pro-Communist, nor did it have any desire to support another Communist revolution. The repatriated prisoners' subsequent failure to contact the Central Committee or to build up a Communist underground was a severe blow to the Moscow Hungarians.[167] This failure has since been rationalized with claims that the repatriated Communists were unprepared to function under the white terror.[168] It is more likely that of the 2 thousand prisoners of war who joined the movement did it out of opportunism — for special privileges in Russia and a speedier repatriation. Unintentionally, *Vörös Újság* contributed to these acts of opportunism when Mátyás Rákosi observed in its pages that in the interest of communism, revolutionary prisoners of war should return to Hungary as soon as possible.[169]

Despite its futility, the Kun faction's revolutionary enthusiasm was further kindled when it launched a new attack on the Vienna Central Committee, now dominated by Landler's supporters, in January 1921. On the pages of *Vörös Újság*, Rudnyánszky charged that the Central Committee's membership consisted only of the defunct Soviet

Republic's top command — men who had not fulfilled their responsibility for building a party organization. He also questioned whether decadent Vienna was the right place for the party's Central Committee. Kun followed up this attack by calling for the transfer of the Central Committee to Hungary. Emigrés whose chances of "being destroyed" were only 60 or 70 percent were urged to return to Hungary and build the party — as were the Communist prisoners of war.[170] Kun was evidently aware that he was not among those who could return and wanted to label his opponents as incompetents and cowards. The slandered Central Committee in riposte charged that the attack from Moscow had had a negative impact on the party and appealed to the Comintern for redress, calling for the punishment of Kun and Rudnyánszky.[171]

The impact of this factional conflict on the party organization was, in fact, negligible, for as Kun himself admitted, a party organization did not exist in Hungary. Party historians, however, cite an increase in the circulation of Communist leaflets in Hungary to prove that 1921 witnessed an increase in Communist activity.[172] Kun is criticized for underestimating this activity. He and Rudnyánszky are also faulted for discussing party issues openly, thus leading the security forces in Hungary to keep the returnees under close observation.[173] This scrutiny, in turn, is cited as the reason for the passivity of the repatriated prisoners of war who had joined the party in Russia. Lastly, a more ingenuous explanation claims that inaction was also due to factionalism and the resulting uncertainty about the source of leadership.[174]

The conflict within the leadership was aggravated in the spring of 1921 when Kun attempted to buy supporters from among the Vienna exiles. He used his follower in Vienna, Béla Vágó, to distribute party funds (two and one-half kilograms of gold coins) in an effort to recruit loyalists and organize the "party-building section" in Vienna. The Central Committee expelled Vágó, a former commissar of the interior, for his corrupt tactics. The incident is known as the program of creating a "two and one-half majority."[175] This oblique reference was to the weight of the gold, but it also equated Kun with the other "two and one-half traitors" — the *Világosság* Socialists who had joined the Two and One-Half International.

The Central Committee's complaint was ruled upon on 21 July 1921, after the Third Comintern Congress. The atmosphere was explosive, for both Kun and Landler were present with their respective supporters.[176] The Comintern called for reconciliation and compromise. It supported Kun's call for the transfer of the party's central apparatus to Hungary, although it exempted the émigrés from returning, noting that this was impractical. In line with the decision of the Third Congress, the party was encouraged to participate in union activities, but with the aim of winning the unions' support rather than destroying them. Vágó was exonerated and a new Central Committee was set up which, though including men from both factions, had a majority supporting Kun. Three people supported him — József Pogány, Dezső Szilágyi, and Endre Rudnyánszky. Only two supported Landler — György Lukács and János Hirossik.[177] Clearly, the Russian-dominated Comintern still favored Kun regardless of his ill-fated machinations.

The editors of the *Proletár,* mainly Landlerites, criticized the decision, pointing out that the Comintern leaders did not understand Hungarian conditions. The *Proletár* tried to indicate that the Comintern's united front slogan "To the Masses," which called for alliance of Communists and noncommunist workers, was irrelevant for Hungary, where the masses showed a total lack of interest. This position was a confession that the Landler group had finally abandoned the idea of a second Communist revolution in Hungary, at least for the time being.[178] Kun castigated the group as "liquidators." The party secretariat, which was being expanded and financed by Vágó, put its weight behind Kun by seconding his accusations.[179]

The clash of the two factions was thus revived with renewed fervor. Kun was now openly attacked by his opponents, Ernő Bettelheim and Henrik Guttman, and charged with the embezzlement of party funds to serve his own ends. Kun's leadership was further discredited by the defection of his close associate Endre Rudnyánszky, whose reputation was enhanced by his membership on the Comintern's Executive Committee. Rudnyánszky, who was ordered by Kun to return to Hungary via Vienna, was awakened to the Hungarian realities during his stay in the Austrian capital and decided to quit the movement. In his letter of resignation to the Comintern's president, Grigorii Zinoviev, he concluded that in 1919 a true Soviet Republic did not exist in Hungary and that he no longer could work with the leaders of the Hungarian party. His message to Moscow, however, was not followed by the return of party and Comintern funds in his possession. Rather, Rudnyánszky absconded with the monies and used the sum to open a jewelry store in Timişoara (Temesvár), Romania.[180]

In response to the infighting, Landler, Lukács, and Hirossik on 24 October resigned from the Central Committee leaving the field to the "party builders." Landler's resignation also led to the resignation of the editors of *Proletár,* which consequently came under the control of the Kun faction. There was now a clear break in the party, and Landler's émigré supporters in Berlin went so far as to consider negotiations with Paul Levi, who had recently been expelled from the Comintern and from the German Communist party. It was hoped that he would be interested in the formation of Communist parties independent of Moscow.[181]

In Moscow the *Vörös Újság* had lost most of its readership due to the repatriation of most of the prisoners of war and had decided to suspend publication.[182] The Landlerites, considering themselves the true heirs of the revolution, established a new paper in Vienna under the same name and used it as a vehicle to level petty accusations against Kun and his partisans. *Proletár,* now edited by the supporters of Kun, responded in kind — until December 1921, when the Comintern cut short the embarrassing press war by suspending the publication of both papers. The cease fire in this war of words led the Kun faction to back its words with action. For this reason, the Central Committee set up an Executive Committee of three and ordered them to cross into Hungary and organize the party on Hungarian soil. The consequences, however, vindicated the Landlerites as the three organizers were quickly arrested in February 1922.[183]

Since the infighting and the mutual recriminations among the Hungarian Communists had the potential of splitting the Communist movement throughout Europe, the Comintern was determined to resolve it and did so in March 1922. It ordered the dissolution of the Hungarian party in exile and instructed its members to join the Communist parties of their host countries. The party's Central Committee was also dissolved and a new one was named consisting of three men who were to transfer their organizational activities to Hungary.[184]

The dissolution of the Party of the Communists in Hungary had eliminated the troublesome Landlerites, while Kun, having a dual party membership, was sent to Ekaterinburg to head the Russian Communist party's Agitprop Bureau in the Ural area. This appointment meant temporary exile and isolation from Hungarian Communist affairs. The decision of the Comintern and of the Russian Communist party leadership was an admission of failure. It marked the abandonment of hopes for a new revolution in Hungary. By the spring of 1922, the first chapter in the history of the Hungarian Communist movement closed on a note of fiasco.

The movement had run its full circle. Initiated in Russia in 1918, it was dissolved there in 1922. It owed its brief success to the humiliation the Hungarians experienced at the hands of the Allies and the successor states. It failed, however, to shape communism to Hungarian needs and therein lay its weakness. Never having been popular even under the optimal conditions of the Soviet Republic, the Communist movement was unable to flourish when it faced nothing but adversity after the Soviet dictatorship's collapse. Not until 1925 was there another attempt to breathe life into the movement. Successful revival came only a quarter of a century later — under the direct tutelage of Moscow.

NOTES

The author wishes to thank the Monclair State College Alumni Association for its financial support of this study.

1. Oszkár Jászi, *Magyar kálvária, magyar feltámadás: A két forradalom jelentősége és tanulságai* (Munich: Aurora, 1969), p. 109.

2. Elemér Mályusz, *The Fugitive Bolsheviks* (London: Grant Richards, 1931), pp. 13, 220–223; Bálint Hóman and Gyula Szekfű, *Magyar történet* (Budapest: Egyetemi nyomda, 1936), V: 603–604; Albert Kaas and Fedor de Lazarovics, *Bolshevism in Hungary* (London: Grant Richards, 1931), pp. 16–17, 20–21. For a recent but similar view see, Bennett Kovrig, *Communism in Hungary, from Kun to Kádár* (Stanford, Hoover Institution, 1979), pp. 10, 20.

3. Aladár Mód, *Válaszutak 1918–1919* (Budapest: Magvető, 1970), pp. 94, 105; Aladár Mód, *400 év küzdelem az önálló Magyarországért* (Budapest: Szikra, 1951), pp. 339–348; Erzsébet Andics, *Munkásosztály és nemzet* (Budapest: Szikra, 1949), pp. 89–96; György Milei, *A Kommunisták Magyarországi Pártjának megalakításáról* (Budapest: Kossuth, 1962), pp. 6–15; János Kende, *Forradalomról forradalomra* (Budapest: Gondolat, 1979), p. 5.

4. István Deák, "Budapest and the Hungarian Revolutions of 1918–1919," *The Slavonic and East European Review,* 66, no. 106 (1968): 138.

5. András Siklós, *Az 1918–1919. évi magyarországi forradalmak, források, feldolgozások* (Budapest: Tankönyvkiadó, 1964), p. 104. For an annotated bibliography of the early activities of the Communist party, see Tibor Hajdu, *Az 1918-as magyarországi polgári demokratikus forradalom* (Budapest: Kossuth, 1968), pp. 428–434. Additional bibliography in: Tibor Szamuely, *A Kommunisták Magyarországi Pártjának megalakulása és harca a proletárdiktaturáért* (Budapest: Kossuth, 1964); Mrs. Sándor Tasnádi, ed., *Kalauz az 1918–1919. évi magyarországi forradalmak válogatott irodalmához* (Budapest: Kossuth, 1978).

6. For an American bibliography see Ivan Völgyes, *The Hungarian Soviet Republic,* Bibliographical Series, no. 43 (Stanford: Hoover Institution, 1970).

7. Richard Löwenthal, "The Hungarian Soviet Republic and International Communism," in Andrew C. János and William B. Slottman, eds., *Revolution in Perspective* (Berkeley: University of California Press, 1971), pp. 174–175. Similar observations were made by Árpád Szélpál, *Les 133 jours de Béla Kun* (Paris: Fayard, 1959), pp. 32–36, 47–48.

8. Robert Michels, *Political Parties* (New York: Dover, 1959), p. 260.

9. Deák, "Budapest and the Hungarian Revolutions," p. 132; William O. McCagg, "Jews in Revolutions: the Hungarian Experience," *Journal of Social History*, 6, no. 1 (1972): 82–86. A recent psychohistorical interpretation of Jewish revolutionaries suggests that they were primarily motivated not by massianism but by self-hatred. Significantly, the author fails to include Hungarian Jews in his monograph. See, Robert S. Wistrich, *Revolutionary Jews from Marx to Trotsky* (New York: Barnes and Noble, 1976).

10. Helmut Gruber, ed., *International Communism in the Era of Lenin* (New York: Doubleday, 1972), p. 119; Branko Lazitch and Milorad M. Drachkovitch, *Lenin and the Comintern* (Stanford: Hoover Institution, 1974), I: 110.

11. Ivan Völgyes, "Soviet Russia and Soviet Hungary," in Ivan Völgyes, ed., *Hungary in Revolution, 1918–1919* (Lincoln: University of Nebraska Press, 1971), pp. 164, 169; Peter Pastor, *Hungary between Wilson and Lenin: The Hungarian Revolution of 1918–1919 and the Big Three* (Boulder, Colo.: East European Quarterly, 1976), p. 5.

12. Mrs. Sándor Gábor and Ferenc Mucsi, eds., *A Magyarországi Tanácsköztársaság 50. évfordulójára* (Budapest: Akadémiai Kiadó, 1970), pp. 313, 326.

13. Ivan Völgyes, "Hungarian Prisoners of War in Russia 1916–1919," *Cahiers du monde russe et sovietique*, nos. 1–2 (1973): 69; Milei, "A magyar hadifoglyok," p. 247.

14. Rudolf L. Tőkés, *Béla Kun and the Hungarian Soviet Republic: The Origins and Role of the Communist Party of Hungary in the Revolutions of 1918–1919* (New York: Praeger, 1967), p. 50. Antal József, *Háború, hadifogság, forradalom, magyar internacionalista hadifoglyok az 1917-es oroszországi forradalmakban* (Budapest: Akadémiai Kiadó, 1970), pp. 103–130; Ivan Völgyes, "Communism Comes to Hungary: An Examination of Some Causes Leading to the Establishment of the Hungarian Soviet Republic" (Ph.D. diss., American University, 1968), p. 138; G. D. Obichkin and H. Vass et al, eds., *A magyar internacionalisták a Nagy Októberi Szocialista Forradalomban és a polgárháborúban. Dokumentumgyűjtemény* (Budapest: Kossuth, 1967), p. 69.

15. Völgyes, "Hungarian Prisoners of War," p. 59; Tőkés, *Béla Kun,* p. 60.

16. Józsa, *Háború, hadifogság,* pp. 142, 167.

17. Tőkés, *Béla Kun,* pp. 56–59; Szélpál, *Les 133 jours,* p. 43.

18. Tőkés, "Béla Kun: The Man and the Revolutionary," in Völgyes, ed., *Hungary in Revolution,* p. 177.

19. György Szamuely, "A Kommunisták Magyarországi Pártjának előkészítése," *Sarló és Kalapács,* 10, no. 4 (1932): 50; László Réti, *Lenin és a magyar munkásmozgalom* (Budapest: Kossuth, 1970), pp. 61–62.

20. Ferenc Münnich, "A magyarországi proletárforradalom hatása a Szovjetoroszországban élő hadifoglyokra," *Sarló és Kalapács,* 9, nos. 3–4 (1931): 77; Milei, *A KMP megalakításáról,* pp. 52–55; L. Davydov, *Revolutionnaires de l'époque de Lenine* (Moscow: Editions du Progrès, 1969), p. 203. Ervin Liptai, *A Magyar Tanácsköztársaság* (Budapest: Kossuth,

1965), p. 45; Réti, *Lenin*, p. 81; Szamuely, *A KMP megalakulása*, p. 130; György Borsányi, *Kun Béla* (Budapest: Kossuth, 1979), p. 65. The Soviet party history fails to treat the organization of international groups in the party; see B. N. Ponomarev, ed., *Istoriia Kommunisticheskoi partii Sovetskogo Soiuza* (Moscow: Politizdat, 1971); another Soviet historian claims that Kun was working under the direction of the Bolshevik party's Central Committee. See Tofik Islamov, "Adalékok a Tanácsköztársaság megalakulásának elözményeihez," in Béla Köpeczi, ed., *A Magyar Tanácsköztársaság 60. évfordulója* (Budapest, Akadémiai Kiadó, 1980), p. 160.

21. Magyar Munkásmozgalmi Intézet, *Dokumentumok a magyar párttörténet tanulmányozásához* (Budapest: Szikra, 1955), pp. 24–29; Völgyes, "Hungarian Prisoners of War," p. 72; Szamuely, *A KMP megalakulása*, p. 129; Obichkin and Vass, *Magyar internacionalisták*, pp. 128–129.

22. Lazitch and Drachkovitch, *Lenin and the Comintern*, p. 44.

23. John W. Wheeler-Bennett, *Brest-Litovsk the Forgotten Peace* (New York: Norton, 1971), p. 405; Borsányi, *Kun Béla*, p. 58.

24. György Milei and Katalin Petrák, eds., *Tanúságtevők* (Budapest: Kossuth, 1979), p. 17.

25. György Milei, *A KMP megalakításáról*, p. 61; Mód, *Válaszutak*, p. 110; Jászi, *Magyar kálvária*, p. 87; Gusztáv Gratz, *Bolsevizmus Magyarországon*, as reviewed in *Vörös Újság* (Moscow), 16 April 1921; Sándor Korcsmáros, *Forradalom és emigráció* (Vienna: n.p., 1923), p. 147.

26. The fascist aspect of the youth revolution is treated by George L. Mosse, "Introduction: The Genesis of Fascism," *Journal of Contemporary History*, 1, no. 1 (1966): 18.

27. Obichkin and Vass, *Magyar internacionalisták*, p. 22.

28. Béla Kun, *La République Hongroise des Conseils* (Budapest: Corvina, 1962), pp. 29–52; Szamuely, *A KMP megalakulása*, p. 137; for a criticism of Kun's intellectual abilities see Tőkés, "Bála Kun: the Man and the Revolutionary," p. 178, and Löwenthal, "The Hungarian Soviet," p. 176.

29. Miklós Zalka, *Szamuely* (Budapest: Kossuth, 1979), pp. 39–45; Borsányi, *Kun Béla*, p. 70.

30. Pastor, *Hungary between Wilson and Lenin*, p. 26.

31. For a brief history of the Károlyi regime see, Gábor Vermes, "The October Revolution in Hungary from Károlyi to Kun," in Völgyes, *Hungary in Revolution*, pp. 31–60.

32. Márton Farkas, *Katonai összeomlás és forradalom* (Budapest: Akadémiai Kiadó, 1969), pp. 326–340; Jászi, *Magyar kálvária*, p. 90.

33. Mód, *Válaszutak*, p. 125.

34. Tibor Hajdu, "Károlyi Mihály a polgári demokratikus forradalomban," in Miklós Stier, ed., *Emlékezés Károlyi Mihályra* (Budapest: Akadémiai Kiadó, 1976), p. 29; Zsuzsa L. Nagy, *A párizsi békekonferencia és Magyarország 1918–1919* (Budapest: Kossuth, 1965), p. 12.

35. V. I. Lenin, *Lenin Magyarországról* (Budapest: Kossuth, 1974), pp. 49–50, 86; Pál Hajdu, "Lenin a Magyar Tanácsköztársaságról," *Sarló és Kalapács*, 4, no. 3 (1932): 51.

36. Lenin, *Lenin Magyarországról*, p. 49; Réti, *Lenin*, p. 75; in this work, the reference to Lenin alone in previous publications is brought to the reader's attention.

37. Béla Kun, *Szocialista forradalom Magyarországon* (Budapest: Kossuth, 1979), pp. 139–142; György Szamuely, "A KMP előkészítése," p. 52.

38. Obichkin and Vass, *Magyar internacionalisták*, p. 48; Völgyes, "Hungarian Prisoners of War," pp. 67, 73.

39. Kun, *Szociális forradalom*, pp. 140–142; Hajdu, *Az 1918-as forradalom*, p. 197.

40. László Kővágó, "Internacionalisták Tanácsmagyarországon," in Zs. L. Nagy and A. Zsilák, *Ötven év* (Budapest: Akadémiai Kiadó, 1967), p. 377.

41. Szamuely, *A KMP megalakulása*, p. 147; Obichkin and Vass, *Magyar internacionalisták*, pp. 197–200, 269.

42. Szamuely, *A KMP megalakulása*, pp. 145–147; Liptai, *A Magyar Tanácsköztársaság*, p. 46; Réti, *Lenin*, pp. 82–83; Hajdu, *Az 1918-as forradalom*, p. 197.

43. Dezső Nemes, ed., *A magyar forradalmi munkásmozgalom története* (Budapest: Kossuth, 1972), p. 135.

44. György Lukács, *Lenin* (Budapest: Magvető, 1970), p. 9.

45. Tibor Zsuppán, "The Early Activities of the Hungarian Communist Party, 1918–1919," *Slavonic and East European Review*, 63, no. 101 (1965): 317; Tibor Hajdu, *Az 1918-as forradalom*, pp. 193–204.

46. Szamuely, *A KMP megalakulása*, p. 213.

47. Mrs. Sándor Gábor, "A szovjet és a magyar pártprogram és alkotmány," in *Ötven év*, p. 328; Magyar Munkásmozgalmi Intézet, *Dokumentumok*, II: 64–66.

48. Magyar Munkásmozgalmi Intézet, *Dokumentumok*, II: 66–67; Szamuely, *A KMP megalakulása*, p. 220.

49. Zsuppán, "The Early Activities," p. 318.

50. Milei, *A KMP megalakításáról*, pp. 75–76; Nemes, *Forradalmi munkásmozgalom*, p. 140; Tőkés, *Béla Kun*, p. 103.

51. Völgyes, "Soviet Russia and Soviet Hungary," in Völgyes, ed., *Hungary in Revolution*, p. 162.

52. János Kende, *Forradalomról forradalomra* (Budapest: Gondolat, 1979), p. 83; Milei, *A KMP megalakításáról*, p. 76; Tibor Hajdu, *Az 1918-as forradalom*, p. 212; Tibor Hajdu, *A Magyarországi Tanácsköztársaság* (Budapest: Kossuth, 1969), p. 248; Tőkés, *Béla Kun*, p. 109; Jászi, *Magyar kálvária*, p. 123.

53. *Vörös Újság*, 21 Dec. 1918; *Szociális forradalom* (Moscow), 15 Jan. 1919; Tőkés, *Béla Kun*, p. 105.

54. Szamuely, *A KMP megalakulása*, p. 205.

55. Hajdu, *Az 1918-as forradalom*, p. 215; Borsányi, *Kun Béla*, p. 90.

56. *Vörös Újság*, 18 Dec. 1918.

57. Rózsa Köves and Tibor Erényi, *Kunfi Zsigmond életútja* (Budapest: Kossuth, 1974), p. 109; Zsigmond Kunfi, et al., "Emlékirat a nemzetközi

Szociális Értekezlethez a Magyarországi Szociáldemokrata Pártnak a proletárdiktatura alatt a Kommunista Párthoz való viszonyáról," *Világosság* (Vienna), 23 Feb. 1921.

58. *Vörös Újság*, 25 Dec. 1918.

59. Gábor, "A Szovjet és a magyar pártprogram és alkotmány," in *Ötven év*, p. 342; Eva S. Balogh, "Nationality Problems of the Hungarian Soviet Republic," in Völgyes, *Hungary in Revolution*, p. 96; Tőkés, *Béla Kun*, p. 210.

60. Richard Pipes, *The Formation of the Soviet Union* (New York: Atheneum, 1968), p. 110; László Kővágó, "A nemzeti kérdés a Tanácsköztársaság idején," *Párttörténeti közlemények*, no. 3 (1979): 163.

61. Gyula Hevesi, *Egy mérnök a forradalomban* (Budapest: Európa, 1969), p. 171.

62. *Vörös Újság*, 11, 18, 21, 23 Jan. 1919.

63. Szamuely, *A KMP megalakulása*, p. 296.

64. Pastor, *Hungary between Wilson and Lenin*, p. 113.

65. As quoted in Frank Eckelt, "The Rise and Fall of the Béla Kun Regime," (Ph.D. diss., New York University, 1965), p. 254.

66. Jakab Weltner, *Forradalom, bolsevizmus, emigráció* (Budapest: Weltner, 1929), p. 131.

67. Mrs. Sándor Gábor, ed., *A magyar munkásmozgalom történetének válogatott dokumentumai* (Budapest: Kossuth, 1956), V, 547–548, hereafter cited as *MMTVD*; Szamuely, *A KMP megalakulása*, p. 296; Liptai, *A Magyar Tanácsköztársaság*, p. 75.

68. Vilmos Böhm, *A Magyar Tanácsköztársaság keletkezése és öszszeomlása* (New York: Hungarian Socialist Labor Federation, 1920), p. 25.

69. Mrs. Béla Kun, *Kun Béla* (Budapest: Magvető, 1966), pp. 124–125; László Remete, *"Rengj csak, Föld!"* (Budapest: Kossuth, 1968), pp. 295–298; Ernő Garami, *Forrongó Magyarország* (Vienna: Pegazus, 1922), p. 103.

70. Tibor Hajdu, "A KMP vezetőinek 1919 február 21-i letartóztatása a Minisztertanács elött," *Párttörténeti közlemények*, 11, no. 2 (1965): 173; Michael Károlyi, *Memoirs of Michael Károlyi, Faith Without Illusion* (New York: Dutton, 1957), p. 148; Tőkés, *Béla Kun*, p. 127; The favorable reexamination of the Károlyi era in the last decade leads Hajdu to criticize those Marxist publications which merely noted the government's attack on the extreme left. See, Tibor Hajdu, "Adatok a Tanácsköztársaság kikiáltásának történetéhez," *Párttörténeti közlemények*, 18, no. 3 (1972): 137.

71. Lajos Németi, "Küldetésben Leninnél," in Jurij Ilnickij, ed., *Lenin velünk van* (Uzhorod: Kárpáti Könyvkiadó, 1970), p. 127.

72. Szamuely, *A KMP megalakulása*, p. 313.

73. Mrs. Mihály Károlyi, *Együtt a forradalomban, Emlékezések* (Budapest: Európa, 1967), p. 460.

74. Kunfi et al., "Emlékirat," in *Világosság*; Böhm, *A Magyar Tanácsköztársaság keletkezése*, p. 25.

75. Köves and Erényi, *Kunfi Zsigmond*, p. 118.

76. *Vörös Újság*, 13 March 1919; Eckelt, "Rise and Fall," p. 156.; Oscar

Jászi, *Revolution and Counter-Revolution in Hungary* (London: P. S. King and Son, 1924), p. 88.

77. Kun, *La République Hongroise*, pp. 99–107.

78. Mrs. Mihály Károlyi, *Együtt*, p. 466; Peter Pastor, "Franco-Russian Intervention in Russia and the Vix Ultimatum: Background to the Loss of Transylvania," *The Canadian Review of Hungarian Studies*, 1, nos. 1–2 (1974): 21; György Litván, "Documents des relations franco-hongroises des années 1917–1919," *Acta Historica Scientiarium Hungaricae*, 21 (1975), p. 184; Mária Ormos, "Mégegyszer a Vix-jegyzékről," *Századok*, no. 2 (1979): 30–32; Tibor Hajdu, *Március huszonegyedike* (Budapest: Kossuth, 1979), pp. 68–69.

79. Pastor, *Hungary between Wilson and Lenin*, p. 110.

80. Budapest, Országos Levéltár, *Minisztertanácsi jegyzőkönyvek,* K 27 MT jvk. No. 29, 20 March, 1919; Hajdu, *Március,* pp. 69–73.

81. Mrs. Sándor Gábor, *A két munkáspárt egyesülése 1919-ben* (Budapest: Kossuth, 1961), p. 21.

82. Ede Gerelyes and Sándor Tarjányi, eds., *Dicső napok* (Budapest: Kossuth, 1960), p. 91; Hajdu, *Március,* pp. 83–84.

83. Magyar Munkásmozgalmi Intézet, *Dokumentumok*, II: 120–121; Gábor, *MMTVD*, V: 688–689; Gábor, *MMTVD*, VI/A: 13–14.

84. Peter Kenéz, "Coalition Politics in the Hungarian Soviet Republic," in János, ed., *Revolution*, p. 61; Böhm, *A két forradalom*, p. 202; Kunfi et al, "Emlékirat," in *Világosság*.

85. Kun, *La République Hongroise*, pp. 361–362.

86. *Vörös Újság*, 23 March 1919.

87. Gábor, *MMTVD*, VI/A: 63; *Budapest — Moszkva, Szovjet-Oroszország és a Magyarországi Tanácsköztársaság kapcsolatai táviratok tükrében 1919. március 22. — augusztus 1.* (Budapest: Kossuth, 1979), pp. 31–32; Borsányi, *Kun Béla*, p. 140.

88. Tőkés claims that it is doubtful that Kun himself believed what he told Lenin. Rather, according to Tőkés, Kun accepted participation in order to bring about a bloodless revolution. See, Tőkés, *Béla Kun*, pp. 148, 135; Tibor Hajdu, Peter Kenéz and Eva S. Balogh argue that the ideological dividing lines between the Communists and the Socialists were not that sharp in 1919; hence unity was easy to achieve. See Tibor Hajdu, *A Magyar Tanácsköztársaság*, pp. 35–36; Kenéz, "Coalition Politics," in János, ed., *Revolution*; Eva S. Balogh, "The Hungarian Social Democratic Centre and the Fall of Béla Kun," *Canadian Slavonic Papers*, 18, no. 1 (1976): 17. The most ingenious explanation comes from Mrs. Sándor Gábor who argues that unification and taking power was needed in order to prevent the Entente occupation of Budapest, which would have led to the destruction of the Communist movement. See, Gábor, *A két munkáspárt*, p. 21.

89. The circumstances of Károlyi's resignation are still debated. See Tibor Hajdu, "Adatok," pp. 149–152; Pastor, *Hungary between Wilson and Lenin*, pp. 140–142.

90. Károlyi, *Faith without Illusion*, p. 154.

91. Mihály Bihari, *Egy gyorsíró feljegyzései* (Budapest: Kossuth, 1969), pp. 145–149.

92. Magyar Munkásmozgalmi Intézet, *Dokumentumok*, II: 122–123; Gábor, *MMTVD*, VI/A: 7; *Vörös Újság*, 22 March 1919.

93. József Rabinovits, "Az egyesűlt 'szocialista-kommunista párt,'" *Sarló és Kalapács*, 4, no. 3 (1932): 44.

94. Tőkés, *Béla Kun*, p. 152.

95. György Lukács, "Önkritika," *Proletár* (Vienna), 12 Aug. 1920; a similar criticism of the lack of party organization is voiced by Mód, in *Válaszutak*, p. 364.

96. "Zoltán Rónai ancien commissaire du people de la Republique des Sovjet de la Hongrie," *Proletár*, 18 Nov. 1920.

97. *Vörös Újság*, 16, 29 April 1919.

98. Gábor, *MMTVD*, VI/A: 489.

99. Gábor, *MMTVD*. VI/B: 53–58.

100. Mrs. Sándor Gábor, *A Magyar Tanácsköztársaság történelmi jelentősége és nemzetközi hatása* (Budapest: Kossuth, 1960), pp. 10–11; Lenin, *Lenin Magyarországról*, pp. 78–80.

101. Lenin, *Lenin Magyarországról*, p. 81; Lazitch and Drachkovitch, *Lenin and the Comintern*, p. 112.

102. Gábor, *MMTVD*, VI/A: 63.

103. Magyar Munkásmozgalmi Intézet, *Dokumentumok*, II: 126.

104. Völgyes, "Soviet Russia and Soviet Hungary," Tőkés, "Béla Kun: The Man and the Revolutionary," in Völgyes, ed., *Hungary in Revolution*, pp. 163–165, 181; Lazitch and Drachkovitch characterize Lenin's attitude toward Kun as a "mixture of affection and annoyance"; see *Lenin and the Comintern*, p. 448.

105. Magyar Munkásmozgalmi Intézet, *A Magyar Tanácsköztársaság 1919* (Budapest: Szikra, 1949), p. 190; Mód, *400 év küzdelem*, p. 417; Mód, *Válaszutak*, p. 110; Borsányi, *Kun Béla*, pp. 391–392.

106. Gábor, *MMTVD*, VI/A: 16, 372.

107. Lenin, *Lenin Magyarországról*, pp. 108–109; Richard Löwenthal claims that at this point Lenin himself was not a Leninist yet, see Löwenthal, "The Hungarian Soviet," in János, ed., *Revolution*, p. 177; Borsányi notes that he does not know whether Lenin meant what he said, or whether he said it merely out of consideration for a struggling comrade, Béla Kun. See Borsányi, *Kun Béla*, p. 145. A recent Soviet article on Lenin and the Hungarian revolution speaks only of Lenin's suspicion of the Social Democrats, see L. N. Nezhinskii, "Revolutsiia 1919 g. v Vengrii," *Voprosy istorii (USSR)*, no. 3 (1979): 63–65.

108. This type of behavior by Lenin is accented in Stanley Page, *Lenin and World Revolution* (New York: McGraw-Hill, 1972), p. 13.

109. Isaac Deutscher, *The Prophet Armed, Trotsky: 1879–1921* (New York: Vintage, 1954), p. 434; Jan M. Meijer, ed., *The Trotsky Papers, 1917–1922* (The Hague: Mouton, 1964), I: 381.

110. Ludmilla Chizhova and Antal Józsa, *Orosz internacionalisták a Magyar*

Tanácsköztársaságért (Budapest: Kossuth, 1973), pp. 26–28; Párttörténeti Intézet, *Nagy idők tanúi emlékeznek* (Budapest: Kossuth, 1959), p. 46.

111. V. I. Fomin, "Szovjet-Oroszország segítsége a Magyarországi Tanácsköztársaságnak," in *Magyar internacionalisták Szibériában és a Távol-Keleten, 1917–1922* (Budapest: Kossuth, 1978), pp. 242–244; Ervin Liptai, *A Magyar Tanácsköztársaság* (Budapest: Kossuth, 1965), p. 452; Réti, *Lenin*, p. 147.

112. Kunfi et al, "Emlékirat," *Világosság*.

113. Gábor, *MMTVD*, VI/A: 230. The Marxist evaluation of the activities of the youth organization is overwhelmingly laudatory; see: László Svéd and Lajos Gál, *Eleven erő* (Budapest: Kossuth, 1969), pp. 22–25; Tibor Hajdu, *A Magyar Tanácsköztásaság*, pp. 258–259.

114. Vera Szemere, *az agrárkérdés 1918–1919-ben* (Budapest: Kossuth, 1963), pp. 108–111; Károly Mészáros, *Az őszirózsás forradalom és a Tanácsköztársaság parasztpolitikája* (Budapest: Akadémiai Kiadó, 1966), pp. 100–106; Szélpál, *Les 133 jours*, pp. 159–161; Tőkés, *Béla Kun*, pp. 181–188. Charles Ira Stastny, "The Hungarian Communist Party, 1918–1930: Days of Power and Years of Futility" (Ph.D. diss., Harvard University, 1967), p. 120.

115. Andrew C. János, "The Agrarian Opposition at the National Congress of Councils," in Andrew C. János, ed., *Revolution*, p. 87.

116. Jenő Varga, "A magyar diktatúra gazdasági tanulságai," *Vörös Újság* (Moscow), 26 Aug. 1920.

117. *Vörös Újság*, 16 April 1919.

118. Gábor, *MMTVD*, VI/B: 214–222; for the English language translation of the constitution, see Gruber, ed., *International Communism*, pp. 123–132.

119. Gábor, *MMTVD*, VI/B: 222.

120. György Milei and Anton Smutny, eds., *Dokumentumok a Szlovák Tanácsköztársaságról* (Budapest: Kossuth, 1970), pp. 121–123; László Kővágó, "A Szlovák Tanácsköztársaság: magyar hódítás vagy internacionalista segítségnyújtás," in László Kővágó, *A Magyarországi Tanácsköztársaság és a nemzeti kérdés* (Budapest: Kossuth, 1979), pp. 85–98; Sándor Györffy and Pavol Kanis, eds., *1919. A szocialista világforradalom útján* (Budapest: Europa-Tatran, 1981), p. 158.

121. Franz Borkenau, *World Communism* (Ann Arbor: University of Michigan Press, 1962), p. 122; Szélpál, *Les 133 jours*, p. 123; Völgyes, "Soviet Russia and Soviet Hungary," in Völgyes, ed., *Hungary in Revolution*, p. 169.

122. Tőkés, *Béla Kun*, p. 211.

123. László Kővágó, "Előszó," in László Kővágó, ed., *A Tanácsköztársaság és szomszédaink* (Budapest: Kossuth, 1979), p. 22; Tibor Hajdu, "A nemzeti kérdés és az 1918–1919-es forradalmak," in Erzsébet Andics, ed., *A magyar nacionalizmus kialakulása és története* (Budapest: Kossuth, 1964), p. 265; Gábor and Mucsi, eds., *A Magyarországi Tanácsköztársaság*, pp. 313, 366.

124. For an overview of Czechoslovak historiography on this topic, including

criticism of the "subjective" interpretations of the 1968–1969 publications of Vietor and others, see Kővágó, "Előszó," in Kővágó, ed., *A Tanácsköztársaság*, pp. 20–25. In a recent review of *Slovenská republika rád. Materiály z ideologickej konferencie k 60. virociu SRR konanej v Prešove 17–18. mája 1979* (Bratislava, 1980). Kővágó praised the Czechoslovak historians, teachers and ideologists for turning against the "twists and slanders" presented by their compatriots in 1969 during the fiftieth anniversay of the Hungarian and Slovak republics, see László Kővágó, "Szemle — A Szlovák Tanácsköztársaság," *Párttörténeti Közlemények*, 27, no. 4 (1981): 214–217; for Vietor's position in 1968–1969, see Martin Vietor, "A Szlovák Tanácsköztársaság jelentősége és helye a csehszlovák történelemben," in Kővágó, ed., *A Tanácsköztársaság*, p. 236; also Martin Vietor, "A polgári forradalom kettős célja, a Szlovák Tanácsköztársaság visszhangja és a fejlődési fázisok kérdése," in Gábor and Mucsi, eds., *A Magyarországi Tanácsköztársaság*, p. 313. For a recent Slovak essay reflecting a return to the pre-*Prague Spring* interpretation, see Pavel Hapák, "A Szlovák és a Magyar Tanácsköztársaság," in Köpeczi, ed., *A Magyar Tanácsköztársaság 60. évfordulója*, pp. 153–156. Hapák's criticism is reduced to the traditional view that Hungarian policy confused Lenin's concept of national self-determination with Bukharin's proletarian self-determination. According to Hapák, popular Slovak hostility to the Hungarian Red Army was due to false fears that the Hungarians intended to reestablish the old order. For a history of Czechoslovak-Hungarian relations and for a favorable appraisal of pre-1968 Czechoslovak Marxist scholarship, see Ferenc Boros, *Magyar-csehszlovák kapcsolatok 1918–1921-ben* (Budapest: Akadémiai Kiadó, 1970), p. 78.

125. Yeshayahu Jelinek, "Nationalism in Slovakia and the Communists, 1918–1929," *Slavic Review*, 34, no. 1 (1975): 67–69; Keith Hitchins, "The Rumanian Socialists and the Hungarian Soviet Republic," in János, ed., *Revolutions*, pp. 136–144.

126. Borkenau, *World Communism*, pp. 129–130.

127. Mrs. Sándor Gábor, *Ausztria és a Magyarországi Tanácsköztársaság* (Budapest: Akadémiai Kiadó, 1969), p. 154; Lazitch and Drachkovitch see the Bettelheim Putsch as a Communist attempt to export the revolution to the West. They see this policy as the cause for the collapse of the Commune, *Lenin and the Comintern*, p. 121.

128. For the text of the speech, see Böhm, *Két forradalom tűzében*, pp. 356–357.

129. Lenin, *Lenin Magyarországról*, pp. 117–121; Gábor, *MMTVD*, VI/B: 561–564.

130. Kun, *La République Hongroise*, pp. 242–244.

131. *Hivatalos Közlöny*, 3, 7 Aug. 1919.

132. Tőkés, *Béla Kun*, p. 214.

133. András Fehér, *A Magyarországi Szociáldemokrata Párt és az ellenforradalmi rendszer* (Budapest: Akadémiai Kiadó, 1969), p. 94; András Fehér, "A Magyarországi Szociáldemokrata Párt újjászerve-

zése és politikája," *Párttörténeti Közlemények*, 41, no. 1 (1963): 83–86.

134. Erika Rév, *A népbiztosok pere* (Budapest: Kossuth, 1969), pp. 13–22; Ágnes Szabó, *A Kommunisták Magyarországi Pártjának újjászervezése (1919–1925)* (Budapest: Kossuth, 1970), pp. 12, 29.

135. Magyar Munkásmozgalmi Intézet, *Dokumentumok*, III: 51; Szabó, *A KMP újjászervezése*, p. 85.

136. Szabó, *A KMP újjászervezése*, p. 20; Nemes et al, *A magyar forradalmi munkásmozgalom*, p. 212.

137. Aleksandr Tivel', *5 let Kominterna v resheniiakh i tsifrakh* (Moscow: Comintern, 1924), p. 13; Sándor Haraszti, "Baranyai Köztársaság," *Valóság*, 20, no. 1 (1977): 37–38; Gyula Hajdú, *Harcban elnyomók és megszállók ellen* (Pécs: Városi Tanács, 1957), p. 354; Szabó, *A KMP újjászervezése*, p. 74.

138. Hajdú, *Harcban elnyomók ellen*, p. 384; András Babics and László Szita, *Válogatott dokumentumok a baranyai-pécsi munkásmozgalom történetéhez* (Pécs: Janus Pannonius Múzeum, 1970), vol. II (1918–1929), p. 124.

139. Péter Lőrinc, "A vajdaság és Magyarország forradalmi kapcsolatai," in Gábor and Mucsi, eds., *A Magyarországi Tanácsköztársaság*, p. 393; Hajdú, *Harcban az elnyomók ellen*, p. 361.

140. "Pécs és Baranyamegye," in *Világosság*, 20 Oct. 1920.

141. *Vörös Újság* (Moscow), 30 May 1920.

142. *Proletár*, 23 December, 1920, 17 Feb. 1921; Mályusz, *Fugitive Bolsheviks*, pp. 104–105.

143. For a discussion of the revolutionary expectations of the Hungarian Communists, see Béla Kirschner, "A nemzetközi forradalom lehetőségének meítélése és a magyar forradalom kérdése a KMP-ben 1919 augusztusa és 1921 tavasza között," *Párttörténeti Közlemények*, 21, no. 1 (1975): 115–116.

144. *Proletár*, 26 May 1921.

145. *Proletár*, 18 Aug. 1921.

146. Hajdú, *Harcban az elnyomók ellen*, pp. 406–421; Mályusz, *Fugitive Bolsheviks*, p. 112. Leslie Charles Tihany, *The Baranya Dispute 1918–1921* (Boulder, Colo.: East European Quarterly, 1978), pp. 58–68.

147. Szabó, *A KMP újjászervezése*, pp. 31–32; Nemes et al, *A magyar forradalmi munkásmozgalom*, pp. 211–212; Dezső Nemes, *Az ellenforradalom története Magyarországon 1919–1921* (Budapest: Akadémiai Kiadó, 1962), pp. 428–430.

148. Szabó, *A KMP újjászervezése*, p. 74.

149. *Vörös Újság* (Moscow), 15, 23 Jan. 1921; *Proletár*, 25 Aug. 1921.

150. Ágnes Szabó, "A Csuvara űgy: Részletek Prónay Pál naplójából," *Párttörténeti Közlemények*, 8, no. 3 (1962): 135–137; Hevesi, *Egy mérnök*, p. 294.

151. Borsányi, *Kun Béla*, pp. 202, 256.

152. Obichkin and Vass, *Magyar internacionalisták*, pp. 315–316.

153. Ferenc Boros, "A csehszlovák-magyar forradalmi és haladó kapcsolatok néhány kérdéséről a Magyar Tanácsköztársaság leverése utáni időszakban (1919–1921)," *Történelmi Szemle*, 7, no. 3–4 (1964): 620; Béla Kirschner, *A KMP stratégiai irányvonalának alakulása (1919–1921)* (Budapest: Akadémiai Kiadó, 1980), p. 25; Kirschner, "A nemzetközi forradalom," p. 93.

154. "Kommunista pártmunka Magyarországon," in *Vörös Újság* (Moscow), 30 May 1920; Szabó, *A KMP újjászervezése*, p. 29; Nemes et al, *A magyar forradalmi munkásmozgalom*, p. 212. None of the above sources gives a specific date for the formation of the party; for the "Temporary Party Rules," see *Proletár*, 8 July 1920.

155. *Vörös Újság* (Moscow), 21 May, 27 June 1920; *Proletár*, 8 July 1920.

156. *Világosság*, 23 March 1921; Köves and Erényi, *Kunfi életútja*, p. 360.

157. *Vörös Újság* (Moscow), 21 March 1920.

158. Gábor and Mucsi, eds., *A Magyarországi Tanácsköztársaság*, p. 474; Tibor Hajdu, *A Magyarországi Tanácsköztársaság*, p. 357; Mód, *Válaszutak*, p. 371.

159. Korcsmáros, *Forradalom és emigráció*, p. 147; Göndör, *Vallomások könyve*, pp. 197–198; Mályusz, *Fugitive Bolsheviks*, pp. 147–148, 259.

160. Szabó, *A KMP újjászervezése*, p. 103. The biographies of Landler pass over the conflict. His selected works published by the Hungarians also lack material pertaining to this conflicts with Kun. See Béla Godanecz and Ágnes Szabó, eds., *Landler Jenő, Válogatott beszédek és írások* (Budapest: Kossuth, 1960), p. 54; Béla Godanecz, *A forradalom vezérkarában*, p. 171. A popularized biography of Landler makes no mention of the factional war; see Péter Földes, *Az utca hadvezére* (Budapest: Kossuth, 1970).

161. György Borsányi, *Kun Béla*, p. 256 and p. 264. The dean of party historians, Dezső Nemes, published a seventy-five page rebuttal of the censured book. In a curious way, the essay will enlighten the reader about the controversial contents of Borsányi's monograph, including the factional conflict and corruption in the party. See Dezső Nemes, "Észrevételek Borsányi György: Kun Béla politikai életrajza című munkájához," *Párttörténeti Közlemények*, 25, no. 3 (1979): 70, 76.

162. Tőkés, "Béla Kun: The Man," in Völgyes, ed., *Hungary in Revolution*, p. 182.

163. *Vörös Újság* (Moscow), 15 Aug. 1920.

164. *Vörös Újság* (Moscow), 10 Oct. 1920.

165. *Vörös Újság* (Moscow), 10 Oct. 1920.

166. "Tézisek," *Vörös Újság* (Moscow), 20 Oct. 1920.

167. Vörös Újság (Moscow), 17 Oct. 1920.

168. Szabó, *A KMP újjászervezése*, p. 96; Borsányi, *Kun Béla*, p. 256.

169. *Vörös Újság* (Moscow), 4 July 1920.

170. *Vörös Újság* (Moscow), 23, 29 Jan. 1921.

171. "Nyilatkozat," *Proletár*, 24 Feb. 1921.

172. Tibor Hetés, *Stromfeld Aurél* (Budapest: Kossuth, 1967), p. 298; Nemes, *Az ellenforradalom története*, p. 430.

173. Szabó, *A KMP újjászervezése*, p. 160; Borsányi, *Kun Béla*, p. 256.

174. Ágnes Szabó, "A Kommunisták Magyarországi Pártjának első kongresszusa," *Párttörténeti Közlemények*, 8, no. 2 (1962): 4–5. An "Old Communist" rejected Szabó's interpretation and claimed that the factional struggle had no impact on Communists in Hungary; see Nándor Szekér (Alajos Heriszt), "Hozzászólás a Szabó Ágnes 'A Kommunisták Magyarországi Pártjának első kongresszusa' című tanulmányához," *Párttörténeti Közlemények*, 8, no. 4 (1962): 125.

175. Mályusz, *Fugitive Bolsheviks*, pp. 148–150; Korcsmáros, *Forradalom és emigráció*, p. 147; Göndör, *Vallomások könyve*, p. 198.

176. Mrs. Tibor Szamuely (Jolán Szilágyi), *Emlékeim* (Budapest: Zrinyi, 1966), p. 157; Mályusz, *Fugitive Bolsheviks*, pp. 147, 259.

177. Nemes et al, *A magyar forradalmi munkásmozgalom*, p. 225; Szabó, *A KMP újjászervezése*, pp. 133–134; Magyar Munkásmozgalmi Intézet, *Dokumentumok*, III: 60–62; Mályusz, *Fugitive Bolsheviks*, p. 152.

178. *Proletár*, 25 Aug. 1921; Magda Aranyos and Árpád Gönczöl, eds., *Lengyel Gyula válogatott írásai* (Budapest: Kossuth, 1965), p. 55.

179. Mályusz, *The Fugitive Bolsheviks*, p. 153.

180. Borsányi, *Kun Béla*, p. 264.

181. Szabó, *A KMP újjászervezése*, p. 143; Tőkés, "Béla Kun: The Man," in Völgyes, ed., *Hungary in Revolution*, pp. 190–191.

182. Obichkin and Vass, *Magyar internacionalisták*, pp. 558–559.

183. Nemes et al, *A magyar forradalmi munkásmozgalom*, p. 226; Szabó, *A KMP újjászervezése*, pp. 151, 157.

184. Szabó, *A KMP újjászervezése*, p. 144.

Communism in Romania 1918–1921

LUCIEN KARCHMAR

Marxist socialism first made its appearance in Romania in the 1870s. Its early history in this environment was unpromising. Romania before the First World War was an agricultural country with an overwhelmingly illiterate peasant population. There was practically no industry, and little mining apart from the oil fields of the Prahova valley. The urban population, as late as 1900, comprised only 13 percent of the total; of this, slightly more than half consisted of Jews, still treated socially and to a large extent legally as unassimilable foreigners.[1] The working class was tiny, and artisans outnumbered industrial workers. The middle class was smaller still. Of all European countries, Romania most closely resembled tsarist Russia in its social and economic structure, but was even less developed.

The Origins of Romanian Social Democracy

Two groups of intellectuals were instrumental in introducing socialism into Romania. One was inspired by contacts with French ideas and consisted to a large extent of sons of well-to-do families who had studied in France. The other was headed by a small band of Russian revolutionaries who had taken refuge in Romania, and who had introduced some of the populist and anarchist ideas characteristic of the Russian radical movement, as well as orthodox Marxist ideology. In 1893 these intellectuals founded the Romanian Social-Democratic Workers' party, whose program derived from that of the German socialists. Acknowledging the primitive stage of Romanian social development, the new party limited itself to advancing moderate demands for reforms of both political and economic conditions and promoting the organization of trade unions among the small working class. In the mid-1890s, it also tried to recruit adherents among the peasantry, but these efforts were quickly thwarted by the government.[2] The party also began to stand candidates for election, and on one occasion actually got two into parliament, but this form of political activity was frustrated by the extremely restricted franchise and the endemic corruption of the Romanian political system. By 1900 a number of the most prominent leaders had left the movement and joined the Liberals and, for the next several years, there was no socialist party in Romania, only isolated groups and individuals.

Slowly, however, the movement revived under the leadership of two men. One was Constantin Dobrogeanu-Gherea, a Russian Jewish revolutionary émigré who had fled to Romania in 1885.[3] More important in the reorganization of socialist forces was Christian (Hristo) Rakovsky, a Bulgarian from the Dobruja, probably the most remarkable and cosmopolitan personality produced by Balkan socialism. Rakovsky studied in Western Europe and had many contacts among socialist leaders there. He played an important role in the foundation and development of the Bulgarian Social Democratic party. In 1905 Rakovsky returned to Romania, where he inherited the family estate, and revived the socialist journal *România muncitoare* [Workers' Romania], which he thereafter edited and financed largely out of his own pocket.[4] Around this periodical, the Romanian socialist forces began once more to coalesce. *România muncitoare* clubs were founded in several cities, and a committee was established to coordinate them. Contemporary events in Russia stimulated interest in socialism, and the trend was reinforced by the progress made in the development of labor unions in Romanian industry.

There were, at this time, a number of conflicting viewpoints among Romanian socialists as to the form their activities should take. Some adhered to an "economist" position, maintaining that capitalism was still so feebly developed in Romania that the foundation of a socialist political party should be deferred until capitalism was more advanced. In the meantime socialists should confine themselves to a struggle for the economic betterment of the working class through trade union organization. There was also an anarcho-syndicalist current, which maintained that a political party was not necessary because the labor unions must be the primary vehicle of the proletarian society. These various opinions were thrashed out at the conference of labor unions and socialist groups in August 1906 and at a second conference in 1907.[5] The conference established a federation of trade unions and decided to revive a social-democratic party as soon as possible.

Unfortunately for the socialists, however, the great peasant rebellion of 1907 negated what little progress the socialist movement had achieved. The socialists generally opposed the uprising, holding that the rebelling peasants were merely tools in the hands of capitalist interests, but the government nevertheless took the opportunity to persecute them for subversion. Some of the socialist organizations were broken up, their publications were suppressed, and a number of leaders, notably Rakovsky, were expelled from the country on the grounds that they were not Romanian citizens. Thus, it was not until early 1910 that conditions eased sufficiently for the Social-Democratic Party of Romania to be established. Rakovsky was generally recognized as its leader. In addition to him, Alecu Constantinescu, and Ion C. Frimu, the first executive committee included Mihai G. Bujor, the new editor of *România muncitoare,* D. Marinescu, N. Georgescu, and C. Vasilescu.[6]

The Romanian Social Democratic party displayed a number of peculiarities, the most interesting of which was that, unlike other socialist movements in Eastern Europe, it attracted very few adherents from the intelligentsia.[7] There were two reasons for this. First, given the general backwardness of Romania and the disproportionally large size of the state's bureaucratic apparatus, the major ladder to success was the civil service. Appointment to the civil service, to the vastly inflated number of government sinecures and even to the private sector, was controlled by the two major political parties, the Conservatives and the Liberals, and most intellectuals therefore joined one of these parties.[8]

Second, the major ideological current in Romanian intellectual circles was a fervid nationalism, the principal aspects of which were irredentism, violent anti-Semitism and xenophobia, and a distorted historical consciousness.[9] Socialist attacks on nationalism and on war as a means of national unification thus repelled Romanian intellectuals, who fulminated against socialist demands that Jews and other national minorities have equal rights. They were also repelled by the ethnic composition of the socialist party; neither Rakovsky nor Dobrogeanu-Gherea was an ethnic Romanian, and the socialist program of equality attracted a disproportionate number of Jews and other minorities, to whom the orthodox parties denied any participation in national life. This stigma continued to plague Romanian socialism, and later communism, throughout its history. One consequence was that teachers and university professors, who in other countries often embraced socialism and propagated it among the young, tended in Romania to drift toward the chauvinistic and anti-Semitic National-Democratic party.

Deprived of support among intellectuals, Romanian socialism tended to depend more than elsewhere in Eastern Europe on the working class for its membership and its cadres. Though a significant proportion of its top leadership appears to have been recruited from the labor movement, its recruiting potential was limited because the working class was so small. In prewar Romania, the industrial proletariat amounted to about 100,000, or 2 percent of the population.[10] If one counts artisans of all kinds, service workers, and seasonal laborers in the lumber industry, one can at most claim that the working class contained 200 to 250,000 members.[11] Since this limited strength had to be recruited primarily through the labor movement, the Social Democratic party was, from the beginning, closely linked with the trade unions; indeed, the two were at first practically indistinguishable and only in 1912 was the formal autonomy of the trade unions proclaimed. Though the prewar labor movement numbered only 12,000 to 14,000 workers at its peak,[12] the Romanian unions, immediately became notable for their aggressive spirit and the virulence of their demands.[13] This bellicosity was manifested in the party as well, partly in its increasing willingness to support the use of strikes, boycotts, and industrial sabotage as forms of political action, and partly in the rise of a radical faction among the leadership, particularly among the proletarians.[14]

Nevertheless, the top leadership adhered to a very orthodox Marxist position and retained a moderate, reformist political orientation. Dobrogeanu-Gherea argued that the socialist revolution would have to take place in the industrially advanced countries of Western Europe before it could occur in backward states such as Romania.[15] Rakovsky rejected as anarchism the concept of a militant vanguard whose deeds would blaze the trail for the rest of the proletariat.[16] The party adhered strictly to the principle of legal activity, following the example of the German socialists.[17]

The socialists' position on the agrarian question is especially noteworthy. Here, again, Dobrogeanu-Gherea formulated the party doctrine. He argued that given the semi-feudal nature of peasant-landowner relations, the theoretical formulations of advanced Western countries were not applicable in Romania. These feudal relations must be abolished to clear the way for the development of new capitalist relations. Dobrogeanu-Gherea reasoned that the removal of feudal servitudes would by itself probably lead to the establishment of bourgeois-capitalist forms in rural society. It would force the landlords to become modern capitalist farmers and to sell much of their land to the peasants, giving rise to a class of small capitalist cultivators. Thus, only a partial expropriation of the estates, not full-scale redistribution of the peasants, might be necessary.[18] Dobrogeanu-Gherea was, on the whole, opposed to socialist agitation in the villages; revolutionary propaganda merely incited peasant *jacqueries* that were essentially reactionary and that failed to attack the real problem, and the capitalist smallholder of the future would be, in any case, antisocialist.[19] The party thus refrained, on the whole, from propaganda among the peasantry, limiting itself to demands for the abolition of feudal servitudes and for partial expropriation of the estates. In addition, it maintained that the expropriated lands, as well as crownlands, should be nationalized and given to the peasants on long-term leases, not in ownership. Although individual lessees would not be excluded, this measure would be used to promote communal cultivation by villages and peasant associations.[20] The concept was reminiscent of the shortcut to socialism championed by the Russian *narodniki* and perhaps reflected Dobrogeanu-Gherea's own populist origins.

For the next several years, the socialists concentrated on organizational works. The party entered candidates, although unsuccessfully, in the elections of 1912, and propagandized such unexceptionable demands as a universal and equal franchise, proportional representation, the extension of education, separation of church and state, reduction of military service, and the eight-hour day. But its two major campaigns were the struggle for legal recognition of the labor unions and the struggle against the "artisan corporations." The latter, introduced in small enterprises by the law of 1900 and extended to large industrial enterprises in 1912, included workers and employers and ensured that the employers held the dominant voice.[21] A 1910 law that prohibited government employees, including railroad workers, from striking or organizing trade unions benefited the socialists, for some of these employees joined the party as an alternative. On the eve of the First World War, however, the party still numbered only about 1,000 members, and, in addition, controlled some 10,000 to 12,000 unionized workers.[22]

Of particular importance was the vigorous campaign that the socialists conducted in 1912 and 1913 against Romania's participation in the Balkan Wars. Consistently adhering to the antiwar and antimilitarist principles advocated by the Second International, Romanian socialists gained little credit for their ethical position from an ardently nationalist public. Indeed, dissension occurred even among the socialists, the membership of the party and the unions declined somewhat, and the circulation of *România muncitoare* shrank.[23]

Nevertheless, when the war broke out in 1914, the Romanian socialists again took an antiwar position, demanding the neutrality of Romania and the other Balkan states. Rakovsky turned out a rash of antiwar articles in the new socialist daily, *Luptă*.[24] On the whole, Romanian socialists, like most of their fellow citizens, showed more sympathy toward the Allies than toward the Central Powers, but the articles of Rakovsky and Dobrogeanu-Gherea demonstrated a particular hostility toward tsarist Russia, which they considered the greatest threat to the Balkan nations.[25] (According to some sources, Rakovsky may have accepted financial aid from the Germans to carry on his peace propaganda.)[26]

In pursuit of peace, the Romanian Social Democratic party expanded its contacts with the socialists of the other Balkan countries. In February 1915, Romanian and Serbian representatives attended a Balkan socialist conference in Sofia, which issued a proclamation calling for the neutrality of their countries.[27] In July the Romanians hosted the second Balkan Socialist Conference in Bucharest, attended by the Greek socialists and the Bulgarian "Narrows," which resulted in a manifesto denouncing the war and calling for a federated Balkan democratic republic that would be strong enough to protect itself from rapacious imperialists.[28] The Romanians were among the parties invited to participate in the Zimmerwald Conference in September 1915, where they were represented by Rakovsky. He adopted a centrist position, criticizing the Second International but opposing Lenin's drive for a final break with the old organization.[29] At the Bern meeting of the Zimmerwald Organization's International Socialist Committee in February 1916, Rakovsky again took a conciliatory stand, sharply criticizing "social-patriotism" and passivity toward the war, but rejecting a schism in world socialism.[30] Surprisingly, no Romanian delegate was sent to the Kienthal Conference in April 1916.

At home, the Romanian socialists pursued the antiwar struggle not only through the press, but also through mass meetings, demonstrations, and twenty-four-hour political strikes.[31] Their campaign could only antagonize the chauvinistic middle classes and intelligentsia, who saw the war as an opportunity to recover the Romanian-inhabited lands from Austria-Hungary, and it found little echo among the peasants, who benefited from the rising price of grain. The working class, however, which suffered from war-induced unemployment and the rise in the price of food, greeted the antiwar campaign with increasing sympathy.[32] The government's attitude toward these socialist activities was relatively tolerant until the summer of 1916, when the decision to enter the war on the side of the Allies led the authorities to bear down heavily on every manifestation of antiwar activity. When the socialists organized a strike and demonstration in Galaţi in June to protest economic hardship and to demand continued neutrality, the marchers were fired on by troops; ten workers were killed and several dozen wounded.[33]

Feeling that war was imminent, Dobrogeanu-Gherea left the country in July, taking refuge in Switzerland.[34] Several weeks later, on 27 August 1916, Romania declared war on the Central Powers. On that day, a last socialist mass meeting took place in Bucharest, and was dispersed by the army. Within two weeks socialist periodicals were suppressed, the premises of socialist clubs were sealed, and all meetings were forbidden. Rakovsky was imprisoned as a dangerous political criminal, and a number of other cadres were jailed, including the secretaries of five trade unions.[35] The mobilization of an overwhelming number of its adherents completed the disorganization of the socialist movement. Only two members of the Central Committee, Ecaterina Arbore and Gheorghe Cristescu, were left in Bucharest, and they were soon arrested. At this point, some of the more radical elements proposed forming a clandestine organization and adopting more revolutionary methods of struggle — a suggestion that provoked indignation among the many who maintained that a social-democratic movement could only act openly and legally.[36]

Before this argument could be resolved, however, the Romanian armies had been defeated and driven back. The Germans entered Bucharest in the beginning of December and by the end of 1916 they had occupied two-thirds of the country. The Romanians retained control only of part of Moldavia, including Iaşi, which now became the seat of the government. The front was stabilized with the assistance of nearly fifty Russian divisions. The rump of Romania was crowded with troops, including hundreds of thousands of Russians, army logistic services, evacuated government agencies, and refugees. Since the free area did not have the resources to support the continuation of the war effort, the Romanians now became completely dependent on Russia, or on Allied lines of supply through Russia, for their supplies and munitions. Many of the logistic services of the army — supply units and depots, hospitals, training units, military schools — had to be reestablished on Russian territory, principally in Bessarabia, the southern Ukraine, and even the Crimea. At the same time, the navy and merchant marine took refuge in Russian ports; Odessa in particular became an important Romanian supply and training base. Many civilian refugees were moved into Russia, and a number of evacuated war industries with 15,000 Romanian workers were relocated around Odessa.

Romanian Socialism and the Russian Revolution

The Romanian socialists now found themselves separated by the front line. The Iaşi socialist section was the most important in the free territory, but since there was practically no industry in Moldavia, most of its sections were not very strong, and some of its leaders were already under arrest.[37] In addition, there were many Romanian socialists who had been transferred to the area with the army, including such leaders as Bujor, the editor of the party organ, and Dobroganeau-Gherea's son Alexander, who had been head of the Ploeşti section. Others, such as Dr. Ottoi Călin, a member of the Central Committee, had arrived as civilian refugees. In the occupied zone were the remnants of party and labor organizations and those adherents who, through age, health, or other reasons, had escaped military service, including four members of the Central Committee. Most of the arrested leaders had been left behind and were released by the Germans, but Rakovsky, who was considered too important, was evacuated and held in a Iaşi prison.[38]

Before the socialists could really pull themselves together, the February Revolution took place in Russia, completely altering the situation in the unoccupied zone around Iaşi. The revolutionary ferment began to engulf the Russian army on Romanian soil. Soviets were formed among the troops, and the adherents of the various radical parties began to campaign for a republican system, land reform, and every conceivable freedom. There was, from the point of view of the Romanian government, every danger that this ferment would infect the Romanian troops and the peasantry of Moldavia. The bulk of the troops were peasants who, along with their comrades who were not in uniform, would certainly be attracted by the slogans of land reform. The revolt of the army would mean the end of the dynasty and the ruling classes, as well as the collapse of the front and German control of the entire country. Only the scarcity of Romanian radicals able to channel mass emotions into concerted action appeared to be holding up the outbreak, but the Russian radicals, with their internationalist convictions, were beginning to direct their propaganda toward the Romanians as well.[39]

The Romanian situation in the spring of 1917 was truly revolutionary, and the government, aware of the danger, resolved on radical measures. In April King Ferdinand issued a proclamation promising land reform and universal, equal male franchise,[40] and the parliament voted the necessary constitutional amendments. The Romanian troops accepted this promise and morale improved. Unlike the Russians, the Romanian soldiers had a direct interest in continuing to fight in order to end foreign occupation of their lands. The reorganized army won minor local victories over the Germans later in the year. With the troops well in hand, the revolutionary situation had passed. It would not recur.

The Romanian socialists failed to seize the moment because they were so few and so disorganized, because nothing in their doctrine had prepared them for a revolutionary opportunity at this stage of development. Nevertheless, contacts with Russian radicals and the heady atmosphere of revolution excited them, and some, particularly from the radical wing of the party, resumed their activities, making speeches and spreading socialist propaganda even among the troops. Some, like Bujor and Alexander Dobrogeanu-Gherea, were not even deterred by the fact that they were still in uniform.[41] Their actions were mostly spontaneous and unorganized, although the Iaşi section, which many of them visited, acted as a sort of information exchange. But they were welcome at the Russian meetings and demonstrations, and Russian army soviets often provided assistance, facilities, and even protection from the Romanian police.[42] On May 1 Alexander Dobrogeanu-Gherea, with the help of revolutionary Russian troops, organized Rakovsky's rescue from jail and his safe passage to Russian territory.[43]

Although the revolutionary moment had passed, neither the government nor the radicals recognized this for many months. To all appearances, the situation not only persisted but became ever more dangerous. The progressive radicalization of the Russian revolution, the accelerated disintegration of the Russian army, and the threatening military situation increased the likelihood that Russia would make peace unilaterally and leave the Romanians stranded. The government was therefore determined to protect its army's integrity at all costs, and dealt harshly with any socialist agitation. It could do little about the Russians in Romania, but repression of the disorganized Romanian radicals was prosecuted successfully. Most of the socialist rank-and-file adherents in the army remained loyal, and their leaders were not numerous. Many were arrested,[44] some were actually murdered,[45] and it was ordered that socialist agitation among troops be punished by execution.[46]

Despite this pressure, the more orthodox socialists, who in Iaşi were led by Dr. Chelerter, still maintained that a social-democratic party could only work openly, and refused to participate in clandestine activities.[47] The more radical elements fled to Russia, where Rakovsky himself was being sought by Russian authorities for extradition. Those who followed him congregated mainly in Odessa, where in June they organized the Social-Democratic Action Committee. Its leader was Bujor, who had escaped arrest, and among its members were the labor leader Al. Nicolau, Gheorghe Stroici, I. Dicescu-Dic, and A. Zalic.[48] Many of these men appear to have been members of the "proletarian" group who had entered the party through trade union organizations.

Romanian Socialists in Revolutionary Russia: The Action Committee (Odessa)

The Action Committee soon began turning out leaflets and pamphlets, and in September renewed publication of the periodical *Luptă* under the editorship of Bujor and Nicolau. The first targets of its activity were the Romanian refugees, workers, and military and naval units in Russian territory. A number of sympathizers were soon recruited and affiliated groups established in several Russian cities. Another target were the 100,000 Transylvanian Romanians who, as soldiers in the Austro-Hungarian army, had surrendered or been captured and were now in prisoner-of-war camps scattered throughout southern Russia. Revolutionary Russian soldiers distributed propaganda among Romanian troops at the front and in Moldavian towns and delivered it to clandestine groups of adherents in Romania.[49] The Romanian government demanded the suppression of these activities, but the Russian Provisional Government was not strong enough to challenge the soviets that protected the committee.

Although the Action Committee represented the left, "revolutionary" wing of the socialists, it was not Leninist. It still accepted the idea that neither Romania nor Russia was ready for a socialist revolution, and instead looked forward to a Romanian equivalent of the February Revolution.[50] Nor did it agree with the policy of peace at all costs; *Luptă* maintained that the February Revolution had turned an imperialist war into a just war of liberation. The committee concentrated on denouncing the monarchy and the oligarchy that dominated Romania, and called for a republic.[51]

At the beginning of November (25 October, Old Style), the Bolsheviks seized power in Petrograd, but their authority was not immediately recognized in the South. The soldiers' soviets on the southern front, and particularly the supreme military soviet in the south, *Rumcherod,*[52] which sat in Odessa, were dominated by Mensheviks and Social Revolutionaries. General Shcherbachev, the commander of the armies on the Romanian front, adopted a noncommittal attitude. Behind the front, Ukrainian nationalists raised their flag in various cities and proclaimed independence. In Bessarabia, the Romanian-speaking population organized a separatist assembly, the *Sfat Ţarii,* which declared the autonomy of the province. The Bolsheviks unleashed their activists and a barrage of propaganda, using the appeals of immediate peace and land, to draw the military soviets over to their side, and began to concentrate their forces to seize the cities and overthrow their rivals. As incredible confusion developed throughout southern Russia, the Romanians, dependent on the Russian hinterland for their existence, watched anxiously and arrested any Bolshevik agitator found approaching Romanian troops; soon they had some four hundred locked up, and many others were spirited over the border into Russia.[53]

During this period, the Action Committee moved steadily leftward.

Immediately after Lenin's seizure of power, it organized a military-revolutionary committee, headed by Bujor, Dicescu-Dic, Nicolau, and other militants, with the aim of promoting a Romanian uprising.[54] In December Bujor traveled to Petrograd for an interview with Lenin.[55] The committee gave up its support of a united socialist government in Russia and established close ties with the Bolsheviks; *Luptă* and the other committee publications printed the decrees of the Bolshevik government, took up the cry for immediate peace, and called for solidarity with Soviet Russia.[56]

Unable to control his troops any further, General Shcherbachev agreed to recognize the suspension of military operations ordered by the Soviet government, and on December 5 signed the armistice for the Russo-Romanian front. The Romanians, confronted with a hopeless military situation, followed suit on 9 December.[57] They anxiously watched the progress of the Russo-German talks, in the meantime trying to preserve the best possible military posture for the coming negotiations. Their first concern was to get rid of the demoralized Russian forces, and many Russian units were disarmed and shipped across the border. Simultaneously, however, the Bolsheviks were reorganizing their military followers and reinforcing them with party cadres and Red Guards. By the beginning of 1918, they felt strong enough to begin the reconquest of the South. In the first days of January, they advanced against the Ukrainian nationalists, and on 14 January Bolshevik units also seized Kishinev and other towns in Bessarabia. The *Sfat Tarii* appealed for help to the Romanian government, and Romanian troops entered Bessarabia.[58] This decision was motivated both by military necessity and by a desire to avenge the Russian seizure of Bessarabia in 1812 and 1878. The Russian forces were driven from the province and Bessarabia was declared an independent republic, but on 9 April it was annexed by Romania. The Romanian occupation was accompanied by a ruthless suppression of all resistance, which meant, first of all, Bolsheviks, Red Guards, and socialists of all kinds; many of those caught were executed, and others fled across the Dneistr into the Ukraine.[59]

In protest against the takeover of Bessarabia, the Soviet government broke off relations with Romania on 26 January. *Rumcherod,* which was now in Bolshevik hands, began to organize countermeasures. The Action Committee was soon drawn into this effort to provoke a revolt in the Romanian armed forces. On 25 January a Romanian revolutionary battalion under the command of Vasile Popovici was formed in Odessa; it numbered 700 men, and was recruited largely from the thousands of Romanian deserters who hid out in Odessa and the southern Ukraine.[60]

Activists from the committee succeeded in penetrating both the Romanian navy, which was lying inactive at the Russian ports of Ismail and Kilia, and the workers of the Naval Arsenal, which had been transferred to Kilia, and organized a revolutionary committee.[61] Around 20 January, a plot was discovered for an uprising among the troops and population of the Danube delta, in which sailors of the cruiser *Elisabeta* were implicated.[62] The sailors fled to Odessa and formed the nucleus of a second revolutionary battalion, which started with 300 men but later grew to 800. On 27 January, the Bolsheviks launched an attack to secure Odessa and expel the Ukrainian nationalists. The battle lasted three days, and the Romanian battalions took part.[63] After the victory, the Action Committee had effective power over all Romanians in Odessa and imprisoned several dozen members of parliament and other prominent refugees.

To coincide with the seizure of Odessa, the committee provoked an uprising on several warships at Kilia and Ismail which was joined by Romanian and Russian workers and soldiers ashore. The revolt, led by Gheorghe Stroici, was quickly put down by the Romanian army.[64] The survivors who got through to Odessa joined the revolutionary battalions, which were next sent to Bessarabia, where they joined Soviet troops fighting the Romanian army at Bendery.[65] Later, they were used to oppose the German advance into the Ukraine.[66] In February 1918 the Action Committee organized mutinies on board several Romanian auxiliary and merchant vessels at Sevastopol and other Black Sea ports, and seized the ships.[67]

Rakovsky arrived in Odessa in early February.[68] After hiding in the Petrograd district, he had traveled to Stockholm to attend the Third Zimmerwald Conference and other socialist meetings. After the October Revolution, he had jettisoned his earlier doubts and joined the Bolsheviks wholeheartedly, thereafter making his career in the Russian Communist party. He had now come to the southern Ukraine to coordinate all efforts against the Romanians and to direct the Action Committee — the last time he would personally lead Romanian socialists.

The Germans occupied the Ukraine on March 13. Before Odessa fell, the Romanian battalions were evacuated to the Crimea and later disbanded.[69] Most of their members were incorporated into the Red Army and, from this point, the activities of the Romanian revolutionaries in Russia largely merge with those of the Russian Communist party (bolshevik) (RKP[b]). Bujor and Zalic went underground in Odessa and created a clandestine Romanian Communist group attached to the illegal Odessa regional committee of the RKP(b).[70] The bulk of the committee went to Moscow, where they established the Romanian Committee, led by Nicolau.[71] There was already in Moscow a small Romanian Group of the RKP(b), recruited both from Romanian workers evacuated to Russia and from Transylvanians, and led by a Transylvanian, Pesceriu. The main tasks of this group had been to agitate among Transylvanian prisoners-of-war, to recruit them for the Red Army, and to prepare propaganda for distribution in the Romanian inhabited areas of Austria-Hungary.[72] This group published leaflets and pamphlets, as well as the journal *Fosis țăranului*. The Romanian Group and the Communist Committee were merged in the fall of 1918 (at a conference apparently arranged at the insistence of Rakovsky) and in December became the Romanian Section of the RKP(b), part of the Central Federation of Foreign Groups of the RKP(b), under the leadership of Nicolau. It appears there was some desire among the member to keep Romanians and Transylvanians independent, however.[73]

The Communist Committee, and later the Romanian section, was in part responsible for producing literature, training agitators, and smuggling both into Romania. But throughout 1918 and 1919, much, if not most, of their energy was spent in recruiting Romanian-speaking volunteers to fight in the Russian civil war. Various Romanian detachments, none of them very large, appeared in the Red Army. In 1918, there was one at Astrakhan, commanded by Vasile Popovici, and one at Samara, where a branch of the section was established under Dicescu-Dic. In 1919, the Romanian Revolutionary Regiment was formed in the Ukraine under Ion Săceanu, with Todor Dismandescu as a commissar, and was later merged with some Hungarians into the International Regiment. This regiment was in turn combined with some further Romanian and foreign units into an International Brigade of 2800 men under Popovici.[74] Other groups of Romanians were scattered through various Red Army formations.

After the German surrender, the Red Army began its reconquest of the Ukraine, and by March 1919 it had approached the borders of Romania. It appeared probable that it would try to recapture Bessarabia, or even to cross Romania to aid the Hungarian Soviet Republic. The Romanian Section was consequently transferred south, first to Kiev and then to Odessa, where it merged with Bujor's Odessa group. It began to publish the periodical *Comunist*, as well as other political literature, and intensified the propaganda effort aimed at Romania.[75] In the summer of 1919, however, the advance of Denikin's army forced the section to return to Moscow. In September it began to publish the journals *Scânteia* and *Dozrobirea sociale*; but most of its members were now sent off on political assignments to the various fronts of the

Russian civil war.[76] The Federation of Foreign Groups was abolished in the spring of 1920, and the Romanian Section was transformed into the Central Romanian Agitation and Propaganda Office of the RKP(b). It was transferred to Kharkov to work under the direction of the Central Committee of the Ukrainian Communist party, that is, directly under the eye of Rakovsky, who had been appointed head of the government of the Soviet Ukraine.[77] Nevertheless, this group of Romanian socialists had now become mere Soviet functionaries; many, such as Dicescu-Dic, for example, would never return to Romania.

Revival of Socialism in Moldavia

The Soviet decision to sign a peace treaty with Germany had left the Romanian government helplessly isolated, and it had no choice but to make peace as well. The terms of the preliminary treaty of Buftea (5 March 1918) and of the Peace of Bucharest (7 May) were very harsh. Among other things, partial demobilization of the army was ordered and the Germans would continue to occupy the territory they had captured until a general peace. The Romanian government therefore remained at Iaşi, exercising direct control only over most of Moldavia.

Still, this territory was now nominally at peace and a semblance of normal political life could be restored. The social-democratic forces began to reorganize under the leadership of the Iaşi section, headed by Ion Sion and Dr. Ghelerter. The Iaşi group began to publish a weekly, *Social-democraţia,* which became the organ of the Moldavian branch of the party and trade unions. Since all the more radical leaders had gone off to Russia (except those who, like Alexander Dobrogeanu-Gherea, were in jail), the field was dominated by rather moderate elements, a situation reflected in the program elaborated at the regional congress of Moldavian socialists and labor unions on 1 July 1918.[78] The congress limited itself to reform proposals: universal franchise, agrarian reform through total expropriation of the estates, freedom of the press, equal rights for Jews. It carefully avoided all mention of revolution, and warned the trade unions to adjust their actions to the immediate interests of the workers; in other words, no political strikes. The congress demanded the right to organize trade unions, as well as the introduction of the eight-hour day, a minimum wage, and so on. It proposed a peace without annexations or reparations, and the right of self-determination for all peoples. It did not mention Russia.

The return of demobilized workers and the partial demilitarization of the economy led to the resurgence of the labor unions.[79] These were still not recognized legally, but given uncertain political and economic conditions, they were finally officially tolerated as an alternative preferable to continuous disruption.[80] Nevertheless, labor relations during this period were very disturbed. The severe economic dislocation, and shortages of food and goods were compounded by spiralling inflation. The government, deprived of its normal sources of income, financed itself largely by printing money. This worked a particular hardship on the urban population, particularly those, like the railroad workers, who depended on the state budget for their salaries. There were consequently numerous strikes, as workers in various industries tried to keep up with the rising coast of living; there were also demands for improved working conditions. The result was a general strike of the railroad workers in March, another in June, and a third in August;[81] metalworkers, arsenal workers, and printers struck in turn. Although the government resorted to the usual arrests and reprisals, the workers won many concessions, such as shorter hours and the end of martial law in various industries. It appears that these strikes had basically economic, not political, motivations.

In both the party and the trade unions, however, there were groups that under the impact of the Russian experience and the propaganda of the Action Committee, had moved leftward and embraced the idea of immediate revolution. These groups, which were still small, called themselves "maximalists," since they proposed the "maximum program," that is, the dictatorship of the proletariat. In imitation of the Bolsheviks, they demanded immediate and continuous political action at all costs, in order to intensify the class struggle and to raise the militancy of the working class to the revolutionary level. They were able to maintain contacts with the Communist center in Odessa, and through it with the Communist Committee in Moscow.[82] Via this route, they received literature, funds, and a few trained agitators, one of whom, Gheorghe Stroici, fell in the hands of the police, was tried for desertion and treason, and spent the rest of his life in jail.[83] Though the maximalists were not strong enough to do much more than distribute occasional leaflets denouncing the government and calling for a republic and solidarity with the Russian revolution,[84] they tried to organize demonstrations and to give some strikes a political cast.[85] These activities attracted the police, and some maximalist groups were imprisoned.[86] Nevertheless, by the fall of 1918 they appear to have had sufficient influence to get a declaration "concerning the goals of the Party" into the pages of *Social-democraţia*, reminding the world that these goals were internationalism, class war, socialization of all the means of production, and a Communist society.[87]

Echoes of Revolution in Occupied Romania

A quite different situation existed in the German-occupied zone of Romania. Here, many socialists had expected an improvement of their situation under German rule, but they were soon disabused of this notion.[88] The Germans released imprisoned socialists, allowed socialist clubs to reopen, and for the first three months did not interfere with small meetings, but they would not allow the publication of a periodical, the opening of a party school, or mass rallies.[89] Labor unions were slowly able to reorganize but led a semi-legal existence; the only officially recognized socialist body was the mutual aid society *Muncă*, headed by Ion Frimu.[90]

The news of the February Revolution provoked a flurry of excitement among socialist groups in the occupied regions. These events coincided with unrest resulting from the economic hardships, particularly for the families of mobilized workers, which stemmed from the shortage of food, the mounting inflation due to the flood of occupation currency, and the dislocation provoked by the ruthless German exploitation of the Romanian economy. In March 1917 several thousand women demonstrated in Bucharest, demanding peace and bread.[91] The Bucharest socialists distributed a leaflet praising the revolution and demanding immediate peace; this brought some arrests and searches by the German police.[92]

Of particular importance for the Romanian socialists was their renewal of contacts with the German and Bulgarian socialist movements.[93] In the summer of 1917, the European-wide negotiations related to the proposed socialist conference in Stockholm led to the establishment of close contacts with the Russian revolutionary parties.[94] Later that summer, the Odessa Action Committee managed to smuggle agents and literature through the front.[95] Under the impact of these influences, the socialists of the occupied zone began to drift apart ideologically, with Alecu Constantinescu emerging as the leader of an increasingly radical left wing.[96]

Thanks to the intervention of the German socialists, the Romanians were allowed to send two representatives, Constantinescu and Frimu, to the third Zimmerwald Conference in Stockholm in September 1917.[97] It is unclear whether Constantinescu, as is sometimes affirmed, also traveled at this time to Petrograd to make personal contact with the Bolsheviks.[98] After his return to Bucharest at the beginning of 1918, however, Constantinescu set up an Action Committee, headed by himself, L. Filipescu, and Constantin Ivănuş, to organize clandestine left-socialist groups in the occupied zone.[99] These groups, which were beginning to call themselves "Communist" as well as "maximalist," disseminated propaganda that hailed the Russian revolution and called for worker solidarity and the overthrow of the monarchy. The Action Committee also maintained intermittent contacts with the Romanian groups in Moscow and Odessa, which became much easier after the treaties of Brest-Litovsk and Bucharest. Couriers could travel across Transylvania with returning Austro-Hungarian war prisoners, or across Moldavia with returning Romanian soldiers and workers. Later, travel on a more ambitious scale became possible, and in October 1918 Constantinescu was in Moscow with a maximalist delegation to assist at the conference that merged the Romanian Communist groups in Russia.[100]

The left-wing groups nevertheless represented only the most extreme aspect of a trend that was observable among most socialists in the occupied zone, where the continued atmosphere of illegality and the more visible impact of defeat and hardship were producing greater radicalization. The rump party leadership in Bucharest put out a manifesto acclaiming the October Revolution and calling on Romanians to overthrow the capitalist oligarchy. As a result, the Germans arrested three socialists (but gave them light sentences) and intensified their surveillance of the movement.[101] Further leaflets denounced the Peace of Bucharest and the Romanian occupation of Bessarabia. But a major problem for the socialist movement was that, excited by the Russian revolution, all kinds of independent groups, and even isolated individuals, were spontaneously putting out leaflets demanding revolution. These groups — the "Bolshevik Federation of Romania," "Communist Workers of Romania," and so on — were not coordinated by any party authority, and their ideological concepts were often far removed from communism.[102] The proliferation of such groups became more acute as party adherents were demobilized and returned home after the Peace of Bucharest.

On 1 May 1918, the Bucharest section held a clandestine meeting attended by the members of the party's Executive Committee and by representatives of the General Commission of Trade Unions, the youth movement, and party sections in other cities. It was decided to prepare a new, revolutionary socialist program for presentation to a party congress, to intensify party propaganda and extend it to the countryside, and to boycott future elections.[103] These proposals clearly show the strong influence of the left wing. A provisional Executive Committee was approved, which included Constantinescu, Frimu, Gheorghe Cristescu, Ecaterina Arbore, and D. Marinescu. Two weeks later, the Germans arrested thirteen activists who had participated in the meeting of 1 May; among them were all the members of the Executive Committee but Frimu, who escaped arrest by chance. The German and Bulgarian socialists once more intervened, and the Romanians were released after two months in jail.[104] At about the same time, it became possible to establish firm contacts with the Moldavian regional committee in Iaşi.[105] Romanian socialism now had two centers with rather different attitudes, and no overall direction.

Currents of Romanian Socialism: The Immediate Postwar Period

By late 1918 most socialists in the occupied zone were willing to consider a change of tactics by the party and wanted a party congress, now long overdue, to meet as soon as possible to discuss the possible changes. Yet the gamut of opinions among the scattered socialist groups ranged all the way from anarchist to "social-patriotic." Even the coalescing left wing was not very clear in its ideology, and had not fully adopted Leninist concepts; it still spoke mostly in terms of peace first and revolution after.[106] None of the factions had moved beyond the stage of general slogans to concrete planning, and none had produced a program that could arouse the masses.

This deficiency was of crucial importance when Germany suddenly collapsed and its army of occupation began a rapid withdrawal from Romania in November 1918. For some days — perhaps for as much as two weeks — until the government mobilized and moved sufficient military units into position, a vacuum existed in much of the former occupied zone and in the capital. Communist writers have frequently claimed that a revolutionary situation existed during November 1918. But whatever the merits of this claim, the Romanian proletariat was neither strong nor militant, and its socialist leadership was disunited and oddly ignorant of the practical measures necessary to seize power. Although workers' councils and militias were formed in a few places, they were isolated, spontaneous growths that soon withered. In particular, no attempts seem to have been made, even by the maximalists, to incite the peasantry with the slogan of immediate seizure of the land. This default can only be explained by assuming that Dobrogeanu-Gherea's views on the agrarian question still predominated and that Lenin's pragmatic approach had not been accepted. The opportunity to exploit the peasant issue passed almost instantly, because the government moved with great speed to defuse it. On the day after the armistice, the king issued a proclamation assuring the nation that the promised electoral and agrarian reforms would be implemented quickly.

On 16 November universal male suffrage was introduced by decree. On 29 December another decree initiated agrarian reform by expropriating large estates for distribution to the peasantry.[107] Although parliament, which had authority for defining the nature of the distribution, took another two-and-one half years to elaborate the terms, the king's prompt action succeeded in defusing peasant discontent. To be sure, the usual peasant riots, clashes with the gendarmerie, burnings of manor houses, and pogroms against Jews continued, and may have been somewhat aggravated by the mood of uncertainty as the parliament went on arguing. But the catalogues of such incidents conceal the major fact that the peasants accepted the promise of land reform as genuine and were thereafter impervious to revolutionary appeals.[108]

The socialists in Bucharest did, however, take quick action on a number of issues. The first was to resume publication of a party organ before censorship could be reimposed. The new journal *Trăiască socialismul* appeared on 14 November and contained a fiery manifesto that hailed the October Revolution and forecast the imminent fall of the monarchy.[109] Although the authorities did not feel strong enough to make arrests,[110] their threat to suspend the journal did persuade the editors to submit to censorship and to change the name of the journal to the slightly less provocative *Socialismul*.[111] The government made another attempt to suspend its publication on 6 December, but worker demonstrations and the threat of a general strike forced its reappearance three days later.[112] In its pages, and in those of party periodicals published in Iaşi, Ploeşti, and Braila,[113] a brisk debate tried to thrash out the principles of the new program. The return to Bucharest of evacuated party leaders and workers intensified this debate. The Iaşi organization generally represented a "minimalist" position, whereas the Bucharest organization contained a strong "maximalist" group, but even more "centrists" who generally made common cause with the maximalists, and also a far left, quasi-anarchist faction.[114] Ploeşti and the oil fields were heavily maximalist, and the various factions appeared in different combinations in other towns.

The war and the incarceration of many socialist leaders had prevented the holding of a regular party congress since 1914. Deaths, retirement, and emigration had depleted the Executive Committee, but on 11 December it was brought up to strength through the cooption of four members.[115] Rakovsky retained his seat in courtesy, but remained inactive; of the seven active members, Constantinescu represented maximalism, and Ion Sion, minimalism, but most of the rest were centrists, although leaning toward the left. Ilie Moscovici became the new secretary general, and Cristescu, the treasurer. It was decided to hold the new party congress in January 1919.

The Executive Committee appeared already to have resolved the problem of international affiliation. As late as the Stockholm Conference, the party and Rakovsky were unwilling to break altogether with the Second International, and in the summer of 1917 the Odessa Action Committee called for the "reconstitution" of the International,[116] thus implying its rejection of Lenin's drive to split the world socialist movement. Since the October Revolution, however, the maximalists had accepted the idea of a Third International, and the centrists now appeared to follow them. In late November the Executive Committee adopted the name Romanian Socialist party in order to dissociate itself from the social-democratic Second International.[117] In December *Socialismul* published an article that pronounced the Second International "dead."[118]

On 22 December the Executive Committee published the new "Declaration of Principles."[119] The new program announced that the only goal of the party was the immediate seizure of power by the working class through "any method," and the installation of the dictatorship of the proletariat for the realization of Communist ideals.[120] Although its language was not yet fully Leninist, the Romanian party appeared to be moving inexorably toward Lenin's position.

During these same days, the maximalists were trying to take advantage of the strong strike movement that had broken out in Romania immediately after the armistice and spread to all industrial branches.[121] Though the strikes were disorganized and spontaneous, economic in their aims, and quite out of the control of the Socialist party,[122] the maximalists saw them as an opportunity for revolutionary action and tried to inject them with political demands. In Bucharest an increasing number of strikers paraded slogans hailing the Russian revolution and the International and condemning the monarchy.[123] Though still too insecure to act, the government nonetheless viewed these developments with growing alarm. The showdown came on 26 December, when a group of maximalist militants led by Constantin Ivănuş called for a general strike at a workers' demonstration organized in support of the printers' strike. Among the organizers was a young teacher, Ana Rabinovici, who later became famous as Ana Pauker. Government troops met and fired upon the demonstration, killing and wounding a number of people.[124] The military and police then arrested hundreds of strikers, who were savagely beaten in jail, some fatally. Scores of socialist leaders were arrested and similarly maltreated; they included three members of the Executive Committee, Moscovici, Cristescu, and

Frimu, the last of whom was so badly injured that he later died.[125] Socialist offices and clubs were pillaged by the soldiers, *Socialismul* was suspended, and martial law proclaimed. Some days later, workers were also fired on in Ploeşti.[126]

This violent reaction frightened both the workers and the socialist leaders. Many of the former backed away from the movement, while the latter came to realize that the situation was not yet ripe for revolution. It had become obvious that the most urgent task was not revolution but the integration of the socialist movement of the *Regat*[127] with those of the newly acquired territories and the creation of a united socialist party.

Socialism in the Newly Acquired Territories

At the end of the First World War, Romania's territory and population were doubled by the acquisition of Transylvania (*Ardeal*), Crişana, the Banat, and Bukovina from Austria-Hungary, as well as Bessarabia from Russia. The new territories contained important natural resources and considerably more industry than existed in the *Regat,* but they also contained large national minorities. Each of the new provinces had a socialist and trade union movement of its own, usually older and better rooted than that of the *Regat,* but each of these had peculiarities that would complicate the task of integration.

Transylvania and the Banat

The socialist movement in Transylvania, Crişana, and the Banat had been part of the Hungarian Social Democratic party, a party with a strong internationalist outlook and a platform of equal rights for all of the nationalities of Hungary. In 1905 it had created special Slovak and Romanian national sections to facilitate contacts with workers of those nationalities. The Romanian section did not become a separate or autonomous party, however, but instead a part of the larger unit. This integration was reinforced by the fact that the trade unions, with which the Social Democratic party was closely connected, were not divided into national sections.

Since ethnic Romanians of Transylvania were overwhelmingly agricultural, a large proportion, if not the majority, of the region's union members were Hungarians and Germans, rather than Romanians. The extremely restricted franchise and the government's extralegal electoral practices were designed to exclude or nullify the vote of the lower classes, as a result of which the socialists never gained even one parliamentary seat. In Transylvania, then, the politically conscious Romanian worker was more attracted by the Romanian National party, a catch-all that claimed to represent the national interests of the entire Romanian community and that was able to get a few deputies into parliament.[128] Like the unions, the Social Democratic party in Transylvania was heavily Hungarian and German. At the same time, however, there were concentrations of Romanian workers in the cities of Hungary proper, particularly in Budapest, and the Romanian Section thus had a constituency that extended well beyond Transylvania and the Banat.

Until the war, the Romanians in Hungary had demanded equal rights, universal suffrage, and the restoration of Transylvanian autonomy. Equal rights and the franchise were also basic points in the socialist program, but since the socialists supported the idea of a multi-national state, they advocated cultural rather than territorial autonomy. When war broke out, the Social Democratic party, including its Romanian section, adopted a "defensist" position and became quiescent. Hungarian Romanians in general did the same, although they were not eager to die for Hungary; thus they surrendered or deserted in large numbers. When Romania entered the war, many of them had a crisis of conscience, joined Austria-Hungary's enemies, but most remained loyal, or at least noncommittal. But by 1917, the hardships, shortages, casualties, and the prospect of defeat had eroded the morale of the population. Labor troubles and strikes began once more, occurring in Transylvania and the Banat as well; the workers demanded not only food and higher wages but peace.[129]

In the fall of 1917, the Romanian Section became active again, changing its name to Romanian Central Committee of the Social Democratic Party of Hungary, which suggested a greater autonomy and a more national orientation. It also resumed publication of its prewar organ, *Adevărul*.[130] Its program of "peace, rights, and bread" was reaffirmed, at a Romanian social-democratic congress in May 1918,[131] and the point that Romanian workers existed under a double yoke, social and national, was added.[132] The Central Committee set up a number of new party groups, particularly in the mining areas of Transylvania and the Banat, and worked hard to recruit Romanian workers into the trade unions then being reorganized; but the unions were reestablished once more in multinational form.[133]

In early October 1918, when the disintegration of the Central Powers had become evident, Romanian socialists began to negotiate with the Romanian National party for a united national front against the Hungarians. Both groups demanded self-determination for the Romanians, which to the Hungarians signified the Romanian annexation of Transylvania and other territories — a course of events that no Hungarian could accept. Count Mihály Károlyi, leader of the Radicals, tried to offer the minorities autonomy on the cantonal system. On 13 October, the congress of the Social Democratic party recognized the right to self-determination of all nationalities, but implied that it should be exercised only in case of the failure to establish a democratic Hungary with equal rights for all.[134] The Romanian socialists rejected this position.

The Hungarian Radicals and Social Democrats formed a National Council, which seized power in Budapest on 31 October and proclaimed the independence of Hungary. On the same day, a Romanian National Council was formed, with six members each from the Romanian National party and the Romanian Central Committee.[135] This act constituted the definite break between the Romanian socialists and the parent party. The council moved from Budapest to Arad, issued a manifesto affirming the right of self-determination, and began to organize local Romanian councils and a national guard. On 10 November, it notified Károlyi's government that it was assuming power in all counties where the majority of the population was Romanian. It also issued a call for an assembly of the Romanian people, which would decide the future of Transylvania.

Great confusion now reigned in Hungary's eastern provinces. Austria and Hungary surrendered and signed an armistice on 3 November. Allied forces began to appear in the area. On 10 November Romania reentered the war and marched its troops into Transylvania, but the Allied command allowed them to occupy only its eastern and southern fringe. Everyone knew that Romania had been promised territorial gains at Hungary's expense, but nobody knew how much. In the Banat, on 31 October, the local Social Democrats tried to set up an autonomous republic based on all the nationalities, but the attempt failed, and the Banat was occupied by Allied forces.[136]

On 1 December the National Assembly of the Romanians of Hungary met at Alba Iulia in Transylvania and proclaimed union with Romania; of its 1228 delegates, about one-tenth were socialists. As to the form of the union, the delegates ranged from those who wanted immediate, unconditional annexation by Romania to those who visualized a broad autonomy. Many Transylvanians were aware that political and social conditions in the *Regat* were in many ways worse than in Austria-Hungary and wished to preserve their advantages. The socialists, in particular, were divided: a militant faction, including Ion Mihuţ and Iosif Ciser, wanted to use the union to force democratic reforms on

Romania, but a moderate wing, led by Ion Flueraş and Iosif Jumanca, the most prominent Transylvanian socialists, were willing to settle for a milder list of conditions.[137] The final wording of the proclamation provided temporary autonomy for Transylvania until a constituent assembly could be called from the entire country, and guaranteed equal rights for all nationalities, civil liberties, labor rights, and radical agrarian reform. The assembly appointed a fifteen-member provisional provincial government, the Directing Council, two of those members, Flueraş and Jumanca, were socialists.[138] The union was accepted by the king on 24 December, and the Romanian army occupied the rest of Transylvania.

The assembly at Alba Iulia represented only Romanians. The Hungarians had their own national councils and national guards; but they were helpless before the Allied armies, and could only protest. The Germans of Transylvania accepted the union. In January 1919 the Romanian Section became the Romanian Social Democratic party of *Ardeal* and Banat, and adopted a moderate program demanding a series of democratic reforms.[139] In this, it reflected its Austro-Hungarian past.

In the summer of 1918, Communist groups began to form in Hungary, largely the work of former prisoners of war returning from Russia. Similar groups began to appear among the Romanian population of Transylvania and the Banat, and among the Romanian workers in Budapest. By the end of December, most of the members of the Romanian Group of the RKP(b) had been sent home from Moscow.[140] Also in December, a Romanian Communist Group was founded in Budapest and published the periodical *Steagul roşu* and later *Glasul poporului.*[141] A strong Communist organization appeared in Oradea; others, in the Jiu Valley, Reşiţa, Braşov, Hunedoara, and other centers. The Communists distributed leaflets and manifestos in the parts of Transylvania not yet occupied by the Romanian army; even when that occupation was extended, they were able to operate freely in the neutral zone, which included most of Crişana.

On 31 December, the Communists organized a congress of "Romanian socialist internationalist factions of Austria, Hungary, and Transylvania" in Budapest. It was attended by representatives from various Transylvanian towns, including some "centrists" who could not quite swallow the Romanian Section's rush to embrace nationalism, and even some "social-patriots." The Communists presented a program calling for the immediate establishment of the dictatorship of the proletariat, expropriation of all land, nationalization of industry and banks, and the establishment of a Third International.[142] The program was accepted by the majority of the delegates, and in January 1919 the Romanian

Communist Federation of Austria, Hungary, *Ardeal,* and Banat, later known as the Romanian Communist Group of Hungary and *Ardeal,* was founded.[143] On 22 March, after the proclamation of the Hungarian Soviet Republic, it was transformed into the Romanian Socialist-Communist Party of Hungary, whose chief organ was the journal *Revoluția socială.*[144] The cadres of this group came from the *Regat* as well as from Transylvania. Some were socialists who had been expelled from Romania in 1907; others came from the Romanian revolutionary battalions of Odessa, some from the maximalist groups of the *Regat,* and still others came from the Communist Committee in Moscow.[145] By whatever name, the group maintained contact with Moscow and with the maximalists in the *Regat,* and worked closely with the Hungarian Communist party.[146]

The most interesting aspect of the activities of this branch of Romanian socialism was the attitude it held on the question of union with Romania. The amalgamation of the Romanian group of the RKP(b) and the Romanian Communist Committee in Moscow, just a couple of months previously, presumably signified Soviet acceptance, if not approval, of the unification of Transylvania and Romania. But the Romanian Communist Group of Hungary and Transylvania, in its various incarnations, began a violent attack on the Social Democrats, particularly Flueraş and Jumanca. The latter were accused of having betrayed the working class by cooperating with a bourgeois party, of selling out to the king and the landowners, of reformism and opportunism. The workers were reminded that Hungarian workers were their brothers, and Romanian gentry their enemies. Although in some of their propaganda the Communists admitted the principle of self-determination, even including secession, they put far more stress on the importance of social revolution, asserting that the dictatorship of the proletariat per se would resolve the national problem.[147] Their actions demonstrated that they preferred union with Hungarian Communists to union with Romanian capitalists. It is impossible to determine whether this position was their own idea or whether it was imposed by Moscow.

After the establishment of the Soviet Republic in Hungary, the Romanian Communist Group concentrated primarily on supporting it against foreign intervention. This support took two forms: propaganda, and recruitment of Romanians for the Hungarian Red Army. The propaganda was aimed at Romanian workers and peasants, stressing their solidarity with Communist Hungary, and at Romanian troops, inciting them to refuse to fight. Recruitment was carried out in Crişana, Hungary, and among deserters; several hundred were enlisted.[148] Many Hungarian volunteers from Transylvania, now technically Romanian subjects, also joined, among them Elek Köblös, later secretary general of the Romanian Communist party. Such activities were naturally considered treasonous by the Romanian government. When the Hungarian Communist forces were defeated in August 1919 and the Romanians occupied Budapest, great efforts were made to confine the Romanian Communists, and a large number received prison sentences.[149] The Communist Group broke up; some members fled abroad, some infiltrated back into Romania, and the surviving adherents in Transylvania went on organizing factions within the Romanian socialist movement.

Bukovina

In Bukovina, the socialists had been a branch of the Austrian Social Democratic party, which was designed as a federation of regional parties in order to accommodate the various nationalities of the Austrian half of the monarchy. Austrian social democracy had grown rapidly since the turn of the century, and had won the struggle for universal manhood suffrage in 1907. The electoral law was peculiar. To ensure a proportional distribution of seats among the nationalities, it had allowed the socialists to capture over a million votes and 87 out of the 516 parliamentary seats. This victory over the franchise question satisfied their most important immediate goal, and thereafter they became moderate and "reformist," inclined to seek solutions through legislation.

The industrial working class in Bukovina was very small, only 7,500 out of a population of 800,000. In addition, there were several thousand miners and seasonal lumber workers, and over 9,000 artisans.[150] Nevertheless, the Bukovina branch of the Social Democratic party drew a large vote in elections, and its chief, Gheorghe Grigorovici, sat in the Austrian parliament from 1907 to 1918. The population of the province was only 35 percent Romanian; the Ukrainians were the largest group, and there were also large communities of Jews, Germans, and Poles. The working class reflected this mixture: the artisan class was almost entirely Jewish and German; the miners, mostly German; and the industrial workers, heavily Slavic and German. Grigorovici himself was of Ukrainian descent.

Romanian troops entered Bukovina after the German surrender. On 28 November 1918, Romanian nationalists held an assembly at Cernăuţi, the capital of the province, and declared for unconditional annexation to Romania. The Ukrainians were not consulted, although the Poles and Germans participated in the assembly and voted for union out of fear of annexation by Soviet Russia.[151] Soon thereafter, the local socialists transformed their party branch into the Social Democratic Party of Bukovina, and adopted a moderate, reformist position decrying revolution.[152]

Bessarabia

Bessarabia was the least industrial province of Romania. The processing industries employed only some five thousand workers; there were also perhaps twice that many artisans.[153] Romanian-speaking Moldavians, who occupied the central rural districts of the province, constituted roughly one-half the population. Ukrainian and Russian peasantry inhabited the northernmost and southernmost districts and amounted to about 28 percent of the total. The cities, which were mostly quite small, were inhabited largely by Jews (about 10 percent of the total population), and by Russians and Ukrainians, who constituted the bulk of the working class, the bourgeoisie, and the intelligentsia. The political consciousness of the Moldavians expressed itself primarily through the Moldavian National party, whose program had originally been Bessarabian autonomy, and since the October revolution, union with Romania. Some Moldavians had been attracted by the agrarian socialism of the Russian populists, and later by that of the Socialist Revolutionaries; but the Moldavian SR party supported the National party on the union issue.[154] And, while Marxian socialism had appeared in Bessarabia before the turn of the century as a branch of the Russian social-democratic movement, it was confined essentially to the Slavic and Jewish populations of the towns; there was hardly a Romanian name to be found among either Bolsheviks or Mensheviks.

In 1917 workers', peasants', and soldiers' soviets were set up in Bessarabia, and the struggle for supremacy began between Bolsheviks, Mensheviks, and SRs. At first, the latter two groups were strongest, controlling the soviets of Kishinev, Bendery, and other towns.[155] But the Bolsheviks merged with the left wing of the Mensheviks to form the united socialist-internationalists, and by the end of the year had won the struggle, not always by clean methods. In December the Bolsheviks split the internationalists and set up their own organization in Kishinev.[156] They were reinforced by activists from Petrograd and Odessa. Their victory in the soviets, however, brought on the Romanian occupation of Bessarabia. In the aftermath, many Bolshevik adherents fled across the Dniestr, and many others were executed by the Romanians.[157] These refugees organized a Bessarabian Central Executive Committee and some military units at Mogilev-Podolsk, but the occupation of the

Ukraine by the Germans forced them to retreat eastward with the Red Army.[158]

The remains of the Bolshevik groups in Bessarabia immediately began to reorganize themselves clandestinely and to construct an underground network.[159] For the next three years, the Communists in Bessarabia functioned primarily as a resistance organization, whose principal purpose was to assist in the reconquest of the province by the Red Army. For that reason, the party was able to attract support from many who normally would have shied away from its policies and even gained a strong following among the Ukrainian and Russian peasantry. But for the same reason, it found support only among those who resented Romanian rule, that is, among the Slavs and the Jews, and virtually cut itself off from any possibility of recruiting among the Moldavians. The latter turned instead to Constantin Stere's rather radical Bessarabian Peasant party, which in 1921 fused with the Peasant party of the *Regat*.

In the summer of 1918, some of the Bessarabian Bolsheviks reached Moscow, where they established the Bessarabian Communist Group of the RKP(b). G. I. Borisov ("Staryi"), from the Bendery group, and I. K. Diachishin secretly returned to Bessarabia to set up a network among the surviving groups. Contacts were established with the illegal Odessa regional committee.[160] The Communists concentrated on creating fighting groups and guerilla bands, and on sabotaging the lines of communication — all in preparation for a revolt. It was dangerous work, because the Romanian government was ruthless in suppressing such resistance. When the Germans retreated at the end of 1918 and the Red Army approached, the Communists precipitated an uprising among the Ukrainian peasants of the Hotin district in January 1919 and in the town of Bendery in May. Both were premature and were bloodily quashed.[161] In the following month, the Romanian police broke many of the underground groups and arrested the Communist regional committee for Bessarabia. A mass trial, the "trial of the 108," followed, culminating in long prison terms for many and nineteen death sentences.[162]

A Bessarabian Provisional Government, headed by I. Krivorukov, was created in Odessa in April 1919 as part of the preparations for the Soviet invasion of Bessarabia.[163] When Denikin's offensive compelled the Red Army to withdraw before mounting the invasion, however, the Bessarabian Communists were left to rebuild their shattered organization. By this time, most of the older activists had either fallen into the hands of the police or had fled to Russia where they were absorbed into the Red Army or the party bureaucracy. Leadership in Bessarabia passed into the hands of a group of young men and women, many in

their early twenties, the most prominent of whom was Pavel Tkachenko.[164] In October 1919 a party conference in Kishinev elected a new
regional committee, which included Tkachenko and other newcomers.[165] The network of local groups was soon restored and the Bessarabian branch of the *Komsomol* was founded. The emphasis in party work
began to shift to long-term political preparation.

The Communist movement in Bessarabia remained a part of the
Russian Communist party, and, as such, received its directives and
material assistance from Moscow. Since the basis of their activity was
refusal to acquiesce to the Romanian annexation, the Bessarabian
Communists militantly refused to have any intercourse with Romanian
socialists, thinking that it might be interpreted as a tacit acknowledgment of Romanian sovereignty. Thus, any arrangements between the
two movements had to be made through Moscow.[166] More surprisingly,
the Romanian Socialist party appears to have refrained from any
attempt to organize either party or trade union branches in the province, even among the Moldavians. There is no indication whether this
forebearance originated with the Romanians or was due to Russian
pressure.

Nevertheless, at the end of 1919, the Bessarabian Communists initiated a number of contacts with the Romanians. In December they sent
two members of the Kishinev committee to Bucharest to talk with
Romanian Communist groups. Throughout 1920 contacts were established between Bessarabian and Romanian trade unions, and some
cooperation resulted; in particular, the Bessarabians joined in the
general strike in October.[167] In the fall of 1920, to reduce the danger
from the police, the Bessarabian Executive Committee decided to set up
two headquarters outside the province, at Iaşi and Cernăuţi; this
project also involved cooperation with local Romanian Communist
groups.[168] Yet all these approaches were limited and tentative. The
major step came in December 1920, when two members of the regional
committee went to Bucharest to meet delegates of the Central Committee of Romanian Communist groups, and to set up a coordinating body
with parity of membership, the Contact Center, whose decisions would
be binding on both parties.[169] Although the formal incorporation of the
Bessarabian organization into the Romanian party did not take place
until August 1922, the Romanian and Bessarabian Communists were
now effectively united. This policy decision was so important that it can
have taken place only on instructions from Moscow. It reflects, undoubtedly, the decision to adapt tactics to a more long-term strategy,
one in which legal forms would be combined with the completely illegal
ones hitherto practiced.[170] Since a branch of the Russian Communist

party could not hope to be legalized in Romania, it had to merge with an organization whose legality was recognized. Henceforth, the Bessarabians were able to exercise great influence on Romanian communism, but within Bessarabia they went their own way, continuing to act as an extension of the Russian party and still hoping to return to the Soviet fold.

Schism in Romanian Social Democracy: The Emergence of the Communist Party

At the beginning of 1919, the economic situation of Romania was disastrous. Oil and coal production were reduced to half the prewar figure; in other branches of the mining industry, conditions were even worse. There was a critical transport crisis; railroad facilities had been wrecked, and most of the rolling stock had vanished. Lack of transport, fuel, and minerals made industrial recovery almost impossible. Agricultural production was similarly disorganized. The cultivated area in the *Regat* had declined by one-quarter, and the tonnage output of most cereals by one-half. Though Transylvania and the Banat had escaped destruction during the war, the agricultural and transport situations were bad there as well, and the sudden severance from their traditional markets paralyzed many industrial branches.

Even more pernicious in its long-term effects was the monetary situation. By 1921 the paper money in circulation was twenty times the prewar figure. The steady decline of the leu on the world market made it difficult to buy machinery and materials, and obstructed recovery. Internally, the general price index rose ten-fold by 1919, and 24-fold by 1923. The shortage of food, fuel, and housing was extremely severe in the urban and mining areas, and inflation struck hardest at the middle and working classes, whose standard of living declined sharply. The industrial stagnation created about 100,000 unemployed.[171]

The economic crisis continued for the next three years. Uncertainty over the terms of the agrarian reform created nervousness among the peasants, which was reflected in low productivity. This was compounded by undercapitalization and primitive methods of peasant agriculture. Furthermore, peasants with too little or no land, who formerly provided seasonal labor, now stayed on their farms, creating labor shortages in mines, factories, and oilfields, as well as in agriculture. In Transylvania and the Banat the emigration of Hungarian engineers and skilled workers aggravated the crisis. Until 1922, the balance of trade remained heavily adverse, and the national budget showed large deficits. The poor financial situation made it very difficult for Romania to attract foreign loans and investments, and the apparent increase in internal capitalization was merely the effect of inflation.

The socialist party of the *Regat* had pulled itself together after the events of December 1918, but in the process it swung away from revolutionary fervor and toward moderation and, at least temporarily, toward nationalism.[172] The shift was partly a reaction to government repression. At the same time, however, it seems to have been influenced by the fact that the many new members were interested in reform and economic gains rather than revolution. In addition, more moderate leaders such as Toma Dragu and N. D. Coces, who had earlier been drummed out for excessive patriotism, were now rejoining the party. Most of the leadership was in jail awaiting trial, and a provisional Executive Committee was in charge. In February 1919 it held unification talks with representatives of the Transylvanian Social Democratic party. The Transylvanians were anxious to have the union with Romania firmly and universally recognized. On 26 February the committee issued a declaration affirming the right of national self-determination, recognizing the union of the new provinces with Romania on the basis of the resolutions voted by their Romanian assemblies, and calling on the socialist movements of Bessarabia, Bukovina, and Transylvania to unite with that of the *Regat* in one proletarian party.[173]

The trial of the socialists arrested in the aftermath of the demonstration of 26 December (see pages 000–000, above) had finally occurred at the end of March 1919. All were acquitted, except the four who were accused of contacts with foreign Bolsheviks; Alecu Constantinescu was condemned to death *in absentia*.[174] The party congress, which had been rescheduled for April, had to be put off once more because the arrested leaders were unable to make the necessary preparations. It was decided instead to hold a party conference, with delegates from the socialist organizations of all the provinces, in late May.[175] In the meantime, the First Congress of the Comintern had met in Moscow at the beginning of March, formally inaugurating the Third International. Although an invitation to attend had been issued by radio broadcast to the revolutionary groups of the world, few delegates were able to penetrate the Allied blockade and reach Moscow. Under these circumstances, Rakovsky appointed himself to represent the "Revolutionary Balkan Federation," and voted in the name of the Bulgarian Narrow party and the "Romanian Communist Party."[176] No such party existed as yet, of course, and Rakovsky had no mandate from the Romanian Socialist party, even though he still was a member of its Executive Committee by courtesy. Nevertheless, one of the problems facing the party conference was whether to accept this affiliation with the Third International and to transform itself into a Communist party.

The conference demonstrated that Romanian socialism was becoming badly split ideologically. The left wing demanded the official adoption of the "Declaration of Principles" of December 1918, with its maximum program, and adhesion to the Third International. The right wing, particularly the Transylvanians and Bukovinians, declared that they would not support a revolutionary program. The opposition of the leaders from the new provinces appears to have been decisive. The centrists, who had earlier inclined toward the Third International, decided, in the interest of unifying the movement, to accept a moderate party platform. The compromise statement of party principles and the electoral program were patterned on those of the Italian Socialist party, whose general strategy increasing numbers of Romanian socialists regarded as more applicable to Romanian conditions than the Bolsheviks'.[177] Although eventual adherence to the Third International was promised, the final decision was left to the future party congress. It was decided to participate in elections, and the program put forward a long list of democratic demands, including partial nationalization of industry, transport, and credit. The agrarian program still echoed Dobrogeanu-Gherea's doctrine; it called for nationalization of all land and its communal cultivation by groups of landless and poor peasants.[178]

The socialist movement now began to prepare for the coming elections, the first under the new law granting universal male suffrage. At the same time, however, the labor unions were involved in a continuing wave of strikes. Thanks to its collective action the working class was able to increase wages by 50 to 90 percent in all major branches of industry, thus keeping up to some extent with the rising cost of living.[179] There were also gains in the struggle for the eight-hour day and improved working conditions. But these strikes were also a battle-ground between the Communist militants and the moderates in the socialist party, as the former sought to stimulate working-class militancy and to link political demands to the economic goals of the strikers. The strikes replaced street demonstrations as the chief Communist tactic. Under their influence, strikes were called for all kinds of reasons and with such frequency that in some centers, notably Bucharest, there was hardly an industrial establishment that did not have at least one work stoppage that year.[180] It is notable that of the 250 strikes officially recorded in 1919, 210 occurred in the *Regat*, where the Communist groups had most of their strength.[181] Clearly, Communist influence was increasing in the towns with large working-class concentrations.

Presumably the Communist groups were still being coordinated by

Constantinescu, who had gone underground, but increasingly these groups were rent by factional struggles. There was, in particular, an ultra-left "antiparliamentary" faction, led by Constantinescu and Gheorghe Teodorescu, which opposed participation in elections on the grounds that the dictatorship of the proletariat could be established only through revolutionary action.[182] The more moderate wing, which included Alexander Dobrogeanu-Gherea and Boris Ştefanov, saw parliament as a useful forum from which to rally the masses. There was even an anarchist fringe that advocated terrorism. All factions, however, were united in their denunciation of the centrists and Transylvanian social democrats, in their appeals to the working class to imitate the Russian example, and in their demand for immediate adhesion to the third International. To this end, a clandestine printing press was set up in Bucharest, to publish pamphlets and the journal *Revoluţia sociala.*[183]

During this period, the Romanian Communists were also able to make inroads into the socialist-controlled Working-Class Youth. This organization, which had some 4,000 members throughout the country, resumed the publication of its organ, *Foaia tineretului,* in December 1918 (replaced in July 1919 by *Tineretul socialist*). Although the organization's stated purpose was educational and cultural, the Communists who infiltrated it soon gave it a political orientation and changed its name to Socialist Youth Movement. In November 1919 delegates of this movement participated in the founding congress of the Communist Youth International in Berlin.[184]

The Romanian Communists received considerable assistance from Soviet Russia. Romanian Communist committees in Odessa and Moscow established special training courses for propgandists, at least forty-one of whom were dispatched to Romania in 1919.[185] Courier routes were developed, through which the Romanians received Communist literature, propaganda materials, and, we may safely assume, instructions. According to Romanian authorities, they also received large sums of money.[186] That claim is only too probable: the Bolsheviks had sequestered the Romanian treasury deposited in Moscow and therefore had plenty of funds to pass along.

By the end of 1919 the Communists had become dominant in the Bucharest section of the Romanian Socialist party, the largest section in Romania. From this base, the Communists tried to push the Executive Committee into affiliation with the Third International. In January 1920, it proclaimed its own adherence.[187] And in July 1920, it began publication of the periodical *Luptă de clasă,* which became the chief legal organ of the maximalists.[188]

Throughout 1919, both Communists and moderates participated in a propaganda campaign to prevent Romanian involvement in the Russian civil war. France and Britain pressured Romania to render military assistance and, since the Romanians were (for political purposes) making a great display of anti-Bolshevism at the Paris Peace Conference, it appeared quite possible that they would give in. Socialists of all factions joined in demanding peace with Soviet Russia and an end to any collaboration with anti-Bolshevik Russian forces. The legal socialist press, hampered by censorship, worked throughout the year to popularize Russia and to proclaim solidarity with the revolution. In editorials and at rallies and mass meetings, these pledges of solidarity were accompanied by the demand that the Romanian army be demobilized.[189] Communist groups worked even harder; indeed, their underground printing press appears to have been dedicated chiefly to the articulation of these points.[190] In addition to sounding the same themes, they also tried to erode military morale by urging soldiers to mutiny or desert. A special section spread propaganda among the French units stationed in Romania.[191]

The Romanian intervention against the Hungarian Soviet Republic was, however, a different matter. Although Moscow appears to have demanded that the Romanian socialists assist Soviet Hungary by every means, including sabotage against the Romanian army, even the Romanian Socialists in Transylvania failed to follow this suggestion.[192] In the *Regat,* things were not much better. Although books are written today to prove that the Romanian working class stood by the embattled Hungarians,[193] the evidence for this claim is almost nil: a one-day general strike, and the publication of a few articles and a few resolutions by local party sections.[194]

There was actually a considerable amount of demoralization, insubordination, desertion, and even mutiny in the Romanian army during the year, but this situation stemmed from the peasant conscripts' resentment of the prolongation of their military service, not from the success of the Communist propaganda effort.[195] The only sizable subversive group was established in the navy, but it was discovered by the authorities.[196] A similar ineffectiveness was evident in the attempts to exploit peasant discontent. Throughout the year, the delays in instituting the agrarian reform led to many incidents in which lands were seized and manor houses looted. But the socialists showed little zeal or skill in their approach to the exasperated peasants, and the bulk of peasant resentment was thus translated into support for either the Peasant party or General Averescu's People's League. Only in the Prahova valley were a significant number of socialist clubs established among the peasantry, and this was because of the large numbers of oil workers in this region who came from, and continued to live in, the local villages.[197]

In addition to their "peace" campaign, the socialists threw themselves with enthusiasm into the electoral campaign. It was soon evident, however, that the Liberal government would seek to control the election's outcome through the chicanery and intimidation that were traditional in Romanian politics. In the midst of the campaign, the socialist leaders were approached by Averescu, who was organizing a boycott of the elections and had adopted a very radical platform that included the overthrow of the monarchy and peace with Russia.[198] Essentially, Averescu was disappointed because he had expected to be asked to form a government; his radical talk and the threatened boycott were intended merely to force the king's hand. But the socialists, already exasperated by the government's tactics, in mid-October assembled an "extraordinary congress," representing all socialist parties. This congress agreed to join the People's League and the Conservative Democrats in the boycott.[199] This was undoubtedly a mistake; the elections were relatively honest, and the Liberals were overthrown. The socialists even won seven seats (out of 568) in constituencies in which candidates had been entered before the boycott decision. The party then reversed itself and allowed these seven to take their seats. They included several members of the Executive Committee of the *Regat*; but, except for Dobrogeanu-Gherea, all were center or right-wing socialists.

The "extraordinary congress" made a number of other decisions designed to advance the unification of the socialist movement in Romania. The Executive Committee of the *Regat* was to admit four delegates from Transylvania and Banat and one from Bukovina, thus becoming a kind of general staff for the movement. In addition, the new General Council, which included representatives of all the socialist organizations and trade unions of Romania, was created and charged with making policy for the whole movement. Its first task was to set the date for the congress that would officially establish a united socialist party. At the end of January 1920, conference of the General Council and of the General Commission of Trade Unions settled on mid-April for both the trade union unification congress and the general congress of the party.[200] The question of affiliation with the Third International was referred to the congress.

Both party and union membership increased in 1920, the first to perhaps 140,000 and the second to nearly a quarter of a million.[201] The two were largely overlapping, and, in fact, nearly all party members were organized workers, since in many areas (e.g. in Transylvania), enrollment in the party was automatic upon receipt of a union card.

There was still a paucity of intellectuals in the movement, however, and consequently the political indoctrination of many recruits was at best rudimentary.[202] But the new strength was reflected in the elections of May 1922, when the socialists won nineteen seats in the Chamber of Deputies (out of 369) and three in the Senate.[203] The General Council cited the need to concentrate on electoral victories as the reason for postponing the party congress until August.[204] As a sop to the leftists, the council declared that it considered the party to have been totally separate from the "yellow" Second International since the Zimmerwald Conference in 1915.

The left wing had become very active in early 1920 and was pushing hard for a confrontation. The Romanian Section in Moscow sent directives appointing Constantinescu the Comintern representative in Romania and exhorting the Communist group to action.[205] Similar instructions were transmitted through the Bulgarian Communists at the Balkan Socialist Conference in January 1920 and thereafter.[206] The Romanian response was rapid. A Committee of Communist Factions was set up by Bujor and Constantinescu, the Bucharest section took the lead demanding affiliation with the Third International, and *Luptă de clasă* began to appear. In the party press, leftists attached the more prominent right-wing socialists. The favorite tactic for mobilizing left-wing opinion, however, remained the strike.

In the coalition government of Vaida-Voevod, which came to power in December 1919, the minister of the interior was Dr. Lupu, a quasi-socialist. He promptly removed military guards from the factories, partially abolished censorship, ended the state of siege in the *Regat,* and projected other reforms.[207] The response was a wave of demonstrations which peaked at the end of February 1920,[208] and a huge wave of strikes, which continued until fall.[209] Altogether some 750 strikes took place in 1920; of these, 345 occurred between March and October, 112 in Bucharest alone.[210] There was even a large increase of strikes in Transylvania, where over a hundred were declared by October.

It is difficult to determine the extent to which the strikes politicized the workers, but inevitably they provoked a powerful response from the government. In March the Vaida-Voevod cabinet was replaced by that of Averescu, who immediately introduced a "strong-hand" policy of repression, putting the army back in the factories. After the May elections, which were "managed" to assure him a great victory, Averescu introduced a "law on collective conflicts" (commonly nicknamed the Trancu-Iaşi law), which imposed an obligatory conciliation period before a strike could take place and outlawed strikes for causes other than working conditions.[211] In the spring of 1921, a "law on professional associations" was adopted. Though it for the first time recognized the legality of labor unions, it forced them to divorce themselves from political parties and to eschew any but economic and cultural objectives.[212]

The government also sought to emasculate the Communist groups by eliminating their leaders. The arrest and conviction of Bujor was a bad blow.[213] In June 1920 the police captured a clandestine Communist organization led by Nicolau and Marcovici and arrested a number of "legal" leaders of Communist groups, disrupting a conference they were planning for that month.[214] In July Constantinescu was seized and again condemned to death. Particularly surprising was the vigor with which many socialists and trade unionists denounced illegal activity and dissociated themselves from the "irresponsible" clandestine group.[215] Nevertheless, the Communists continued to denounce moderate leaders and proclaim the necessity of transforming the socialist party into a Communist one. For this reason, the socialist Executive Committee seized the opportunity to postpone the party congress once more, pleading that the reintroduction of censorship, the state of siege, and the prohibition of public meetings, made its preparation impossible.[216] In reality, they feared a split. Of course the Communists, encouraged by Moscow, continued to voice their demands for the congress.

The new date of the party congress was to be set after the regional party conference in Transylvania, Banat, and Bukovina, scheduled for August and September. At these conclaves, the regional parties came out unequivocally for the unification of the socialist movement of Romania, and the Transylvanians and Banaters expressed a guarded sympathy for the Third International.[217] As another sop to the leftists, the General Council declared its intention to send a delegation to Russia to investigate the question of affiliation with the Third International. The delegation, consisting of Cristescu, Dobrogeanu-Gherea, Constantin Popovici, Flueraş, Eugen Rozvany, and David Fabian,[218] finally reached Moscow only however, in mid-October,[219] too late to attend the Second Congress of the Comintern. In a meeting with its Executive Committee (ECCI) the Romanians learned of the Twenty-one Conditions for affiliation approved by the Congress. They were then sent off to Kharkov to confer with Rakovsky. There Cristescu, and possibly others, quarreled with Rakovsky over the latter's (and Moscow's) intention to dictate the composition of a new executive committee of the Romanian party; Cristescu also had reservations about the requirement that there be an illegal organization parallel to the legal party.[220] The delegation returned to Moscow in a huff, though the two leftists, Dobrogeanu-Gherea and Fabian, were first given a special tour of the Ukraine as a mark of favor.

In Moscow, the reunited delegation was confronted by the Comintern leadership's attempt to browbeat them into submission. They were hectored about the errors of their party and pressed to admit their guilt. Bukharin demanded that Flueraş be excluded from the delegation, and the Romanians agreed.[221] Zinoviev delivered the most bitter attacks against the Romanian party.[222] Although the Romanians tendered apologies for various sins, they did not capitulate entirely. Cristescu and Popovici composed an answer in the name of their Executive Committee, which rejected most of the accusations and pointed out that the Romanian masses were not ready for revolution and cared little for the Third International.[223] Nevertheless, the Russians succeeded in extorting a declaration in which the Romanian delegation approved the principles of the Third International and the Twenty-one Conditions, and promised to work for the affiliation of their party. It is not clear whether this declaration was signed by the entire delegation (minus Flueraş) or only by the leftists.[224] The delegates had an audience with Lenin. Before returning home in January 1921, Dobrogeanu-Gherea remained in Russia for three more months.

In the meantime, crucial events had shaken the Romanian Socialist party. The introduction of the "law on collective conflicts" had angered all socialists, because it facilitated strikebreaking and could easily be used to justify the imprisonment of union leaders and organizers. The law also prohibited strikes by government employees and in those private enterprises that were "of public interest." The party fought this legislation in parliament, in its press, and through rallies and demonstrations, but could not prevent its passage on 5 September.[225] On 10 October, the General Council of the party met to consider the resolutions of the recent regional conferences. It declared that a single, centralized Socialist party of Romania would come into being on 1 January 1921.[226] It also decided to present an ultimatum to the government demanding the suspension of the Trancu-Iaşi law and various other concessions: amnesty, abolition of censorship, and so forth. Should the government refuse, the party announced that it would resort to a nation-wide general strike.[227] The ultimatum was signed by nearly all the important socialist leaders, regardless of faction. The government did refuse, and the general strike was declared on 20 October.

The general strike of 1920 has become one of the great myths of the Romanian Communists, but, half a century later, it is difficult to assess its true extent and effectiveness. The facts were veiled at the time by censorship and thereafter by propaganda. The government claimed that 65,000 workers participated;[228] Communist writers today claim 400,000, or even half a million.[229] Since the latter number exceeds the total number of workers in Romania in 1920, the government estimate is certainly closer to the truth. The best estimate that can be made is that perhaps as many as 200,000 stopped work, however briefly; that the strike caused considerable disruption in certain branches, such as the railroads, but not in others; that it was pursued much more vigorously in the *Regat* than in Transylvania; that it failed to paralyze the country; and that it was broken in a week.

Unquestionably, however, the general strike was a disaster for both the Socialist party and the labor movement. The government proclaimed martial law and moved ruthlessly to crush its opponents. The majority of party and union leaders found themselves in jail, where they remained for many months. Courts-martial handed out long prison sentences to hundreds of strikers, party periodicals were suspended, and offices wrecked. By 26 October the Transylvanian unions had ordered an end to the strike, and the *Regat* unions followed suit on 28 October. This did not, however, put a stop to government reprisals. On 8 December a small ultra-left group, led by Max Goldstein of Iaşi, bombed the Senate, killing a minister and a bishop and wounding several others.[230] This incident provided the incentive for further government reprisals. At the end of the year, there were still between 1,000 and 2,000 militants in detention.[231]

The result was the virtual collapse of the trade unions, and consequently of party membership, as tens of thousands of frightened workers left the movement. In 1921 the number of organized workers fell to about 32,000; some 60 of the 239 unions went out of existence.[232] When the trade union congress was held in October 1921, it represented only 81 unions with 20,000 workers. The important miners' union lost over 13,000 of its 22,000 members.[233] Although union membership slowly rose to some 50,000 in 1923, and perhaps 70,000 in 1924, it never recovered from the blow, and since organized labor constituted the backbone of party membership, neither did the socialist movement.

Still, the movement tried hard to reorganize itself, in November setting up a provisional Executive Committee and a provisional General Commission of Trade Unions, both in Bucharest.[234] With so many leaders in jail, however, these governing bodies had to be reconstituted with second-string personalities, and local sections had to draw upon rank-and-file workers. Since the less radical members had dropped away and since the strike had left much bitterness, these new cadres were, on the whole, considerably more radical than their predecessors. The result was a shift to the left in the lower and intermediate levels of party leadership, and recognized leftists even got into the Executive Committee and the General Commission.[235] This developed presented the left wing with an excellent opportunity to gain control of the party, and on November 16 representatives of the Communist groups held a clandestine conference to coordinate plans for the capture of the socialist movement.[236] The conference chose a Communist Central Committee to direct the effort; its secretary was Belbert Moscovici, who went under the name of Alexander Bădulescu.[237] A propaganda campaign was unleashed, which blamed the right-wing leadership for the failure of the general strike and demanded an immediate party congress to decide on affiliation with the Comintern.[238] In December the leftists were strengthened by the establishment of formal collaboration with the Bessarabian Communists; the first Bessarabian delegate to the Contact Center was Pavel Tkachenko.

The leftist campaign forced the provisional Executive Committee to call a General Council for 31 January 1921. By that time, the party delegation had returned from Russia and joined in the fray. Three major groupings emerged. The right wing consisted of those leaders who had escaped arrest because they had not signed the ultimatum or had openly dissociated themselves from the general strike: Grigorovici, Flueraş, Jumanca (who was freed from jail in December), Dunăreanu, Şerban Voines, and Pistiner. This group, particularly the Transylvanians and Bukovinians, had begun to feel that the party would have to be purged of the leftists and turned toward moderation.[239] Unfortunately for them, most of their natural allies were in jail. The left wing had also decided that the party would have to be purged, but of the rightists. It was led openly by Stoiculescu, P. Becheanu, M. Macavei, Fabian, Gh. Vasileacu-Vasia, Rozvany, Köblös, and others, and directed from underground by men such as Bădulescu, Ivănuş, and Filipescu.[240] It was now better organized than the right wing, and more difficult to disrupt, because the men who mattered were underground. In the middle were the centrists, whose main interest was to hold the party together. They too were hampered because some of their most influential personalities, including Moscovici, Alexander Oprescu, Emil Socor, had been imprisoned after the general strike. Those who were at liberty, such as Cristescu, Popovici, and Theodor Iordăchescu, had no common policy.

In the General Council, the right wing presented a resolution proposing strict adherence to the program of May 1919 and the affiliation of the trade unions to the Amsterdam International. The centrists proposed temporary adherence to the program of May 1919, free discussion in the party on tactics and affiliation, and a caretaker Executive Committee evenly allotted among the three factions. The leftists' resolution declared that the division between the left and right wings was unbridgeable, and that the party should adopt a platform of class warfare and affiliate with the Third International. The rightists obtained eight votes, the centrists twelve, and the leftists eighteen.[241] The leftist resolution was declared binding on the party. The rightists thereupon stated that they were quitting the party to create a socialist movement of their own. The centrists, unwilling either to support the leftist resolution or to follow the rightists, decided to take a neutral stand, refusing to vote further measures or to accept party office. The leftists then elected a new Executive Committee of their own, with Cristescu, who now joined them unreservedly, as secretary, and set the date of the party congress for 8 May.

In the next few days, the rightists set up a "Provisional Central Committee of Romanian Social Democracy" and began to organize their following in the provinces.[242] The Bukovinian journal *Vremea nouă* was moved to Bucharest to become their central organ. The committee obtained the allegiance of nine of the socialist deputies, and of all three senators. The centrists constituted themselves into a "Socialist Unitarian Group," led by Iordăchescu, and published a declaration outlining their differences with the leftists but committing themselves, with reservations, to the Comintern.[243] The leftists, now openly calling themselves Communists or the "Communist stream" (*curentul comunist*), continued their takeover of the party apparatus. Voinea was ousted from the editorship of *Socialismul* and the newspaper was taken over by Fabian and Vasilescu-Vasia.[244] In its pages, the Communists pounded away at the rightists and at the "opportunism" of the centrists, and prepared the ground for the congress.[245] In mid-February a conference of the *Regat*'s trade unions endorsed the Communist position.[246] Of the parliamentary socialist faction, six deputies declared for the Communists.[247]

The Communists may have gained the upper hand in the *Regat,* but in Transylvania and Bukovina the bulk of the regional socialist parties and of the trade unions appear to have remained loyal to their old social-democratic leaders. On 12 February, the Communists assembled a conference of some Transylvanian union locals and members of the party committees of Braşov, Cluj, Tîrgu-Mureş and Oradea "who remained faithful to the [Transylvanian] congress of 1920" (i.e. to the decision to unify the Romanian parties). The conference anathematized the Transylvanian executive committee, created a "provisional Transylvanian Council of the Romanian Socialist Party," and tried to assume the mantle of the socialist legitimacy in the province, but does not seem to have gained any sizable following.[248] The organizations that participated in the conference came from towns that were overwhelmingly

Hungarian, places where Flueraş and Jumanca would be unpopular as Romanian nationalists. The Communists had greater success in penetrating the youth organization, the Union of Working-class Youth of Transylvania and Banat, which affiliated with the Communist Youth International.[249] Its membership seems to have been largely Hungarian.

In the first days of March 1921 another clandestine conference of Communist groups took place in Iaşi. This meeting was attended not only by delegates from groups in the *Regat,* Dobruja, and Banat, but also by representatives of the Bessarabian Communists and of the Ukrainian and Jewish Communist organizations of Bukovina.[250] The conference marked a further step in the incorporation into the Romanian movement of Communist forces from territories claimed by Soviet Russia; as such, it must have represented a further accommodation by Moscow to the political realities of the 1920s. But the extravagant praise lavished by the conference on the Bessarabians, who were held up as a model, leads one to suspect that they were to be used to supervise the Romanians. The main business of the conference was to discuss the procedure for transforming the Romanian socialist movements into a centralized Communist party. It was felt that the Communist groups, too loosely connected for proper discipline, must be consolidated further and must begin legal as well as illegal activity in order to secure victory at the coming congress.

This increased Communist activity, and particularly the attempts to distribute revolutionary literature in army barracks, attracted the attention of the authorities. Arrests followed; Filipescu, Becheanu, Ivănuş, Fabian, Vasilescu-Vasia, and other leaders were jailed in March and April. *Socialismul* was temporarily suspended.[251] The arrangements for the congress went forward, however. A complex scheme for indirect election of delegates was instituted, which favored small party sections and gave some scope for manipulation.[252] Ultimately, 27 party sections chose to participate in the congress; of the total of 540 "mandates," 380 were Communist and 160 were centrist.[253] No right-wing delegates were elected. The centrists suffered badly from lack of focus. Some were still desperately hoping for a formula that would reunite the party, while others had concluded that the future lay with the Communists and sought to emulate Cristescu.

The fourth General Congress of the Romanian Socialist party took place on 8–12 May.[254] When the question of the Third International was finally put to the vote, 428 mandates were cast in favor of unconditional affiliation, and 111 in favor of affiliation with reservations. The party was declared a section of the Comintern, and the meeting became, in fact, the first congress of the Romanian Communist party, although the name proposed at the congress (and retained until the end of 1922) was "Socialist-Communist Party of Romania." The more extreme activists, led by Rozvany, now proposed to expel the centrists. After some debate, it was decided to allow them provisionally to retain membership, but to exclude them from further decision making and from the congress.[255] Before any further action could be taken, however, the government on 12 May arrested all the members of the congress who had voted for unconditional affiliation and various other Communist leaders (some 72 persons in all), charging them with treason.[256] Among those imprisoned were all the Communist parliamentary deputies and most of the leaders of the youth movement. The Romanian Communist party thus found itself in an anomalous situation: it at last had a formal existence, but now found itself with no leadership, no party structure, and no statute. All that existed were the local sections that had opted for the Comintern and the network of clandestine groups with their underground leadership.

The faithful could also turn for guidance to a number of position papers that had been published prior to the opening of the congress. Dobrogeanu-Gherea again handled the agrarian question. Although it retained strong traces of the elder Gherea's ideology (in its refusal to consider the peasantry a revolutionary force), the proposed program was more realistic in that it did accept the idea of individual proprietorship, albeit with incentives for collective farming.[257] It was thus hardly a Leninist program; in fact, in the eyes of Leninists, the Romanian party never succeeded, at least in the 1920s, in developing a satisfactory approach to the peasant.[258] The nationality program proposed cultural autonomy, reminiscent of Austrian social-democratic concepts, and denied the need for territorial separatism.[259] Here again, the Romanians departed from Lenin's ideas.

In June 1921, such Communist leaders who had escaped arrest, as well as some centrists, assembled in Iaşi and set up a provisional party council.[260] Though little information is available on its composition and functions, we can assume that the clandestine Communist Central Committee and the Bessarabians played a major part. Leonte Filipescu, Constantinescu's former collaborator, was an important member. He was sent to Bucharest under the alias Iorgu to revive the organization there. He soon set up an illegal Local Committee of the Socialist-Communist party and began propaganda work,[261] trying whenever possible to disseminate the party line through the local party sections that could still publish their journals legally. In June the Socialist Youth Movement reconstituted a provisional central committee, including N. Popescu-Doreanu and Lucreţiu Pătrăşcanu, who was to play an important role in Romanian communism, and began to reorganize its local groups. For "tactical" reasons, the Youth Movement declared itself independent of all other working-class organizations, but the Communist members of the Central Committee kept it well under control. In August they resumed publication of the journal *Tineretul socialist* and, at Filipescu's request, made its columns available to the Bucharest Local Committee.[262] *Tineretul socialist* remained for several months the most important legal Communist mouthpiece. In October, however, Filipescu fell into the hands of the authorities and was murdered by the police some months later.[263]

At the end of 1921, a power shift occurred in the Romanian Communist movement. The details are still obscure, but we do know that the change was associated with the sudden rise of a group of young intellectuals led by Marcel Pauker. Grouped around Pauker were his wife Ana, Lucreţiu Pătrăşcanu, Vasile Luca, Popescu-Doreanu, Ştefan Teodorescu, and others who would play major roles over the next thirty years. Pauker was included with N. Simulescu in Filipescu's Local Committee, and was apparently sent to Switzerland to report to unspecified Comintern contacts on the Romanian situation.[269] On his return to Romania, he proceeded to seize control; whether he had Comintern authority to do so is unknown, but, in view of his later career, probable. By late fall, a large number of those arrested during the general strike were being released. On 4 December, Pauker organized the Provisional Committee of the Bucharest Section, consisting of himself, Simulescu, and the recently released veteran, Ivănuş. On 8 December, he added Pătrăşcanu, the just-released Mihail Macavei, and an unidentified sixth member, and converted his group into the Provisional Executive Committee of the Socialist-Communist party, apparently dismissing the existing provisional party council on his own authority.[265] The centrist Gheorghe Tănase replaced Simulescu in January, but this move did not succeed in attracting any other centrist elements to the party. In mid-December, Pauker revived *Socialismul* as the chief party organ.[266] His control of the Bucharest organization, the strongest in Romania, and of the party publications allowed him to arrogate the highest authority in the movement, but the immediate recognition of his Provisional Executive Committee by both the Balkan Communist Federation and the Comintern implied that his action had the blessing of Moscow.[267] In January 1922 a Romanian delegation took part in the conference of the Balkan Communist Federation in Vienna.

The consolidation of the youth movement took place at the same time. During the trade union conference at Braşov in October 1921, delegates from the provisional committee of the Socialist Youth Movement and from the Working-Class Youth of Transylvania discussed the unification of their organizations. This consolidation was actually effected in March 1922, creating the Socialist Youth of Romania, which became the Union of Communist Youth in 1924.[268]

The Bessarabian Communist organization, while slowly integrating itself into the Romanian movement, was still fighting a separate battle, and, unlike the semilegal Romanian party, it remained entirely illegal. Pavel Tkachenko was now the head of the regional committee of the RKP(b), as well as its representative in the Contact Center. Other important activists and members of the regional committee were S. Bubnovsky and I. Badeev. At the end of 1920 and early 1921, the party was seriously hurt by a series of arrests, especially in Ismail and Orgeev (Orhei).[269] In March 1921 Tkachenko and a large number of activists from the Iaşi base were arrested. Within a month, Bubnovsky, who replaced Tkachensko in the Contact Center, was captured in Bucharest; Dobrochaev succeeded him in the center.[270] In July and August, the police broke several clandestine groups in Kishinev and in southern Bessarabia, and apprehended several more in December. At the end of 1921 about a dozen captured activists were executed.[271]

Nevertheless, the Bessarabians survived and scored some successes. In February 1921 a new underground journal, *Bessarabskii bol'shevik,* began to appear; in April, after the Iaşi conference, the Bessarabian party began to put out its first periodical in Romanian, *Bolşevicul basarabean.* The Kishinev and Bendery sections remained particularly active and the youth organization was extended. The Communists were also very successful in establishing themselves in the villages of the southern districts, which three years later led to the Tatar Bunar uprising.[272] Throughout the year, a number of sabotage and guerrilla groups continued to operate in the province, although not very intensively.[273] But one area in which the Bessarabian Communists could make no progress was in organizing union support. The police successfully choked off all union activity, and by mid-1922 there was no organized labor in Kishinev.[274] When legal unions reappeared late that year, they were led by Romanian social democrats, and Communist efforts to penetrate them were not particularly effective.

While the Communists passed through a period of disorganization, the socialists regrouped. In Bukovina, they had retained control of almost all, and in Transylvania, of most, party sections and labor unions. Thus the Social Democratic party of Bukovina, the Transylvanian Socialist party and the Socialist party of the Banat simply continued in existence under their old leaders. In the *Regat,* a few sections, especially in Moldavia, remained loyal, and in June 1921 they were organized into the Romanian Social Democratic party. That same month, the socialists held a congress at Ploeşti and founded the Federation of Socialist Parties of Romania,[275] which affiliated with the International Workers' Association of Vienna, the so-called Two-and-one-half International. Grigorovici became the chairman of the Executive Committee and its representative in Vienna; Şerban Voinea, its secretary.

In December 1921 a number of centrist leaders who had been imprisoned after the general strike were released from jail. This group, which appeared to dislike the social democrats at least as much as the Communists, started a party of its own, the Romanian Socialist party, based in the *Regat* and taking up a "unitarian" position, with which it hoped to salvage the unity of the workers' movement and to reverse the decisions of the May congress.[276] Its leaders were Moscovici, Emil Socor, Al. Oprescu, and Spiridion Calu. In February 1922 Iordăchescu and his "unitarians" joined them, having quit the Communist party because of fundamental differences over its program.[277] In August 1922, the "unitarians" gave up their hopeless task, and, apparently concluding that the social democrats were more congenial to their ideas, merged with the Romanian Social-Democratic party into a new Socialist party of Romania. A single, centralized socialist party was not established until 1927.

A struggle began between the socialists and Communists over the control of the organized labor movement, which still constituted the bulk of potential supporters. It was complicated by the fact that the second Trancu-Iaşi law, the "law on professional associations," came into force in May, forbidding labor unions to have political objectives. The social democrats, not seeking revolution, were the first to come to terms with this statute. On 21 June, in Ploeşti, they held a conference of the labor unions of Transylvania, Banat, and Bukovina, and issued a declaration urging workers to organize themselves on the basis of the Trancu-Iaşi law. They also founded the Central Labor Union Council, with headquarters at Cluj, to serve as the new trade union center.[278] Although they declared that their unions would be "neutral," they knew as well as anyone that leadership could be translated into political support. There followed a second conference in Ploeşti, on 26 June, called by a number of unions of the *Regat,* Banat, and Transylvania which had been inclined toward the Third International; it set up a rival Provisional General Commission.[279] Because the Communists had been ordered by their imprisoned leaders to have nothing to do with the Trancu-Iaşi law, the General Commission fell into the hands of centrists, who declared that their goal was the unification of the labor movement. The Communists realized belatedly that any worker organization they could control, even if it could not stage political strikes, was much better than none. They were thus forced to try to infiltrate the centrist trade unions or to create new ones. To this end, they now tried to stimulate the enrollment of workers in legal trade unions, using *Tineretul socialist* for this campaign.[280]

In October the General Commission called a trade union congress in Braşov. It had hoped to make this a unity congress, but the Central Council refused to participate except on its own terms. The eighty-one union locals that sent delegates represented at most 20,000 workers, showing the decline of organized labor in Romania.[281] A number of Communists attended the congress, and, in particular, the Socialist Youth leaders Popescu and Pătrăşcanu were sent to inject some militant ideology; but the centrists were firmly in control, and the Socialist Youths were excluded. The congress, fortified by a message from Moscovici and other imprisoned centrist leaders, came out flatly for union neutrality. However, the unification of the two labor groupings was not accomplished until the labor congress at Sibiu in June 1922, when a National Commission of Trade Unions was established; its executive committee was dominated entirely by social democrats.[282] Unification did not last long. The Communist program of infiltration proceeded so well that at the general labor congress at Cluj, in September 1923, the socialists decided to split the movement, and expelled all the infected unions from the National Commission.[283]

Now that the Trancu-Iaşi laws were in force, and almost all unions conforming to them, the number of strikes fell by some 80 percent.[284] The economic upturn that began in 1921 also helped, although inflation continued. The Communist tactic of radicalization through strikes was thus paralyzed for the next decade.

It is difficult to estimate how much working-class support was being given at this time to each of the rival socialist currents. However, a Comintern source stated that in 1921, 36 percent of the total Romanian union membership adhered to the Communists.[285] This was an estimate not of the membership of Communist-led unions but of Communist sympathizers in all unions, and therefore would err in the Communists' favor. Two years later, at the Cluj congress, the expelled Communist-dominated unions contained 45 percent of the total union membership. It would thus appear that the socialists always retained the loyalty of a larger share of the working class. This situation was reflected in the parliamentary elections of March 1922, which were "managed" by the Liberal government of Bratianu. The socialist Federation won about 2.5 percent of the vote nationwide, and nearly 10 percent in Bukovina, electing one deputy. The Communists took about 0.3 percent of the total vote, and no seats; their best showing was in Muntenia, where they won 1.3 percent.[286]

The policy of the "united front" was introduced by the Comintern after its Third Congress, being promulgated by ECCI in December 1921. From its first issue for that month, *Socialismul* began a campaign for a united front with the centrists and social democrats, but met with a categorical rejection from the socialist Federation.[287]

In January 1922 the government finally opened the trial of 271 Communists, the so-called Dealul Spirii Trial. The accused included all those arrested at the May congress and a mixed bag of Romanian revolutionary militants and Bessarabian Communists picked up since the general strike. The trial dragged on for nearly five months, until an amnesty in June set free 213 of the prisoners.[288] With this large number of Communist leaders back into circulation, it at last became possible to reorganize and consolidate the Communist movement. In October the second party congress was held in Ploeşti. This congress elected the first regular unified Central Committee, with Gheorghe Cristescu as general secretary, voted a provisional statute, and adopted the name Communist Party of Romania. This, rather than the May congress, can be considered the true inception of the Romanian party.

NOTES

1. R. W. Seton-Watson, *History of the Roumanians* (Cambridge, 1934), p. 349.

2. H. L. Roberts, *Rumania* (New Haven, 1951), p. 244; M. Gillard, *La Roumanie nouvelle* (Paris, 1922), p. 141. There is no individual history of pre-Second World Romanian socialism and communism in English, and no reliable history of any other language. Robert's *Rumania* and Ionescu's *Communism in Rumania 1944–1962* contain brief accounts of early Romanian socialism and of the Communist Party in the interwar period. These are the best available in English, but both contain gaps and errors. There is an even briefer and gappier account, from the Romanian socialist viewpoint in *Politics and Political Parties in Roumania*. Possibly the least unreliable source on early Romanian socialism in Romanian is C. Titel Petrescu's *Istoria socialismului în România* (Bucharest, 1944). Trotsky's articles in *Ocherki politicheskoi Rumynii* give some shrewd views of the situation before 1913. The flood of books which has appeared in Romania since 1945 is extremely untrustworthy, because repeated purges since the inception of the Romanian Communist Party have left us with so many un-persons and non-events.

3. L. Trotsky and Ch. Rakovsky, *Ocherki politicheskoi Rumynii* (Moscow, 1922), pp. 70–71.

4. J. A. Rothschild, *Rakovski* (St. Anthony's Papers on Soviet Affairs, no. 12) (Oxford, 1955), pp. 2–6.

5. Akademiia nauk SSSR, *Istoriia Rumynii 1848–1917* (Moscow, 1971), pp. 429–432, 474–475; Gillard, p. 34.

6. *Istoriia 1848–1917,* pp. 480–483.

7. Ecaterina Arbore-Ralli, "Le mouvement socialiste en Roumanie," *Bulletin Communiste,* year 4, no. 47/48 (9 Dec. 1920), p. 21; Trotsky and Rakovsky, pp. 69, 76–77.

8. Gillard, pp. 52–60; Trotsky and Rakovsky, pp. 60–61; E. Turczynski, "The Background of Romanian Fascism," *Native Fascism in the Successor States* (Santa Barbara, 1971), p. 108; D. Mitrany, *The Land and the Peasant in Rumania* (London, 1930), pp. 532–533.

9. Turczynski, pp. 102–108.

10. *Classe operaia e movimento contadino in Romania* (Bucharest, 1974), p. 121n22; G. Alexiano et al, *Roumanie* (La via juridique des peuples: Bibliothèque de droit contemporain) (Paris, 1933), p. 283. The numbers given in *Istoriia 1848–1917,* pp. 359–360, appear much exaggerated.

11. Trotsky and Rakovsky, p. 67; Juliusz Demel, *Historia Rumanii* (Wroclaw, 1970), pp. 357–358; *Classe operaia,* p. 104.

12. Trotsky and Rakovsky, p. 67; Arbore-Ralli, p. 21.

13. Gillard, pp. 34–35.

14. *Istoriia 1848–1917,* p. 484.

15. *Istoriia 1848–1917,* pp. 428–429, 483–484.

16. *Istoriia 1848–1917,* pp. 474–475.

17. Arbore-Ralli, p. 21; *Istoriia 1848–1917,* pp. 425–426.

18. Roberts, pp. 276–283; *Classe operaia,* pp. 104–109.

19. Ibid., p. 278.

20. Arbore-Ralli, p. 21; *Classe operaia,* pp. 111–112; *Istoriia 1848–1917,* pp. 482–483; *Politics and Political Parties in Roumania* (London, 1936), pp. 246–247. The agrarian program is given in W. E. Walling et al, *The Socialism of Today* (New York, 1916), pp. 185–187.

21. *Politics and,* p. 247; *Istoriia 1848–1917,* pp. 488–489; Gillard, pp. 33–34; G. D. H. Cole, *A History of Socialist Thought* (London, 1956), vol. 3, pt. 2, p. 599.

22. Arbore-Ralli, p. 21. W. E. Walling, *The Socialists and the War* (New York, 1915), p. 210, gives 3,000.

23. Roberts, p. 245; *Istoriia 1848–1917,* pp. 494–497; Rothschild, p. 9. L. S. Stavrianos, *Balkan Federation* (Smith College Studies in History, vol. 27, no. 1–4, October 1941–July 1942), pp. 189–190, 192; N. Copoiu, *Le socialisme européen et le mouvement ouvrier et socialiste en Roumanie 1835–1921* (Bucharest, 1973), pp. 148–150; Walling et al, p. 183.

24. *Lupta, passim.* See also: C. Dumas and Ch. Rakovsky, *Les socialistes et la guerre* (Bucharest, 1915).

25. Walling, *The Socialists and the War,* pp. 210–211, 400–401; Rothschild, p. 11; Ionescu, p. 4.

176 LUCIEN KARCHMAR

26. Z. A. B. Zeman, *Germany and the Revolution in Russia 1915–1918* (London, 1958), pp. 85–86.

27. Arbore-Ralli, pp. 21–22.

28. Ibid., p. 22; Stavrianos, pp. 198–199; Copoiu, p. 154; *Politics and,* pp. 248–249; Trotsky and Rakovsky, pp. 132–133.

29. Rothschild, p. 12; O. H. Gankin and H. H. Fisher, *The Bolsheviks and the World War* (Stanford, 1940), pp. 316, 341; Copoiu, pp. 156–157.

30. Rothschild, pp. 12–13; Gankin and Fisher, p. 380.

31. *Istoriia 1848–1917,* pp. 546–552; Arbore-Ralli, p. 22.

32. N. N. Constantinescu et al, *Situaţia clasei muncitoare din România 1914–1944* (Bucharest, 1966), pp. 10–43; *Istoriia 1848–1917,* pp. 544–546.

33. Arbore-Ralli, p. 22; Trotsky and Rakovsky, pp. 133–134; *Istoriia 1848–1917,* p. 552.

34. Arbore-Ralli, p. 22; Trotsky and Rakovsky, p. 134.

35. M. Cruceanu and F. Tănăsescu, *Al. Dobregeanu-Gherea* (Bucharest, 1971), p. 24.

36. Arbore-Ralli, p. 22.

37. Trotsky and Rakovsky, p. 134.

38. Ibid.

39. S. M. Parkhomchuk, *Velikii zhovten' i revoliutsiine pidnesennia v Rumunii* (Kiev, 1967), pp. 53, 57.

40. D. Mitrany, pp. 99–107; Gillard, pp. 147–148; Seton-Watson, pp. 503–505.

41. Cruceanu and Tănăsescu, p. 27.

42. *Istoriia 1848–1917,* p. 558.

43. Cruceanu and Tănăsescu, p. 28; Trotsky and Rakovsky, pp. 134–135.

44. Cruceanu and Tănăsescu, pp. 29–30; Trotsky and Rakovsky, p. 135; "Delo tov. Buzhora," *Kommunishcheskii Internatsional,* year 3, no. 17 (June 1921), p. 4425.

45. Trotsky and Rakovsky, pp. 136–137; Gh. Rădulescu, *Anii furtunilor* (Bucharest, 1962), pp. 25–26.

46. *Istoriia 1848–1917,* p. 559; Rădulescu, p. 26.

47. Parkhomchuk, p. 58; *Istoriia 1848–1917,* p. 560; V. Liveanu, *1918: din istoria luptelor revoluţionare din Romînia* (Bucharest, 1960), p. 131.

48. Parkhomchuk, p. 60; *Istoriia 1848–1917,* p. 559.

49. Parkhomchuk, p. 61.

50. *Istoriia 1848–1917,* p. 560; Parkhomchuk, pp. 61–70.

51. *Documente din istoria mişcării muncitoreşti din România 1917–1921* (Bucharest, 1966), pp. 55–63.

52. "Rumcherod" was an acronym for "Executive committee of the soviets of soldiers', sailors', workers', and peasants' deputies of the RUManian front, the Black Sea (CHERno morski) fleet, and the ODessa military district."

53. C. J. Vopicka, *Secrets of the Balkans* (Chicago, 1921), pp. 157, 159.

54. Parkhomchuk, p. 85; Copoiu, p. 177.

55. Akademiia Nauk SSSR, *Istoriia Rumynii 1918–1970* (Moscow, 1971), p. 14; *Forta creatoare a ideilor Leniniste* (Bucharest, 1970), p. 49.

56. Ibid., *Documente*, pp. 66–68; *Marea revoluţie socialistă din octombrie şi mişcarea revoluţionară şi democratică din România: Documente şi amintiri* (Bucharest, 1967), pp. 3–6, 9–12.

57. S. D. Spector, *Rumania at the Paris Peace Conference* (New York, 1962), pp. 45–46; Vopicka, pp. 146–151.

58. Akademiia Nauk Moldavskoi SSR, *Istoriia Moldavskoi SSR* (Kishinev, 1968), vol. 2, pp. 70–81; Stefan St. Graur, *Les rélations entre la Roumanie et l'URSS depuis le traité de Versailles* (Paris, 1936), pp. 15–16; A. Popovici, *The Political Status of Bessarabia* (Washington, D.C., 1931), pp. 152–158; Alex. Boldur, *La Bessarabie et les rélations Russo-Roumaines* (Paris, 1927), pp. 73–74.

59. *Istoriia MSSR*, pp. 77, 80–81; Ch. G. Rakovsky, *Roumania and Bessarabia* (London, 1925), pp. 32–37; Comité pour la libération de la Bessarabie, *Mémoire sur la situation de la Bessarabie* (Paris, 1919), pp. 28–29.

60. Liveanu, pp. 216–217; Parkhomchuk, p. 86; Copoiu, p. 177; Pantazzi, p. 189.

61. Ibid., p. 218.

62. Ibid., pp. 214–215.

63. Ibid., p. 217; Copoiu, p. 177; Pantazzi, pp. 192–194.

64. Liveanu, pp. 218–221; Parkhomchuk, p. 85.

65. Liveanu, pp. 217–218; Parkhomchuk, p. 86.

66. Copoiu, p. 177.

67. Liveanu, pp. 223–225; Parkhomchuk, pp. 84, 87.

68. Rothschild, pp. 17–18; Pantazzi, pp. 195–209.

69. Parkhomchuk, p. 90.

70. Parkhomchuk, pp. 169–170; *Istoriia 1918–1970*, p. 25. The group eventually numbered 15 members.

71. Parkhomchuk, p. 102; *Istoriia 1918–1970*, p. 25; *Marea revoluţie*, pp. 34–35.

72. Parkhomchuk, p. 102; *Istoriia 1918–1970*, pp. 25–26. Its orientation was Transylvanian — and directed toward the peasant population; part of its membership had formed the Romanian Revolutionary Peasant party (Ionescu, p. 9).

73. Parkhomchuk, pp. 102, 105; *Istoriia 1918–1970*, p. 26; Ionescu, pp. 9–10; *Marea revoluţie*, pp. 55–56.

74. Copoiu, pp. 178–182; Parkhomchuk, pp. 173–179; *Marea revoluţie*, pp. 57, 62.

75. Parkhomchuk, pp. 170–172, 174; *Marea revoluţie*, pp. 86–89.

76. Parkhomchuk, p. 181; *Marea revoluţie*, pp. 66, 78, 86–89.

77. Parkhomchuk, p. 184.

78. Documente, pp. 92–97.

79. Ibid., pp. 85–86.

80. Parkhomchuk, p. 92.

81. Alexandre Marghiloman, *Note politice 1897–1924* (Bucharest, 1927), vol. 3, p. 541; *Istoriia 1918–1970*, pp. 28–29; Parkhomchuk, pp. 92–93.

82. Parkhomchuk, pp. 103, 104, 170.

83. Ionescu, pp. 8, 357; Trotsky and Rakovsky, p. 141.

84. Documente, pp. 86, 99–100, 109–111.

85. Documente, p. 86.

86. Marghiloman, vol. 3, pp. 520–521.

87. Documente, pp. 105–106.

88. Arbore-Ralli, p. 92.

89. Ibid., Trotsky and Rakovsky, p. 137.

90. Istoriia 1848–1917, p. 562; Parkhomchuk, pp. 50–51.

91. Arbore-Ralli, p. 23; Istoriia 1848–1917, p. 561; Parkhomchuk, p. 51; Trotsky and Rakovsky, pp. 137–138.

92. Arbore-Ralli, p. 23; Istoriia 1848–1917, pp. 561–562; Parkhomchuk, p. 51.

93. Arbore-Ralli, p. 23; Istoriia 1918–1970, p. 27.

94. Arbore-Ralli, p. 23.

95. Ibid., p. 23; Parkhomchuk, p. 61.

96. Rădulescu, p. 42; Parkhomchuk, p. 50.

97. Arbore-Ralli, p. 23; Gankin and Fisher, pp. 664, 674. For unknown reasons, a number of present-day Communist writers state erroneously that the two delegates were Frimu and Gheorghe Cristescu. Cf. C. C. Giurescu et al, Chronological History of Romania (Bucharest, 1972), p. 261, and Copoiu, pp. 159–160.

98. Bol'shaia Sovetskaia Entsiklopediia (3d edition), vol. 13, p. 46 ("Konstantinescu"). No such trip is mentioned by Arbore-Ralli, the best source for this period.

99. Rădulescu, p. 43; Demel, p. 374; Istoriia 1918–1970, p. 26.

100. Parkhomchuk, p. 105; Ionescu, pp. 9, 13.

101. Arbore-Ralli, p. 23; Documente, pp. 71–74; Rădulescu, pp. 35–38; G. Unc (Unk), Solidarnost' rumynskogo rabochego i demokraticheskogo dvizheniia s Velikoi oktiabr'skoi sotsialisticheskoi revoliutsiei (Bucharest, 1968), pp. 15–16.

102. Arbore-Ralli, p. 23; Istoriia 1848–1917, pp. 561–562; Parkhomchuk, pp. 94–95.

103. Arbore-Ralli, p. 23; Istoriia 1918–1970, p. 27.

104. Arbore-Ralli, pp. 23–24; Rădulescu, p. 48; Parkhomchuk, p. 96.

105. Documente, p. 91.

106. Arbore-Ralli, p. 24; Liveanu, pp. 140, 258–259; Istoriia 1918–1970, pp. 561–562; Parkhomchuk, p. 97; Rădulescu, pp. 44–45.

107. Mitrany, pp. 110–112; Seton-Watson, pp. 535–536; Giurescu, pp. 266, 269.

108. F. Borkenau, World Communism (Ann Arbor, 1962), pp. 99–100. It is quite true that "the agrarian reform in Roumania [sic] was perhaps the strongest single obstacle that opposed the advance of Bolshevism."

109. Liveanu, pp. 372–373; Parkhomchuk, p. 106; Copoiu, p. 193.

110. Liveanu, pp. 365–366.

111. Rădulescu, p. 52; Liveanu, p. 373. "Trăiască socialismul" means "Long live socialism."

112. Liveanu, pp. 376–377.

113. Arbore-Ralli, p. 24.

114. Arbore-Ralli, p. 24; Liveanu, pp. 407–414.

115. Documente, pp. 121–122.

116. Ibid., pp. 60–63.

117. Copoiu, pp. 192–193; Liveanu, pp. 405–406.

118. Documente, pp. 116–119.

119. Ibid., pp. 123–128.

120. "Pis'mo ispolkoma Rum. sots. partii de IKKI," *Kommunisticheskii internatsional,* year 2, no. 16 (31 March 1921), 3815.

121. Liveanu, pp. 374–393; Parkhomchuk, pp. 117–118; Rădulescu, pp. 54–55.

122. Arbore-Ralli, p. 24.

123. Marghiloman, vol. 4, pp. 187–188; Vopicka, p. 288; Ion Duca, *Memoirs* (unpublished; typescript in the Hoover Institution, Stanford), chap. 44, p. 463.

124. Liveanu, pp. 616–622; Rădulescu, pp. 57–64; Documente, pp. 137–138, 143–144; Arbore-Ralli, pp. 24–25; Marghiloman, vol. 4, p. 188. The number of victims has been the object of one of the usual shell games of political mythology. The government claimed that six were killed and fifteen wounded (Marghiloman, vol. 4, p. 191). The unofficial estimate was twenty killed (and 40–50 wounded), and this was accepted by contemporary writers, both pro- and anticommunist (Marghiloman, vol. 4, p. 188; Arbore-Ralli, p. 25; Trotsky and Rakovsky, p. 138). But in December 1920, Zinoviev, head of the Comintern, claimed that there had been more than 100 killed and several hundred wounded (*Kommunisticheskii internatsional,* year 2, no. 16 [31 March 1921], 3808–3809). This figure has now become enshrined, the number of killed usually being given as 102 or 104, and of wounded, as 200 or more (V. Dembo, *Rumyniia* (Moscow, 1937), p. 123; Giurescu, p. 268; Liveanu, p. 621; Rădulescu, p. 62; Parkhomchuk, p. 123). The socialist leadership in Bucharest apparently had no knowledge of what the maximalists were planning (Arbore-Ralli, p. 25; Roberts, p. 246n3).

125. Arbore-Ralli, p. 25; Liveanu, pp. 621–622; Documente, pp. 162–164; Marghiloman, vol. 4, pp. 188, 240–241; Duca, pp. 463–464. Duca, who was then minister of agriculture, claims in his unpublished memoirs that the repression far surpassed anything the government had intended, and that it proved impossible at the time to establish who was responsible for issuing such orders; but that several years later, he discovered that a military commander, General Rasoviceanu, had done so on his own responsibility, because he decided that the government was not sufficiently energetic in fighting Communist subversion.

126. Marghiloman, vol. 4, p. 209.

127. The *Regat,* or "Old Kingdom" was Romania in the boundaries of 1916.

128. Cole, pp. 566–569.

129. Liveanu, pp. 423–448; M. Constantinescu et al, *Unification of the Romanian National State: the Union of Transylvania with Old Romania* (Bucharest, 1971), pp. 172–174; *Istoriia 1848–1917,* pp. 565–567.

130. Constantinescu, pp. 172–173.

131. Documente, pp. 63–65.

132. Constantinescu, pp. 174–177; Documente, pp. 77–84.

133. Constantinescu, pp. 173; N. G. Munteanu and Gh. Ioniță, *Un veac de istorie a minerilor de pe Jiu* (Bucharest, 1971), pp. 20–21.

134. Constantinescu, pp. 180–182, 232–233.

135. Ibid., pp. 184, 235. Later in November, its composition was apparently changed to six socialists and thirty National Party members, which corresponded far better to their relative strengths in Transylvania (ibid., p. 191).

136. Ibid., pp. 268–270.

137. Ibid., pp. 192, 240, 264–267.

138. Ibid., pp. 282–285; Seton-Watson, pp. 533–534; Documente, pp. 141–143. Many of the provisions of the Act of Union were later disregarded or mutilated by the Romanian government.

139. Documente, pp. 151–160; Constantinescu, p. 194. It also decided to publish periodicals in German and Hungarian and to recruit among those nationalities.

140. Liveanu, pp. 593–594.

141. G. Unc. *Die Solidarität der Werktätigen Rumäniens mit der proletarischen Revolution in Ungarn* (Bucharest, 1970), p. 82.

142. Liveanu, pp. 595–597.

143. Ibid., pp. 597–598. "Austria" meant essentially the Bukovina.

144. *În sprijinul Republicii ungare a sfaturilor 1919: Documente şi amintiri* (Bucharest, 1969), p. 33.

145. Ibid., p. 33; Unc, *Die Solidarität*, p. 82.

146. Liveanu, p. 594; *În sprijinul*, p. 33.

147. Liveanu, pp. 594, 596–599.

148. *În sprijinul*, pp. 35–39, 66–69, 73, 80–86; Rădulescu, p. 73; Unc, *Die Solidarität*, pp. 84–90.

149. *În sprijinul*, pp. 143–149, 152–153, 158–159, 162–163, 195.

150. C. G. Rommenhöller, *Gross-Rumänien* (Berlin, 1926), p. 70; Gillard, p. 50.

151. Parkhomchuk, pp. 114–115; *Istoriia 1918–1970*, p. 35.

152. Liveanu, p. 607. However, already in the spring of 1918, Communist groups were founded in Bukovina by war prisoners returning from Russia (Parkhomchuk, pp. 100–101). There was also, apparently, direct penetration of the RKP among the Ukrainians of north Bukovina, who were encouraged to demand annexation to Soviet Ukraine; a Ukrainian Revolutionary Organization was set up, led by intellectuals, and drawing its membership from the peasantry (*Pod znamenem velikogo oktiabria* [Kishinev, 1967], pp. 167–168). Lastly, an odd body, the Organization of Communist Jews, appeared among the Yiddish-speaking Jewish community which formed 12 percent of the population of Bukovina (Ionescu, p. 18).

153. Rommenhöller, p. 70; *Istoriia MSSR*, vol. 2, p. 237.

154. *Istoriia MSSR*, vol. 2, p. 22.

155. Ibid., pp. 26–27.

156. Ibid., p. 46. The Kishinev organization had about 160 members, of which 100 were soldiers, and only 60 workers and intellectuals, i.e., unquestionably

local inhabitants. It may be noted that of the seven named as chief activists of the latter group, three were Slavs, four were Jews, and not one was Moldavian.

157. Ibid., pp. 74–84.

158. Ibid., pp. 81–82.

159. Ibid., p. 91.

160. Ibid., pp. 92–93.

161. Ibid., pp. 96–99, 105–106; *Pod znamenem,* pp. 76–77.

162. *Istoriia MSSR,* vol. 2, p. 114.

163. Ibid., pp. 104–110. The names indicate that all the members of the new committee were, once more, Slavic or Jewish. In July, delegates from the various local groups assembled in Odessa for a regional party conference; a new regional committee of nine men was selected.

164. *Pod znamenem,* pp. 89–90.

165. Ibid., p. 66; *Istoriia MSSR,* vol. 2, p. 115.

166. *Pod znamenem,* p. 96. Within Bessarabia, the Communists appear to have had a monopoly of socialist activity. The Mensheviks and the Jewish *Bund* seem to have disappeared altogether after 1917.

167. *Istoriia MSSR,* vol. 2, pp. 117, 129–130.

168. *Pod znamenem,* pp. 90–94, 138–142.

169. Ibid., pp. 95–99, 161–163.

170. *Istoriia MSSR,* vol. 2, p. 249.

171. For the economic situation of postwar Romania, *vide* Gillard, pp. 95–128; F. E. Manoliou, *La réconstruction économique et financière de la Roumanie et les partis politiques* (Paris, 1931), pp. 62–108; Constantinescu, pp. 7–147.

172. The membership of the socialist parties in Romania increased rapidly to a total of perhaps 90,000. (*Politics and,* pp. 252–253). Romanian writers today give a total of 100,000 members at the end of 1919 (Constantinescu, p. 140; Goldberger, p. 84). Arbore-Ralli, (p. 25) gave the membership as 37,500 in the *Regat,* 75,000 in Transylvania and 15,000 in Bukovina, Rakovsky claimed that there were 20,000 party members and 120,000 unionized workers in the *Regat* alone (Trotsky and Rakovsky, p. 140) and that total socialist party membership was 60,000 ("Kommunisticheskoe dvizhenie v Rumynii," *Kommunisticheski internatsional,* year 2, no. 13 [28 Sept. 1920], 2563).

173. Documente, pp. 165–167; Rădulescu, p. 70; Musat and Ardeleanu, p. 276. This declaration later caused arguments with more internationalist comrades, and the implicit recognition of the annexation of Bessarabia particularly infuriated the Russians. The declaration constituted a major point in Zinoviev's violent attack on the Romanian Socialist Party in 1920 (*Kommunisticheskii internatsional,* year 2, no. 16 [31 March 1921], 3809–3810). Cf. also the reply of the Romanian Executive Committee (ibid., 3816–3817). Parkhomchuk (p. 162) writes that "The spirit of national-chauvinism completely permeates the entire Declaration." The Transylvanian party went through a number of cosmetic changes in 1919. The party name was changed from "social-democratic" to "socialist," (*Documente,* pp. 243–246) and, in accordance with a resolution of the Romanian party conference of May, it pulled Flueraş and Jumanca out of the Directing Council (ibid., pp. 234–236). In December, the party was reorga-

nized so as to create within it an autonomous sub-party for the Banat (ibid., pp. 273–275). In effect, this reorganization was one of the adjustments made to accommodate the nationality problem in the new provinces. The Transylvanian party and trade unions were recruiting large numbers of Hungarian and German workers, who had recognized that the peace settlement had eliminated alternatives. The miners' union, for example, now included only 65 percent Romanians, the rest being mainly Hungarian (ibid., p. 231). The Transylvanian party took steps to assure that the nationalities would be represented in its central secretariat, as well as in the governing body of a united Romanian socialist party (ibid., pp. 274–275).

174. Arbore-Ralli, p. 25; Marghiloman, vol. 4, pp. 274, 281; *Bulletin périodique de la presse roumaine,* no. 14 (28 May 1919), p. 2.

175. *Bulletin,* no. 14, p. 4.

176. *Kommunisticheskii internatsional,* year 1, no. 1, 131–132.

177. Documente, pp. 199–210.

178. Arbore-Ralli, p. 25; Muşat and Ardeleanu, pp. 277–279.

179. Constantinescu, p. 129; Munteanu and Ioniţă, p. 27.

180. Duca, chap. 45, p. 468; *Bulletin,* no. 14, p. 4, and no. 15 (10 July 1919), p. 2; *Istoriia 1918–1970,* pp. 47–48; Goldberger, pp. 70–79.

181. *Istoriia 1918–1970,* p. 49; Constantinescu, p. 140.

182. Cruceanu and Tănăsescu, p. 40; *Forţa creatoare a ideilor leniniste* (Bucharest, 1970), p. 72.

183. Parkhomchuk, p. 166; Marghiloman, vol. 4, p. 372.

184. Parkhomchuk, pp. 120–121, 166–167.

185. Ibid., p. 172.

186. Duca, *loc. cit.*; Marghiloman, *loc. cit.*; *Bulletin,* no. 27 (21 August, 1920), p. 2.

187. Documente, pp. 281–283, 299–303.

188. Rădulescu, pp. 99–100.

189. Copoiu, pp. 163–168; Unc, *Solidarnost',* pp. 39–62; Rădulescu, pp. 81–84.

190. Unc, *Solidarnost',* pp. 42–43; *Istoriia 1918–1970,* p. 49.

191. *Istoriia 1918–1970,* pp. 43–45; Parkhomchuk, p. 158.

192. Documente, p. 231; Ionescu, p. 14.

193. Cf., Unc., *Die Solidarität,* and *În sprijinul,*; also Copoiu, pp. 185–188.

194. *Istoriia 1918–1970,* pp. 46–47; *În sprijinul,* pp. 26–30, 124–142; Documente, pp. 224–229; Marghiloman, vol. 4, p. 348.

195. Marghiloman, vol. 4, pp. 225, 415; Rădulescu, pp. 86–89; Parkhomchuk, pp. 157–159.

196. Marghiloman, vol. 4, p. 371; Rădulescu, p. 88.

197. Fl. Dragna, "Momente din activitatea desfăşurată la sate de militanţii aripii revoluţionare a mişcării muncitoreşti în frunte cu grupurile comuniste 1917–1921," *Studii şi materiale de istorie contemporană* (Bucharest, 1962), vol. 2, pp. 28–30; *Istoriia 1918–1970,* p. 69; *Classe operaia,* pp. 132–133.

198. Muşat and Ardeleanu, pp. 220–225, 284; V. Liveanu, "Data privind pregătirea şi desfăşurarea Congresului I al Partidului comunist din Ro-

mînia," *Studii şi materiale,* p. 137n2, and p. 172; Roberts, p. 94n2; *Kommunisticheskii internatsional,* year 2, no. 16, 3811, 3818.

199. Documente, pp. 246–247; 258–262; Muşat and Ardeleanu, pp. 283–284; Marghiloman, vol. 4, p. 407.

200. Documente, pp. 305–308.

201. Liveanu, "Date," p. 130n1; Goldberger, p. 88; *Istoriia 1918–1970,* p. 65. The party membership in the *Regat* was supposedly 45,000, in Transylvania 80,000, and in Bukovina 15,000. Some current Romanian writers even claim 160,000 party members and up to 300,000 union members. There are indications that all these figures may be grossly inflated. *Bol'shaia Sovetskaia Entsiklopediia* (first edition), vol. 49 (1941), 572, gives union membership in 1920 as 90,000, organized in 156 locals. If we assume that nearly every union member was also a party member, total party membership might then have been also about 90,000.

202. Documente, p. 399.

203. *Politics and,* p. 253; *Kommunisticheskii internatsional,* year 2, no. 13 (28 Sept. 1920), 2563. Muşat and Ardeleanu (pp. 286–288) wrongly give 21 seats in the Chamber and one in the Senate. In addition, Bujor was elected, while under sentence, to a seat from Galaţi, but could not fill it, since the government refused to liberate him.

204. *Documente,* pp. 348–349, 403–404; Ch. Rakovsky, "Kommunisticheskoe dvizhenie v Rumynii," *Kommunisticheskii internatsional,* year 2, no. 13 (28 Sept. 1920), 2563.

205. *Documente,* p. 394; Parkhomchuk, p. 237.

206. V. Kolarov, "Kommunisticheskaia partiia i politicheskoe polozhenie v Bolgarii," *Kommunisticheskii internatsional,* year 3, no. 17 (July 1921), 4337–4348.

207. Muşat and Ardeleanu, pp. 284–285; Goldberger, p. 85; *Istoriia 1918–1970,* p. 56.

208. Goldberger, p. 86, *Documente,* pp. 325–326.

209. *Istoriia 1918–1970,* pp. 65–66; Goldberger, pp. 94–150; Parkhomchuk, pp. 203–212; Rădulescu, pp. 98–103.

210. Alexiano et al, p. 283; *Greva generală din Romînia 1920* (Bucharest, 1960), pp. 108, 134–135; Constantinescu, pp. 140–141.

211. Alexiano, pp. 291–292.

212. Ibid., pp. 305–306.

213. *Documente,* p. 400.

214. Rakovsky, "Kommunisticheskoe," 2565–2566; *Greva,* p. 126.

215. *Bulletin,* no. 27 (21 Aug. 1920), p. 2; *Kommunisticheskii internatsional,* year 2, no. 16, 3814–3815 and 3819–3820.

216. *Documente,* pp. 451, 452–454; "Pis'mo iz Rumynii," *Kommunisticheskii internatsional,* year 2, no. 14 (6 Nov. 1920), 2881–2884.

217. *Documente,* pp. 473–488; *Greva,* p. 135; Liveanu, "Date," pp. 135–136.

218. Cristescu and Popovici represented the Executive Committee of the *Regat.* Flueraş and Rozvany, the Executive Committee of the Transylvanian party, Dobrogeanu-Gherea, the trade unions, and Fabian, the youth movement. Flueraş was a right-wing socialist, Cristescu and Popovici were centrists,

Alexander Dobrogeanu-Gherea and Fabian were leftists, and Rozvany inclined that way.

219. Cruceanu and Tănăsescu, pp. 48–51; Muşat and Ardeleanu, p. 289; Liveanu, "Date," pp. 136–137.

220. *Documente*, pp. 701–703, 712–713; Cruceanu and Tănăsescu, pp. 49–50.

221. *Documente*, p. 702; Liveanu, "Date," p. 137.

222. Zinoviev, "Chlenam Rumynskoi kommunisticheskoi partii i vsem soznatel'-nym rabochym," *Kommunisticheskii internatsional,* year 2, no. 16 (31 March 1921), 3807–3816.

223. "Pis'mo Ispolkoma," ibid., 3815–3820. It is interesting to observe that the Comintern was still sufficiently tolerant at this time to publish this defiant document in its official organ.

224. Liveanu, "Date," p. 137. The declaration was allegedly signed on 5 December, whereas Cristescu and Popovici's answer to Zinoviev is dated 10 December. It may be questioned whether they would have written the latter if they had assented to the former. However, the dates of the various events in Moscow are confused, and the sources not entirely dependable. Rozvany was the mover of a resolution, at the party congress in May 1921, admitting all past party errors as required by the Comintern; thus it is probable that he would have signed the declaration along with Gherea and Fabian.

225. *Documente*, pp. 456–463, 466–473, 500–502.

226. *Istoriia 1918–1970*, p. 71; Goldberger, pp. 156–157; Liveanu, "Date," p. 138.

227. *Documente*, pp. 509–529; Goldberger, pp. 158–170.

228. Constantinescu, p. 145; Goldberger, p. 351.

229. Ibid.; *Istoriia 1918–1970*, p. 72; T. Georgescu, *Progress and Revolution in the Traditions of the Romanian People* (Bucharest, 1971), pp. 55–58; Goldberger, pp. 351–356; Rădulescu, p. 109.

230. Marghiloman, vol. 5, p. 99; V. Spiru, *Aus den Totenhäusern Grossrumäniens* (Berlin, 1926), p. 20.

231. *Documente*, pp. 530–541; Goldberger, pp. 361–416; *Istoriia 1918–1970*, pp. 73–74; Parkhomchuk, pp. 217–230; Marghiloman, vol. 5, pp. 87–88; *Bulletin*, no. 30 (12 Feb. 1921), p. 10; *The Times*, 25 Oct. 1920, p. 9, and 9 Nov. 1920, p. 11; *The New York Times*, 26 Oct. 1920, p. 21, and 12 Dec. 1920, II, p. 9.

232. *Bol'shaia sovetskaia entsiklopediia* (1st ed.), vol. 49, 572. *Politics and,* p. 253, states that union membership in Transylvania and Banat fell from 92,000 to 28,000; since the unions there remained about twice as strong as in the *Regat,* this would give about 42,000 organized workers nationwide.

233. Munteanu and Ioniţă, pp. 28, 42.

234. *Documente*, pp. 542–543; Goldberger, pp. 429–430.

235. *Forţa creatoare*, p. 73; Georgescu, p. 62.

236. *Istoriia 1918–1970*, pp. 75–76; *Forţa creatoare*, p. 70; Georgescu, pp. 59–60; Rădulescu, p. 116. The directives are given in *Documente*, pp. 546–556. There were, at this time, allegedly 50 Communist groups in Romania.

237. *Pod znamenem*, pp. 97–98. *Istoriia 1918–1970*, (p. 76) states erroneously that Constantinescu became the secretary; Constantinescu was in jail at this time.

Since Bădulescu-Moscovici was not hitherto prominent in the movement, and there were more notable personalities available, it may be concluded that he was Moscow's choice; the more so since the next year he was in Moscow as a member of ECCI.

238. *Documente*, pp. 536–538, 557–560.

239. Liveanu, "Date," p. 145 and n. 1.

240. At the beginning of December, Constantinescu with a group of Communist activists escaped from Jilava prison. The police pressure was, however, too great to allow him to remain in the country. He fled to Bulgaria, from there to Russia. Marghiloman, vol. 5, pp. 95–98.

241. *Documente*, pp. 564–571; Liveanu, "Date," pp. 148–152; Georgescu, pp. 64–66; *Forţa creatoare*, pp. 74–75; *Bulletin*, no. 31 (12 April 1921), p. 11; *The Times*, 15 Feb. 1921, p. 9.

242. Liveanu, "Date," pp. 153–154; M. C. Stănescu, *Mişcarea muncitorească din România în anii 1921–1924* (Bucharest, 1971), p. 67. The members of the committee were Grigorovici, Jumanca, Dunareanu, Voinea, and I. Mayer.

243. *Documente*, pp. 571–576.

244. Liveanu, "Date," p. 151; *Istoriia 1918–1970*, pp. 77–78.

245. *Documente*, pp. 576–582, 589–591; Liveanu, "Date," p. 161.

246. *Documente*, pp. 586–588; Liveanu, "Date," pp. 155–156; Georgescu, pp. 69–70.

247. Cristescu, Dobrogeanu-Gherea, Dumitru Stoiculescu, Kosta Stoev, Ev. Stanev, and Boris Ştefanov. The last three were Bulgarians from the Dobruja. Gheorghe Tănase joined the Communists later.

248. *Documente*, pp. 597–598; Liveanu, "Date," p. 155.

249. Georgescu, p. 70; Stănescu, p. 65.

250. Liveanu, "Date," pp. 157–158; Parkhomchuk, p. 249; *Istoriia MSSR*, vol. 2, p. 255; *Forţa creatoare*, pp. 79–80; *Istoriia 1918–1970*, p. 78.

251. Liveanu, "Date," pp. 162, 165; Stănescu, p. 42; *Istoriia 1918–1970*, p. 78; *Documente*, pp. 602–603.

252. *Documente*, pp. 617–621.

253. Rădulescu, pp. 141–142; Liveanu, "Date," pp. 162–163. "Mandates" were votes allocated to the various sections on the basis of size of membership. Communist mandates were those committed to unconditional affiliation with the Third International. Centrist mandates were committed to affiliation with reservations ("Unitarians") or uncommitted. The actual number of delegates was far smaller, since each one exercised a large number of mandates; of the 62 delegates present at the congress, 57 ultimately voted Communist, and 5, centrist. Of the 27 sections, eight were in Transylvania, two in the Banat, one in Dobruja, the rest in the *Regat*. It is claimed that they represented 45,000 workers (*Documente*, p. 681; Rădulescu, p. 142). This may have been so before the general strike, but is certainly an exaggeration in May 1921; the actual number then had probably fallen at least by half. This was pointed out at the congress (*Documente*, p. 682).

254. *Documente*, pp. 680–733; Liveanu, "Date," pp. 163–192; Rădulescu, pp. 141–149; Cruceanu and Tănăsescu, pp. 56–59.

255. *Documente*, pp. 724–726.

256. *The New York Times,* 16 May 1921, p. 17; *Bulletin,* no. 33 (21 June 1921), p. 8; Liveanu, "Date," pp. 192–193; Rădulescu, p. 149; Stănescu, pp. 36–37, 40–41.

257. *Documente,* pp. 656–675.

258. V. Kolarov, "Foreword," in Hr. Kabakchiev et al, *Kommunisticheskie partii Balkanskih stran* (Moscow, 1930), pp. 13–14, 21–23.

259. *Documente,* pp. 675–680.

260. Stănescu, p. 52; Rădulescu, p. 155; Dembo, p. 132.

261. Rădulescu, pp. 155–157; Stănescu, pp. 52–53; *Documente din istoria partidului comunist şi a mişcării muncitoreşti revoluţionare din România (mai 1921–august 1924)* (Bucharest, 1970), pp. 30–32.

262. Stănescu, pp. 52–54.

263. Rădulescu, pp. 157, 170–171.

264. Ionescu, pp. 19, 355.

265. Ibid., p. 355; Stănescu, pp. 54–55.

266. *Documente (1921–1924),* pp. 85–87, 89–91; Stănescu, pp. 54–55.

267. Stănescu, pp. 54, 58. It did, however, cause indignation among the Communist leaders in prison since the party congress (Ionescu, p. 355). In January 1922, a Romanian delegation took part in the conference of the Balkan Communist Federation in Vienna.

268. *Documente (1921–1924),* pp. 73–77; Stănescu, pp. 65–66; Georgescu, p. 81.

269. *Istoriia MSSR,* pp. 249–250; *Pod znamenem,* p. 158.

270. Ibid., p. 98.

271. Ibid., pp. 147, 159; *Istoriia MSSR,* p. 252.

272. *Istoriia MSSR,* pp. 252, 259–261.

273. Ibid., pp. 250, 259–260.

274. A. Bădulescu, "Le reveil syndical," *Bulletin communiste,* vol. 4, no. 6 (8 Feb. 1923), p. 90.

275. *The New York Times,* 7 Aug. 1921, II, p. 3; *Bulletin,* no. 34 (3 Aug. 1921), pp. 9–10; Stănescu, pp. 68–73; *Politics and,* p. 254. The 83 delegates claimed to represent 43,000 organized workers, which is certainly exaggerated.

276. Stănescu, pp. 56–57; Giurescu, p. 278.

277. Liveanu, "Date," p. 56.

278. *Documente (1921–1924),* pp. 19–22; Stănescu, pp. 73–75.

279. *Documente (1921–1924),* pp. 23–26; Stănescu, pp. 75–78.

280. *Documente (1921–1924),* pp. 40–45.

281. A. Bădulescu, "Trade Union Congress in Rumania," *Inprecorr,* vol. 1, no. 11 (25 Nov. 1921), p. 87; Stănescu, pp. 80–85; *Documente (1921–1924),* pp. 45–73, 78–81. Two-thirds of these workers were in Transylvania and Banat, one-third in the *Regat.*

282. Bădulescu, "Le reveil," pp. 90–91.

283. *Politics and,* p. 256.

284. Manoliou, p. 207. It can be argued that this decline occurred largely because the unions had shrunk so much, because the workers were cowed, and because the Trancu-Iaşi laws gave employers the upper hand.

285. Quoted in R. V. Burks, *The Dynamics of Communism in Eastern Europe* (Princeton, 1961), p. 65.

286. Burks, p. 225.

287. *Documente (1921–1924)*, pp. 87–89; Stănescu, pp. 55, 57–58. Since this campaign began immediately after the establishment of the Provisional Executive Committee, it may be that Pauker was selected by the Comintern specifically to institute a united front policy.

288. Rădescu, pp. 158–174; Cruceanu and Tănăsescu, pp. 63–73; Trotsky and Rakovsky, pp. 141–146.

The Communist Party of Yugoslavia during the Period of Legality, 1919–1921*

IVO BANAC

> [In 1918–1921] the movement of the masses blew over with the vehemence of a torrent of which nothing remained except gullies. . . . As the result of the [Communist] party's very composition (along the completely detached individual provinces, lands, and peoples), in our country the revolutionary wave has assumed the form of a left phrase, declamatory, hysterical, nervous, provocative, unbalanced, in seething agitation, blood boiling, full of affectation.
>
> — Miroslav Krleža (1935)[1]

Basic Determinants of Communist Politics in Yugoslavia, 1919–1921

The Communist movement has changed considerably since Lenin's time, and it is therefore not surprising that the party that has dominated Yugoslavia since 1945 is rather different from the organization founded in Belgrade in 1919.[2] Indeed, the conduct of the Communist Party of Yugoslavia during the past four decades owes more to certain acquired and transformed organizational strictures of the thirties and to the political-ideological style of Tito's circle than to the inspiration of the heterogeneous little group that banded together at Slavija Square in Belgrade on Easter Sunday 1919.

The history of indigenous communism during the so-called period of legality — the first two years of the Yugoslav state — is one of great strides and sharp reversals.[3] The Unification Congress of the *Komunistička partija Jugoslavije* (Communist Party of Yugoslavia, KPJ) —or *Socijalistička radnička partija Jugoslavije (komunista)* (Socialist Workers' Party of Yugoslavia [Communist], SRPJ [k]), as the party was called until June 1920 — marked the end of the first phase in the consolidation of the Comintern's South Slav section. Despite its considerable successes, the KPJ was not destined to become a compact entity during its two years of legality. As a result of being forced underground in 1921, the party was decimated. In the next decade and a half, though it increasingly bent to the requirements of Moscow, it was at the same time weakened internally by factionalism. Thus it became saddled with the ballast of "Russism" (less of a discredit in Yugoslavia than in the other East European countries), but, until Tito's advent in 1937, it had little of the discipline of the Moscow central party.

Yugoslavia's Marxist historians and latter-day party theoreticians have viewed the KPJ's period of legality as a time of missed opportunities, attributable to a variety of factors. The KPJ was supposedly burdened with the outdated formulas of social democracy, especially the Austro-Marxism found in Croatia and Slovenia. The party line discouraged the disaffected non-Serbian nations and the peasantry, the KPJ's "natural allies." The party never struck a "correct" balance between legal and illegal work. Its leaders had illusions about their ability to ride the tiger of "bourgeois parliamentarianism." They actually believed that the government would permit them to enjoy electoral gains. In short, they made strategy out of a tactic, while failing to develop any insurrectionary or underground apparatus. Their "cadre policy" was practically nonexistent, since they preferred numbers to quality. Clamorous and provocative, they needlessly taunted the ruling classes (as well as potential allies) with inflammatory verbiage. This imprudent behavior left them open to attack from the authorities, and when it came they were shown to be defenseless, naive, and without allies.

To a degree, all these criticisms are justified and constitute a fair summary of the KPJ's course in 1919–1921. Yet it is difficult to imagine how Yugoslavia's Communists could have overcome all these failings if similar tasks eluded their much more skillful comrades in, for example, Germany, a defeated country with a numerically significant and sophisticated working class, which was in addition nationally homogeneous.

The various challenges to the legitimacy of the new Yugoslav kingdom did not necessarily make revolutionary initiatives any easier there than elsewhere; indeed, it is more likely that these challenges complicated the task of the revolutionary left. A predominantly agrarian country, the eastern regions of which had been thoroughly devastated during the war, Yugoslavia was burdened with a seemingly insoluable national problem. The 1918 unification had not come about as the result of a democratic agreement between the freely elected representatives of the country's constituent nations but had been more in the nature of an obeisance. It was a recognition by largely unrepresentative political groups of the fact of the Serbian military occupation of the formerly Austro-Hungarian territories and Montenegro; similarly, of certain powerful ideological currents, most notably that of integral Yugoslavist unitarism based on the ideology of *narodno jedinstvo* (national oneness or unity), whereby the Serbs, Croats, and Slovenes were taken to be three "tribes" of one single "Yugoslav nation" rather than settled and separate national individualities; and also of specific external and internal menaces including Italian irredentism and widespread rural violence, the latter viewed by many as "Bolshevik inspired."

Whereas the proponents of unitarism, notably the newly formed *Demokratska stranka* (Democratic Party, DS), especially its radical wing led by Svetozar Pribićević, were eager to use the centralized state as a means for obliterating all historically derived differences among the Serbs, Croats, and Slovenes, the majority of purely Serbian parties, best represented by the *Narodna radikalna stranka* (National Radical Party, NRS) of Nikola Pašić and Stojan Protić, were counting on centralism to further the hegemony of the Serb nation. Their strength lay in two already established Serbian institutions: the monarchy, headed all but formally by the Prince Regent, Aleksandar Karadjordjević, and the military. In the cabinets and the highest representative bodies (including some appointive legislatures), the centralists combined numerical power and political horse trading to maintain their dominance. In other words, the country was run more or less like an expanded prewar Serbia, a situation not without precedent in the history of the modern Serbian state.

From the very beginning of the new Yugoslavia, then, the Serbian hegemonists were in basic disagreement with the non-Serb national movements, which were committed to pluralistic state institutions consistent with Yugoslavia's multinational characer. Of these national movements, the Croat peasant movement of Stjepan Radić was the most significant, though not the most militant. Radić's *Hrvatska republikanska seljačka stranka* (Croat Republic Peasant Party, HRSS) was rapidly expanding its base through republican and (con)federalist agitation. Though in fact inseparable from the overall social conditions, the national question emerged predominate among all the other seemingly distinct political, economic, and social problems.

For a number of reasons, the founders of the KPJ did not regard the struggle against centralism as a cause they could support, much less as one they could lead. They objected to the government's high-handed attacks on the non-Serb national movements, but they considered themselves to be clearly distinct from the nationally disaffected — and clearly distinct, too, from the peasantry, from the anarchistic rural jacqueries, and from the primitive rebelliousness of the *zeleni kader* (Green Cadres), whose protagonists in some cases hardly concealed their identification (however idiosyncratic) with revolutionary Russia.[4] The distinctions were not always clear-cut or self-evident, but the official Communist movement of its own choosing developed separately from the spontaneous popular outbursts.

Whether or not the Communists could have remained legal by allying themselves with the national and peasant movements is highly debatable: it could be argued that the likelihood of an interdict would have been all the greater had the Communists espoused a different policy on the national question. It is clear, however, that the KPJ did not take advantage of the considerable revolutionary optimism that the October Revolution engendered among the South Slavs.

Even before the collapse of Austria-Hungary the Russian example inspired a series of military mutinies, culminating in the Boka Kotorska rebellion of the Austro-Hungarian fleet in February 1918.[5] During the course of wartime hostilities, approximately two hundred thousand Croat, Slovene, and Serb soldiers fighting in Austro-Hungarian units were captured by the Russians on the Eastern front. More than twenty thousand of these prisoners-of-war fought in the ranks of the Red Army after October 1917 — an impressive figure, since the total number of the Red Army's foreign troops was only a little more than 50 thousand.[6] Many Croat, Slovene, and Serb repatriates also fought in the defense of the 1919 Soviet Republic in neighboring Hungary.[7] Most of these veterans of Red units from Russia and Hungary returned to newly established Yugoslavia as Communist adherents or sympathizers. (A southern Slav section of the Bolshevik party, which also included the Bulgarians, was formed in Russia in April 1918).[8] Their influence strengthened the local "torrent of the masses" and contributed to the already pronounced radicalization of Yugoslavia's politics, a precondition for differentiation in the ranks of the existing social-democratic groups and for initiatives to create a united Communist party.

From Social Democracy to Communism: The Gestation of the KPJ

Before unification, the area subsequently encompassed by Yugoslavia had been the domain of three sovereign states, one of which (Austria-Hungary) included numerous internal subdivisions, some at least partially autonomous. Complex territorial makeup was an obstacle to the organizational unity of socialist groups and explains their numerousness. Depending on the count, six or more South Slav social-democratic organizations operated before 1914. Of these, the four most important were (in chronological order of founding): the *Socijaldemokratska stranka Hrvatske i Slavonije* (Social Democratic Party of Croatia and Slavonia, SDSHS), founded in 1894; the *Jugoslovanska socialnodemokratična stranka* (South Slav Social Democratic Party, JSDS), founded in 1896, essentially a Slovene socialist party with branches among the Croats in Istria and Dalmatia; the *Srpska socijaldemokratska partija* (Serbian Social Democratic Party, SSDP), founded in 1903; and the *Socijaldemokratska stranka Bosne i Hercegovine* (Social Democratic Party of Bosnia and Hercegovina, SDSBH), founded in 1909.[9] The unification of these groups would have been difficult even under conditions of full ideological unanimity. As it happened, socialist organizations among the South Slavs took shape under diverse influences and developed distinct traditions.

The Croatia-Slavonia (SDSHS) and South Slav (JSDS) parties were essentially reformist parties, mostly concerned with trade union questions. They were established by and were primarily led by the most articulate and politicized of the working class. They attracted few intellectuals, and this lack was reflected in their neglect of theory and their generally pragmatic approach. In Serbia, the situation was exactly the opposite. Because of Serbia's slower pace of industrialization, socialism developed there independently of the trade union movement and was largely the handiwork of left-wing intellectuals and the student youth. Not surprisingly, the SSDP was considerably more doctrinaire than the JSDS and SDSHS, and was much preoccupied with the "purity" of theory and the independence of the socialist movement.

The Serbian socialists had a different attitude, too, on the national and agrarian questions. Whereas the SDSHS and the JSDS broke away from the Austro-Marxist strictures against reducing the national question to the struggle for "cultural-national autonomy," and eventually came to espouse an integralist-unitarist Yugoslavism (and after 1917 the establishment of an integral Yugoslav state), the Serbian socialists steadfastly shunned national preoccupations as activities that properly belonged to the sphere of purely bourgeois concerns.[10] To a great extent, the Serbian socialists' lack of interest in the national question was due to the fact that Serbia, before 1913, was a nationally homogeneous state. It is less easy to explain why they were so determined not to bring the peasants into the socialist masses.[11] It may be noted, however, that in Croatia-Slavonia, where latifundian landholding dominated the most fertile agricultural areas, no "higher" doctrinal imperatives could induce an aloof attitude toward the peasantry. But after the SDSHS

attempts to organize in the countryside met with determined governmental restrictions, the entire effort had to be abandoned in exchange
for unencumbered agitation in the cities.[12] It should be noted, too, that
the Bosnian socialist party had much the same attitude as the Serbian
socialists toward mobilization of the peasants. On the national question,
although they echoed the views of the Austro-Marxists, temperamen-
tally they were closer to the SSDP, in believing that the problem should
not be part of socialist concerns.[13]

The First World War brought South Slav social democracy to a
standstill. Except in Bosnia-Hercegovina, where it barely subsisted, the
movement was proscribed among the Dual Monarchy's South Slavs. In
Serbia, it suffered the fate of all the other political parties, although
some SSDP members may have joined Bulgarian socialist organizations
in Bulgarian occupied parts of Serbia.[14] Similarly, as much as circumstances permitted, Serbian Social Democrats continued their organized
work in emigration, especially in France.[15] The socialist movement
began to recover only after the 1917 February Revolution in Russia and
with the beginning of appeals for an international socialist conference.
Hoping to defend the monarchy's territorial integrity, the Austro-
Hungarian authorities sought to utilize the abortive Stockholm gathering by permitting the revival of South Slav socialist and unionist activities.

A multitude of internal differences hampered the socialist revival,
and these tensions were exacerbated by the Bolshevik seizure of power
in Russia. For in addition to the long-standing ideological differences
among the sundry South Slav socialist parties, their memberships were
increasingly preoccupied with the question of which attitude to take on
the Bolshevik venture. The parties in Serbia and Bosnia-Hercegovina
were at least formally pro-Bolshevik, but the divisions in the ranks of
the SDSHS and the JSDS assumed contours typical of the collision
between the left and right currents throughout the European socialist
movement.[16]

A differentiation in the ranks of the SDSHS was hastened by the
leadership's hostility to bolshevism and any revolutionary initiatives.[17]
Croatia's veteran socialist Vitomir Korać (1877–1941) best represented
the attitudes of the party's old guard — the right wing that then dominated the party. He believed that the goal of social reform could be
achieved through strictly legal means, which included prodding the
liberal bourgeoisie into a course of social reform. The right welcomed
the dissolution of Austria-Hungary and participated in the local administrative bodies (including the *Narodno vijeće* or National Council)
which functioned during the brief interlude before the unification with

Serbia and Montenegro. This cooperation brought some immediate improvements in labor legislation, the only really tangible results of Korać's strategy. In line with the SDSHS's adherence to the concept of *narodno jedinstvo,* Korać welcomed the creation of Yugoslavia, and became a minister in the first post-unification cabinet, headed by Stojan Protić.

The right's "ministerialism" was a necessary result of a strategy for which the SDSHS's left had nothing but scorn. Committed to a course that in principle, at least, did not shy from insurrection, and disdainful of any cooperation with the bourgeoisie, the left instinctively welcomed the October Revolution as a signal for socialist initiatives of their own, although it was hardly in a position to grasp any but the most rudimentary implications of Bolshevik strategy. Philo-Bolshevik elements in the SDSHS were particularly active among the Zagreb socialist youth. A circle of leftist intellectuals, among whom Djuro Cvijić (1896–1937?), August Cesarec (1893–1941), and Miroslav Krleža (1893–1981) exercised decisive influence, stimulated actions for a determined break with the SDSHS leadership.[18] Their efforts forced the socialist movement in Croatia, which according to Korać, was "neither spiritually nor organizationally unified," to decide whether to continue with its old strategy or to cultivate the Bolshevik example.[19]

The trickle of organized Communists returning from Russia aggravated the disagreements within the SDSHS. According to one source, "a total of 114 emissaries, i.e., only a fifth (20.86 percent) of all party-organized Yugoslav cadres in Soviet Russia," returned to Yugoslavia by 20 December 1918 (amounting at most to only one percent of all repatriates, since even the Red Army veterans usually were not Bolshevik cadres).[20] This was a vigorous minority, however. Among them were members of the South Slav Communist leaderships in Russia, such as Vladimir Ćopić (1891–1939), Nikola Kovačević (b. 1890), Lazar Vukićević (1887–1941), and Nikola Grulović (1888–1959). After their return to Zagreb in early December 1918, Ćopić and Kovačević were instrumental in creating an underground Communist network in Croatia-Slavonia and Bosnia.[21] Vukićević and Grulović, who like most organized returnees settled upon Vojvodina as a base, initiated the so-called Pelagić alliance of Communists in early March 1919 soon after they came to Novi Sad.[22] All the activist returnees advocated unconditional adherence to Bolshevik positions, a break with social democracy, and the building of illegal Communist organizations.

The activities of the repatriates complemented the somewhat less militant, though no less pro-Bolshevik, stance of the SSDP and SDSBH. A few of the leaders of these parties were quite as radical as the returnees. Some, most notably Filip Filipović (1878–1937), a leading Serbian socialist who since 1912 had been the secretary of the Serbian Workers' Chamber, participated in the work of the underground Communist network.[23] Filipović is believed to have been the first South Slav social democrat to advocate bolshevism in the public press.[24] In addition to his action, as early as 25 December 1918, the SSDP called on all of Yugoslavia's social-democratic groups to start the preliminary work for the establishment of a statewide party dedicated to class struggle.[25] Only the SDSBH accepted this call. The chief obstacle to the unification remained Korać's sway in Croatia-Slavonia and the complex situation within the JSDS.

Contending factions in Croat social democracy clashed at the SDSHS conference, held in Zagreb on 26–28 January 1919. On the eve of the gathering, Filipović spoke in Zagreb calling for the dictatorship of the proletariat in the form of "Soviet power" and for the unification of "workers' Yugoslavia" on the principles of the Third International.[26] The left was divided between those who favored a determined break with Korać and those who still hoped for a compromise, and that division allowed the right's resolution, which approved Korać's strategy and indirectly condemned bolshevism, to win with 54 ballots against the opposition's 39.[27] Some 64 delegates were not even present to vote.[28] Since the right was favored in the election for party leadership, the left decided not to participate in the final vote and withdrew its candidates.[29]

The right's victory proved to be a pyrrhic one, however. Shortly before the SDSHS conference the left had succeeded in gaining the support of the most important trade unions, and now, with party control in the hands of the right, it pressed for a split.[30] After the conference the left leaders held a secret meeting attended by the delegates of the Serbian and the Bosnian-Hercegovinian socialist parties, who had been observers at the SDSHS conference. The leftist gathering elected a unified leadership, known as *Akcioni odbor ujedinjene opozicije* (Action Committee of the United Opposition, AO).[31] The break in the SDSHS was final. The AO directed the SSDP to organize a congress of all Yugoslav socialist parties and groups that supported a revolutionary program and tactics.[32] It also managed to get the support of the Zagreb political organization of the SDSHS at its annual meeting in March 1919, to which the official leadership of the SDSHS responded by formally excluding the "Bolsheviks" from the party on 22 March.[33]

Unlike the SDSHS, the Slovene JSDS emerged from the war remarkably unified.[34] Ideological disagreements in its ranks were not considered a sufficient cause for factionalism. The Slovene socialists were, however, divided over political priorities. In view of the precarious position of the numerically weak Slovenes, most members were in favor of cooperating with the other Slovene parties and postponing the struggle for socialism for a more propitious time after the unification of all the South Slav lands. Acting on these majority opinions, the JSDS leaders Anton Kristan (1881–1930) and Albin Prepeluh (1881–1937) entered the postunification Slovene regional government. (The former ultimately became a minister in Ljuba Davidović's cabinet of August 1919.) The minority of the JSDS, best represented by Dr. Henrik Tuma (1858–1935), was opposed to "national concentrations" and favored a Danubian confederation based on socialist industrial cooperatives rather than on ventures founded on ethnic kinship. To Tuma, class struggle was paramount, and only after it had been waged successfully would the Slovenes become nationally emancipated. Surprisingly, both sides expressed sympathy for the Bolsheviks, although the majority was not yet prepared to join in creating a statewide party based on a Leninist program.

The attitude of the JSDS invoked condemnation from pro-Bolshevik forces elsewhere in Yugoslavia. Despite all of A. Kristan's efforts to reach a compromise with the widest spectrum of socialist forces outside Slovenia, he could not evade the charges of "ministerialism" coming from the Communist left, nor the mistrust of Korać and the other rightists.[35] One more year would pass before a Communist opposition emerged within the JSDS.[36] In the meantime, the JSDS took no part in the movement for the unification of Yugoslavia's pro-Bolshevik socialists.

The Congress of Unification

After the authorities thwarted an attempt to hold the Unification Congress in Slavonski Brod, the pro-Bolshevik socialists, led by the Serbian and Bosnian-Hercegovinian parties, finally gathered in Belgrade on 20–23 April 1919 for the declared purpose of organizing a Communist workers' party.[37] The official SDSHS was excluded from the preparations for the congress, and the Slovene socialists chose not to send a delegation. In addition to the Serbian and the Bosnian-Hercegovinian parties, the gathering was attended by the representatives of Croatia-Slavonia's socialist left and leftist groups from Dalmatia and Vojvodina, bringing the total number of delegates to 432.[38]

The creation of the SRPJ(k), effected at the Unification Congress, was based on a set of principles largely derived from the program and statutes of the SSDP, which in turn were based on the 1891 Erfurt Program of German social democracy. In spite of the gathering's condemnation of the Second International and the "ministerialist" strategy, as well as the new party's decision to join the Comintern, the SRPJ(k) was essentially wedded to certain "orthodox" — but not quite Bolshevik — traditions of the old Serbian social democracy.

That the principal direction of the congress amounted to a compromise between the centrist and the Communist left can be deduced from the difficulties in arriving at a name for the party. The adjective "Communist" was tacked on in parentheses, almost as an afterthought, but only at the insistence of the pro-Bolshevik elements, who also encountered difficulties in obtaining the majority's unreserved adherence to the Comintern. Neither the center nor the left of the new party recognized the significance of the national and the agrarian questions, and there were many problems still to be solved, but at least a united Communist party had finally been established in Yugoslavia.[39] This act, as well as the unification of the pro-Communist trade unions[40] and the creation of *Savez komunističke omladine Jugoslavije* (League of the Communist Youth of Yugoslavia, SKOJ),[41] laid the foundations of a movement that would ultimately find its way to power.

The precarious compromise that characterized the party's line was also reflected in the composition of the leadership, for in addition to the leftists, represented by the SRPJ(k)'s first secretary, Filip Filipović, the Central Party Council included the men of the center, who only formally tolerated the leftist course of the Unification Congress. The extent of the divisions in the leadership can be gauged from the bitter assessment that several members of the SRPJ(k) liaison center in Vienna expressed in a report to the Comintern in the autumn of 1919. Writing on the role of the Bosnian socialists in preventing divisions before the Unification Congress, the authors of the report noted that "these same comrades, out of love for unity, have coopted comrades Lapčević, Košanin, Radošević, Kaclerović, and others into the Central Party Council [although they] did not want to receive the mandate at the Congress, 'because of its extremism.'"[42]

The report included the prediction that the current leadership "must fall, and that also will happen probably in the shortest time under the influence of the revolutionary disposition of the masses." The leadership did not fall immediately and it was changed only at the Second Congress in 1920, but the twelve months that separated the two congresses were marked by a subsurface confrontation between the left and the center, a matter that did not diminish the growing Communist influence.

Between the Two Congresses

The conflicts within the party during 1919–1920 developed under conditions of Communist militancy and substantial successes in the acquisition of a mass following. At the same time, the civil authorities began their first measures designed to curb the nascent SRPJ(k). Conclusions to be derived from this paradoxical situation were moot, and provided ample arguments for both the center and the left. While the left drew inspiration from the party's rising numerical strength, which according to one internal report (as well as other estimates) amounted to over 50,000 members in late May 1920, the SRPJ(k) center was increasingly disturbed by governmental attacks.[43] Before the 1919 May Day manifestations, over a thousand leading Communists were arrested throughout Yugoslavia, including all members of the Central Party Council.[44] Repression was most intense in Bosnia-Hercegovina, where the SRPJ(k) trade union organizations were disbanded, their offices and newspapers closed, and property confiscated. This interdict was lifted only some six weeks later.[45]

Repressive measures failed to curtail Communist initiatives. A two-day general strike paralyzed the country in late June, and several days after that the army mutinied in Maribor, Slovenia, and Varaždin, Croatia.[46] Although there is no evidence that the SRPJ(k) organized these rebellions, the insurgent soldiers certainly drew inspiration from Communist slogans, and these events were sufficiently serious to cause alarm in the highest government circles. A semblance of composure was restored only after the fall of the Hungarian Council Republic later that summer. This was followed by several intensive drives to put down the Communist activists. In August, the police arrested two of the leading Zagreb Communists, Vladimir Ćopić and Simo Miljuš (1894–1938), as well as several other persons who were denounced by a certain Alfred Diamantstein, an erstwhile emissary of the Kun government who had become an agent provocateur. Diamantstein confessed that he transmitted money and material from Hungary to the Communists in Yugoslavia. The "Diamantstein Affair" soon engulfed some of the top SRPJ(k) leaders, as the authorities attempted to substantiate a perfectly plausible supposition that certain SRPJ(k) leaders were a link in a chain of conspiracy leading from Moscow via Budapest. A large number of the leaders, including Filipović and Sima Marković (1888–1937?), were arrested. Although many of those arrested were released by early 1920 and the trial of Ćopić and Miljuš in April 1920 ended with a verdict of "not guilty," the authorities had at least succeeded in temporarily disrupting SRPJ(k) activities.[47]

Despite these reversals, Communist influence and membership grew steadily, even in the overwhelmingly rural southern provinces of former Serbia, Macedonia, and Kosovo, as well as in equally nonindustrial Montenegro.[48] But the SRPJ(k) was mainly interested in gaining adherents among the urban wage laborers, who, on account of extremely unfavorable economic conditions resulting from wartime dislocations and the slow pace of recovery, had strong incentives to embrace radical political alternatives to the existing social order.[49] The workers' disaffection was being amply demonstrated by the growth of the strike movement, in which Communist cadres played a visible role, and in 1920 their discontent was reflected in a series of Communist electoral successes that caught the authorities by surprise.

In the 1920 municipal elections in Croatia-Slavonia, Dalmatia, and Montenegro, the Communists won a significant portion of the vote, in some towns (Slavonski Brod, Duga Resa, Našice, Virovitica) even pluralities.[50] In Zagreb, the SRPJ(k) gained 7,011 votes (or twenty mandates) out of the total of 17,950 ballots cast.[51] An impressive showing was made in many other towns of Croatia-Slavonia, in Split and a few localities in Hrvatsko Primorje, as well as in Podgorica and Petrovac in Montenegro.[52] In Zagreb, Karlovac, and Slavonski Brod, Communist mayors were elected.[53] The authorities responded by invalidating the ballots in the Zagreb mayoralty race, and also the ballots in all elections in Croatia where the SRPJ(k) won municipal seats.[54] Many elected Communists were arrested.[55]

Rhetorical sallies aside, the Communist response to these administrative attacks was in most instances half-hearted, and this same lack of forcefulness also undercut some of the most spectacular initiatives in the strike movement. In April, a statewide railroad workers' strike that lasted for more than two weeks succeeded in completely shutting down this vital branch of transportation, but the Communists seemingly did not dare to initiate work stoppages in other sections of transportation and communications, though boldness might have been the most effective response to governmental countermeasures.[56] In some cases, restraint was obviously the wisest course considering the severity of the government's actions. The army was sent in to occupy the Trbovlje mines in Slovenia, and in Ljubljana fourteen demonstrators were killed and some seventy wounded during the bloody incident at Zaloška Cesta.[57]

The Vukovar Congress

The failure of the railroad workers' strike and the growing repression against the Communist movement brought the internal SRPJ(k) confrontations to a head. The center was increasingly disassociating itself from the party's reputed adventurism, while the extreme left, notably in the ranks of the SKOJ, started questioning the advisability of the party's electoral tactic.[58] Such factionalism was checked briefly at the SRPJ(k)'s Second Congress by the removal of the center. This congress, held in Vukovar on 20–24 June 1920, and attended by the Slovene pro-Bolshevik socialists (signifying the party's full territorial consolidation), marked the victory of the left.[59]

The leftists succeeded in passing a new program and statutes of the KPJ (as the party was renamed), which anticipated the directives of the Second Comintern Congress to break decisively with the remnants of "reformism" in the Communist movement. The KPJ called for open propagation of the socialist revolution, the dictatorship of the proletariat, and the conversion of Yugoslavia into a Soviet republic within a Balkan-Danubian federation of Soviet republics.[60] The delegates elected a new, exclusively leftist leadership.[61] Despite the sharp turn in the party program, the KPJ still discounted the significance of the national question and it did not adopt any concrete proposals for agitation among the peasants.

The defeated center immediately proceeded to organize against the new course initiated at Vukovar. It objected not only to the initiation of the openly revolutionary line of the KPJ but also — especially the Croat "centrists" — to the decision to undertake a thorough centralization of the party.[62] Centralization had been discussed pro and con, but at Vukovar it was decided with definite swiftness that all existing regional executive committees would be liquidated and replaced with secretariats whose leadership would be appointed by the KPJ's Central Party Council.[63] When the Croat centrists refused to yield the party newspaper, archives, and treasury to the Liquidation Executive Committee, headed by Kamilo Horvatin, they were expelled.[64] Their Serbian and Bosnian-Hercegovinian counterparts, who were more opposed to the new party program than to the centralization, then began agitating for a revision of the policies set in Vukovar. They particularly questioned the reaffirmation of the KPJ's adherence to the Third International and called for an extraordinary party congress. In

November, the "centralists" published a "Manifesto of the KPJ Opposition." The Central Party Council condemned this action on December 10 and expelled all the signatories, including Lapčević, Topalović, Košanin, and others.[65]

Post-Vukovar: Deceptive Advances

It is not clear to what extent the consolidation of the KPJ in a leftist platform and the centralization contributed to the Communists' ability to influence events and broaden their base. All the Comintern sections, including the KPJ, were still far from conforming to the principles of "democratic centralist" cadre policy or "bolshevization" that were imposed within the Communist movement in the late twenties. Nevertheless, for as long as it could operate legally, the KPJ was able not only to retain its considerable (albeit disparate) membership, but actually to make gains.

The results of the municipal elections in Serbia and Macedonia, which took place on 22 August 1920, demonstrated the party's electoral potential. The KPJ succeeded in gaining control of numerous municipalities, particularly in southern Serbia, Kosovo, and Macedonia.[66] To the dismay of the authorities, the KPJ ticket, headed by Filip Filipović, won the election for the Belgrade municipal government. This and numerous other municipal successes were reversed by governmental action. The minister of the interior, Milorad Drašković, made it plain to a protesting delegation of the KPJ leaders that "while monarchy and bourgeois power exist in this country, the Communists cannot hold the capital city's municipality in their hands."[67] Nor was the government happy with the Communist showing at the elections for the Constituent Assembly. The KPJ gained 198,736 votes, or 59 mandates, ranking fourth, after the ruling Democratic and Radical parties and the oppositional Croat Republican Peasant party, in ballots cast.[68] Its parliamentary club was the third largest (after those of the Democrats and the Radicals).

The KPJ's considerable electoral gains do require some comment. If the total number of ballots cast in the elections for the Constituent Assembly is compared with the Communist showing and is distributed according to Yugoslavia's constituent regions, the the following pattern emerges:[69]

Region	Total vote cast	KPJ vote	KPJ vote in relation to total vote (in %)	Regional contribution to the total KPJ vote (in %)
Macedonia, Kosovo, and Sandžak	182,075	49,449	27.16	24.88
Serbia proper	325,380	48,376	14.87	24.34
Croatia-Slavonia	438,799	31,641	7.21	15.92
Bosnia-Hercegovina	330,958	18,074	5.46	9.09
Slovenia	158,265	16,289	10.29	8.20
Vojvodina	93,226	13,955	14.97	7.02
Montenegro	28,612	10,869	37.99	5.47
Dalmatia	49,964	8,074	16.16	4.06

Nationwide, the KPJ polled 12.36 percent of the total vote. If this is taken as the party's average strength, then it is evident that the Communists performed below their own national average in the industrialized regions of the country and did best in the areas with few or no industrial workers.

The KPJ's successes, therefore, cannot be accounted for in terms of the base to which the Communists appealed or in terms of class orientation. In Macedonia and Montenegro, where the KPJ had its most impressive successes, there were no organized national parties that could wage legal struggles against centralism and Serbian hegemonism. The KPJ's successes in these areas were an electoral protest against the regime. As an avowedly revolutionary party, the KPJ was the only outlet for the recusant nationalities in these areas. In the other areas of intense national disaffection, such as Croatia-Slavonia, Slovenia, and Bosnia-Hercegovina, the non-Serbs generally voted for the parties that best represented their national and confessional interests: the Croats for Stjepan Radić's HRSS, the Slovenes for the Slovene People's party, and the Bosnian-Hercegovinian Muslims for the Yugoslav Muslim Organization. Here the KPJ's showing was less impressive. In the more populated Croatia-Slavonia, for example, though the KPJ vote was third in terms of the total KPJ vote nationwide, Radić's party got 52.55 percent of the vote and the KPJ only 7.21 percent.

The Social Democratic opponents of the KPJ henceforth would delight in pointing out that the Communists were not appealing to the working classes but to a patchwork of "motley malcontents."[70] This was certainly not the party's intention. The KPJ still tended to discount the strategic potential of the national question and made no attempts to capitalize on this issue. The Communist leaders were overconfident of their ability to ride the continental red wave, and were not inclined to reexamine their position.

The subsequent events repudiated the stance of the KPJ leadership. The postwar revolutionary wave in Europe had already reached its peak and was visibly receding. The defeat of the Red communes in Germany and Hungary and Soviet reversals in Poland hastened the stabilization of the anti-Communist governments and the social order that they safeguarded. But in Yugoslavia, where peasant insurgency was still seething — as in Croatia in 1920 — the KPJ failed to appreciate the importance of national and peasant movements and lost the opportunity to aid the rebel peasants. The Communist deputies in the Constituent Assembly, who affected a self-assured pose, hardly appreciated the resilience of the regime that they continued to attack with an assortment of rhetorical devices.[71] Nor did the KPJ leadership recognize the extent of the party's isolation, widened by the Communist inability to differentiate between the centralist government and the opposition parties. In the long run, the revolutionary bravado, as yet untested in direct conflict, proved counterproductive and exposed the party to governmental reprisals. By the end of 1920, the KPJ itself had given the government the opportunity for a decisive denouement.

Obznana and Oblivion

The government's determination to curb the Communists once and for all came in December, after a series of Communist-led strikes had shut down a number of mines in Slovenia and Bosnia. The gendarmerie and the army were mobilized against the miners' enclave in the Bosnian village of Husino. During a clash between the miners and the government forces on the night of 27 December, seven miners were killed, and some seven hundred were arrested.[72] This bloody nocturnal clash encouraged the government to muzzle the KPJ, and two nights later (29–30 December), pleading the discovery of a revolutionary plot, it issued a sweeping directive, the so-called *Obznana* (Proclamation), which banned Communist propaganda, prohibited the work of the party organizations, and in addition to numerous other restrictions ordered the seizure of the KPJ offices and newspapers.[73]

Although this decree was no more than a culmination of a series of constraints against the Communists, the KPJ leadership was caught completely by surprise. The party was quite unprepared for any sort of

countermeasure, and it was powerless to resist the systematic implementation of the provisions of the Obznana.[74] And because it was so isolated
from the other parties of the opposition, it had to stand alone in its
extreme distress. Though there were a few scattered protests, they could
hardly blunt the ferocity of the governmental assault. Before the Obznana, the KPJ had had a highly conspicuous apparatus, sustained by
tens of thousands of members and sympathizers. Lulled by its fairly won
successes, it had not bothered to develop any underground organizational apparatus, and therefore once its open organization fell away, or
was destroyed as under the Obznana, the whole party was brought to a
halt. An underground apparatus had to be started and built under
exceedingly difficult circumstances, and meanwhile, faced with the
party's apparent inability to revive its political and trade union
branches, which had been completely decimated, the vast majority of
the KPJ members became disillusioned and demoralized, and lapsed
into inactivity.

While the KPJ leadership was still hoping that the trend initiated by
Obznana could be reversed and that the government could be pressured
to withdraw the proclamation, the government moved to fix it even
more firmly.[75] The passage of the 1921 (Vidovdan) Constitution
(28 June 1921) by the majority in the Constituent Assembly — a vote
that the Communist deputies boycotted — strengthened the centralists
and removed the last possibility of lifting the Obznana. Some segments
of the KPJ membership, unreconciled to the leadership's passive reaction to the Obznana, responded with terrorist tactics in hopes of forcing
the government to a reconsideration. On 29 June, Spasoje Stejić, a
Communist house painter, tried to assassinate Regent Aleksandar.[76]
This attempt failed, but on 21 July Alija Alijagić, a member of a
conspiratorial group called *Crvena pravda* (Red Justice), which included
some Communist youths from Zagreb and Bijeljina in Bosnia, succeeded in assassinating the former minister of interior, Drašković.[77]

The results of these terrorist acts were precisely the opposite of what
the perpetrators had envisioned. Governmental reprisal was swift and
harsh. By the end of July the Communist parliamentary club was
dissolved. On 2 August the National Assembly passed a special anti-
communist act, the "Law for the Defense of Public Security and Order
in the State," better known as the "Law for the Defense of the State"
(*Zakon o zaštiti države*, ZZD), which formally banned the KPJ.
Known Communist leaders were arrested as initiators of terrorist actions.

In the aftermath of the ZZD, the KPJ organizations were so weakened that for all intents and purposes they ceased to exist. Many

Communist leaders fled the country; those who did not were arrested. The majority rank and file simply ceased all political activities, though a few joined noncommunist and even anticommunist parties. The Communist movement in Yugoslavia would not become a massive force for a generation. The organizational weakness of the KPJ was best described in this 1924 report to the Comintern:[78]

When the Party was banned it entered illegality, but without *any* real organizations. In organizational regard the Party actually did not exist. The First Conference in July 1922 did not spring up from the organizations; instead, certain comrades were designated as delegates to that conference. The failure of that conference, which was supposed to create organizations for the party and to ready it for work, are well known. In May 1923, the Second Conference was held, whose delegates were chosen from organizations which were created before that. All the decisions of this conference were arrived at unanimously and it can be said that somewhat more serious and more planned work in the Party begins only with this conference.

Today [1924] the Party has a total of 70 organizations [with] 688 members. According to regions:

	Org[anizations].	with	members
Serbia	15	"	124
Macedonia	5	"	68
Montenegro	6	"	40
Dalmatia	5	"	168
Slovenia	10	"	84
Croatia	11	"	99
Bosnia	10	"	64
Vojvodina	8	"	41
Total	70	with	688

If such a balance sheet three years after the ZZD could be considered a partial improvement, one sees the magnitude of the KPJ's organizational weakening. The fact that a remnant of 688 actually represented somewhat less than 2 percent of the KPJ's membership in 1920 speaks for itself: the gullies after a torrent. . . .

The KPJ and Yugoslavia's National Question

The KPJ's recovery was a slow and a painful process. Certainly no real gains were possible until the KPJ undertook a careful examination of the causes and the implications of its demise and scrutinized the inherent weaknesses of its stand on the national question.[79] The energies that the KPJ ultimately consigned to the elucidation of its position on the national question had no parallel in any other Comintern section. Under the circumstances the KPJ's preoccupation with the national question was not in itself extraordinary. What was exceptional was that from 1919 to 1941, as one observer put it, "the KPJ programmatically tested all the viewpoints that are at all possible about Yugoslavia and about the national question in Yugoslavia."[80] And it was equally exceptional that it moved to such an examination after the total lack of awareness of the revolutionary potential of the national question which it had expressed earlier.

In the relatively lengthy documents of the Unification Congress, the national question is alluded to in only one sentence, in which it is noted that the SRPJ(k) favored "a single national state with the widest self-government in the regions, districts, and communes."[81] Again in the documents of the Vukovar Congress, the subject is mentioned only briefly, though the tone is more unitarist: "The KPJ will further remain on the bulwark of the idea of national oneness [*nacionalno jedinstvo*] and equality of all the nationalities in the country."[82] Evidently, the KPJ in 1920 placed no importance on the matter of Yugoslavia's deteriorating national relations. As far as the Communists were concerned, national tensions were a curse of the old regimes, specifically of the Austro-Hungarian monarchy, and they would be eradicated with the creation of the new "national" state of the South Slavs. As one local SRPJ(k) organ in Croatia noted:

> From now on the bourgeoisie in all of its parties will have to conform exclusively to the disposition of the people and its needs here, and not to Vienna or Pest, and that is precisely why we are hoping for the healing of our public conditions. . . . political equality and the enormous needs of the exhausted people will further contribute to this; national phrasemongering will have to yield to economic and social policy, and Social Democracy [Communists] will also look after that.[83]

The roots of Communist unitarism were disparate. It has already been noted that the South Slav Social Democratic parties in Austria-Hungary accepted *narodno jedinstvo* as their programmatic approach to the national question in the period before 1918. Thus the Communsts in the formerly Austro-Hungarian regions were all in favor of Yugoslavism, and the tenor of certain statements made by the party leaders in those areas was completely out of tune with the decisively defeatist line with which the Leninists responded to the Great War.

The Croat "centrist" Bornemissa, for example, spoke glowingly of "our *narodno jedinstvo,* which we won with our blood in arduous and painful struggles,"[84] and no criticism could stir the Communists in Dalmatia as much as the disparagement of their commitment to the unification. Charges of that sort were met with responses to the effect that, "if the national and the class consciousness of our working people were not as developed before and during the war as it is now, the fault cannot be laid on it [the people], but on our intelligentsia which did nothing to arouse its awareness."[85] In their wounded pride, the authors of the same protest made much of the claim that "the Communist party firmly embraced national unification, and if someone opposes that, he will not approach [the SRPJ(k)] but the other [*sic*] separatist parties: the Radicals, *frankovci* [followers of the late Dr. Josip Frank in Croatia], and the like."[86] Not only were such positions indistinguishable from vintage unitarist nationalism, but, in isolated instances, the Communists' devotion to Russia carried a ring of traditional Pan-Slavism. In the years before the fall of tsarism, claimed the Split organ of the SRPJ(k), "Lenin worked incredibly arduously, with the patience that perhaps nobody but a Slav can understand."[87]

The heterodox opinions of Communist militants in Yugoslavia's western regions were to a considerable extent a carry over from the prewar days, when a number of future Communist intellectuals (Cvijić, Horvatin, Cesarec, Klemenčić, etc.) belonged to the revolutionary nationalist youth.[88] At the beginning of their political activity they differed from the other unitarist forces in Croatia and Slovenia in that their Yugoslav integralism was revolutionary and uncompromising. It was, therefore, not accidental that these "left Pribićevićists" evolved toward socialism, and that they found fault with the form, but not with the method, of the 1918 unification.[89] Typical of their perceptions were the opinions expressed by Cesarec in an article published within a week after the unification, but, as Cesarec stressed, "written even before the [December 5th] events on the Jelačić Square."[90] The article highlighted the contradiction between Cesarec's positive appraisal of the unification and his growing dismay at the popular dissent to this act. Cesarec blamed the monarchical form of the unification for the Vendée-like passions of the Croat and Slovene republicans:

> Having examined the interrelations of the republican and the monarchic current in Yugoslavia, we reach crushing conclusions. The more intelligent and the more progressive current, which seeks unitarism, is actually retrogressive when contrasted to Europe, because it seeks to realize its unitarism by means of a monarchy, [whereas] the more conservative and completely reactionary current which seeks a republic, is in reality, from the European standpoint, more progressive in comparison with its adver-

saries. But black and egoistic plots are concealed in it, seeking to realize
their separatist aims via the vehicle of a republic: *and that is what must be
refuted — separatism, and not the republic!*[91]

Consistent in his views, Cesarec called for the voluntary abdica-
tion of King Petar. It was singularly unfortunate, in Cesarec's opinion,
that the national unification had not been brought about by the united
revolt of the people themselves. Had it been so, "the problem of a
monarchy vs. a republic, and even of centralism vs. a federation, would
have been solved in one stroke in favor of a *centralist republic.*"[92]

The concept of *narodno jedinstvo* on which the Communists of the
formerly Austro-Hungarian areas based their unitarism was a concept
that denied the individuality of the indigenous South Slav nations and
instead, as in the case of Svetozar Pribićević and the Democratic
party, insisted on their common nationhood. All the differences among
the nationalities were summed up as mere "tribal" idiosyncracies, which
would disappear in a unified nation in which they no longer had a
historical foundation. The Serbian Communists also adopted the terminology of *narodno jedinstvo,* but their reasons were less ideological —
as Nikola Grulović put it, their unitarism was more a matter of
expediency than of a total commitment to *narodno jedinstvo.*

As will be recalled, Grulović belonged to the Pelagić alliance, a
group largely made up of returnees from Soviet Russia. The Russian
experience implied that the alliance's views on the national question
were influenced by the Bolshevik example. Thus the Pelagićists foresaw no impediments to the promotion of the national individuality of
the Serbs, Croats, and Slovenes, and their demand for a Soviet-style
federalization of Yugoslavia was a logical consequence of these views.
The approach of the SSDP was rather different. A delegation of
Pelagićists — Vukićević, Grulović, and another returnee — which
came to Belgrade on 17 February 1919, to consult with the SSDP's left
on the prospects for the unification of Yugoslavia's pro-Bolshevik
factions soon realized how ambiguous the attitude of its Serbian counterparts was to the national question. According to Grulović:

On the national question, Filip [Filipović] expressed himself in a twofold
way. He said that he is not opposed to the assertion that the Serbs,
Croats, and Slovenes are three peoples, but as far as the Macedonians and
the Montenegrins were concerned he said that they were not nations and
that he is in favor of centralism, just as the majority [in the SSDP] is. All
the rest [of the SSDP participants] also agreed with him and some
furthermore stated that it would be unpopular to recognize the existence
of several nations. Essentially, the standpoint taken was that all the

peoples had accepted *narodno jedinstvo* and that we also must assert the same in our declaration.

After Vukićević accepted that suggestion, we changed our original principled stand about the federative arrangement [of Yugoslavia] and substituted it with centralism.[93]

The attitude of Filipović and his comrades was in perfect accord with the traditions of the SSDP, a party rooted in an independent and — before 1913 — nationally homogenous state. Under Serbian conditions there existed no compelling need for recourse to a supranational Slavic identity, precisely the ideology of *narodno jedinstvo* in the defensive strategy of the unitarist-minded sections of the Croat, Serb, and Slovene opinion in Austria-Hungary. Furthermore, the rigidly orthodox tradition of the SSDP relegated national concerns to the exclusive tutelage of the bourgeoisie. It was part of the SSDP belief that the bourgeoisie had a duty to advance Serbian national interests, while the socialists were to concern themselves with the imperatives of class struggle. Since the victorious bourgeoisie effected *its* 1918 unification under the banner of *narodno jedinstvo,* and since that fact seemed to have been universally accepted, there was no need — and certainly no obligation — on the part of the Serbian militants to challenge the concept of *narodno jedinstvo,* particularly since the socialists from the other regions seemed to be fully committed to it.

There are many indications that the former SSDP's division-of-labor approach (with the bourgeoisie attending to national concerns and the proletariat to class struggle), so typical of the classic two-stage concept of revolution, quickly became the common property of the entire nascent SRPJ(k). In numerous party statements throughout the country, *narodno jedinstvo* was repeatedly referred to as the principal "historical task of the bourgeoisie."[94] Nevertheless, since the realities of centralization and the resistance it provoked increasingly detracted from the nimbus of this presumed mandate, the Communists could claim yet another argument against the regime — that of failing even in an area all its own. The SRPJ(k) Central Party Council's "Manifesto to the Working Class of Yugoslavia," issued in September 1919, was typical of this line of argument: "The general position of the working class in Yugoslavia is all the more difficult and more complicated inasmuch as the bourgeois government is demonstrating unfitness and evasiveness in executing its historical task in regard to national unification."[95]

If the bourgeois regime was incapable of achieving *narodno jedinstvo,* who could come to the rescue? The fiasco of the centralizing measures found the Communist party in the uncomfortable role of being the voluntary retriever of an untenable policy. With a determination that in retrospect defies credence, the Communists made every effort to establish their credit as unflinching champions of unitarism. Since the bourgeoisie had proved that it could not establish *narodno jedinstvo,* the Communist party, claiming that it represented "one of the strong pillars of national unification," took over the task.[96] So infatuated were the Communists with their newly discovered mission that the divisions that had marked the ideological approaches to *narodno jedinstvo* in Yugoslavia's various regions practically disappeared. Thus, the Serbian Communists became as vocal in the defense of this principle as any of their Croat or Slovene counterparts with a more solid unitarist pedigree.[97]

The Communist defense of *narodno jedinstvo* should not be interpreted as an indication that the KPJ as a whole abandoned its original position, which placed the national question among its secondary (really paltry) concerns. On the contrary, the unitarism of the KPJ was different from that of certain non-Communist politicians (Pribićević) inasmuch as the Communist insistence on the common nationhood of the Serbs, Croats, and Slovenes implied that the entire matter ought not arouse any further controversy, and that they should concentrate on the really important social questions. Nor should the party's increasing accusations of the bourgeoisie's "betrayal" of *narodno jedinstvo* be seen as merely a matter of expediency. Here also, the key to the Communist attitude lay in the party's accent on the imminence of sharp class confrontations, and in the conception of the socialist revolution that the KPJ shared with the entire Communist movement in the immediate postwar period, when victory seemed but a step away.

Expectations of the nearness of the revolution were so high in the party's left wing that this assumption actually cut off a systematic analysis of Yugoslavia's national question. The dominant opinion in the Communist rank and file was that since the bourgeoisie had failed to achieve *narodno jedinstvo,* the task would not only fall to the proletariat, but it would in fact become an aspect of Yugoslavia's forthcoming socialist revolution: "Neither federalism nor centralism, nor any other arrangement is in the position to realize *narodno jedinstvo,* or to solve any [other] problem. All of that will remain unsolved and unrealized until the working people take possession of power."[98]

A paradox, which the KPJ never quite resolved, was implicit in this prognostication. *Narodno jedinstvo,* was, after all, a variant of nationalism: specifically, the prototype of South Slav supranationalism. Yet, in Communist perception, it somehow managed to coexist with a different, but no less powerful, strain of decisively Marxist derivation, that is, the concept of internationalist humanity, which, as the liberated entity of the postrevolutionary, genuinely historic epoch, would shed all the elements of the alienation characteristic of class societies, including nationality.[99] Paradoxically, however, although the unitarism of Pribićević contained only extenuated elements of universalism, the KPJ's defense of *narodno jedinstvo* drew much of its inspiration from the universalist/internationalist element of Marxism, which was especially influential during the period under consideration. *Narodno jedinstvo* could not ultimately be reconciled with apocalyptic revolutionary universalism, but it did permit the termination of national pluralism within the KPJ itself, a structural endeavor with far-reaching implications.[100]

The KPJ's unitarism and universalism were not corollaries. The former was rooted in the native soil, whereas the latter was greatly inspired by a dominant strain of Marxism. Yugoslavia's Communist leadership did not yet perceive the implications of the latent tension between these two aspects of the party's national program. With the program of internal centralization, there was no inconsistency. Here, the Comintern's directives perfectly complemented the policy that unitarism also demanded. The Comintern was conceived as a thoroughly centralized international party, with one center and a single global strategy that brooked no local allowances. Although the KPJ's Vukovar statute faithfully reflected all of the Comintern's specifications, it was also an offshoot of Yugoslav national unitarism. The Comintern's monolithic aspirations were thus in perfect harmony with the implications of *narodno jedinstvo*. In the case of the KPJ, both policies prescribed centralism. Analogies between the centralizing measures of the Belgrade cabinets and the centralization of the KPJ thus became inescapable; but whereas such correspondence could only dim the Communist luster among the disaffected South Slav nations, it was not immediately apparent that the centralization of the Communist movement necessarily implied still less desirable trends, foremost among which was the preeminence of the Serbian cadres in the party leadership.

Just as the Comintern came to reflect primarily the interests of one party and of one state, so the rudiments of hegemonism, typical of Yugoslavia's wider national relations, were to a considerable extent reproduced within the KPJ.[101] The next phase of the KPJ's history was dominated by the opening of a debate on the national question, the outcome of which determined the party's altogether different course in the late twenties, including certain inescapable changes in its leadership.

Conclusion

The KPJ's undervaluation of the peasantry was no less persistently wrongheaded than the party's position on the national question.[102] A revolutionary alliance with the country's most numerous stratum was regarded as unlikely, an appraisal perhaps not lacking in insight. As a result, the Communists did not undertake a policy of base building in the countryside. A seeming inability to advance an attractive agrarian program coupled with a campaign of ill-timed broadsides against the emerging peasant parties contributed to the KPJ's nonexistence in the countryside. These self-defeating attitudes were not to be overcome during the period under consideration.[103]

Communist attempts to develop a following among the urban intellectuals, writers, and artists were at best uneven.[104] Nevertheless, the allegiance of such mainstays of intellect as Miroslav Krleža, who would rapidly earn the dominant position in Croat letters (and beyond), became a source of powerful attraction to the student youth, especially in the late twenties and throughout the thirties.[105] At the time, however, this influence was hardly sufficient. The party's downward slide was not about to be reversed.

Conditions in the new Yugoslavia were largely favorable to the rapid growth of the Communist movement. These advantages were considerably diminished by omissions and blunders for which the Communists were themselves to blame. This statement should not, however, be interpreted to mean that the KPJ's fortunes would have been markedly different if all the self-created obstacles could have been avoided. A disciplined party, led by a more reflective and bolder directorate, committed to a far more perceptive political program, would certainly have been more effective. Nevertheless, it is unwarranted to claim that such a party could have organized a successful seizure of power, or even approached that goal.

The KPJ's hour would come under quite different circumstances precisely two decades after its retreat into the underground. By then, the party could bring into play all the experiences and insights accumulated during the intervening twenty years of illegality. More important, by April 1941 those who maintained the interdict over the KPJ for an entire generation would themselves be on the run.

Abbreviations

AO	*Akcioni odbor ujedinjene opozicije* (Action Committee of United Opposition)
CRSVJ	*Centralno radničko sindikalno vijeće Jugoslavije* (Central Workers' Trade Union Council of Yugoslavia)
DS	*Demokratska stranka* (Democratic Party)

HRSS *Hrvatska republikanska seljačka stranka* (Croat Republican Peasant Party)

IHRPH *Institut za historiju radničkog pokreta Hrvatske* (Institute for the History of the Workers' Movement of Croatia)

JSDS *Jugoslavanska socialnodemokratična stranka* (South Slav Social Democratic Party)

KPJ *Komunistička partija Jugoslavije* (Communist Party of Yugoslavia)

NRS *Narodna radikalna stranka* (National Radical Party)

SDSBH *Socijaldemokratska stranka Bosne i Hercegovine* (Social Democratic Party of Bosnia and Hercegovina)

SDSHS *Socijaldemokratska stranka Hrvatske i Slavonije* (Social Democratic Party of Croatia and Slavonia)

SKOJ *Savez komunističke omladine Jugoslavije* (League of the Communist Youth of Yugoslavia)

SRPJ(k) *Socijalistička radnička partija Jugoslavije (komunista)* (Socialist Workers' Party of Yugoslavia [Communist])

SSDP *Srpska socijaldemokratska partija* (Serbian Social Democratic Party)

ZZD *Zakon o zaštiti države* (Law for the Defense of the State)

NOTES

* Research work on portions of this article was done under grants from the International Research and Exchanges Board, the Fulbright-Hays Commission, and Stanford University. The author takes pleasure in acknowledging the generous assistance of these institutions as well as the kind help of the staffs of *Institut za historiju radničkog pokreta Hrvatske* (Institute for the History of the Workers' Movement of Croatia, IHRPH) in Zagreb, *Sveučilišna i nacionalna knjižnica* (University and National Library), also of Zagreb, and of the Hoover Institution and the Stanford University libraries at Stanford University.

1. Miroslav Krleža, *Deset krvavih godina i drugi politički eseji*, 2d. rev. ed. (Zagreb: Zora, 1971), p. 568.

2. The official name of the Yugoslav state during the 1918–1929 period was the Kingdom of Serbs, Croats, and Slovenes. In this article the term "Yugoslavia" will, for the sake of convenience, be used throughout instead of its unwieldy official equivalent.

3. The history of the KPJ has been studied more than that of any other of Yugoslavia's twentieth-century political groups. A staggering body of literature dissecting the party's course has accumulated since 1945, representing the findings of adulators, detractors, and others. The quality of much of this material defiantly challenges the third law of materialist dialectics. Nevertheless, no student of the KPJ can afford to bypass the monumental bibliography of monographic literature (thus, unfortunately, no articles) on the KPJ, its socialist

predecessors, and the workers' movement, published in Yugoslavia in the 1945–1969 period. See Žarko D. Protić, Milan Vesović, and Milan Matić, *Socijalistički i radnički pokret i Komunistička partija Jugoslavije: 1867–1941; Bibliografija posebnih izdanja: 1945–1969* (Belgrade: Institut za savremenu istoriju, 1972). This bibliography lists all the general studies on the KPJ and its activities, both statewide and along the narrower confines of the current republic boundaries, and permits me to forgo bibliographic suggestions, except in certain important cases. Of these, studies that should certainly be mentioned are: Rodoljub Čolaković, Dragoslav Janković, and Pero Morača, eds., *Pregled istorije Saveza komunista Jugoslavije* (Belgrade: Institut za izučavanje radničkog pokreta, 1963); Pero Morača, *Istorija Saveza komunista Jugoslavije: Kratak pregled,* 2d ed. (Belgrade: Rad, 1966); Pero Morača and Dušan Bilandžić, *Avangarda: 1919–1969* (Belgrade: Komunist, 1969). For a chronology of important events in the KPJ history see Marija Sentić, Sofia Sigetlija, and Mijo Potočki, *Kronologija SKJ: 1919–1969* (Zagreb: Stvarnost, 1970). As far as the published sources on the KPJ's history in the twenties are concerned, see especially: *Istorijski arhiv Komunističke partije Jugoslavije, Tom II: Kongresi i zemaljske konferencije KPJ: 1919–1937* [Cyr.] (Belgrade: Istorijsko odeljenje Centralnog komiteta KPJ, 1949); Edib Hasanagić, comp., *Komunistička partija Jugoslavije, 1919–1941: Izabrani dokumenti* (Zagreb: Školska knjiga, 1959). Of the memoir literature see especially: Pero Morača et al, eds., *Četrdeset godina: Zbornik sećanja aktivista jugoslovenskog revolucionarnog radničkog pokreta, Knjiga prva: 1917–1929* (Belgrade: Kultura, 1960); Rodoljub Čolaković, *Kazivanje o jednom pokoljenju,* vol. 1 (Zagreb: Naprijed, 1964). Of the general works on the KPJ published outside Yugoslavia see: Ivan Avakumovic, *History of the Communist Party of Yugoslavia,* vol. 1 (Aberdeen: Aberdeen University Press, 1964); U.S. Congress, Senate, Committee on the Judiciary, *Yugoslav Communism; a Critical Study,* by Charles Zalar, Committee Print (Washington, D.C.: Government Printing Office, 1961). See also Fedor I. Cicak, "The Communist Party of Yugoslavia between 1919–1924: An Analysis of Its Formative Process," Ph.D. dissertation, Indiana University, 1965. Literature on the more specialized aspects of the KPJ activities will be listed separately under the appropriate topics.

4. There are still many questions to be answered about the *zeleni kader,* the picturesque generic term for the deserters who found refuge from the military cadres of the Austro-Hungarian army in the green forest expanses, especially in northern Croatia. An important summary of the issues that remain controversial is Bogdan Krizman, "O odjecima Oktobarske revolucije i zelenom kaderu," *Historijski zbornik,* Zagreb, 10 (1957), no. 1–4: 149–157. Published sources on the *zeleni kader* include: Bogdan Krizman, "Gradja o nemirima u Hrvatskoj na kraju g. 1918.," ibid., pp. 111–129; Josip L. Vidmar, comp., "Prilozi gradji za povijest 1917–1918. s osobitim obzirom na razvoj radničkog pokreta i odjeke Oktobarske revolucije kod nas," *Arhivski vjesnik,* Zagreb, 1 (1958), no. 1: 11–173; Josip I. Vidmar, comp., "Prilozi gradji za historiju radničkog pokreta i KPJ 1919. god.," ibid., 2 (1959), no. 2: 7–227; Josipa Paver, comp., *Zbornik gradje za povijest radničkog pokreta i KPJ 1919–1920: Dvor, Glina,*

Ivanić-Grad, Kostajnica, Kutina, Novska, Petrinja, Sisak (Sisak: Historijski arhiv, 1970). An interesting case study of a *zeleni kader* unit with a pronounced anarcho-Bolshevik program, the *"Kolo gorskih tiča* or "Circle of Mountain Birds" of Božidar Matijević, active in the environs of Djakovo, is Lavoslav Kraus, "O dvjema manifestacijama 'odjeka Oktobra' u Slavoniji," *Naučni skup "Oktobarska revolucija i narodi Jugoslavije,"* 1 (Belgrade and Kotor: Zajednica institucija za izučavanje radničkog pokreta i SKJ, 1967), pp. 1–46.

5. On the revolutionary stirrings in the South Slav lands inspired by the October Revolution, and particularly on the Boka Kotorska naval mutiny, see F[erdo]. Chulinovich, *Otkliki Oktiabria v iugoslavianskikh zemliakh* (Moscow: Progress, 1967); Ferdo Čulinović, *1918 na Jadranu* (Zagreb: Glas rada, 1951); Bernard Stulli, *Revolucionarni pokreti mornara 1918* (Zagreb: IHRPH, 1968).

6. For a detailed analysis of the South Slav participation in the October Revolution and Russia's Civil War, see Ivan D. Ochak, *Iugoslavianskie internatsionalisty v bor'be za pobedu sovetskoi vlasti v Rossii (1917–1921 gody)* (Moscow: Izdatel'stvo Moskovskogo universiteta, 1966). The Serbian translation of this work is Ivan D. Očak, *Jugosloveni u Oktobru* [Cyr.] (Belgrade: Narodna knjiga, 1967). Memoirs of the South Slav Red Army veterans are collected in *Jugoslovani v Oktobru: Zbornik spominov udeležencev Oktobarske revolucije in državljanske vojne v Rus:ji (1917–1921)* (Ljubljana: Zavod "Borec," 1969).

7. The establishment of Béla Kun's Hungarian Council Republic was on the whole a stimulus to Leninist ideology in neighboring Yugoslavia, despite certain thoughtless actions, such as the disparagement of the peasantry. For details, see: Šandor Mesaroš, "Madjarska Sovjetska Republika i revolucionarne perspektive u Jugoslaviji," *Historijski institut Slavonije. Zbornik,* Slavonski Brod, 1970, 7–8: 47–66.; Iurii A. Pisarev, "Vengerskaia Sovetskaia respublika i slavianskie narody," *Uchenye zapiski Instituta slavianovedeniia,* Moscow, 11 (1955): 119–153.

8. Očak, *Jugosloveni u Oktobru,* p. 103. For a brief period in November and early December 1918, the Serb, Croat, and Slovene Communists in Russia had an independent party, *Komunistička partija (boljševika) Srba, Hrvata i Slovenaca,* (Communist Party [Bolshevik] of the Serbs, Croats, and Slovenes), with its own leadership, but there is no evidence that the Russian Bolsheviks ever recognized it as a parallel but separate party. For details see Bogumil Hrabak, "Komunistička partija (boljševika) Srba, Hrvata i Slovenaca," *Jugoslovenski istorijski časopis,* Belgrade, 1969, 1–2: 7–27.

9. There is no single comprehensive work on social democracy among the South Slavs. The subject is treated extremely summarily in the following textbooks: Stjepan Blažeković, *Priručnik za historiju medjunarodnog radničkog pokreta i historiju KPJ* (Zagreb: Naprijed, 1960), pp. 97–106; Dušan Bole, *Razvoj delavskega gibanja do prve svetovne vojne* (Ljubljana: Cankarjeva založba, 1963), pp. 90–96; 138–140; Mijo Haramina and Blagota Drašković, *Pregled historije radničkog pokreta,* 3d. rev. ed. (Zagreb: Prosvjeta, 1969), pp. 47–52; Ljubinka Krešić, ed., *Priručnik za istoriju medjunarodnog rad-*

ničkog pokreta (Belgrade: Rad, 1964), pp. 413–450. On the wartime activities
of the Social Democratic parties in the area, see: Vlado Strugar, *Jugoslavenske
socijaldemokratske stranke: 1914–1918* (Zagreb: JAZU, 1963), and Sergije
Dimitrijević, "Balkanski socijalisti i prvi svetski rat," *Prilozi za istoriju socijalizma*, Belgrade, 1 (1964): 67–78. Vitomir Korać, one of the three most
important leaders of the SDSHS and its only elected deputy in the Croat Sabor
before World War I, has written a partisan but thorough three-volume work on
the workers' movement and social democracy in Croatia-Slavonia, and on its
ties with similar movements in the other South Slav lands. See Vitomir Korać,
Povjest Radničkog Pokreta u Hrvatskoj i Slavoniji, 3 vols. (Zagreb: Radnička
komora, 1929–1933). On the same subject see also Mirjana Gross's remarks in
Jaroslav Šidak et al, *Povijest hrvatskog naroda: g. 1860–1914* (Zagreb: Školska knjiga, 1968). For the published sources on Croat social democracy see
*Istorijski arhiv KPJ, Tom IV: Socijalistički pokret u Hrvatskoj i Slavoniji,
Dalmaciji i Istri 1892–1919* (Belgrade: Istorijsko odeljenje CK KPJ, 1950). Nor
is there a systematic history of Serbian social democracy. Dragiša Lapčević,
one of its leaders, has written a brief summary on this subject, which should be
used cautiously. See Dragiša Lapčević, *Istorija socijalizma u Srbiji* [Cyr.]
(Belgrade: Izdavačka knjižarnica Gece Kona, 1922). See also *Institut za
istoriju radničkog pokreta Srbije, Srpska socijaldemokratska partija* [Cyr.]
(Belgrade: Naučna knjiga, 1965). For the published sources on Serbian social
democracy, see *Istorijski arhiv KPJ, Tom III: Socijalistički pokret u Srbiji
1900–1919* [Cyr.] (Belgrade: Istorijsko odeljenje CK KPJ, 1950). Published
sources on social democracy in Bosnia-Hercegovina, Vojvodina, and Macedonia are to be found in *Istorijski arhiv KPJ, Tom VI: Socijalistički pokret u
Bosni, Vojvodini i Makedoniji* [Cyr.] (Belgrade: Istorijsko odeljenje CK KPJ,
1951).

10. This subject, too, still has not received definite treatment, but there exists
a substantial literature that can be consulted with some profit. See especially:
Vlado Strugar, *Socijalna demokratija o nacionalnom pitanju jugoslovenskih
naroda* (Belgrade: Rad, 1956); Vlado Strugar, *Socijal-demokratija o stvaranju
Jugoslavije* (Belgrade: Rad, 1965); Mirjana Gross, "Socijalna demokracija
prema nacionalnom pitanju u Hrvatskoj 1890–1902," *Historijski zbornik*, Zagreb, 9 (1956), no. 1–4: 1–27; Fedora Bikar, "Nacionalna politika hrvatske
socijalne demokracije od 1902 do 1905," in Vasa Čubrilović, ed., *Jugoslovenski narodi pred prvi svetski rat* [Cyr.] (Belgrade: Naučno delo, 1967); and
two articles by Fedora Bikar: "Prijedlog za promjenu kompozicije i nadopunu
teksta o socijalnoj demokraciji u 'Pregledu istorije Saveza komunista Jugoslavije,'" *Putovi revolucije*, Zagreb, 2 (1964), no. 3–4: 135–142, and "Razvoj
odnosa izmedju hrvatske i srpske socijalne demokracije i pokušaji usklad-
jivanja njihovih koncepcija o nacionalnom pitanju od 1909 do 1914," ibid., 3
(1965), no. 5: 165–192. Bikar's findings have been challenged in Šidak, p. 352.

11. For a detailed study of the SSDP views on the peasant question, as
expressed in the thinking of Dragiša Lapčević, see Desanka Pešić,
"Dragiša Lapčević i 'seljačko pitanje' (1903–1914)," *Prilozi za istoriju
socijalizma*, Belgrade, 3 (1966): 65–102.

12. For details on the SDSHS agitation in the countryside, see: Andrija Radenić, *Položaj i borba seljaštva u Sremu od kraja XIX veka do 1914* [Cyr.] (Belgrade: Naučno delo, 1958); Arpad Lebl, "Pokret poljoprivrednih radnika u Sremu 1906–1907" [Cyr.] *Matica srpska. Zbornik za društvene nauke,* Novi Sad, 17 (1957): 5–28; V[ladimir]. I. Freidzon, "Sotsialdemokratiia i klassovaia bor'ba v khorvatskoi derevne v kontse XIX — nachale XX v.," *Ezhegodnik po agrarnoi istorii Vostochnoi Evropy: 1959 g.* (Moscow: Izdatel'stvo Akademii nauk SSSR, 1961), pp. 331–343.

13. Ibrahim Karabegović, *Radnički pokret Bosne i Hercegovine izmedju revolucionarne i reformističke orijentacije (1909–1929)* (Sarajevo: Svjetlost, 1973), pp. 20–23.

14. Bogumil Hrabak, "Srpski socijaldemokrati prema februarskoj i oktobarskoj revoluciji 1917–1918 godine," [Cyr.] in *Institut za istoriju radničkog pokreta Srbije,* p. 261.

15. For published sources on the subject see Mihailo Todorović, comp., *Srpski socijalistički pokret za vreme Prvog svetskog rata: Materijali* [Cyr.] (Belgrade: Rad, 1958).

16. It is common knowledge that the SSDP and the SDSBH were Bolshevik oriented practically from November 1917. The SDSBH, especially, was apparently single-minded on this question, if one takes *Glas slobode* [The voice of liberty], the party organ, as a reliable indicator. In the emigré SSDP ranks there were apparently some hesitations in backing the Bolsheviks. Sava Muzikravić, for example, declared: "Bolshevism is the greatest negation of Marxism and of the Marxist conception of social development. If there is still somebody who recommends bolshevism, or that foolishness of Lenin and Trotsky, after the terrible example that they gave in practice, then he is worthy of pity" (Muzikravić in Paris to Dušan Popović in London, 29 July 1918, ibid., p. 137). Muzikravić would ultimately become an important publicist of inter-war Yugoslavia's anticommunist socialists. Nevertheless, it seems unwarranted to question the predominance of pro-Bolshevik sentiments in both parties, although this commitment would be somewhat mitigated in competition with the activist South Slav returnees from Russia, who in effect questioned the value of everything in the socialist movement that was not explicitly Bolshevik. There is no question, however, that the SSDP and the SDSBH decisively influenced the shaping of the SRPJ(k) and entered the new party *en bloc.* It is therefore regrettable that there exist no detailed studies of the roots and the growth of the two parties' identification with the Bolshevik cause. Vlado Strugar's study of the South Slav socialist parties during the war is far too general in dealing with the rise of Bolshevik influence to answer the question definitively. Strugar suggests that the SSDP's espousal of bolshevism was the logical outcome of the party's antiwar stand. Indeed, the position of the SSDP on this matter was unique, and constituted an act of considerable political courage. Serbia was a small country ravaged by a major power. Its people were not receptive to arguments that questioned a determined stand against a basically defensive war. In fact, the SSDP did not prevent its members, or even its leaders, from fighting on the fronts. (Dimitrije Tucović [1881–1914], the foremost Serbian socialist, died as

an army officer during the celebrated Kolubara battle.) Nor could the SSDP attempt to disrupt Serbia's military. This would have been an act of folly, indeed treason, given the absence of such campaigns on the part of Austro-Hungarian socialists, who had greater reasons to sabotage the war effort. The SSDP's parliamentarty deputies did, however, vote against Serbia's war credits, the only party of the Second International to do so. One does not doubt the correctness of Strugar's conclusion that the SSDP's stand on the question of war, a feeling that a new International had to be built, and the sensitivity to the cause of the small Balkan peoples were bonds between the Bolsheviks and the SSDP. Yet, these points are rather intuitive, not explicitly documented. See Strugar, *Socijaldemokratske stranke*, pp. 103–111. Strugar's explanation (p. 185) of the SDSBH's vociferous espousal of bolshevism is less convincing. It seems overly facile to accept the party's junior status and smallest membership among all the other South Slav socialist groups, as well as Bosnia-Hercegovina's backwardness (which supposedly instilled the idea that the province's transformation could only be accomplished by a "world alliance of proletarians"), as sufficient causes for the party's exceptionally radical, pro-Bolshevik stance. Similarly, one is not convinced by Korać's explanation that the SDSBH's philo-bolshevism developed under the tutelage of Austro-German and Hungarian socialists and their influential immigrant worker conationals in Bosnia-Hercegovina; that is, therefore, consituted an "opportunist" stratagem designed to please Count Czernin, "who wanted to divert social radicalism as a trump card against national radicalism, because the latter was far more dangerous for the Monarchy's survival" (Korać, 3: 344). Other authors throw no light on this subject. On the history of Lenin's (and the Bolshevik party's) interconnections with the South Slav (especially Serbian) socialists, see G. M. Slavin and M. M. Sumarokova, "V. I. Lenin i rabochee dvizhenie v Iugoslavii (1904–1924 gg.)," in *V. I. Lenin i obrazovanie kommunisticheskikh partii v strankakh Tsentral'noi i Iugo-Vostochnoi Evropy*, ed. L. B. Valev et al (Moscow: Nauka, 1973). On the influence of Leninism on the growth of Yugoslavia's Communist movement, see Sergije Dimitrijević, "Usvajanje iskustava Oktobarske revolucije u jugoslovenskom radničkom pokretu," *Jugoslovenski istorijski časopis,* Belgrade, 1968, 3–4: 71–99.

17. For a synthesis of the origin of the socialist left wing in Croatia and the group's path to communism, see especially: Dušan Bilandžić et al, eds., *Komunistički pokret i socijalistička revolucija u Hrvatskoj* (Zagreb: IHRPH, 1969); Dušan Bilandžić et al, eds., *Revolucionarni radnički pokret u Zagrebu izmedju dva svjetska rata* (Zagreb: IHRPH, 1968). For an analysis of the 1918–1919 ideological confrontations and factional struggles in the SDSHS, see: Vujica Kovačev, "Ideološke i političke borbe u radničkom pokretu Hrvatske i Slavonije 1917–1919 godine," *Istorija radničkog pokreta; Zbornik radova,* Belgrade, 4 (1967): 73–180; Leopold Kobsa, "Socijaldemokratska stranka Hrvatske i Slavonije od obnove pokreta do Kongresa ujedinjenja s posebnim akcentom na procese u zagrebačkoj organizaciji," in Bilandžić et al, eds., *Revolucionarni radnički pokret,* pp. 133–169. For a social-democratic view of these conflicts, see Korać, 1: 256–272.

18. For the contributions of Cesarec and Krleža in the creation of the Communist organization in Croatia, see Zorica Stipetić, "Uloga Augusta Cesarca i Miroslava Krleže u stvaranju Komunističke partije Jugoslavije," *Časopis za suvremenu povijest*, Zagreb, 5 (1973), no. 3: 71–96.

19. Korać, 1: 256.

20. Hrabak, "Komunistička partija," pp. 17–18.

21. Ibid., pp. 21–22. The activist returnees' extensive organizational undertakings in Croatia-Slavonia and Bosnia are best detailed by Ivan Očak. In an excellent recent study he reconstructed the exploits of Ćopić, Kovačević, and others from December 1918 to early spring 1919. This group created tens of illegal Communist organizations in cooperation with the local leftists (an underground Communist group functioned in Zagreb as early as December 1918) and financed the network with funds obtained in Council Hungary. It also established a liaison system and even a number of insurgent units (frequently referred to as "Red Guards"). The returnees' bold initiatives did not, however, culminate in a planned uprising. See Ivan Očak, "Povratnici iz Sovjetske Rusije u borbi za stvaranje komunističkih organizacija uoči prvog kongresa SRPJ(k)," *Historijski zbornik*, Zagreb, 27–28 (1974–75): 1–26, esp. pp. 2–8.

22. Conceived as a strictly conspiratorial revolutionary organization, the Pelagić alliance nevertheless advertised its existence and aims. As a result, it may be considered the first openly Communist organization in Yugoslavia. After careful preparation, the group was constituted at an illegal congress held on 9 March 1919, in Stražilovo (Srijem). The gathering was attended by 48 delegates from most of Yugoslavia, although the majority of the participants were then active in Vojvodina. Based largely in this province, the Pelagićists branched out throughout the country (except, apparently, in Slovenia). Their underground organizations also functioned in some army units. The group's leadership was dominated by returnees from Soviet Russia; the membership, according to some sources, numbered as many as 20,000 persons. On the genesis, organization, and program of the group, see ibid., pp. 10–24. See also Toma Milenković, "Uticaj Oktobarske revolucije na koncepcija i delatnost Jugoslovneskog revolucionarnog saveza pelagićevaca," *Istorija XX veka; Zbornik radova*, Belgrade, 10 (1969): 227–244.

23. Filipović's Russian revolutionary ties dated back to 1899, when he first went to St. Petersburg as a university student. He participated in the 1905 revolution and became a Bolshevik propagandist. Subsequently, he wrote for *Pravda* and other Russian revolutionary journals. Interned by the Austro-Hungarian occupation authorities in Aschach and then Vienna, he joined a Russian Bolshevik group in Vienna but was expelled from Austria in November 1918. After that he worked briefly with the Hungarian Communists in Budapest and with the South Slav Communist returnees from Russia. Throughout this time he wrote articles in defense of the Bolsheviks, using the Sarajevo SDSBH organ as his chief outlet. He returned to Belgrade in December 1918 and immediately started recruiting members for an illegal Communist network. For details on Filipović's Russian connections and his stay in Budapest, see: M. M. Sumarokova, "Novye dannye o nachale revoliutsionnoi deiatel'nosti Filipa

Filipovicha," *Sovetskoe slavianovedenie,* Moscow, 1967, 1: 56–59; I. D. Ochak, "Neizvestnoe pis'mo Filipa Filipovicha," ibid., 1966, 1: 66–68. After his return to Yugoslavia, Filipović carried out the duties previously agreed upon with his Budapest contacts. In short, despite his SSDP pedigree, Filipović's activities were identical to those of the actual repatriates from Russia. For example, in January 1919 he organized a 200-strong, Belgrade-based, Communist network, with branches throughout Serbia. Similarly, according to some reconstructions, he was a member of a conspiratorial troika that headed Communist underground work in the western areas of Yugoslavia. (Other members were Ćopić and Kovačević.) See Očak, "Povratnici," pp. 4, 9, 11.

24. Dimitrijević, "Usvajanje iskustava," pp. 77–78.

25. Strugar, *Jugoslavenske socijaldemokratske stranke,* pp. 102–103; cf. Slavin and Sumarokova, pp. 386–387.

26. Dimitrijević, "Usvajanje iskustava," p. 80.

27. Kobsa, p. 165.

28. Korać, 1: 259.

29. Kobsa, p. 165.

30. The leftist *Kartel stukovnih saveza* (Cartel of Trade Unions) was formed on 16 January 1919, outside the official SDSHS trade unions. Syndicates representing printers, railwaymen, shop attendants, tanners, construction workers, bookbinders, and so on — the strongest trade unions in northern Croatia — joined. Ibid., p. 164.

31. Ibid., p. 166.

32. Korać, 1: 259.

33. Kobsa, pp. 167, 168.

34. For an analysis of ideological controversies within the JSDS and for the party's course in 1918–1919, see Strugar, *Jugoslavenske socijaldemokratske stranke,* pp. 283–310. See also Metod Mikuž, *Oris zgodovine Slovencev v stari Jugoslaviji: 1917–1941* (Ljubljana: Mladinska knjiga, 1965), pp. 34–37, 129–135.

35. Korać, 3: 289–290. Korać's contempt for A. Kristan and the latter's supposed habit of seeking "rotten compromises" are hardly concealed in the passage cited.

36. For an analysis of the final division between the Social Democrats and the Communists in the Slovene trade union movement and the JSDS, see especially France Klopčič, *Velika razmejitev: studija o nastanku komunistične stranke v Sloveniji aprila 1920 in o njeni dejavnosti od maja do septembra 1920* (Ljubljana: Državna založba Slovenije and Inštitut za zgodovino delavskega gibanja, 1969).

37. For the documents of the Unification Congress, see *Istorijski arhiv KPJ,* 2: 10–26. The dominant role of the SSDP in the creation of the SRPJ(k) and the implications of this contingency will be discussed below. This was the subject of a recent study that occasioned critical replies. See: Neda Engelsfeld, "Kako je došlo do ujedinjenja radničkog pokreta u Kraljevini SHS," *Hrvatsko sveučilište,* Zagreb, 6 October 1971; Neda Engelsfeld, "Formiranje SRPJ (u[sic!])," *Hrvatsko sveučilište,* 13 October 1971; Stanislava Koprivica-Oštrić, "O

jednom prikazu ujedinjenja radničkih pokreta u jugoslavenskim zemljama," *Časopis za suvremenu povijest,* Zagreb, 3 (1971), no. 2–3: 242–253.

38. Unlike the Social Democrats from northern Croatia, Dalmatian socialists apparently were united in their determination to join the new Communist party. They were represented by eight delegates at the Unification Congress. See Bilandžić et al, eds., *Komunistički pokret,* p. 68. Socialists from Vojvodina were represented at the congress by two distinct groups with different ideological platforms. One was the already noted Pelagić alliance, undoubtedly the most consistent pro-Bolshevik tendency at the Unification Congress. The "regular" Social Democrats from Vojvodina were represented by the Agitational Committee of Serb and Bunjevci (Bačka Croats) organizations of the former Hungarian social democracy. For a detailed analysis of political currents in Vojvodina's socialist and communist movements, before and after the Unification Congress, see Toma Milenković, *Radnički pokret u Vojvodini; 1918–1920; (od kraja prvog svetskog rata do Obznane)* (Belgrade: Institut društvenih nauka — Odeljenje za istorijske nauke, 1968); see also Aleksandar Fira, "Kongres ujedinjenja SRPJ(k) i Vojvodina," [Cyr.], *Matica srpska. Zbornik za društvene nauke,* Novi Sad, 22 (1959): 7–24. The same issue of the cited journal contains numerous other important articles on the origins of the Communist movement in Vojvodina, the "Pelagićists," some of their leaders, etc. See also Danilo Kecić, *Klasne borbe u Vojvodini: 1918–1941* (Novi Sad: Pokrajinsko veće Saveza sindikata Jugoslavije za Vojvodinu, 1969).

39. The inconsistencies and compromises in the SRPJ(k)'s position do not, however, justify Živko Topalović's assertion that the Unification Congress was a mere Social Democratic gathering. The "Congress held in Belgrade in April of 1919 did not create the Communist party," Topalović says: "That party was created in Vukovar [i.e., at the KPJ's Second Congress in June 1919], one year later. In Belgrade [at the Unification Congress], however, the Communists succeeded in one thing: they managed surreptitiously to worm their way into the Socialist party and then later to misuse the honest faith of democratic socialists on behalf of alien aims." Živko Topalović, *Začeci socijalizma i komunizma u Jugoslaviji* (London: Peasant Jugoslavia Ltd., 1960), p. 65. Topalović's *post festum* opinion rests on a static, formalistic, and even legalistic appreciation of the gathering. By the same logic one could discount the authenticity of most Communist founding congresses during the immediate postwar period.

40. The integration of Yugoslavia's trade unions was a very complex process, which necessarily reflected political regrouping within the regional socialist parties, since by and large the revived trade unions were affiliated with the Social Democratic movement. The tug-of-war between the "ministerialists" and the leftists — and later between the left-center and the Communist left — was reproduced in the trade unions, with the difference that the Communists never quite extirpated the influence of their socialist rivals in the syndicates, in any case not as successfully as in the Communist party itself. The founding congress of Yugoslavia's united trade unions literally overlapped with the SRPJ(k)'s Unification Congress. Held in the same city (Belgrade), at the same time

(22–23 April 1919), under the same auspices (SSDP), and attended largely by the same persons who were delegates at the party congress, the unionist gathering effected the unification of all the trade union federations from Serbia (with Macedonia), Bosnia-Hercegovina, Dalmatia, Vojvodina, and Montenegro. These complete unionist leaderships were also joined by Croatia-Slavonia's dominant leftist unions and by Slovenia's railwaymen. The new organization was called *Centralno radničko sindikalno vijeće Jugoslavije* (Central Workers' Trade Union Council of Yugoslavia, CRSVA); its statutes stressed centralism, a determined class struggle, and allegiance to the Third International. (The Profintern had not yet emerged as an organization with its specific contours.) At its inception, the CRSVJ represented 250,000 organized workers. An additional 25,000 unionists still belonged to syndicates loyal to the old social democracy (largely in Slovenia and Croatia-Slavonia). But it proves easier to unify the leaderships of the old federations, even under a relatively radical program, than to effect the unification of all craft unions into centralized statewide organizations; and it was still less easy to promote industrial unions. Nevertheless, this process proceeded apace despite the resistance of special regional and political interests. For example, after their removal from the KPJ, the "centrists" remained in the CRSVJ and frequently promoted a rapid centralization of certain craft unions when they felt they could use them against the Communists, or, alternately, hindered the centralization of Communist-dominated professional associations. On the whole, however, the Communists had the upper hand in the CRSVJ until 1920, when the authorities tipped the balance in favor of the anti-Communist unionists. The genesis and the early stages of Yugoslavia's united trade union movement are vividly described in the works of Josip Cazi, Yugoslavia's foremost authority on the subject. Cazi, however, was once a leading Communist unionist, a matter of some import for the tenor of his observations. See especially Cazi's *Revolucionarni sindikati Jugoslavije, 1919–1920* (Belgrade: Rad, 1959); *Komunistička partija Jugoslavije i sindikati* (Belgrade: Kultura, 1959), pp. 5–23; and *Nezavisni sindikati*, 1 (Zagreb: IHRPH, 1962): 1: 9–29.

41. On the twenties phase of the Communist youth movement in Yugoslavia and the role of the SKOJ, see especially: Slavoljub Cvetković, *Napredni omladinski pokret u Jugosaviji 1919–1928* (Belgrade: Institut društvenih nauka — Odeljenje za istorijske nauke, 1966); Slobodan Petrović, *Sedam sekretara SKOJ-a* (Belgrade: Rad, 1962).

42. AIHRPH KI Br. 4/I ("Dorogie tovarishchi" [Vienna, 21 October 1919]). The report was signed by Franjo Ljuština, Lazar Vukićević, and D. Majusovič(?). Dragiša Lapčević (1874–1939), Nedeljko Košanin (1874–1934), and Mijo Radošević (1884–1942) were among the important leaders of the center, the first two in Serbia, the third in Croatia. Other important "centrists" included Živko Topalović (1886–1972) in Serbia, and the Jakšić brothers in Bosnia-Hercegovina. Triša Kaclerović (1879–1964), a noted Serbian socialist, continued in the Communist ranks despite his apparent "centrist" proclivities in 1919. He rose to the position of secretary of the KPJ, and

withdrew from the Communist movement in 1926. He held several responsible positions in post-1945 Yugoslavia.

43. AIHRPH KL I/9 ("Revoliutsionnaia volna v Iugoslavii" [20 May 1920]). According to Ilija Milkić (1884–1968), a representative of the SRPJ(k) in the Comintern and the author of this report, Yugoslavia's party numbered "over 50,000 members, and the trade union organizations, which go together with the Communist party, over 150,000 members." Milkić also claimed that the SKOJ numbered "almost 10,000 members." In a report that was sent to the Communist Youth International (KIM) in June, two members of the SKOJ Central Committee claimed that the SKOJ "numbered twenty-eight organizations with 5,500 members." They added that if the membership of certain organizations which were banned by the authorities was added to this number "then our League numbers over 8,000 members in total." AIHRPH KI 7/I ("Bratskomu Soiuzu kommunisticheskoi molodezhi" [7 July 1920]). According to official Comintern publications, the Communist party membership in Yugoslavia in July 1920 amounted to 60,649 members — 20,500 in Serbia and Macedonia, 7,432 in Bosnia and Montenegro, 3,335 in Vojvodina, 2,092 in Dalmatia, 15,500 in Croatia, and 11,790 in Slovenia. Cited in Avakumovic, p. 41, no. 53.

44. AIHRPH KI Br. 4/I.

45. Karabegović, pp. 140–141.

46. For a detailed account of the general strike, see Dejan Gajić, *Generalni štrajk 1919* [Cyr.] (Belgrade: Narodni univerzitet, 1951). On the Maribor mutiny, see Milan Ževart, "Vojaški upor v Mariboru julija 1919," *Prispevki za zgodovino delavskega gibanja,* Ljubljana, 7 (1967) no. 1–2: 129–133. The Varaždin rebellion was republican and leftist and clearly under the influence of Béla Kun's Hungarian Council Republic. What made it particularly noteworthy was the fact that the insurgent soldiers and the local Communists made every effort to draw in the peasants from the neighboring villages, and were partly successful. This was a rare instance of Communist agitation in the countryside and can be attributed to local inspiration. For more details, see Vidmar, "Prilozi gradji za historju radničkog pokreta," pp. 160–172, 179–180, 190–194, 196–197.

47. The essential facts about the Diamantstein Affair can be found in Ivan Ramljak, "Afera Diamantstein; (na marginama arhivske gradje i zagrebačkih novina)," in *Zagreb: Jučer danas sutra,* ed. Zdravko Blažina (Zagreb: Epoha, Matica Hrvatska, Mladost, Naprijed, Panorama, Znanje, Zora, 1965), pp. 207–217. Yugoslavia's post-1945 historiography generally has insisted that Miljuš and Ćopić were completely innocent. Other accounts give credence to the authorities. Cf. Avakumovic, p. 35. Miroslav Krleža, in his recently published diary, in an entry dated 17 April 1968, notes that "forty years ago," in a room in his Zagreb apartment in Prilaz 3, "in a cabinet, Sima Miljuš's carbine was left behind (from the Diamantstein days, when Sima wanted to take Zagreb with Captain Metzger, in August 1919); during those days my room in Prilaz 3 was a warehouse full of carbines and ammunition." See "Fragmenti dnevnika iz godine 1968," *Forum,* Zagreb, July–August 1972, p. 75.

48. Even before the end of 1919, eleven SRPJ(k) organizations were operating

in Macedonia (Skopje, Veles, Bitola, Kavadarci, Negotino, Štip, Tetovo, Kumanovo, Gevgelija, Prilep, and Ohrid). In 1920 numerous other village party branches were created. For details, see Ivan Katardžiev, "Prilog pitanju nastanka i razvitka komunističkog pokreta u Makedoniji i aktivnost KPJ u periodu od 1919. do 1920. godine," *Istorija radničkog pokreta: Zbornik radova*, Belgrade, 5 (1958): 7–157. On the growth of Communist organizations in Kosovo, see Miodrag Nikolić, *Revolucionarni radnički pokret na Kosovu i Metohiji 1895–1922*. (Priština, Istorijska komisija OK SKJ za Kosovo i Metohiju, 1962, pp. 14–40. At least two party organizations existed in Montenegro by mid-1920: In Podgorica (300 members) and in Cetinje (188 members). Some reports mention an additional organization in Danilovgrad. At a KPJ conference held in Podgorica on 31 October 1920, the Regional Council and the Regional Secretariat of the KPJ for Montenegro were established and their members elected. See Batrić Jovanović, *Komunistička partija Jugoslavije u Crnoj Gori 1919–1941* [Cyr.] (Belgrade: Vojno delo, 1959), pp. 58–60. See also Niko S. Martinović, *Radnički pokret u Crnoj Gori pod rukovodstvom Jovana Tomaševića (1918–1924)* [Cyr.] (Belgrade: Rad, 1955), pp. 37–47.

49. On the occupational structure and other characteristics of the Croat working class, especially in Zagreb, see two excellent studies by Mira Kolar-Dimitrijević: "O socijalnoj strukturi radništva Hrvatske u razdoblju izmedju dva rata," *Časopis za suvremenu povijest*, Zagreb, 2 (1970), no. 1: 77–103; and *Radni slojevi Zagreba od 1918. do 1931.* (Zagreb: IHRPH, 1973). For the condition of Serbia's urban laborers, see Petar Milosavljević, *Položaj radničke klase Srbije 1918–1929* [Cyr.] (Belgrade: Rad, 1972). On the economic situtation of Yugoslavia's wage laborers in the aftermath of the war, see Dragoslav Janković, "Društveni i politički odnosi u Kraljevstvu Srba, Hrvata i Slovenaca uoči stvaranja Socijalističke radničke partije Jugoslavije (komunista) 1.XII.1918–20.IV.1919," *Istorija XX veka: Zbornik radova*, Belgrade 1 (1959): 48–51.

50. Čolaković et al, eds., *Pregled istorije SKJ*, p. 55.

51. Bilandžić et al, *Komunistički pokret*, p. 73.

52. Ibid., p. 74. Cf. Čolaković et al, *Pregled istorije SKJ*, p. 55.

53. Bilandžić et al, *Komunistički pokret*, p. 74.

54. Ibid.

55. Čolaković et al, *Pregled istorije SKJ*, p. 55.

56. Ibid., p. 56.

57. Ibid., pp. 56–57.

58. Bilandžić et al, *Komunistički pokret*, pp. 74–75.

59. The representativeness of this victory was widely disputed, although the conclusion of at least one vote taken at the congress is known. According to Klopčič, (p. 149): "The result of the vote for the list of candidates of the Central Party Council was as follows: out of the 374 delegates who were verified by the Congress 305 voted; of those there were 63 blank paper ballots and 242 filled ones." It is also known that of the 242 active ballots, some included votes for persons not on the list of candidates. For example, Živko Jovanović (1888–1923) received 55 votes and Triša Kaclerović 20. We do not know

whether any other persons received some additional votes. The 242 votes cast for the leftist leadership would indicate that 64.7 percent of the verified delegates favored the left, and by implication, rejected the center. The 63 blank votes (or 16.8 percent of verified delegates) would therefore constitute the "centrist" core. In his study of the labor movement in Croatia-Slavonia, Korać provides the following account of the balloting at the Vukovar Congress: "In addition to the makeup of the Congress [Korać claims that the different regional organizations of the SRPJ(k) were not represented according to their actual strength, resulting in the disproportionately large delegation from Serbia with Macedonia], the methods at the Congress itself were decisive. Even physical violence was applied, so that the majority of delegates from Slovenia and Croatia-Slavonia demonstratively left the Congress even before its conclusion, and thus by the end of the Congress only 305 out of 374 delegates remained. During the elections for the administration 65 blank ballots were turned in, and therefore only 240 delegates voted, and out of these there were again 125 crossed ballots, so that a mere 115 delegates were unanimous, therefore *not even a third of the Congress*" (Korać, 2: 197). Korać's account differs from Klopčič's in one minor and one major respect. Instead of Klopčič's 63 blank ballots and 242 filled ones, Korać talks of 65 and 240, respectively. More important, however, Korać introduces the question of 125 crossed ballots, although he does not cite his source. Neda Engelsfeld follows Korać's account in every detail, but also does not cite any evidence. See Engelsfeld, "Centralizacija Partije 1920. i *rasap* — 1921. godine," *Hrvatsko sveučilište*, Zagreb, 1 (1971), no. 25: 16. According to Stanislava Koprivica-Oštrić, "In the report of the government commissioners, who . . . followed the Congress, crossed ballots are not mentioned" (Koprivica-Oštrić, p. 250). As an outspoken opponent of the Communists, Korać was not, of course, an impartial observer, but since he was a contemporary of the events and intimate with the "centrist" version of the Vukovar procedures, his account cannot be dismissed out of hand. Nevertheless, until additional evidence emerges, the accepted estimate of the left's strength in Vukovar will have to be considered as a clear plurality.

60. For the documents of the Second (Vukovar) Congress of the KPJ, see *Istorijski arhiv KPJ*, 2: 28–58.

61. Pavle Pavlović (1888–1971) and Jakov Lastrić were elected presidents of the KPJ; Filipović and Sima Marković, party secretaries; and Vladimir Ćopić, technical secretary.

62. Writing to Ilija Milkić on 14 July 1920, from Zagreb, Sima Marković noted that "Although the provincial party princes were up in arms against the centralization more than against everything else, the Vukovar Congress accepted both the new statute and all the proposed resolutions with an overwhelming majority" AIHRPH KI I/11 (Dragi druže Milkiću, 14 July 1920).

63. Bilandžić, et al, *Komunistički pokret*, p. 75.

64. Izvršni Odbor Centralnog Vijeća K.P.J. i Likvidacioni Izvršni Odbor K.P.J. za Hrvatsku i Slavoniju, "Dole izdajnici komunizma," *Radnička straža*, Vukovar, 24 July 1920.

65. "Odluke plenarne sjednice C.V.K.P.J.," *Oslobodjenje*, Split, 24 December 1920.

66. Čolaković et al, eds., *Pregled istorije SKJ*, p. 70.

67. Morača et al, eds., *Četrdeset godina*, p. 121. The recollections are those of Vladimir Mirić, a member of the delegation.

68. Bilandžić, p. 76.

69. These figures are a result of calculations done by the author, and are based exclusively on the statistical data found in Čulinović, *Jugoslavija izmedju dva rata*, vol. 1 (Zagreb: JAZU, 1961), table between pp. 312 and 313.

70. A typical example of such commentaries is "Na dohvat, Prirodni saveznici," *Glas slobode*, Sarajevo, 23 March 1922.

71. On the attitudes and the initiatives of the KPJ deputies in the Constituent Assembly, see Neda Engelsfeld, "Rad Kluba komunističkih poslanika u plenum Ustavotvorne skupštine (u prosincu 1920. i u siječnju 1921.)," *Radovi Instituta za hrvatsku povijest*, Zagreb, 1972, 2: 181–262.

72. Branko Djukić and Slobodan Djinović, *Husinska buna* [Cyr.] (Belgrade: Rad, 1958), pp. 41–42.

73. Čolaković et al, eds., *Pregled istorije SKJ*, p. 76.

74. On the reaction of the KPJ leadership to the *Obznana*, see Miroslav Nikolić, "Stav rukovodstva Komunističke partije Jugoslavije prema Obznani," *Jugoslovenski istorijski časopis*, Belgrade, 1970, 3–4: 51–70.

75. Čolaković et al, eds., *Pregled istorije SKJ*, p. 77.

76. Ibid., p. 83.

77. On the background of *Crvena pravda* and the assassination of Draškov, see the memoirs of two conspirators, Rodoljub Čolaković (b. 1899) and Marijan Stilinović (1904–1959), who survived the subsequent imprisonment to become important KPJ leaders: Čolaković, *Kazivanje*, 1: 129–240; Marijan Stilinović, *Bune i otpori* (Zagreb: Zora, 1969), pp. 56–71. Alija Alijagić (1896–1922) was executed on 8 March 1922. Despite the KPJ's official repudiation of terrorism, the cult of Alijagić was encouraged, leading to frequent Communist demonstrations at Alijagić's tomb in Zagreb's Mirogoj cemetery, even after his remains were disinterred by the gendarmerie and removed to the vicinity of Bihać (Bosnia) in 1925. AIHRPH ZB –XVIII–L–9/187: Mjesna organizacija, Zagreb/Komunistička Partija & Mjesna organizacija, Zagreb/ Savez Komun[ističke]. Omladine: Radnici i siromašni gradjani grada Zagreba [1925].

78. AIHRPH KI/69 or 69/II ("Izvještaj o stanju Partije" [1924]).

79. Literature on the KPJ's evolving positions on Yugoslavia's national question is considerable, although much of it is not necessarily enlightening. The reasons for this are to be sought in the still continuing importance of Yugoslavia's nationality relations, in which the former positions of the ruling party assume a relevance far in excess of their original significance, by which to support any number of contradictory stands (from unitarism and centralism to the breakup of Yugoslavia). As a result, a large number of seemingly scholarly studies on the KPJ's "national line" tell us more about the current controversies than their authors originally intended. Certainly the most serious and the best

documented recent contribution on the subject is a monograph by Dušan Lukač: *Radnički pokret u Jugoslaviji i nacionalno pitanje 1918–1941* (Belgrade: Institut za savremenu istoriju i NIP Export-press, 1972). Among the other general studies and statements published in Yugoslavia, see: Janko Pleterski, *Komunistička partija Jugoslavije i nacionalno pitanje 1919–1941* Belgrade: Komunist, 1971); Janko Pleterski, "Nacionalno pitanje u Jugoslaviji u teoriji i politici KPJ—KPS," *Jugoslovenski istorijski časopis*, Belgrade, 1969, 1–2: 28–68; Janko Pleterski, "Komunistička partija Jugoslavije i nacionalno pitanje u prvoj jugoslavenskoj državi," *Nastava povijesti*, Zagreb, 1969–1970, 2: 10–19; Leopold Kobsa, "O gledištima KPJ na nacionalno pitanje u Jugoslaviji u razdoblju izmedju dva svjetska rata," *Naše teme*, July 1969, pp. 1078–1091; Gordana Vlajčić, "KPJ i nacionalno pitanje 1919–1941," in *Socijalizam i nacionalno pitanje* (Zagreb: Centar za aktualni politički studij, 1970), pp. 71–95; Gordana Vlajčić, *KPJ i nacionalno pitanje u Jugoslaviji* (Zagreb: "August Cesarec," 1974); Dušan Lukač, "Doprinos revolucionarnog radničkog pokreta u razrešavanju ključnih problema nacionalnog pitanja u Jugoslaviji," *Jugoslovenski istorijski časopis*, Belgrade, 1969, 4: 163–170; Petar Kozić, "Nacija i nacionalno pitanje u shvatanju jugoslovenskih socijalista-komunista," *Pravno-ekonomski fakultet. Zbornik radova*, Niš, 1966, pp. 95–103; Rodoljub Čolaković, "Borba Komunističke partije Jugoslavije za rješenje nacionalnog pitanja," in *Izabrani govori i članci*; vol. 1, ed. Milica Borić (Sarajevo: Svjetlost, 1960), pp. 281–310. Of the works published outside Yugoslavia, see especially, Wayne S. Vucinich, "Nationalism and Communism," in *Contemporary Yugoslavia: Twenty Years of Socialist Experiment*, ed. Wayne S. Vucinich (Berkeley: University of California Press, 1969); Paul Shoup, *Communism and the Yugoslav National Question* (New York: Columbia University Press, 1968). On the more specialized aspects of the KPJ stand on the national question, see especially: Jozo Ivičević, "Odrednice unitarističkog nacionalnog programa I i II kongresa KPJ," *Hrvatski znanstveni zbornik*, Zagreb, 1971, 1: 135–179; Novica Vojinović, "Federalizam u koncepcijama KPJ u periodu 1919–1928. godine: Prilog diskusiji o nacionalnom pitanju," *Medjunarodni radnički pokret*, Belgrade, January–March 1972, pp. 41–71; Novica Vojinović, "Diskusija o nacionalnom pitanju u KPJ od 1919. do 1926. godine," *Prilozi za istoriju socijalizma*, Belgrade, 1971, 8: 213–274; Kiril Miljkovski, *Makedonskoto prašanje vo nacionalnata programa na KPJ (1919–1937)* (Skopje: Kultura, 1962); Stephen E. Palmer, Jr., and Robert R. King, *Yugoslav Communism and the Macedonian Question* (Hamden, Conn.: Archon Books, 1971).

80. Ivičević, p. 135.

81. *Istorijski arhiv KPJ*, 2: 14.

82. Ibid., p. 42. "The phrase 'of all nationalities' means the equality between the Yugoslavs on one side and the Hungarians, Albanians, Germans, and other ethnic groups on the other." Lukač, *Radnički pokret*, p. 49.

83. "Gradjanske stranke," *Radnička straža*, Vukovar, 1 May 1919.

84. "Javna pučka skupština u Vukovaru," ibid., 21 September 1919.

85. Božidar Radanović, "Povodom jedne radikalske klevete," *Oslobodjenje*, Split, 18 December 1920.

86. Ibid.

87. "Ko je Lenjin?," ibid., 2 February 1920.

88. On this subject see Jaroslav Šidak et al, eds., *Povijest hrvatskog naroda g. 1860–1914* (Zagreb: Školska knjiga, 1968), pp. 279–284.

89. Ante Ciliga, "Uloga i sudbina hrvatskih komunista u KPJ," *Bilten Hrvatske demokratske i socijalne akcije,* Rome, 9–10 (1972), no. 67: 3.

90. On 5 December 1918, a group of soldier-demonstrators was fired upon by the *Narodno vijeće* loyalists. Cesarec wanted to stress that his reaction to the unification was not influenced by this outrage. See August Cesarec, "Povodom najveće i najtužnije slave," *Sloboda,* 7 December 1918, in Davor Kapetanić, "Nepoznati Cesarec," *Rad JAZU,* Zagreb, 1965, no. 342: 580–584.

91. Ibid., p. 583.

92. Ibid., p. 584. My italics.

93. Nikola Grulović, "Jugoslovenska komunistička revolucionarna grupa 'Pelagić'," [Cyr.] *Matica srpska: Zbornik za društvene nauke,* Novi Sad, 22 (1959): 116.

94. The other "historical tasks of the bourgeoisie" were "destruction of feudal remnants and the carrying out of social and political reforms." Izvršni odbor centralnog partijskog veća S.R.P.J.(k.), "Manifest radničkoj klasi Jugoslavije!," *Radnička straža,* Vukovar, 28 September 1919.

95. Ibid.

96. Lukač, p. 35.

97. See, for example, references to Sima Marković's articles on the eve of the Vukovar Congress, ibid., p. 45.

98. "Stjepan Radić," *Glas slobode,* Sarajevo, 9 December 1920.

99. For a detailed analysis of the philosophical foundations of Marxist generic-universalist concept as reflected in the programs of the first two KPJ congresses, see Ivičević, pp. 139–141, 168.

100. Ibid., p. 170.

101. For a detailed and documented discussion of this phenomenon see ibid., pp. 164–167. Drawing from the documents of the AIHRPH KI collection, Ivičević gives a convincing portrayal of the Serbian Communists' preeminence in the KPJ. For example, in one cited document the SSDP's initiative in bringing about the Unification Congress is explained in this way: "This mission the unification of the party was assumed by the Serbian Democratic Workers' Party [sic], because both by its revolutionary traditions and by its organizational competency it could accomplish this task more easily than others [i.e., the other Social Democratic parties in Yugoslavia]. The working masses of Yugoslavia were already aware that the Serbian party always belonged to the left wing of the Second International and that it did not betray socialism in the course of the war, and therefore they related with full confidence to the mandate of the Serbian party in connection with the calling of the First Unification Congress of the Yugoslav proletariat" (ibid., p. 165). The same tendency is reflected in the other documents. Immediate publication of a theoretical journal was considered essential for the ideological cultivation of the working class, "especially for the regions of former Austria-Hungary where the cultural-educational level is very

low in comparison with the level of the working class in former Serbia" (ibid., p. 166). The same document, written by Filip Filipović, also says: "Both in the party and in the trade union organizations the greatest activists are the Serb workers and therefore they represent the greatest force both in the Party and in the trade unions." Although there was more than a grain of truth in the claim that the SSDP took ideological and educational tasks much more seriously than the SDSHS and the JSDS, the attitude of the Serbian party leaders had a strong touch of exclusivism, which was bound to strengthen the preeminence of the Serbian organizations of the KPJ.

102. Works on the KPJ's agrarian policy are few in number and — when summary — largely inadequate. See: Dimitrije Bajalica, *Komunistička partija Jugoslavije i "seljačko pitanje"* (Belgrade: Kultura, 1959); Stipe Šuvar, "Komunistička partija Jugoslavije i seljačko pitanje," *Naše teme*, Zagreb, 13 (1969), no. 7: 1092–1114; Ivan Cifrić, "Agrarno i seljačko pitanje u teoriji i praksi naše Partije (I)," ibid., 19 (1975), no. 3: 403–427; Žarko Jovanović, "Seljačko i agrarno pitanje na Vukovarskom kongresu," in Historijski institut Slavonije, *Drugi kongres KPJ: Materijali sa simpozija održanog 22. i 23. VI 1970. povodom 50-godišnjice Drugog (Vukovarskog) kongresa KPJ 1920.* (Slavonski Brod: Historijski institut Slavonije, 1972), pp. 161–172; Žarko Jovanović, "KPJ prema seljaštvu u Srbiji do 1929.," *Jugoslovenski istorijski časopis*, Belgrade, 1974, 1–2: 115–134; Nikola L. Gaćeša, *Agrarna reforma i kolonizacija u Sremu 1919–1941* [Cyr.] (Novi Sad: Institut za izučavanje istorije Vojvodine, 1975), pp. 46–52. Suspicion of the peasantry as a "petty bourgeois" stratum excessively bound up in traditions of property and land, characterized much of the KPJ thinking on the agrarian question. This attitude, inherited in large measure from the old SSDP, was far different from Bolshevik attempts to influence the impoverished peasant masses and to make them an important part of Bolshevik policy. Even the ultra left within the KPJ (the Pelagić alliance) did not emulate the Bolshevik agrarian program of turning the land to the peasants for their own use under the supervision of local, regional, and central committees and agencies. Instead, following the example of Hungarian communards, the Pelagićists rejected the parceling of large, efficient, and technologically advanced estates, typical of Slavonia and Vojvodina where the alliance's members were most numerous. Without reference to intermediate stages, the Pelagićists proposed that the land be nationalized after the revolution and that the seized property be administered by the agencies of the revolutionary state. See Milenković, "Uticaj Oktobarske revolucije," pp. 237–240.

103. The intervention of the Comintern in 1924 signaled changes in the KPJ's agrarian policy. See Cifrić, pp. 4J9, 416–418.

104. On the impact of the October Revolution in Yugoslavia's cultural and artistic circles and on the Communist successes and failures in mobilizing the intellectuals (especially in Croatia where these attempts were most noticeable), see: Ivo Frangeš, "Poticaji Oktobra u hrvatskoj književnosti," *Forum*, Zagreb, 6 (1967) nos. 11–12: 672–684; Franc Zdravec, "Oktobarska revolucija in slovenski književniki," *Naučni skup "Oktobarska revolucija i narodi Jugo-*

slavije (Belgrade and Kotor: Zajednica institucija za izučavanje radničkog pokreta i SKJ, 1967), pp. 1–29; Zorica Stipetić, "Inteligencija u Hrvatskoj i komunistički pokret za vrijeme legalnog djelovanja KPJ (1919–1921)," in *Drugi kongres KPJ,* pp. 351–365; Mladen Iveković, *Hrvatska lijeva inteligencija 1918–1945* 2 vols. (Zagreb: Naprijed, 1970).

105. It can be said without exaggeration that Krleža's literary work was the single most important factor in shaping the KPJ's intellectual following. Ill-fated Milan Gorkić (Josip Čižinski), secretary of the KPJ during the mid-1930s, bestowed the highest accolade on Krleža when he sent the following directive to the party's representative in the Comintern in 1932: "Explain to the people that he [Krleža] is greater and more important to us than what Gorky is for the Russians and Barbusse for the French." Otokar Keršovani, "Skica za studiju o Miroslavu Krleži," ed. Nusret Seferović, *Forum,* Zagreb, 5 (1966), no. 5–6: 87, n. 13, 66, n. 8. Krleža's influence could be anticipated from the impact of *Plamen* ("Flame," 1919), his first Zagreb-based, left-wing literary journal. Krleža's sway would become all the more powerful during the remainder of the interwar period. Excellent analyses of Krleža's works can be found in the following two *Festschriften*: Marijan Matković, ed., *Zbornik o Miroslavu Krleži* (Zagreb: JAZU, 1963); Ivan Krolo and Marijan Matković, eds., *Zbornik o Miroslavu Krleži 1973* (Zagreb: JAZU, 1975). The first collection contains a superior bibliography of Krleža's publications compiled by Davor Kapetanić. See also Kapetanić's bibliography of literature on Krleža in Vojislav Djurić, ed., *Zbornik o Krleži* (Belgrade: Prosveta, 1967), pp. 335–435. Cf. Gojko M. Tešić, "Literatura o Miroslavu Krleži 1973," in Krolo and Marković, pp. 627–672.

Communism in Bulgaria, 1918–1921

LUCIEN KARCHMAR

In the years immediately after the First World War, the Bulgarian Communist movement displayed a number of fascinating peculiarities. In the first place, its leadership had acquired its Marxist convictions not from the West but from the Russian revolutionary movement, and consequently was closer in mentality and outlook to the Bolshevik leaders than to those of any other Communist group in Europe. Second, the division of the Bulgarian Socialist movement into independent and mutually hostile wings — moderate and radical, or reformist and revolutionary — occurred neither as a consequence of the Russian revolution nor as a result of the founding of the Third International, but took place fifteen years earlier, almost at the time that the Russian Socialists split into Bolsheviks and Mensheviks. Consequently, Bulgarian adhesion to the Comintern was not accompanied by the usual internecine struggle, and the Bulgarian Communist party could pride itself on being the only one, apart from the Bolsheviks, to join the Third International in a body, without splits or defections.[1] Third, despite its rather humble beginnings, the Bulgarian Communist party immediately developed remarkable strength and soon became the second largest political party in Bulgaria, with genuine mass support among the population. Last, throughout this immediate postwar period, as before, the Bulgarian Communists were characterized by a remarkably narrow-minded, almost fanatically dogmatic interpretation of Marxism — an interpretation that was impervious to both the proddings of reality and admonitions from abroad. With this stance they reflected the views of their founder and leader, Dimiter Blagoev, and honored their original name, the Party of the "Narrow" Socialists (*Tesnyatsi*).

Bulgarian Social Democracy: "Broads" and Narrows"

Founded in 1891, the Bulgarian Social Democratic party immediately had fallen prey to factional struggles.[2] It broke apart in 1892 and was reunited in 1894, but the infighting continued and became more embittered. In these internal struggles, Blagoev headed the "hard" faction and Ianko Sakazov became recognized as the leader of the "soft" wing. Despite these internal tensions, the party elected its first parliamentary deputies in 1894, and scored further successes in 1899, 1900, and in 1902, when eight Socialists, including Blagoev, were elected. Nevertheless, these victories only sharpened the splits within the party, for the legitimacy of its electoral support among the population became one of the issues that divided the two groups.

Until 1905 or 1906, industrial workers constituted considerably less than half the membership of the Socialist movement, the majority of whose members came from the intelligentsia, the bourgeoisie, and the artisan class.[3] Blagoev was worried by this situation, which, in his opinion, threatened the degeneration of a supposedly proletarian party. But the number of industrial workers in Bulgaria was infinitesimal, and it increased very slowly. At the time of the foundation of the Socialist party, the industrial work force numbered only five or six thousand;[4] in 1909, it had risen to about twenty thousand,[5] and in 1922 was still only fifty-five thousand out of a population of nearly five million.[6] Under these circumstances, the majority of the ballots cast for Socialist candidates came from the peasantry and the petite bourgeoisie, and represented a protest vote rather than support for social revolution. Nevertheless, the "soft" faction was pleased, and even determined to woo these nonproletarian elements, taking the position that a parliamentary platform would more than compensate for its abandonment of Marxist purity. Blagoev, however, continued to regard the peasants from the orthodox Marxist viewpoint, claiming that they were incorrigibly bourgeois and reactionary, and that a party that attempted to cater to them would soon be corrupted, lose its revolutionary character, and evolve into a merely radical-bourgeois, vote-seeking organization. He began to demand that the Socialists discontinue these dangerous practices and confine their appeal to the genuine proletarians. Blagoev's position on this issue was to become a basic tenet of "Narrow" socialism and, as such, it was in time imprinted on the Bulgarian Communist party.

A second point at issue between the two party factions at the turn of the century concerned the relationship between the Socialist movement and the trade unions that were at last beginning to appear, as a result of Socialist influence. On the one hand, the "soft" faction maintained that these still embryonic organizations should be allowed to operate independently of the party, to enlist all workers regardless of their political views, and to fight, for the time being, to win purely economic goals.

They maintained that political action would expose the tiny unions to destruction by the government, and that, in any case, agitation for economic goals would increase worker solidarity and class consciousness, thus inevitably leading them to adopt a socialist political platform. Blagoev, on the other hand, argued that trade union organization could not be separated from political action, and that trade unions, however small and weak, must participate militantly in the class struggle. This strategy, in turn, demanded full organizational control by the party and the exclusion from its membership of politically suspect or wavering elements.[7] Again, Blagoev's view eventually became one of the basic premises of "Narrow" socialism.

A third point of contention was the possibility of cooperation between the Socialists and other Bulgarian political parties. Blagoev categorically rejected even temporary cooperation with bourgeois movements (among which he classed the recently founded Agrarian Union) as corrupting and unworthy of a proletarian party, whereas his opponents were willing to undertake such alliances if their goals were compatible with socialist objectives.

The dissension over these issues came to a head in 1903, and Blagoev attempted to purge his "broad-minded" opponents from the Socialist party. The result was a split: the two factions set up separate political organizations, thereafter known as the "Narrow" Socialists and the "Broad" Socialists. Until the First World War, both parties remained tiny and approximately equal in strength, their memberships increasing from about one thousand each in 1903 to about three thousand each in 1914. Soon thereafter, the infant trade unions also split, with the workers divided almost evenly between the "Broads" and "Narrows." The fragmented unions were reorganized into two federations: the General Federation of Trade Unions, with about fifteen hundred members, was controlled by the "Narrows," whereas the Federation of Free Trade Unions, with twelve hundred members, followed the "Broads." By 1914, their membership had increased to about seven thousand and four thousand respectively; however, a number of independent unions, which had remained "politically neutral" and unaffiliated, and which included the large transport-workers' and teachers' unions, were on the whole under "Broad" influence.

Within the "Narrow" party, Blagoev now enforced total organizational and doctrinal discipline. Those members who disagreed with his tenets were ruthlessly purged. In 1905 a group led by Georgi Bakalov and Nikola Harlakov was expelled, and in 1908 a similar fate overtook others led by Nikola Sakarov and Koika Tineva. These groups attempted to set up a third, independent Socialist movement, but even-

tually joined the "Broads." Hristo Rakovsky, another of the Bulgarian
Socialists who had, as students in Switzerland, become converted to
Marxism by Plekhanov, also broke with Blagoev and moved to Romania, where he became one of the leaders of the Socialist movement.
Blagoev thus eliminated all the intellectuals unwilling to subscribe to his
dictatorship or likely to question his interpretation of Marxism; thereafter, the Central Committee and all the leading positions in the party
remained safely in the hands of a small clique that accepted his ideas.
The party applied the same procedure to the trade unions that it
controlled, bringing them under strict party control, methodically indoc-
trinating the workers with "Narrow" ideology, and leading them in
"offensive" strikes, whose purposes were primarily political. Such ideological purity had a high price, however: a great reduction in the ranks
of the faithful under Blagoev's control or influence, within both the
party and the labor unions. For the next decade, then, the "Narrow"
party lacked any prospect of transformation into a mass movement and
had to limit itself, as it later admitted, to being a "party of propaganda"
rather than a "party of action."[8]
    The "Narrows'" search for ideological purity inflicted considerable
damage on the Socialist movement as a whole, since the two parties now
invested a larger proportion of their limited intellectual and organizational resources in fighting each other than in opposing the bourgeoisie.
Until the beginning of the First World War, the Second International
continued to attempt a reconciliation between the two wings of Bulgarian socialism, which it considered equally orthodox in their Marxism,
and sent a number of emissaries — including Trotsky and Karl Legien,
secretary of the International Federation of Labor Unions — to plead
for unity. All such efforts foundered on Blagoev's inflexible determination to have no relations whatever with the "opportunists." The fanati-
cism and bigotry with which the "Narrows" maintained their position,
and their demands that their rivals be expelled from the world Socialist
body, scandalized everyone,[9] but the disapproval of foreign Socialist
leaders could not budge Blagoev and his supporters.
    The fortunes of Bulgarian socialism began to turn with the outbreak
of the Balkan Wars in 1912. Both the "Broads" and the "Narrows" took
an impeccably doctrinaire position on the question of war and loudly
denounced Bulgarian participation in their press and in parliament — a
stand that initially made them the target of attacks by outraged patriots
and government sanctions. The Bulgarian military disasters of 1913,
however, induced a complete reversal of public opinion, and in the
elections at the end of that year, both Socialist parties won an enormous
increase in the votes cast for their candidates, though the party member-

ships themselves did not grow noticeably. Each party received slightly over fifty thousand ballots; sixteen "Narrow" and twenty-one "Broad" deputies sat in the new parliament.[10] This electoral triumph, which amounted to some 20 percent of the total vote, was again due to support from the peasantry and, to some extent, the petite bourgeoisie, rather than the working class, and again it represented popular protest against government policy rather than a desire for social revolution. The same election witnessed a great increase in the power of the Agrarian Union, which captured forty-nine parliamentary seats.

Within three months, the government decreed new elections, in which the socialist vote was somewhat reduced: the "Narrow" party obtained nearly forty thousand, and the "Broad" party slightly less than fifty thousand ballots. Their parliamentary representation was reduced to eleven and nine respectively.[11] The "Narrow" faction, however, included most of the party's important leaders: Blagoev, Kolarov, Kabakchiev, Lukanov, and Dimitrov. Since the next elections in Bulgaria did not take place until after the First World War, they retained their parliamentary seats until the fall of 1919.

Bulgarian Socialism and the First World War

Although Bulgaria remained neutral at the outbreak of the First World War, Bulgarian nationalists were well aware that this war provided them with an opportunity to reverse the losses of 1913. They were receptive to offers from each of the opposing alliances but hesitated, wanting to determine which side was more apt to emerge victorious. In 1915 the Bulgarian government finally became convinced that the Central Powers were most likely to triumph. General mobilization was decreed in September, and in October Bulgaria entered the war on the side of the Central Powers, attacking Serbia. The members of the Entente immediately declared war on Bulgaria, and soon thereafter the Bulgarian army found itself holding a front in Thrace and Macedonia against the Anglo-French forces that had landed at Salonika.

During the year-long bidding for Bulgarian support, both the Entente and the Central Powers had attempted to influence Bulgarian political parties toward their cause, an effort that extended even to the Socialist camp. In the fall of 1914, Plekhanov, an avid supporter of the tsarist war effort, wrote to the Bulgarian Socialists, urging them to cooperate with the Entente, and early in 1915 Helfand-Parvus arrived in Bulgaria to recruit them for the German side.[12] A crucial third influence, making himself felt at the same time, was Lenin. Immediately after the outbreak of the war, he had elaborated his thesis on the duty of Socialists in an imperialist war, rejected the "tainted" Second International, and initiated efforts to organize a new and "pure" International. He sent a Georgian Bolshevik named Buachidze to Bulgaria to keep him in touch with the local Socialists and influence them toward his views.[13]

Under Blagoev's leadership, the "Narrow" Socialists once more took an impeccably internationalist and dogmatically orthodox position. They resolutely opposed Bulgaria's entry into the war, vehemently denouncing the possibility in their press, on the floor of parliament, and in public meetings.[14] The Twenty-first Party Congress, held in August 1915, passed an antiwar resolution.[15] Plekhanov, the old mentor of the "Narrow" Socialists, was bitterly attacked for his support of the war, and Parvus' overtures were rebuffed.[16] The "Narrows" also tried to pursue their antiwar policy on an international level. They violently condemned those European Socialist parties that supported their national war efforts, and protested such activities to the International Socialist Bureau. In February 1915 the "Narrows" arranged a Balkan socialist conference in Sofia, attended by the Serbian and Romanian Socialist parties, which issued a rather fatuous declaration calling on their governments to keep out of the conflict.[17] In April, the "Narrows" voted for the antiwar resolution of the International Conference of Socialist Youth at Berne.[18] In July, their representatives attended the Second Balkan Socialist Conference at Bucharest, where, jointly with the Serbian, Romanian, and Greek Socialist parties, they signed a resolution denouncing the war and proclaiming that the Balkan peoples could find salvation only in a federated Balkan republic.[19] Finally, in September, they dispatched Kolarov to Switzerland to represent the "Narrow" party at the Zimmerwald conference of socialist internationalists. Interestingly, the Bulgarians took a relatively moderate position at Zimmerwald. Although they maintained a strong antiwar stand, they refused to go along with Lenin in rejecting the Second International and, for the time being, preferred to preserve whatever could be salvaged from the wreck of socialist unity.[20]

Bulgaria's entry into the war produced no change in the ideological position of the "Narrow" party but did somewhat curtail its ability to make propaganda. The party press was now subject to censorship, and suspensions of publication were imposed when their utterances grew excessively antipatriotic. Nevertheless, the "Narrows" do not appear to have been unduly persecuted. Their representatives continued to sit in parliament, to vote against all war credits, and to make speeches against Bulgaria's military involvement.[21] Their periodicals still published strongly critical articles. The government made no overt attempt to prevent the party's delegates from attending the second conference of the Zimmerwald Left, held at Kienthal, Switzerland, in April 1916; only because the Austrian government refused to allow them to pass through its territory did Kirkov and Kolarov fail to attend.[22] Though some party activists were jailed for subversive activities the biggest obstacle to party activity was probably the fact that so many of its members and activists had been drafted for military service together with all other able-bodied Bulgarian males.[23] Moreover, the party does not appear to have called on its members to refuse to perform their military service or to desert if drafted. Only in 1918 did a major figure from the party leadership advise the troops to imitate the Russians and mutiny.[24]

The attitude of the "Broads" toward the war differed radically from that of the "Narrows." Although they had earlier supported the demand that Bulgaria remain neutral in the world conflict, the "Broads," on the whole, took the position that Bulgaria's territorial claims were just. After the declaration of war, they supported the war effort, though there were differences among them in the degree of that support. Thus, whereas the party leader, Sakazov, and his supporters in the party's parliamentary delegation abstained from voting either for or against war credits and eventually came to doubt the wisdom of remaining in the war, the faction centered around the party's organ *Narod* adopted an extremely chauvinistic line.[25]

Impact of the Russian Revolution

The February revolution in Russia stimulated all the Bulgarian opponents of the war to new efforts. The moment was particularly propitious, for public opinion, under the pressure of wartime hardships, was turning strongly against the government and army morale was beginning to disintegrate. The Russian revolution appeared to herald an early end to the fighting. "Narrow" antiwar propaganda was eagerly read. Circulation of the *Rabotnicheski Vestnik* rose from two thousand in 1914 to eleven thousand five hundred,[26] and the circulation of "Narrow" periodicals and leaflets among front-line troops also began to increase. Favorite propaganda themes now included praise for the Russian revolution and the actions of the Russian proletariat, often couched in speculations about the future of the new society. In April, Blagoev sent a telegram in the name of the party and the trade unions to offer congratulations to the Petrograd Soviet.[27]

The February Revolution also stimulated renewed attempts to reconstruct world socialist unity. The Socialist parties of neutral countries attempted to organize an international socialist conference in Stockholm. Repeatedly postponed, the meeting finally took place in September but misfired, partly because delegations from the Western Entente Powers were prevented from attending, and partly because the groups affiliated with the Zimmerwald movement decided to boycott it.

The Zimmerwald party was supposed to hold a preliminary conference to decide on the attitude to be adopted toward the Stockholm meeting. For this purpose, Kirkov and Kolarov were sent to Stockholm in the spring of 1917, where, because of the repeated postponements, they remained for several months. By this time, the "Narrow" party had moved considerably further to the left on this issue, and was even prepared to endorse Lenin's demand for a new International.[28] In July they added their names to a comprehensive manifesto produced by the Bolshevik delegates, denouncing the proposed Stockholm conference as a tool of the "social patriots."[29] By the time the general Zimmerwald conference assembled at the beginning of September, the Bulgarians had departed for home, after first endorsing the boycott policy; the conference, in fact, voted to make it binding upon the entire Zimmerwald group.[30]

The October Revolution in Russia does not appear to have made much difference, either qualitatively or quantitatively, in the activities of the "Narrow" party. The "Narrows" naturally hailed the revolution and praised the Bolsheviks, whom they now considered their "brothers."[31] They do not seem to have had a clear idea of the implications of the Bolshevik seizure of power, however. Certainly it did not spur them into any new revolutionary activity of their own. They merely continued with their customary barrage of peace propaganda, criticism of the government, and denunciation of the shortages and high prices. The one major innovation was their espousal of the Bolshevik peace proposals. Blagoev took up this question on the floor of the parliament,[32] and the party press and various party assemblies continually demanded that the proposals be accepted and peace negotiations quickly concluded.[33] By extension, the Russian proposals were held up as a model for Bulgaria: it, too, should denounce its alliances and leave the war unilaterally. The party press also carried a considerable number of stories about the new Soviet state and its affairs. Obtaining these stories presumably became easier after the Treaty of Brest-Litovsk, when Russia was no longer officially an enemy, but it does not appear that the new political situation led to any direct contacts between the "Narrow" party and Lenin.

In 1918, the leadership of the "Narrow" Socialists consisted of two groups. Blagoev and a small circle of early collaborators, such as his friend Georgi Kirkov, were by then fifty to sixty years old. Most of them had studied in Russia during the 1880s, there encountering the Russian revolutionaries, first the *narodniki* and later the Marxists. They had participated in the foundation of the Socialist movement in Bulgaria, and had controlled it, or at least its "Narrow" wing, ever since. Blagoev, besides leading the party, edited its theoretical journal, *Novo Vreme*; Kirkov, who had edited the party's central organ, *Rabotnicheski Vestnik,* and had been instrumental in organizing the "Narrow" labor unions, had been the secretary of the Central Committee of the party since 1905. Next to them stood a group of younger men who, at the end of the world war, were all approximately forty years old. These men — Vasil Kolarov, Hristo Kabakchiev, Todor Lukanov, and others — generally had studied abroad also, but in Western Europe, chiefly Switzerland, where they had inbibed their Marxism from exiled Russian Socialists, often from Georgii Plekhanov himself.[34] Of this group, Vasil Kolarov, Blagoev's protégé, was apparently being groomed for the future leadership of the party; he was increasingly being used to represent the "Narrow" Socialists at various international meetings, and to produce some of their more important statements and proclamations. Kabakchiev, who in 1910 had become the editor of the *Rabotnicheski Vestnik,* was the party's chief intellectual and thus wrote most of the important party documents, such as proclamations, reports, leading articles for the Bulgarian and international Communist press, and justificatory pieces to be submitted to the Third International. It is interesting that Georgi Dimitrov, who later became the best-known Bulgarian Communist, overshadowing all the others in international reputation, had at this time a definitely subordinate position.[35] Unlike the other party leaders, who were all intellectuals — most often teachers or lawyers — Dimitrov was a genuine worker and proletarian. He had developed into a brilliant labor organizer at an early age, and had succeeded Kirkov as the secretary of the "Narrow" labor union federation in 1910, but, in the immediate postwar period, he does not appear to have had much voice in the formulation of party policy.

The Radomir Uprising and Its Aftermath

By early 1918, the internal situation in Bulgaria was becoming desperate. The war effort was draining the country economically, and the hardships inflicted on both the civilian population and the front-line troops were destroying morale. Bulgaria had mobilized almost 20 percent of its total population, and about two-thirds of all able-bodied males over twenty years of age.[36] Because manpower was short and many draft animals were requisitioned for the army, the area under cultivation, and consequently the production of foodstuffs, had to be considerably reduced. This difficult situation was compounded by a bad harvest in 1917 and heavy food purchases by Germany. The grave shortages resulted in a disastrous increase in prices; the general price level rose eightfold, with certain items, such as potatoes, going up by 1,200 percent. The effect on the urban lower classes, families of soldiers, and people on fixed salaries was devastating. By the spring of 1918, women were demonstrating and rioting in many towns. Even the peasantry, which at first had benefited from the high food prices, was now suffering. Despite rather frenetic financial activity during the war, and the formation of many new corporations, the tiny Bulgarian industrial base could not begin to meet the demand formerly filled by imports, and shortages of manufactured products became critical. In fact, a number of Bulgarian factories, dependent on imports of now unavailable raw materials, had to shut down. The government, unable to finance the war effort from available resources, increased the national debt and printed vast quantities of paper money, but the resulting inflation, which destroyed the value of the *leva,* only compounded the hardship.[37] The troops at the front were also beset by constant shortages of the most essential supplies, and the reports they received from their families led to a simmering discontent and an increasingly insistent demand for peace. Those who had opposed the war from the beginning now appeared to have been wise prophets, and support for their positions swelled. The "Narrow" party received additional credit for the efforts made by its parliamentary representatives to obtain government assistance for both the working-class and soldiers' families, and for their denunciations of the shortages.[38]

The circulation of the "Narrow" press and other publications increased enormously, that of the *Rabotnicheski Vestnik* rising to over twenty-five thousand.[39] In particular, "Narrow" propaganda was being widely distributed in the army, and was contributing to the erosion of morale at the front. In some cases, individual Socialists or sympathizers in uniform were turning out and distributing their own leaflets and pamphlets.[40] The government, greatly worried, began to take increasingly severe measures against the circulation of subversive literature. Increasing numbers of soldiers were arrested for passing "Narrow" periodicals, and a number of party leaders at last found themselves in jail for sedition; the prisoners included three parliamentary deputies — Dimitrov, Lukanov, and Tsiporanov — the first two being members of the party's Central Committee as well.[41]

In June 1918, the Radoslavov cabinet, which had governed Bulgaria since the beginning of the war, was forced out of office by the general unrest. In what was assumed to be a prelude to peace negotiations, Radoslavov was replaced by Alexander Malinov, leader of the Democratic party and reputedly a man of pro-Entente sympathies. Malinov approached all the political parties in an attempt to organize a government of national unity. The "Narrows," naturally, refused categorically, for Blagoev was determined to remain true to his principle of never forming alliances with the bourgeoisie.[42] The Agrarians and the "Broad" Socialists asked, as a condition for their acceptance, that peace negotiations be opened immediately and unconditionally, and that all territorial demands be renounced; Malinov was not willing to go quite that far, so these parties also remained outside the new cabinet.[43]

None of these measures succeeded in restoring the morale of the army, and discontent continued to mushroom throughout 1918. There were numerous small mutinies; some of them, notably that in the 27th Infantry Regiment, involved "Narrow" party members, whereas Agrarian Union members provided the leadership in others. Desertions increased, and government investigators found that about half of them were soldiers affiliated with either "Narrow" socialism or Agrarianism.[44] Rumors began to circulate in the army that the alliance with Germany had been for three years only, and that the troops therefore would stop fighting on 15 September, the third anniversary of the mobilization.[45]

As it happened, 15 September was the date on which the Entente forces opened their final offensive on the Salonika front. The Bulgarian line was broken, and the army began a retreat that quickly collapsed into a rout.[46] Thousands of troops refused to obey orders and streamed down the railroad lines from Macedonia through Kiustendil and from Thrace through Gorna Dzhumaia, some of them attacking the army headquarters at Kiustendil. The two railroad lines converged on the junction of Radomir, and thousands of mutineers had collected there by 25 September, threatening to march on Sofia and overthrow the government. In desperation the government assembled a delegation of parliamentarians — including Stamboliski and Daskalov, who were quickly released from jail — to go to Radomir and pacify the mutinous troops. Instead, the two Agrarians took command of the mutiny, proclaimed a republic on 27 September, and led the troops on Sofia. Met before the capital by loyal units stiffened with German troops, the rebellious forces were defeated; Stamboliski and Daskalov were forced to flee, and the monarchy was saved.[47]

Nevertheless, even before the proclamation of the Radomir republic, the government had concluded that the war was lost, and, on 26 September, it dispatched emissaries to request an armistice, which was signed on 29 September. It stipulated that the Bulgarian army was to be demobilized, Franco-British forces were to occupy strategic points throughout the country, and the Bulgarian railways were to be placed at their disposal. The disgraced King Ferdinand promptly abdicated and left the country; his son Boris was installed on the throne.

Throughout these eventful days, the "Narrow" party made no attempt whatsoever to exploit the military uprising or to precipitate a social revolution. Moreover, it actively discouraged those of its supporters who attempted to intervene in this situation. On 22 September, while the Allied breakthrough was in progress, the "Narrow" socialists held a conference in Sofia to discuss the general situation and the tasks of the party, finally settling on a program that called for the overthrow of the monarchy and the formation of a Federated Balkan Democratic Republic.[48] A few days later, Stamboliski, before setting out for Radomir, came to Blagoev to propose that they join forces to seize power and proclaim a republic. For his part, he offered to accept the entire socialist program with only one reservation: peasant smallholders were to retain ownership of their land. He pointed out — and he was probably correct — that the peasants and the Socialists together had a very good chance of making a revolution, but that if they acted separately, the situation would be hopeless. Blagoev adamantly rejected the proposal, explaining to Stambolisky that fundamental ideological differences made cooperation between their parties impossible. He told his own followers that a peasant rising against the government would merely be an internecine struggle within the bourgeoisie — an essentially reactionary phenomenon with which the proletariat could not associate itself.[49] When the miners of Pernik wanted to join in the military uprising, their union was informed that the "Narrow" Central Committee had decided that the party must not involve itself in this struggle.[50] Thereafter, the "Narrow" Socialists remained spectators while the uprising ran its course.

Some months later, Blagoev's decision to stand aside was attacked by dissidents within the party who claimed that a crucial opportunity had been missed and pointed out that deeds, not merely words, are required of a revolutionary party. In later years, the Comintern criticized the decision on the same grounds, claiming that a "revolutionary situation" had been present in Bulgaria at that moment, and that the "Narrow" socialists had failed to turn the military uprising into a social revolution because of the "insufficient Bolshevization" of their party and their failure to understand and correctly apply "Leninist principles."

Since the Comintern's criticism is universally accepted and repeated by current Bulgarian historiography,[51] it is worth noting that within a few months of the uprising, the "Narrows" offered their own explanation for their inaction. They claimed that there had been very few party members among the mutineers and that it had therefore been impossible to organize the mutiny and give it a revolutionary character. Furthermore, they argued that the party in Sofia was also quite weak at that time.[52] A later article, apparently written by Blagoev himself in the summer of 1920, offered a fuller explanation. First, the armies of the Entente had been entering Bulgaria, and would never have allowed a proletarian and peasant revolution to take place. Second, there were large German forces in Sofia, which had been sent to put down the mutinies, and while they occupied Bulgaria, no revolution was possible. Third, the "Narrow" party had very few activists available at that time, since most of the membership had been drafted, while Sofia, with its small industrial sector, lacked any kind of proletarian concentration: consequently, the party had been powerless to undertake any kind of mass action. Last, the vast majority of the mutineers were peasants who wanted only to return home. Had they captured Sofia, they immediately would have scattered back to their villages, and at best would have given power to the Agrarian Union. The article concluded that there had been no possibility of turning such a movement into a proletarian revolution of the Soviet kind.[53] Blagoev's reasons were apparently good enough for the "Narrows," because as late as 1923 Kolarov still maintained that the party had convincingly justified its attitude during the Radomir uprising.[54]

Indeed, Blagoev's arguments are quite sound, and there is no reason to suspect that any "Narrow" attempt to seize power would have been anything but a miserable failure. Even had they possessed the strength to attempt to stage-manage the situation, Bulgaria's neighbors would have combined and subjected them to the same fate as the Hungarian revolution. The peasants in uniform were indeed, in their vast majority, interested only in returning to their homes, and would not have lent themselves to any revolutionary attempt. Nevertheless, it is plausible to assume that the arguments advanced in the 1920 article carried relatively little weight in the "Narrow" party's actual decision. It appears that, at the crucial moment in 1918, the "Narrows'" beloved Marxist orthodoxy tied their hands. It probably never occurred to Blagoev that a socialist revolution could or should occur in a country in which the industrial proletariat amounted to only one percent of the population. It probably never occurred to him, either, that such a revolution could take place in Russia, and when it did, he must have assumed that it was a fluke. Moreover, in the early fall of 1918 Lenin's regime was a dubious example to imitate; the civil war was beginning to spread and it was uncertain that the isolated Bolsheviks could retain power. Blagoev accepted the idea that the war would produce socialist revolutions, but, of necessity, only in the industrialized West.[55] He believed that, at most, Bulgaria would emerge as a democratic republic, and he insisted that its installation was the business of the bourgeoisie, not of the proletariat. The later charge that the "Narrow" party was "insufficiently Bolshevized" in 1918 is correct in the sense that the Bulgarians had not accepted Lenin's variations upon Marxism, which, from their doctrinaire perspective, must have appeared heretical. For twenty years Blagoev had preached the ideological and practical impossibility of any alliance with the peasantry, arguing that the peasant hordes would swamp and corrupt the workers' movement with their conservative, petit-bourgeois ideas. This principle had become so deeply ingrained in the "Narrow" party that to jettison it in order to imitate the Russian model — even accepting the doubtful assumption that the Bulgarians were fully informed about Lenin's political tactics — would have been psychologically impossible. These attitudes would remain ingrained in the "Narrow" Socialist movement even after it had transformed itself into the Bulgarian Communist party, and would, within a few years, become the cause of real disasters instead of mere missed opportunities.

The Birth of the Bulgarian Communist Party

Despite the victory of the government forces, the Malinov cabinet was forced to reform itself in order to enhance its appeal to both the population and the victorious Allied powers. In this period of national emergency, it was desirable to have a national coalition, and the reorganized cabinet therefore included a couple of Agrarians and "Broad" Socialists. The reformed government lasted only a little over a month, however, when it was replaced by a cabinet headed by Todor Todorov, the leader of the Nationalist party. This government was composed of representatives of the "left-wing" bourgeois parties, such as the Democrats and Progressives, and also included two "Broad" Socialists and three Agrarians. Among the latter was Stamboliski, who had to be hurriedly pardoned for his participation in the military rebellion.[56] It does not appear that the "Narrow" Socialists were asked to join either cabinet, probably because the Bulgarians knew the Entente's attitude toward Lenin's government and were unwilling to risk any appearance that they were associated with it. The "Narrows" were thus spared the necessity of refusing once more to join a coalition. Moreover, the participation of the "Broads" gave the "Narrow" party a new and powerful grievance against them, particularly after the

"Broad" Socialist Pastuhov was appointed minister of the interior in May 1919. This position put him in charge of the police, and consequently, of the actions undertaken by the government against the Communists during the summer of that year.[57]

Organizational gains in the immediate postwar months must, indeed, have convinced the "Narrow" Socialists that their own way of pursuing the revolution was not only valid but successful. The situation in Bulgaria continued to favor them. The country was still in the grip of an advancing economic crisis, food shortages grew worse, and there was starvation among the urban poor. The depreciation of the *leva* and the rapid rise in prices continued unabated, the cost of living for an average family in 1919 being thirteen times higher than in 1914 and twenty times higher than in 1910. The country had suffered 115,000 killed and twice as many wounded during the war, and over 100,00 were still prisoners of war, thus greatly reducing the available labor force, especially in the villages. At the same time, the rapid demobilization of the army increased the immediate problem of unemployment. The state was further burdened with over 400,000 refugees from Macedonia and the territories that Bulgaria was forced to cede to her victorious neighbors. The peace negotiations already indicated that massive reparations would compound the other economic problems. This socioeconomic distress was accompanied by a general political unrest directed against those considered guilty of precipitating the national disasters and those who had made fortunes from the sufferings of their countrymen. Even in the villages, one constantly heard calls for the punishment of the politicians who had brought Bulgaria into the war and for the expropriation of the war profiteers.[58]

In this atmosphere, the population turned to those parties which had consistently opposed the war, and both the "Narrow" Socialists and the Agrarians thus saw dramatic increases in their popularity and following. The membership of the "Narrow" party, which in 1915 had been only 3,400, grew to 6,000 in December 1918, 10,000 by the end of January 1919, 21,000 by the end of March, and over 30,000 by the end of the year.[59] The number of party sections simultaneously rose from 104 in 1915, to 582 in March 1919, and 1,160 by the end of the year.[60] A similar rise occurred in the membership of the General Federation of Labor Unions. The membership of its thirteen unions had shrunk somewhat during the war, due to the conscription and loss in action of so many workers; at the end of 1918, they had 115 local sections with 5,700 members, compared to 6,500 in 1914. By April 1919, however, the federation had grown to 199 sections with 12,800 members, and by the end of the year it contained 31,700 members, now organized into eighteen unions.[61] To a large extent, the party must have been perplexed by the characteristics of this new membership and the problems it raised. The workers who joined the labor federation were interested primarily in their economic problems, not in revolution; indeed, only one-fifth of them went on to become party members.[62] As a result, industrial workers constituted only 10 percent of the party membership whose ranks contained one and one-half times that number of agrarian laborers and nearly twice that many artisans. Well over half the party membership belonged unequivocally to the bourgeoisie or petite bourgeoisie: professional people, intellectuals, civil servants, and small peasant landholders.[63] The social distribution of the membership by and large reflected those groups which had been most hurt by the economic situation. For instance, the salaries of civil servants, particularly in local and district administration, had fallen scandalously behind the rise in the cost of living making them probably the most hard-hit group in the country. In March 1919, the party membership included over 1,800 civil servants — 8.5 percent of the total — and they had their own union with 900 members. Similarly, "Narrow" ranks were loaded with teachers, and a teachers' union with 1,100 members was affiliated with the party. Moreover, the Labor Federation included a great many unions whose members were hardly industrial workers or proletarians: barbers, waiters, office workers, theatrical employees, tailors. Nevertheless, the party could assume that events were running in its favor. The economic situation was bound to produce a progressive proletarianization of the population; party and trade union membership would continue to grow; both groups, whatever their derivation, would be steadily indoctrinated and converted into militants; and ultimately the party would create the mass proletarian base needed for a revolutionary seizure of power.

In the meantime, apart from the organizational work necessary to incorporate their new recruits, the activities of the "Narrow" party proceeded much as before. One of its most important concerns was to obtain amnesty for all those accused or convicted of sedition in wartime, and, to this end, the "Narrows" repeatedly raised demands for amnesty in parliament, in the press, and at public meetings.[64] Propaganda campaigns against high prices, against unemployment, and against the "war criminals" and profiteers were carried on in the press and through rallies and street demonstrations.[65] Simultaneously, the party exploited the numerous labor conflicts and strikes as much as possible in order to create "class consciousness" and "worker solidarity." Of particular importance were the prolonged labor troubles at the Pernik coal mines near Sofia, in which Georgi Dimitrov was closely involved. The Pernik mines supplied the Bulgarian railways, and the railways, having been placed at the disposal of the occupation forces by the armistice agreement, had to function smoothly. The Pernik troubles therefore placed the government in a delicate political situation, leading to its heavy-handed repression of the workers. Various labor leaders, including Dimitrov, were arrested, giving the party martyrs and a useful propaganda issue.[66]

A watershed in the history of the "Narrow" Socialists was reached with the founding of the Third, or Communist, International. In January 1919, Lenin at last decided to proceed with his cherished idea of creating a new international socialist organization, and on 24 January the revolutionary groups of the world were invited to attend a founding congress in Moscow. With Russia practically isolated from the rest of the world by civil war and blockade, only delegates from the Scandinavian, German, and Austrian parties succeeded in getting through to attend the First Congress of the Comintern at the beginning of March. The other national groups were "represented" by self-appointed individuals who happened to be in Russia at the time, and who certainly had no formal mandate from the organizations for which they claimed to speak. Hristo Rakovsky, the former "Narrow" Socialist who had become a leader of the Romanian Socialist party, had been in Russia since 1917, and had become an important member of the Bolshevik party, rising to head the Soviet government of the Ukraine. For purposes of the First Congress, he undertook to represent the "Revolutionary Balkan Federation" and was allowed to vote in the names of both the "Narrow" party and the Romanian Socialist party.[67] A Bulgarian Communist Group, led by a certain Dzhorov and composed of Bulgarian expatriates in Russia, also participated in the congress, but without a vote.[68] Dzhorov's and Rakovsky's reports to the congress consisted mainly of generalities and demonstrated a lack of contact with events in Bulgaria.[69]

Already on 15 January, however, the Central Committee of the "Narrow" party had issued a proposed new party program, in which it indicated its willingness to join a future Third International.[70] It was now ready to endorse the First Congress, to adopt the platform it had elaborated, and to maintain ever after that the Bulgarians had indeed participated actively in the establishment of the Comintern. This endorsement took place at the Twenty-second Congress of the "Narrow" party, which also became the First Congress of the Bulgarian Communist party.

The "Narrow" Socialists missed the opportunity to be the first group in Bulgaria to call itself a Communist party, however. The "Broad" party contained a left wing, grouped around the periodical *Sotsialisti-*

cheski Pregled and led by the former "Narrow" Socialist Harlakov. In 1917, Harlakov went to Stockholm to endorse, in the name of this group, the position of the Zimmerwald movement.[71] In October 1918 Harlakov's followers, as well as some other left-wing groups, officially abandoned the "Broad" party, and in the beginning of April 1919 they organized a new political body under the name of the Bulgarian Workers' Communist party.[72] It was an odd body, which probably never contained more than a few hundred members, but was itself divided into two factions: an extreme faction under Deliradev, which demanded immediate direct action and formation of revolutionary soviets, and a more moderate and orthodox faction led by Harlakov himself. The new party petitioned for admission to the Third International, but was refused.[73] In the following months, it approached the Final Congress of the Bulgarian Communist party, requesting a unification of forces. The platform of Harlakov's group, however, contained a number of principles that were anathema to the "Narrows": that the situation in Bulgaria was favorable for immediate mass revolutionary action; that such action required immediate consolidation of the working class; that, to achieve this end, the labor unions should be made independent of all political parties and unified; and that the revolutionary action would best be conducted not through political parties but through apolitical peoples' soviets.[74] Since neither side would surrender its principles, the unification proposal was rejected, and Harlakov's party remained independent.

By the time, the "Narrow" Socialists were presumably properly informed as to what constituted orthodoxy in the eyes of the Comintern, since direct contact had at last been established with Russia. Revolutionary agents had been dispatched into the Balkans via Communist Hungary in March,[75] and with the reoccupation of Odessa and the Black Sea coast by the Bolsheviks, it was now possible to send couriers to Bulgaria by sea. In fact, members of the Bulgarian Communist group in Russia were sent home in time to participate in the Bulgarian party's First Congress.[76]

Frist Congress of the BKP

The First Congress, which took place on 25 to 27 May 1919, adopted a platform composed by Hristo Kabakchiev, which changed the name of the party to Bulgarian Communist party (BKP), and declared it a member of the Communist International. Incorporating the principles of the Comintern program, it recognized that the world was now passing through the imperialistic last stage of capitalism, accepted the necessity of the armed overthrow of the bourgeoisie, and proclaimed a socialist soviet republic as its goal. It added, however, that the Bulgarian Soviet Republic would become part of a Balkan Socialist Federative Soviet Republic. The party platform also stated the need for: a people's militia and a Red Army; labor legislation, such as the eight-hour day; the provision of working-class housing; general and free education; the separation of church and state; and the abolition of the national debt and of taxes paid by workers.[77] Of particular interest, however, was the section that dealt with the peasantry. The Communists proposed to nationalize all land, beginning with the expropriation of large estates. Rather contradictorily, the platform maintained that land would not be taken away from the small peasant, but immediately added that all means would be used to promote collective ownership and collective cultivation with the use of machinery. Thus, in effect, the BKP refused to make any concession to peasant views. The expropriation of large estates was an equivocal point, since hardly any existed in Bulgaria; and the talk of nationalization was bound to frighten the peasantry, which, in any case, would not distinguish between collectivization and nationalization. Since the program made no further mention of peasant demands or interests, we can conclude that the BKP had not really accepted, and possibly had not even understood, Lenin's tactics in dealing with the peasant problem and the worker-peasant alliance (*smychka*). The party would make no concessions to peasant desires, and seems to have been interested in attracting only the proletarianized peasant, who, having nothing to lose, would accept it on its own terms.

The congress also voted a resolution presented by Kolarov on the subject of Bulgaria's international political situation. This resolution called for the punishment by a national revolutionary court of the bourgeois politicians guilty of bringing Bulgaria into the war, and for the overthrow of the equally guilty monarchy. As a solution of Balkan territorial problems, the resolution called for the formation of the Balkan Federated Soviet Republic, in which disputed territories, such as Macedonia and Dobrudja, would be component republics. It insisted on the destruction of all the old parties, including the "Broad" Socialists, and of the coalition government, and called for a struggle against any attempt by the Bulgarian government to assist anticommunist intervention in Russia, Hungary, or elsewhere.[78]

The BKP thus adopted a program that explicitly recognized the existence of a revolutionary situation in Europe and that acknowledged its duty to exploit it by organizing an armed insurrection to overthrow the bourgeoisie. Putting this program into action was another matter, however. It became obvious that the party was still firmly in the hands of

Blagoev, not of Moscow, and Blagoev was determined to take no chances and to avoid provocations that might destroy the party.[79] Doubtless, his memories of the Russian revolutionary movement made him conscious of the perils of hasty action. Moreover, Blagoev was very much aware that Bulgaria was still under Entente occupation, and he said openly that the success of the revolutionary movement would depend not merely on the party, but on the occupation regime and on the development of events in other countries; he even added that socialist revolution in Bulgaria was three-quarter's dependent on the victory of socialist revolution in the major capitalist countries.[80] Thus, only lip service was paid to armed insurrection, and the tactics that the party actually decided to pursue consisted primarily of mass demonstrations, mass meetings, rallies, strikes, and similar measures.[81] Such activities were calculated to embarrass and annoy the government, and even more to educate the working class in militancy and solidarity; by provoking official reprisals, they would polarize working-class opinion, but hardly endanger the existence of the regime. In addition, the party intended to continue to exploit the parliamentary rostrum, and, to this end, the First Congress approved the policy of contesting future parliamentary elections.[82]

The BKP Expands Its Base

As a result, by the end of 1919, the BKP had organized nearly five thousand public meetings, rallies, and demonstrations, supplemented by over seven thousand meetings of local party organizations.[83] All possible issues were exploited. The old economic themes of prices, jobs, and housing were always useful, and, as the peace negotiations in Paris continued and the terms imposed on Bulgaria became known, protest against the proposed peace treaty was added to the BKP repertory.[84] As the Communist "action" multiplied, the authorities often responded with repressive violence. On 19 November, in response to a terrorist attack during a demonstration against food and fuel shortages in Plovdiv, the troops opened fire; four people were killed and nearly thirty wounded.[85]

The climax of this policy was arranged for 27 July: mass demonstrations were scheduled to occur simultaneously in all the cities of Bulgaria, and to amplify them, the party's peasant supporters were to be brought into the towns. The pretext was a protest against the government's reactionary policy on every conceivable issue; the purpose was to "take over the streets." The government, suspecting an attempt at revolution, proclaimed martial law and called out the troops and police.

Clashes took place in many cities. Throughout the country, over one hundred people were wounded, several hundred were arrested, and many were beaten by the police, thus providing the grist for further protest demonstrations.[86]

The BKP attempted through its labor unions to flood the country with a wave of systematic strikes. Since economic issues were not lacking, it managed to conduct 135 such wage conflicts in 1919, involving a total of 76,000 workers.[87] This figure, compared to the total number of union members or of industrial workers in Bulgaria, suggests that many of them were involved in several strikes during the year. Nevertheless, the average of over five hundred strikers per incident is impressive given Bulgarian conditions. The largest affair was the strike at the Pernik coal mines in July, in which seven thousand workers participated. Other large strikes occurred in the tobacco and sugar industries. The main issue, apart from higher wages, was the eight-hour day,[88] though from June onward, purely political strikes were also introduced.[89]

Beginning in the summer of 1919, the defense of Soviet Russia against intervention was an increasingly imporant issue. Under pressure from Allied powers, the Bulgarian government supplied arms and ammunition to the anti-Bolshevik forces of A. I. Denikin, sold them foodstuffs, and allowed White Russian representatives to recruit volunteers from among Russian expatriates and former prisoners of war. The BKP mounted a press campaign against this policy, raised the issue in parliament, and organized protest demonstrations.[90] There were even some attempts to sabotage the arms shipments.

Throughout this period, the Communist movement continued to recruit ever more adherents. Between May and September alone, the party increased by 11,600 members, and the Federation of Labor Unions by 12,000.[91] When the first national parliamentary elections since before the war were held in August 1919, the results reflected the realignment of political forces. The bourgeois parties retained 30 percent of the popular vote, and 65 out of 236 seats in parliament, but this vote was split between four major and a couple of minor parties; individually, these formerly powerful bodies appeared to be finished politically. The Communists received 119,000 votes — 18 percent of the total — and 47 parliamentary seats, triple the vote they received in 1914. They now definitely had the upper hand over their "Broad" Socialist rivals, who, while also improving on their 1914 vote, did not do so by nearly such a margin. They received 84,000 votes, 80 percent more than in 1914, and thereby obtained

39 seats. The largest block of votes — 27 percent — had gone to the Agrarian Union, which captured 85 seats.[92]

Stamboliski Bests the BKP

The Communists were overjoyed with their show of strength, which made them the second largest political power in the land. They were still far from being able to form a government, however. This privilege belonged to the Agrarians as the largest party, but since even they had not obtained a majority, the government would have to be a coalition. In this situation, Stamboliski approached, first of all, the Central Committee of the BKP, proposing that they share the government, and leaving the terms of the alliance open. That he was willing to deal with the Communists at all is remarkable, because any new Bulgarian government must negotiate the final terms of the peace treaty with the Allied powers, and the latter would not take kindly to any suggestion of Bolshevik influence. That he made them his first choice, illustrates Stamboliski's radicalism and his views on the most suitable ally for the peasantry. But, as in 1918, he was immediately and adamantly rebuffed. Blagoev would not budge: there would be no "opportunistic" alliances with the corrupting bourgeoisie.[93] Stamboliski then approached the "Broad" Socialists, but they made exorbitant demands for ministerial positions. He finally had to settle for an alliance with a couple of the bourgeois parties.

When, four years later, the BKP tried to justify to the Comintern the rejection of this worker-peasant alliance, it produced two reasons: first, Stamboliski had not meant what he said, because he would never compromise himself in the eyes of the Allied powers through an alliance with Communists; and second, the village bourgeoisie that controlled the Agrarian Union was no less afraid of communism than the urban bourgeoisie and therefore could never actually consent to this arrangement. But why did the BKP not accept the alliance as a tactical move? The BKP explained that even to indicate a readiness to enter a government that retained the monarchy and the present political system would confuse and dishearten the working class. At the same time, to propose an alliance on the only acceptable basis — destruction of the monarchy and establishment of a government of soviets — would be naive, since it would be equivalent to demanding that the Agrarians become Communists. In any case, to let the Agrarians govern for awhile, thereby revealing their true nature to the people, would be the best way to revolutionize the peasantry.[94]

Not content with the rebuff, the Communists over the next months proceeded to irritate Stamboliski with their strikes, demonstrations, and attacks on the peace treaty, which he was determined to conclude on the best terms possible in order to normalize Bulgaria's international position. The results of the communal elections of 7 December must have confirmed their belief in the value of these tactics. The Communist vote increased to 140,000, and the BKP found itself in control of the councils in half the district cities, over forty small towns, and sixty-five villages.[95]

The confrontation with Stamboliski came in December over the issue of the great railway strike. Like all government employees, the railway and postal workers, who belonged to the same unions, had fallen far behind in the struggle against inflation, and the possibility of a strike had been simmering since the summer. The railway men were split among three unions: six thousand in the Communist, seven thousand in the "Broad" socialist, and ten to twelve thousand in the "neutral" union. A joint strike committee had been formed in summer but fell apart because the other unions would not agree to the Communists' insistence that political demands be attached to the wage demands.[96] On 24 December, to coincide with the opening of parliament, both the BKP and the noncommunist labor unions held demonstrations in Sofia and other cities to protest high prices and shortages. The government called out the troops and the armed peasants of the Agrarian Union's Orange Guard to keep the demonstrations in check and there were many clashes. The government, probably conditioned by the events of the past months, reacted with excessive severity and began to dismiss those civil servants and railroad workers who had participated. In response, the railroad workers on 27 December declared a strike in which all three unions joined.[97]

The strike did not have a united leadership. The Communists refused to join a united strike committee, justifying their refusal with the claim that they feared behind-the-scenes maneuvers by the "opportunists."[98] The real reason was doubtless that they would be outnumbered three to one on a united committee, and that they still wanted to turn the strike into a political one by putting forth a list of political as well as economic demands. Two parallel strike committees were therefore established, and the noncommunist one, which controlled the large majority of the railroad men, consistently refused to make demands other than those for better wages and working conditions.[99]

On 29 December, however, the Communist party decided to exploit the political potential of the situation further: they called for a general strike in support of the railroad workers, and issued a strike platform that consisted of a number of purely political demands.[100] The strike itself could not have been very impressive, since only the Communist unions went out (the "Broad" Socialists and the "neutrals" refused to join them);[101] but it was combined with demonstrations and street disorders that produced considerable turmoil.[102] Stamboliski was willing to grant the workers' wage demands, which he considered just,[103] but he refused to be coerced by Communist political action and decided to break the strike by any means possible. Thousands of Orange Guards were brought into the cities to intimidate the urban proletariat, and the police and army were let loose. The arrest of most of the members of the Central Committee of the BKP was ordered; Lukanov was caught, but the others managed to go into hiding. Hundreds of lesser party workers were rounded up, however, and many local party sections were closed down. Hundreds of strikers, especially from the Communist unions, were arrested, and cases of sabotage were dealt with ruthlessly. Suspected saboteurs were shot out of hand, others were condemned to death by court-martial,[104] and some forty people were killed in clashes with troops.[105] These means broke the determination of the BKP within a week, and the general strike was called off.

The railroad strike continued for fifty-six days, but it failed to bring the total paralysis of the economy on which the strikers and the BKP had counted. Partial service was restored by using peasants who had done railroad work during the war and quickly trained engineers;[106] strikers who failed to return to work by a certain deadline were fired, more arrests were made, and the workers finally gave in at the end of February.[107] Throughout the entire episode, Stamboliski maintained firm control. He enjoyed the solid backing of his party and of the peasantry in general, and even of the Inter-Allied Commission in the Balkans, whose troops were held in readiness to assist him if needed.[108]

The Communist party was forced to recognize that it had suffered a notable defeat. Their cherished tactics failed utterly in a trial of strength; the government controlled the means of coercion and the sources of real power. The Orange Guards and the troops made them realize that they had no chance of precipitating a successful insurrection. As Kolarov later explained, it became clear that the government had the peasant masses on its side, and a proletarian revolution could not succeed if the peasants not only refused to support it but would in fact oppose it arms in hand.[109] The loss of face was painful; the Communist railroad workers' union lost more than half its membership, and two years later still numbered only 3,900.[110] The BKP could console itself only by accusing the "Broad" Socialists of having betrayed the cause and by attempting, in later years, to transform the entire railroad strike into a Communist epic. But it is noteworthy that they never again attempted a showdown with Stamboliski, and their policy became more cautious than ever.

Stamboliski saw the chance to exploit his victory to political advantage. Promptly upon the conclusion of the railway strike, he dissolved parliament and decreed new elections, hoping to capture a clear majority of seats and thereby to form a purely Agrarian cabinet. He promised to use discussion to fight Bolshevism in parliament, but elsewhere he would employ the same means that the Bolsheviks themselves used against their enemies in Russia. As soon as the dissolution was announced, therefore, he had a number of Communist ex-deputies, who had now lost their parliamentary immunity, flung in jail until the elections were over.[111] Heavy-handed terror and provocation were applied by the police and the Orange Guards. Despite all expectations, when the elections took place at the end of March 1920, the BKP had once more increased its share of the electorate, picking up 182,000 votes, an increase of 52 percent over 1919; however, since more people went to the polls this time, their share of the total vote rose only from 18 to 20 percent. On the other hand, the Agrarian share went from 27 to 39 percent. The "Broad" Socialists, meanwhile, suffered a sudden collapse: their total vote was only 55,000, considerably less than in 1919, and constituted a mere 6 percent of the total votes cast. In the final distribution of the 229 seats, the Agrarians had 110, the Communists 50, the "Broads" 9, and the various bourgeois parties 60.[112] Though Stamboliski was a little short of the 50 percent he needed to form an all-Agrarian cabinet, there would be no talk of coalition this time. Instead, Stamboliski simply invalidated thirteen of the opposition's seats, nine of which were held by Communists. The by-elections to fill them were never held. Stamboliski now had his parliamentary majority, and thereafter governed entirely through his own party. The BKP was reduced to forty-one seats, but after its recent disasters, it did not dare to make an issue of the matter.[113]

Emergence of the "Iskraists"

The pusillanimous performance of the past months precipitated the first schism in the ranks of the party — a development that had been brewing ever since the First Congress. At this time a left-wing faction in the party, led by Ivan Ganchev, the assistant editor of *Rabotnicheski Vestnik,* had protested against the party's insufficient militancy. They demanded that the party refuse to participate in elections, which were a doomed bourgeois institution, and that it pass immediately to mass revolutionary action and the formation of soviets. Blagoev heaped scorn

on these "anti-parliamentarians," and they were temporarily contained.[114] But the failure of the railway strike produced a new wave of
left-wing criticism, and in addition Blagoev was now accused of having
bungled the opportunity of the soldiers' rebellion. At the end of February 1920, Ganchev and eighty-five other "leftists" were expelled from
the BKP.[115] In September Ganchev founded the new periodical *Iskra* as
a forum for the various left-wing groups, which together perhaps numbered as many as one thousand members.[116] The left-wingers, who were
now collectively known as "Iskraists," included rebels from the BKP,
survivors from Harlakov's party, which disintegrated at the end of that
year, and dissidents from the "Broad" party. They were strongly influenced by German "left" communism, and made contacts with similar
groups in Holland and Italy. For example, the Iskraists demanded that
craft unions be replaced by factory unions, and that these organizations
become the mainspring of revolutionary action.[117] With their emphasis
on the more democratic and nonparty workers' soviets, they increasingly directed their criticism at the growing centralization and dogmati-
zation of the BKP. They derided the party's "barracks discipline,"
decried its "bureaucratized labor unions," and warned that the BKP,
with its bureaucratic organization, was destined for "external catas-
trophe and internal disintegration."[118] They were not far wrong.

The "left" Communists sent delegations to both the Second and Third
Congress of the Comintern, asking that the International either admit
the Iskraists as a separate body or force the BKP to reinstitute them and
to open the party to freer dicussion of disputed points.[119] The Comintern
rejected them both times. Therefore, at the end of 1921, the "leftists"
began planning to form a separate party, taking over the name previously used by Harlakov's group: Bulgarian Workers' Communist party.
They also planned to join the Fourth International then being mooted
by the "left" Communists of western Europe. Nothing seems to have
come of this project, however, and the "left" Communist movement in
Bulgaria disintegrated at the end of 1922 or the beginning of 1923.[120]

The Period of Consolidation, 1920–1923

Although disembarrassed of its left-wing critics, the BKP still had to
decide what tactics to pursue in the near future. The attempts to
establish Communist governments in Hungary, the Baltic States, and
Bavaria had failed; the position of Communist parties in neighboring
countries was not very encouraging; and, although the Red Army's
advance into Poland in the summer of 1920 brought temporary encour-

agement, it too was soon defeated. The tactics hitherto pursued in Bulgaria had not quite produced the desired results. The party had, for example, regarded strikes as a sort of rehearsal for revolution, preparing the workers for the seizure of political power,[121] but the rehearsal produced nothing useful. Thereafter, this tactic was progressively deemphasized. In 1920 the Communist unions engaged in only 68 wage conflicts, in which somewhat over 8,000 workers participated, an average of 125 strikers per conflict; in 1921, almost as many wage conflicts took place, but the number of participants was greatly reduced, with only about 50 strikers per incident. Moreover, the rate of failure in Communist-led strikes increased markedly. In 1919 the party claimed 57 successful and 54 partially successful strikes to 22 failures; in 1920 30 successes and 17 partial successes were balanced by 21 failures; in 1921, there were more failures than real successes: 25 of the former to 23 of the latter, and 18 partially successful.[122]

The Second Party Congress, which met on 23 May 1920, could have been expected to indicate the direction that future tactics should take. But the resolution on the position of the country and the party, presented by Kabakchiev and adopted by the congress, merely attacked the Agrarians for all their sins, and added the usual formula to the effect that the BKP, guided by its program and the principles of the Third International, would energetically pursue the struggle against the whole bourgeoisie until final victory.[123] The resolution presented in the name of the Central Committee and the Control Commission, however, proposed the following tasks: consolidation of an "iron discipline" within the party, creation of district training schools for peasant organizers, the reorganization on a more formal basis of the territorial party network, and the extension of Communist education, especially printed propaganda.[124]

These became, in effect, the tactics emphasized during the period of consolidation — a period that for all practical purposes, continued right up to the overthrow of Stamboliski in 1923. It was decided that particular care would be paid to educational and propaganda activities during this time, the theme being that the BKP was the only organized social force able to overcome the reigning anarchy, misery, and hunger.[125] Centralization was to be pursued with vigor, and dissent from party dogma rooted out. Organizational work would aim to establish not only closer control from the center but also the recruitment of more members, and especially the undermining of the Agrarians in the villages. Finally, the party would continue to contest elections, particularly local elections, and would try to utilize the communities it controlled as additional tribunes from which to propagandize its message.

The BKP and the Comintern

In July 1920, shortly after the party congress, the Second Congress of the Comintern met in Moscow. An authorized BKP delegation was dispatched this time, but its journey was not without vicissitudes. The delegation set off across the Black Sea in two fishing boats. One was blown onto the Romanian coast, and the Romanian authorities imprisoned Kolarov and Dimitrov. They were freed only after an official protest by Soviet Russia, and then returned to Bulgaria.[126] The other boat got through to Odessa, and its three passengers, Kabakchiav, Ivan Nedialkov-Schablin, and Nikola Maksimov arrived safely in Moscow.[127] Schablin had been chosen to remain behind and take over the seat reserved for the BKP on the Executive Committee of the Comintern (ECCI).

The Second Congress produced the famous Twenty-one Conditions, acceptance of which became obligatory for all Communist parties. As far as the BKP was concerned, most of these conditions implied no change in its program, because, in its opinion, it had already put them into practice, in some cases years before the conditions were formulated. It had long ago rid itself of all "reformists" and "centrists" and denounced "social patriotism"; it already controlled a large part of the trade unions in Bulgaria; it was already pursuing "democratic centralism"; it had already purged the untrustworthy and the dissident; and it already called itself Communist and enthusiastically embraced the Comintern. On two points, however, it could be faulted, and on these two issues it was finally prodded by the Comintern into some sort of reluctant action.

One of these conditions required that all Communist parties, even those which could function legally, nevertheless had to maintain a parallel clandestine organization that would, at the decisive moment, carry out the actual revolution. The BKP had hitherto operated entirely legally and openly. It understood this new requirement to mean the creation of a special underground military organization, the nucleus of which already existed. In late 1919, a commission of a few trusted Communists, some of them reserve officers, had been set up under the supervision of Party Secretary Kolarov to produce concrete proposals for military work within the party. By the spring of 1920 they had formulated a few projects and a Supreme Military Revolutionary Commission, under the leadership of Todor Atanasov, was attached to the Central Committee. After that, nothing happened for over a year, until the BKP was criticized at the Third Congress of the Comintern, in 1921, for dragging its feet on the issue. Kolarov was then instructed to expand the military organization. As a first step, the Supreme Military Commission was reorganized into several sections: armaments commission, training commission, and so on. Three-man military committees were attached to district and communal party organizations, and by the end of 1921 a start had been made in organizing secret combat groups. Various local party organizations began to stockpile weapons, and the supreme commission was also charged with the task of penetrating and subverting the armed forces. Nevertheless, it does not appear that this work was being pursued with any special vigor.[128]

The second condition on which the BKP was faulted was the requirement that Communists must make special efforts to win peasant support — to refuse to work in the countryside was deemed antirevolutionary. This requirement appeared to be specifically aimed at the Bulgarians, and the party was therefore obliged to act. Nevertheless, the issue was apparently allowed to slide until the Third Party Congress in May 1921, which appointed a commission to elaborate, for the first time, an agrarian program for the party. Blagoev himself delivered the report on the agrarian question, a measure of the importance accorded to conforming with the requirements of the Third International. He proclaimed that in a country like Bulgaria, wih its large peasant population, the task of the revolutionary proletariat would be much more difficult if these peasant masses were not first recruited for communism, or if they decided to oppose it. He presented the Leninist analysis of the division of the peasantry into classes, stressing the need to separate the "middle" peasants from the large landowners and to neutralize them, while utilizing every means to organize the rural proletarians, semi-proletarians, and "small" peasants.[129] The congress adopted a resolution recognizing the revolutionary potential of the smallholder. Specifically, the BKP proposed to liberate the peasants from "debts to usurers, banks, and the state," from "exploitation by merchants"; it promised that after its seizure of power it would give every support to peasant cooperatives and collectives; and it declared that all land was public property and would therefore be handed over to those who worked it.[130]

This last point appeared to indicate that, whatever Leninist tactics might be, the BKP did not really intend to change its ways. Its goal was still nationalization, with no concessions to petit-bourgeois property consciousness. That the pursuit of this policy would frighten the smallholders who formed the vast majority of the Bulgarian peasants and make life difficult for party organizers in rural areas, did not seem to matter.[131] Many of the other features of the BKP's agrarian program were equally dogmatic and wrongheaded. The point about usury had long been dear to Blagoev's heart. Twenty years before, usury had indeed been a scourge, but since then a combination of factors — including peasant cooperatives, war and postwar inflation, which allowed the peasant to pay off his debts in depreciated *leva,* and the government credit that was extended particularly under Stamboliski's regime —had greatly alleviated the problem.[132] The division of peasantry into classes was done rather arbitrarily on the basis of data from 1910. Owners of less than 7½ acres were considered semi-proletarians; 7½ to 25 acres, "small" peasants; 25 to 50 acres, "middle" peasants; 50 to 250 acres, "large" peasants; over 250 acres, landowners. Blagoev estimated the number of landholders at about 640,000, divided into 44 percent semi-proletarians, 41 percent "small," 11 percent "middle," and 4 percent "large" peasants, and 0.2 percent landowners.[133] These statistics appear to be incorrect per se,[134] for Blagoev seems to have underestimated both the total number and the proportion of dwarf and small landholdings. Furthermore, the postwar distribution differed even more sharply from his figures: most of the large estates had been in Dobrudja, which was no longer part of Bulgaria, whereas the territories annexed in the Balkan Wars added a large number of very small properties. Blagoev also estimated about 160,000 hired laborers, that is, rural proletarians. He was always prone to overestimate the number of wage earners in Bulgaria, and in this case his figure included many younger sons of landed peasants or owners of dwarf holdings working for extra income and therefore hardly apt to consider themselves landless. Most important, these categories hardly corresponded to the Bulgarian peasant's view of himself. The attempt to apply mechanically a Russian model in a situation where landowning nobles and great estates did not exist and the vast majority of peasants thought of themselves as small proprietors was not likely to prove easy.

The BKP and Stamboliski's Agrarian Union

The whole problem of Leninist tactics and of the worker-peasant alliance immediately raised the question of the relationship between the BKP and the Agrarians. Blagoev does not appear to have asked himself how the Communist party was to "neutralize" the middle peasant if it treated the Agrarians as a bourgeois party and continued to attack it so vehemently. The concept of the worker-peasant alliance logically implied the formation of an alliance, however expedient and temporary, with the party that the peasants considered their own political organization.[135] Two factors appear to have influenced the BKP's stance. First, the election returns of the previous two years seem to have given the Communists the impression that their vote would continue to increase at the same rate until they had captured the majority of the electorate: they therefore saw no need for compromise with any other political party. Apparently, the Communists failed to recognize that, although their vote increased, the Agrarian vote increased much more rapidly, and that, whereas their share of the total electorate had hardly increased, the Agrarian share had increased significantly. Thus, it was the Agrarians who appeared to be making the inroads into other parties' constituencies. The new Communist votes seem to have come partly from people who had not voted previously, and largely from former "Broad" Socialist electors, but certainly not from the ranks of the Agrarians.

Second, the "Leninist" classification of the peasantry seems to have convinced the Communists that about 88 percent of the rural population consisted of proletarians or semi-proletarians. In addition, they appear to have thought that a little propaganda would make the peasants conscious of this reality, and that they would then of necessity join the ranks of the proletarian party on its own terms. If this scenario were realized, the Agrarians would ultimately be left with only the nonproletarian part of the rural population, that is, about 12 percent of the total. Such a decline Agrarian fortunes would negate the reasons for considering a deal with them, and time, Communist education, and organizational work would take care of any remaining problems. In the terminology that was to become more familiar a year later, the Communists felt that there was no need for a "united front from above" with the Agrarians, and that what they were doing already amounted to a "united front from below." This construction dovetailed with their assumption that the Agrarian Union was a bourgeois party — a party therefore controlled by the rich peasants, who were deceiving and exploiting the smallholders. The BKP resolutely closed its eyes to the fact that "semi-proletarians" and "small" peasants constituted the bulk of Agrarian membership and the real base of Stamboliski's support.[136]

Since the railway strike, the Communists seemed to consider Stamboliski not only their chief political rival but also their chief enemy; indeed, their most venomous words were now directed against Stamboliski rather than against the reactionaries and capitalists. This attitude stemmed, of course, from resentment at Stamboliski's victory over them and from their misinterpretation of the nature of the Agrarian Union, but it was also a result of the Communists' need to convince themselves that their interpretation of the rural situation was correct, that Stamboliski would not be able to counter its historical inevitability. After all, were Stamboliski able to hold on to his peasant constituency, the new Communist tactics would prove as futile as the old ones; the

BKP would never be able to create the mass base it needed among the peasantry.

This attitude led to ludicrous misrepresentations of Stamboliski's political role. For instance, when Dragiev was expelled from the Agrarian Union, Blagoev wrote that it was because he had tried to protect the "small" peasant and the democratic character of the party and that he had been ejected by the *kulaks* and village bourgeoisie, by Stamboliski;[137] the interpretation of this episode in current Bulgarian historiography is precisely the reverse. Kabakchiev wrote that Stamboliski represented the ruthless and insolent nouveau-riche village bourgeoisie that had profiteered from high food prices and wanted to continue using state power for further enrichment.[138] He was also called the Balkan Mussoloni.[139] Just as dogmatic and negative was the Communist attitude toward the reforms that Stamboliski attempted to introduce. The Second Party Congress declared that these reforms were intended to deceive the peasant masses and turn them from the true path, and the Third Party Congress branded them "counterrevolutionary." They were attacked by the party press and by its representatives on the floor of parliament. The land reform was criticized for its defects, the compulsory labor law was described on the one hand as a reactionary utopia and on the other as disguised military conscription, while the grain trade law was denounced as an attempt to produce great profits for the village bourgeoisie.[140] The only two reforms that the Communist deputies did not vote against were the progressive income tax and the law on the expropriation of buildings.

Organization of the BKP in a Period of Consolidation and Propaganda

The major triumph of the Communist party in 1920 was the splitting of the "Broad" Socialist party and the annexation of its left wing. A moderate left group within the "Broad" party, led by the former "Narrow" Socialists Georgi Bakalov and Nikola Sakarov (who stood somewhat to the right of Harlakov), had, since the end of the war, become unhappy both with the "Broad" policy of participation in the government and with the division of the Socialist movement in Bulgaria. After the election of 1919, they began to publish the periodical *Borba* as a forum for their ideas.[141] During the railway strike, they exerted increasing pressure on the "Broad" party leadership to find a compromise that would allow unification with the BKP. At the end of February 1920, the "Broad" party council finally issued a declaration rejecting any collaboration with the government and declaring its readiness to unite with the Communists.[142] The *Borba* group thought that the rest would be simple, because, in their opinion, the two parties differed only on tactics, not on doctrine. On 29 February, however, the BKP replied that the "Broads" would have to accept the concepts of proletarian dictatorship, the soviet system, and the Third International before unification could take place.[143] The left-wingers now demanded that their party call a congress to endorse these points, and furthermore, that this congress take place before the date of the BKP's Second Congress. The "Broad" leadership, however, scheduled the party congress for late June, and managed to secure enough right-wing delegates to prevent the acceptance of the Communist conditions. Although the congress voted to leave the Second International, it did not agree to enter the Comintern immediately, instead asking the BKP to compromise on the conditions for unification. By this time, the Second Congress of the Comintern had taken place, and the Communists replied that they were bound by the Twenty-one Conditions and could not compromise. Moreover, they demanded that the "Broad" party clean out all the "social traitors" who had supported the war or held ministerial posts, a demand that appeared to end any possibility of unification.[144] In September, therefore, Bakalov called a conference of the "Broad" leftists, and began to organize an exodus. In October and November Bakalov led two large batches of "Broad" Socialists into the ranks of the Communist party, and at the beginning of 1921, Sakarov followed suit.[145] The BKP gained perhaps two thousand new members. More important from the Communist viewpoint was the fact that the "Broad" labor union federation was dominated by Bakalov's followers. At the end of September, they led most of their union membership to join the Communist General Federation of Labor Unions.[146] The "Broad" party thus lost practically all its working-class adherents, while the Communists came to control the bulk of the unionized workers in Bulgaria. The "Broad" Socialists never recovered from this blow; in Communist eyes, they were now completely finished as a political force and could safely be ignored.

At the same time, the small Communist Workers' party of Harlakov had been negotiating for admission into the BKP. In 1920 a party congress voted for unification, but the leadership, unwilling to give up its extreme leftist convictions, dragged out negotiations, finally breaking them off in August. Thereupon their party fell apart, and most of the membership joined the Communists, although Harlakov himself did not.[147]

In May 1920, the Communist party consisted of 1,259 local organizations with somewhat over 35,000 members. In May 1921, the membership had risen to slightly over 37,000 and by the end of 1921 it amounted to slightly under 38,000, organized in 1,512 local sections.[148] A slow but steady increase in membership was thus occurring during this period of consolidation.

The territorial organization of the party had now become more complex. At its head were the seven members of the Central Committee, which decided policy by unanimous vote. The Central Committee's composition had hardly changed for a decade, and still included Blagoev, Kolarov, Kabakchiev, Dimitrov, Lukanov, and Nikola Penev. At the Second Party Congress, however, Tina Kirkova was elected to replace her dead husband, George. The Central Committee was assisted by a secretariat, containing a large number of sections for special purposes, headed by Kolarov. "Democratic centralism" was now well ingrained in the party, and all sections and affiliated organizations were fully subordinated to the Central Committee. The growth of the party and its progressive bureaucratization made it necessary to introduce an intermediate layer, the district committees, which served as limbs of the Central Committee to control propaganda and agitation and to coordinate organizational and educational activities. Below them were the local organizations of the towns and villages. The local committees themselves had various sections for special tasks, such as propaganda and agitation among women, youth sections, aid to "victims of capitalist dictatorship," committees of proletarian culture, publications committees, and so on. The local organizations of the larger urban centers had the special task of ensuring that the weaker groups in the countryside remained under the "favorable influence of the mass Communist movement of the big cities."[149]

An important arm of the party was its parliamentary section, of which Blagoev remained chairman until his death. The Communist parliamentary deputies were tightly organized into a group under a special statute, to ensure that they would carry out the party's precise instructions.[150] Quite a number of control devices had been developed in other areas of the party structure in the name of democratic centralism, including: a Control Commission to supervise the Central Committee in the interests of the party congress; ten traveling party inspectors, each with his own district, to check up on local organizations for the Central Committee; and various other supervisory bodies. Also important were the party school in Sofia, which put party agitators through a one-month course, and the schools that trained candidates for party membership.

The General Federation of Labor Unions was still the most important of the organizations associated with the party. In May 1920 it comprised eighteen unions with 31,700 members.[151] By May 1922, with the addition of the Teachers' Union, which had formerly been attached directly to the Central Committee, the federation included nineteen unions, but even after the absorption of the "Broad" trade unions, its membership inexplicably dropped to 29,100.[152] This situation caused considerable concern, because the trade unions now contained fewer members than the party itself. From the orthodox Communist viewpoint, this anomalous situation meant the labor organizations would never be able to carry out the role usually assigned them in a period of armed revolution. Also worrisome was the small percentage of union members who also joined the party. The membership of the latter contained relatively few workers; although about 30 percent of party members were classified as wage earners, the number of real industrial workers was much lower, perhaps as low as 5 or 6 percent.[153]

The party controlled a large number of other "front" organizations. The League of Bulgarian Communist Youth grew rapidly from 2,500 members in the spring of 1920 to over 13,000 at the end of 1921, split evenly between urban and rural groups. The Central Women's Committee had 72 sections and 4,200 members by the end of 1921. A Communist League of War Invalids was converted in 1921 to the Union of War Victims; its membership rose from 1,100 to 4,200. Various lesser groups existed for engineers, students, and reserve officers.[154]

The workers' cooperative society *Osvobozhdenie,* founded in 1919, had 57,000 members at the beginning of 1922, and consisted of over one hundred branches and agencies. Its publishing division printed all the party publications; its construction division constructed party buildings. It maintained connections with both the Russian and American labor movements.

Of some interest was the so-called Central Emigrants' Committee, founded in April 1920 to organize the refugees from Macedonia and from the territories lost by Bulgaria after the First World War. It was estimated that at least 400,000 such refugees were in Bulgaria, and, as disgruntled victims of nationalism, they should have presented a fertile field for Communist propaganda. In reality, despite a promising start, this organization had relatively little success. After the war, the Macedonian refugees, although confused and stunned by the course of events, began to divide once more into the two traditional camps; the Supremists, who wanted the annexation of Macedonia by Bulgaria, and the Federalists, who wanted an independent or autonomous Macedonia. The former were essentially hangers-on of military and conservative-chauvinistic circles in Bulgaria; but the latter should have been widely attracted by the Communist concept of a federal Balkan republic. In March 1919, the chief surviving Federalists formed a committee in Sofia; early in 1920, this committee split, and one wing under the veteran guerrilla leader Dimo Hadji Dimov joined the Communists. But the emigrants' committee was not the best possible body to deal with the Macedonian question because it lumped Thracian and Dobrudjan refugees, whose only interest was direct reannexation to Bulgaria, with Macedonians whose interest was in federation. As a result, the committee suffered from conflicting viewpoints, and never had much success with its recruiting. At the end of 1921, it had only 1,300 members.[155]

As befitted the period of propaganda and consolidation, the BKP paid a great deal of attention to its publishing activity, which was under the supervision of a special commission attached to the Central Committee. It issued a vast number of periodicals. The party's central organ, *Rabotnicheski Vestnik,* was a daily with a circulation varying from twenty-five to thirty-five thousand. The weekly *Selski Vestnik* was aimed at the peasantry and ran editions of eight to twelve thousand. *Novo Vreme,* edited by Blagoev, was the party's theoretical organ, issued biweekly in over five thousand copies. A women's weekly, *Ravenstvo (Equality)* had an edition of ten thousand; *Mladezh,* a weekly for the Youth League, fourteen thousand; *Cherven Smiakh,* a humoristic weekly, four thousand; *War Victim,* biweekly, four thousand. There were special periodicals for the Macedonians, the Turks, the Armenians, the Jews, and the American Communists in Bulgaria. Furthermore, a vast number of pamphlets and over sixty books poured from the presses. How was such an extensive publishing program financed? Since the reported income of the party and the unions was not large, and since the *leva* was not worth much one is led to conclude that the reports of huge subsidies from Soviet Russia, purportedly twenty million *leva* annually,[156] were probably correct.

The BKP successfully contested the local elections of October 1920, capturing control of 22 town and 65 village councils. When the government dissolved these bodies and held new elections in February 1922, the Communists won control of 9 cities and 113 village communes. Over 3,600 communal and 115 provincial councillors throughout the country were party members. To coordinate party efforts in this special sphere, the Central Commission for Communal Representation was attached to the Central Committee. It gave directives to Communist councillors, who were expected to organize themselves into formal and disciplined groups and to carry out party instructions. The Communist-controlled councils were to be used as forums for party ideology and, if possible, as weapons in the class war, although it is not clear that any specifically Marxist results were achieved in this way.[157]

This massive organizational activity gives the impression that throughout 1921, despite its revolutionary verbiage, the party was becoming something of an institution. Its structures and activities were giving employment to many and keeping a great many more busy. It was developing hierarchies, and a certain smugness, so that Comintern prodding was now required to remind it of its duties. Its activities were conducted through an army of agitators who organized public meetings and rallies, distributed literature, and supervised the work of local party groups. Clashes with the authorities still occasionally resulted in casualties, as during the rallies celebrating the anniversary of the Russian revolution.[158] In May 1921, a school children's procession in Sofia was bombed by unknown perpetrators, but rumor attributed the deed to the Communists; in the ensuing rioting, a couple of Communist clubs were attacked, and one was burned, giving rise to a BKP propaganda campaign against "fascist" organizations.[159]

The major issue during the spring of 1921 was the formulation of a party agrarian program. This matter was finally settled at the Third Party Congress, held in May 1921, which also increased the membership of the Central Committee to nine. Soon thereafter, a delegation of nineteen party leaders traveled to Moscow to attend the Third Congress of the Comintern in June 1921. This congress condemned left-wing extremism and also recommended a policy of "united front" with noncommunist workers' organizations. This Comintern directive made no difference to the work of the BKP, however. It still could not convince itself that the Agrarian Union was a working class and not a bourgeois organization, and it considered the "Broad" Socialists moribund and not worth an alliance. Consequently, finding no partner for a united front on the Bulgarian scene, it went on as before. Bulgarians now participated more extensively in the work of the Comintern. Kolarov had been elected a member of the ECCI at the Third Congress,[160] and earlier that year Kabakchiev had served as an emissary to, and had helped to split, the Italian Socialist party.

In the second half of 1921, the Bulgarian Communists found themselves involved in several lines of agitation concerned with Soviet Russia. Already in December 1920, the Soviet government had proposed the estabishment of diplomatic relations with Bulgaria, and the BKP had taken up this cause both in and out of parliament. The Bulgarian government, however, thought it prudent to refuse. In the summer of 1921, the great famine began in the Volga provinces, and the Soviet government appealed for international help. In August, the BKP began a campaign to collect relief funds for Russia, and ultimately raised about three million *leva* in money and grain. Twelve hundred carloads of foodstuffs were dispatched to the famine areas.[161] Although this aid amounted to only about $21,000, it was the eleventh largest amount raised — less than in the United States, the Scandinavian countries, or England, but more than was raised in Germany.[162] In 1921, the defeated White Russian army of General Wrangel, evacuated from the Crimea, was confined in refugee camps on the Turkish Straits. The Allied powers and various organizations made efforts to find refuge for them in various European countries.[163] Stamboliski agreed, more or less unwillingly, to accept a contingent, and the first shiploads of Cossacks began to arrive in Bulgaria at the end of summer.[164] By December, some 35,000 had entered the country.[165] Since they arrived in uniform, in organized units, and with their weapons, the Soviet government was concerned that Bulgaria might be used as the base for a new counter-revolutionary attempt, especially as the most important of Wrangel's commanders had also come to Bulgaria. The Communist party immediately launched a propaganda campaign, holding rallies and demonstrations, protesting in parliament and in the press against the presence of these White Russians. They demanded that the Russians be disarmed and preferably deported, and certainly that their leaders immediately be banished from Bulgaria. At the same time, the question of relations with Soviet Russia was raised once more. Although this campaign mounted throughout the fall and winter of 1921, its climax really came several months later, in March 1922.[166]

It is also interesting to note that, throughout this period, the Bulgarian Communists remained probably the most assiduous advocates of Balkan federation, in the ultimate form of a federated Soviet Republic, and in the meantime, of a federation of Balkan Marxist parties. The attempts at such federation had begun in 1910, when a Balkan Socialist Conference was held in Belgrade. The policy of consultation between the parties did not get far before the outbreak of the Balkan Wars, but afterward the "Narrow" Socialists cooperated with other Balkan Socialist parties in their attempts to keep their countries out of the war, and to propagate the idea of federated republic as the solution for their national problems. A second Balkan Socialist Conference, which they attended, was held at Bucharest in July 1919. Thereafter, the idea lay dormant; but after the war, the BKP included the concept of the federated Balkan republic, now in its soviet form, in its program, and constantly propagandized this point. In January 1920, in the midst of the turmoil of the railway strike, the BKP assembled a new Balkan Socialist Conference in Sofia, attended by the Greek, Romanian, and Yugoslav Socialist parties, at which the Balkan Communist Federation was founded and proclaimed a section of the Third International.[167] The central office of the federation was established in Bulgaria, and the BKP thereafter held a leading role in the new organization. A second meeting took place in Vienna in February 1921,[168] producing a draft program for the federation,[169] but this meeting really marks the beginning of the takeover by agents from Moscow. A third meeting, scheduled to take place in Sofia in May, was aborted because most foreign delegates could not get to Bulgaria.[170] A congress of Balkan Communist labor unions was also held in Sofia in November 1920, presided over by Dimitrov,[171] but nothing much evolved from it. To the Bulgarian party, Balkan federation had appeared to provide a new approach to solving the previously insoluble territorial problems that beset the region. Once the idea became a mere tool of the Comintern, however, its promise withered.

NOTES

1. The Norwegian Socialist party also joined the Third International in a body, but soon discovered that it had made a mistake and quit.

2. The best account in English of the early history of Bulgarian socialism is Joseph Rothschild, *The Communist Party of Bulgaria* (New York, 1959). From the Bulgarian viewpoint, see *Istoriia na Bulgarskata komunisticheska partiia* (Sofia, 1969), and *Materiali po istoriia na Bulgarskata komunisticheska partiia (1885–1925 g.)* (Sofia, 1968). For a brief "Broad" socialist version, see T. Tchitchovsky, *The Socialist Movement in Bulgaria* (London, 1931).

3. *Bol'shaia sovetskaia entsiklopediia* (1st ed.), vol. 6, p. 732.

4. Rothschild, *Communist Party*, p. 46.

5. Alexander Gerschenkron, "Some Aspects of Industrialization in Bulgaria, 1878–1939," in Gerschenkron, *Economic Backwardness in Historical Perspective* (Cambridge, Mass., 1962), p. 433.

6. *Bol'shaia*, vol. 6, pp. 715–716.

7. Rothschild, *Communist Party*, p. 26; D. Blagoev, *Prinos kum istoriiata na sotsializma v Bulgariia* (Sofia, 1949), p. 542.

8. V. Kolarov, "Taktika Bolgarskoi kommunisticheskoi partii v svete soby-tii," *Kommunisticheskii internatsional*, year 6, no. 1 (1924): 590.

9. G. C. Logio, *Bulgaria — Problems and Politics* (London, 1919), p. 77; Rothschild, *Communist Party*, pp. 58–60.

10. Rothschild, *Communist Party*, pp. 44–45.

11. Ibid., p. 45.

12. Hr. Kabakchiev, B. Boshkovic, H. D. Vatis, *Kommunisticheskie partii Balkanskih stran* (Moscow, 1930), pp. 80, 82.

13. I. Samuilov, *Verbindungen der bulgarischen Revolutionare mit Lenin* (Sofia, 1970), pp. 95–98.

14. Kabakchiev, Boshkovic, Vatis, *Kommunisticheskie partii*, pp. 75–80; *In-*

ternatsionalizmut na BKP — Dokumenti i materiali — 1892–1944 (Sofia, 1974), pp. 78–82, 86–87; *Istoriia*, pp. 173–188.

15. *Internatsionalizmut na BKP*, pp. 86–87; *Materiali po istoriia BKP*, p. 138.
16. Kabakchiev, Boshkovic, Vatis, *Kommunisticheskie partii*, pp. 81–83.
17. *Internatsionalizmut na BKP*, pp. 82–85; *Materiali po istoriia BKP*, pp. 137–138.
18. Rothschild, *Communist Party*, p. 64.
19. *Internatsionalizmut na BKP*, pp. 86–87; S. Blagoyeva, *Dimitrov* (New York, 1934), p. 27. Dimitrov was recognized by the Romanian police as a known subversive, and expelled from the country.
20. O. H. Gankin and H. H. Fisher, *The Bolsheviks and the World War* (Stanford, 1940), p. 341; Samuilov, *Verbindungen*, pp. 110–111; Kabakchiev, Boshkovic, Vatis, *Kommunisticheskie partii*, pp. 84–89.
21. *Materiali po istoriia na BKP*, pp. 139–140.
22. Ibid., pp. 141–142; Samuilov, *Verbindungen*, pp. 112–113.
23. B., "Kommunisticheskoe dvizhenie v Bolgarii," *Kommunisticheskii Internatsional*, year 2, no. 11 (14 June 1920), p. 1823.
24. *Bol'shaia sovetskaia entsikopediia* (3d ed.), vol. 12, p. 183.
25. Rothschild, *Communist Party*, pp. 69–72.
26. H. Hristov, *Revoliutsionnata kriza v Bulgaria prez 1918–1919* (Sofia, 1957), p. 95; F. Hristov, *Voenno-revoliutsionnata deiinost na Bulgarskata komunisticheska partiia 1912–1944 g.* (hereafter: Filiu Hristov), p. 48.
27. *Internatsionalizmut na BKP*, p. 87.
28. Samuilov, *Verbindungen*, p. 118; Rothschild, *Communist Party*, p. 68.
29. Gankin and Fisher, *The Bolsheviks*, pp. 656–663.
30. Ibid., p. 675.
31. *Istoriia na BKP*, pp. 204–205. Blagoev called them "our comrades."
32. *Internatsionalizmut na BKP*, pp. 92–93.
33. Ibid., pp. 93–94; Hristov, *Revoliutsionnata kriza*, pp. 122ff.
34. Cf. *Septemvriiskoto vustanie 1923 — Entsiklopediia* (Sofia, 1973), pp. 30–31, 136, 155, 178.
35. Rothschild, *Communist Party*, p. 50.
36. Hristov, *Revoliutsionnata kriza*, pp. 12–13.
37. Ibid., pp. 13–20, 25–39; Logio, *Bulgaria*, pp. 195–230.
38. Hristov, *Revoliutsionnata kriza*, pp. 51–60.
39. Filiu Hristov, p. 48.
40. Hristov, *Revoliutsionnata kriza*, pp. 145–148.
41. *Istoriia na BKP*, p. 205; *Georgi Dimitrov — biografiia* (Sofia, 1972), p. 112.
42. Logio, *Bulgaria*, p. 192.
43. K. Todorov, *Balkan Firebrand* (Chicago, 1943), p. 99; Tchitchovsky, *Socialist Movement*, p. 21.
44. Hristov, *Revoliutsionnata kriza*, pp. 224–232.
45. Ibid., p. 217; J. Buchan, ed., *The Nations of Today, — vol. 12: Bulgaria and Romania* (London, 1924), p. 137.
46. A. Palmer, *The Gardeners of Salonika* (New York, 1965), pp. 199–232.

47. The Radomir rebellion is discussed in Hristov, *Revoliutsionnata kriza*, pp. 250–323. See also K. Kozhuharov, *Radomirskata republika* (Sofia, 1948), and M. A. Birman, "Narastanie revoliutsionnoi situatsii v Bolgarii v 1917–1918 gg. i Vladaiskoe vosstanie," *Uchennye zapiski Instituta slaviano-vedeniia*, vol. 5 (Moscow, 1952), and for an earlier account, G. Damianov, *Istinata za Septemvriiskata revoliutsiia v Bulgariia* (Sofia, 1921). Cf. Todorov, *Balkan Firebrand*, pp. 101–103.

48. Hristov, *Revoliutsionnata kriza*, p. 300.

49. Ibid., pp. 304–305; F. Borkenau, *World Communism* (Ann Arbor, Mich., 1962), pp. 96–97.

50. Hristov, *Revoliutsionnata kriza*, p. 292.

51. Cf. G. Dimitrov, *Political Report Delivered to the V Congress of the Bulgarian Communist Party* (Sofia, 1949), pp. 13–14; *Materiali po istoriia BKP*, pp. 145–146; H. Hristov and K. Vasilev, *Dimitur Blagoev* (Sofia, 1956), pp. 89–90; and many others.

52. "Deiatel'nost' sotsial-demokratii (testniakov) v Bolgarii," *Kommunisti-cheskii internatsional*, year 1, no. 5 (Sept. 1919), p. 745.

53. B., "Kommunisticheskoe dvizhenie," pp. 1822–1823.

54. Kolarov, "Taktika Bolgarskoi," p. 590.

55. Hristov and Vasilev, *Dimitur Blagoev*, p. 83; *Materiali po istoriia BKP*, pp. 144–145; *Istoriia na BKP*, p. 212.

56. *The Times* (London), 25 October 1918, p. 5, and 16 December 1918, p. 7.

57. Ibid., 27 May 1919, p. 11.

58. Hristov, *Revoliutsionnata kriza*, pp. 331–336; Hr. Kabakchiev, "Bolgariia posle imperialistichesko voiny," *Kommunisticheskii internatsional*, year 2, no. 14 (6 November 1920), pp. 2821–2824; "Die Preisesteigerung in Bulgarien," *International Pressekorrespondenz* (hereafter: *Inprekorr*), vol. 1, no. 7 (8 October 1921), p. 62; Buchan, *Bulgaria and Romania*, p. 152.

59. *Istoriia na BKP*, p. 214; Hristov, *Revoliutsionnata kriza*, p. 417; B., "Kommunisticheskoe dvizhenie," p. 1823; *Bol'shaia sovetskaia entsiklopediia* (1st ed.), vol. 6, p. 732.

60. Ibid.

61. G. Dimitrov, "The Trade Union Movement in Bulgaria," *Inprecorr*, vol. 3, no. 8 (1 March 1923), p. 124; N. Schablin, "Otchet Bolgarskoi kommunisticheskoi partii," *Kommunisticheskii Internatsional*, year 2, no. 15 (20 December 1920), p. 3417; Hristov, *Revoliutsionnata kriza*, p. 417; *Georgi Dimitrov —biografiia*, p. 119.

62. Hr. Kabakchiev, "Die wirtschaftliche Krisis und die Gewerkschaften in Bulgarien," *Inprekorr*, vol. 1, no. 38 (20 December 1921), p. 342.

63. Hristov, *Revoliutsionnata kriza*, p. 417.

64. *Istoriia na BKP*, p. 215; Hristov, *Revoliutsionnata kriza*, pp. 352–354.

65. *Istoriia na BKP*, pp. 215–216; *Materiali po istoriia BKP*, pp. 165–167; Hristov, *Revoliutsionnata kriza*, pp. 344–352, 355–363, 368–369.

66. Hristov, *Revoliutsionnata kriza*, pp. 370–381; Blagoyeva, *Dimitrov*, pp. 30–32; *Georgi Dimitrov — biografiia*, pp. 123–125; *Vasil Kolarov: Important Dates of his Life and Career* (Sofia, 1948), p. 27.

67. J. A. Rothschild, *Rakovski* (St. Anthony's Papers on Soviet Affairs no. 18, Oxford, 1955), p. 15; J. W. Hulse, *The Forming of the Communist International* (Stanford, 1964), pp. 18, 63; Borkenau, *International Communism*, p. 162. Cf. the list of delegates to the First Congress of the Communist International, *The Communist International*, year 1, no. 1 (1919), pp. 131–132.

68. *The Communist International*, loc. cit., Hulse, *Forming of the Communist International*, p. 63.

69. St. Dzhorov, "Bolgariia i imperialisty," *Kommunisticheskii Internatsional*, year 1, no. 1 (1 May 1919), pp. 127–128; Hr. Rakovsky, "Doklad tov. H. Rakovskogo," ibid., year 1, no. 4 (1 August 1919), pp. 555–556.

70. *Materiali po istoriia BKP* (1955 edition), p. 156; *Istoriia na BKP*, pp. 216–217.

71. I. N. Iotov, *Tsentrizmut v bulgarskoto sotsialistichesko dvizhenie 1905–1920* (Sofia, 1969), pp. 272–273; Gankin and Fisher, *The Bolsheviks*, pp. 668n, 675.

72. Iotov, *Tsentrizmut*, p. 316.

73. *Bol'shaia sovetskaia entsiklopediia* (First edition), vol. 6, p. 734.

74. Iotov, *Tsentrizmut*, pp. 399–400.

75. Hulse, *Forming of the Communist International*, p. 41.

76. Dechev, "Tesniaki — Bolgarskaia kommunisticheskaia partiia," *Kommunisticheskii Internatsional*, year 1, no. 4 (1 August 1919), pp. 499–500.

77. "Programnaia deklaratsiia Bolgarskoi Kommunisticheskoi partii (sotsialistov 'tesniakov' sektsii Kommunisticheskogo Internatsionala)," *Kommunisticheskii International*, year 1, no. 4 (1 August 1919), pp. 503–512; *Bulgarskata komunisticheska partiia v rezoliutsii i resheniia na kongresite, konferentsiite i plenumite na TsK* (hereafter: *BKP v rezoliutsii*), vol. 2: *1919–1923* (Sofia, 1957), pp. 5–19.

78. "Rezoliutsiia s'ezda Bolgarskoi kommunisticheskoi partii o polozhenii Bolgarii," *Kommunisticheskii Internatsional*, year 1, no. 5 (September 1919), pp. 689–695.

79. Hristov and Vasilev, *Dimitur Blagoev*, p. 94; Rothschild, *Communist Party*, p. 99.

80. Hristov and Vasilev, loc. cit.; "Deiatel'nost' sotsial-demokratii," p. 747.

81. A. Avramov, *Politicheskata strategiia i taktika na BKP, 1903–1923* (Sofia, 1974), p. 170.

82. *BKP v rezoliutsii*, pp. 35, 129; *Istoriia na BKP*, p. 223; G. Georgiev, *80 godini pod chervenoto zname* (Sofia, 1971), pp. 165–166.

83. *Bol'shaia sovetskaia entsiklopediia* (1st ed.), vol. 6, p. 732; Avramov, *Politicheskata strategiia*, pp. 170–171.

84. Hristov, *Revoliutsionnata kriza*, pp. 455–460.

85. Ibid., pp. 474–476. The Communists claim that a member of the dissident "left" faction of the party was responsible for the attack; cf. S. S. Arabadzhiev, *Borbata na BKP (ts) protiv "levite" komunisti, 1919–1921* (Sofia, 1964), p. 139.

86. Hristov, *Revoliutsionnata kriza*, pp. 440–448; B., "Kommunisticheskoe dvizhenie," p. 1824; *Istoriia na BKP*, p. 225.

87. Avramov, *Politicheskata strategiia,* pp. 171–173; Dimitrov, "The Trade Union Movement," p. 124.

88. Hristov, *Revoliutsionnata kriza,* pp. 438–439.

89. Ibid., pp. 439–440.

90. Ibid., pp. 477–497; B., "Kommunisticheskoe dvizhenie," p. 1826; Ts. Nikolov, *Deinostta na BKP v zashtita na Suvetska Rusiia 1917–1922* (Sofia, 1960), pp. 67–79.

91. Hristov, *Revoliutsionnata kriza,* p. 471.

92. S. G. Evans, *A Short History of Bulgaria* (London, 1960), p. 159; Hristov, *Revoliutsionnata kriza,* p. 449; B., "Kommunisticheskoe dvizhenie," pp. 1824–1825.

93. Hristov, *Revoliutsionnata kriza,* p. 461; *Istoriia na BKP,* p. 227; Tchitchovsky, *Socialist Movement,* p. 23; Avramov, *Politicheskata strategiia,* p. 181.

94. Kolarov, "Taktika Bolgarskoi," pp. 592–594.

95. B., "Kommunisticheskoe dvizhenie," p. 1826; *Materiali po istoriia BKP,* p. 178; Buchan, *Bulgaria and Romania,* p. 152.

96. Hristov, *Revoliutsionnata kriza,* pp. 524–525.

97. Ibid., pp. 523–535; B., "Kommunisticheskoe dvizhenie," p. 1827; *Istoriia na BKP,* p. 231; *Georgi Dimitrov — biografiia,* pp. 128–130.

98. Kolarov, "Taktika Bolgarskoi," p. 596.

99. Hristov, *Revoliutsionnata kriza,* pp. 534–535, 566–569; *Georgi Dimitrov — biografiia,* p. 133.

100. Hristov, *Revoliutsionnata kriza,* pp. 535–536.

101. Ibid., pp. 536–537; B., "Kommunisticheskoe dvizhenie," p. 1828; *Georgi Dimitrov — biografiia,* p. 131. To understand the real magnitude of the "general" strike, one must remember that the total membership of the Communist unions at the end of 1919 was about 30,000. Of these, the railwaymen, some 6,500, were already on strike, as well as about 3,000 coal miners, who had walked out in sympathy; however, the latter, whose employment depended on the functioning of the railways, would have been laid off anyway for the duration. Of the remainder, some, such as tobacco workers and agricultural laborers, would have been seasonally unemployed in December, and others, such as barbers and theatrical employees, had little economic impact. The order for a general strike would thus pull out only about 15,000–16,000 additional employees, which, in a population of nearly 5 million, would hardly amount to economic paralysis.

102. *The Times,* 6 January 1920, p. 9, and 8 January 1920, p. 9; *The New York Times,* 6 January 1920, p. 1.

103. Todorov, *Balkan Firebrand,* p. 128; *The Times,* 21 January 1920, p. 11.

104. *The Times,* 8 January 1920, p. 9, and 10 February 1920, p. 11; *The New York Times,* 25 January 1920, p. 10; Hristov, *Revoliutsionnata kriza,* pp. 554–556.

105. *The Times,* 13 March 1920, p. 15.

106. Todorov, *Balkan Firebrand,* p. 128; *The Times,* 21 January 1920, p. 11, 13 March 1920, p. 15 and 21 April 1920, p. 15.

107. The railway and general strikes are discussed in detail by Hristov, *Revoliutsionnata kriza*, pp. 498–573. N. Penev's very brief *Razvoi na profdvizhenieto na zheleznicharite v Bulgariia* (Sofia, 1949) contains a few pages on the railway strike. A contemporary, but very propagandistic, analysis was Georgi Dimitrov's *Ot porazhenie kum pobeda*, reprinted in vol. 5 of his *Suchinennia* (Sofia, 1952), pp. 289–344. Cf. Todorov, *Balkan Firebrand*, pp. 126–132; *Istoriia na BKP*, pp. 231–235; G. Dimitrov, "Professional'noe dvizhenie v Bolgarii," *Kommunisticheskii Internatsional*, year 2, no. 15 (20 December 1920), pp. 3308–3310.

108. *The New York Times*, 22 January 1920, p. 3.

109. Kolarov, "Taktika Bolgarskoi," pp. 598–599.

110. "The Situation in the Communist Party of Bulgaria," *Inprecorr*, vol. 2, no. 71 (23 August 1922), p. 533. In 1921, it had also been "about 4,000" (*Bol'shaia sovetskaia entsiklopediia* (1st ed.), vol. 6, p. 736). This compares to 6,372 in December 1919 (Dimitrov, "Professional'noe dvizhenie," p. 3306). The membership of the miners' union also fell from 3,300 to 2,400 during the same period.

111. *The Times*, 21 April 1920, p. 15; Buchan, *Bulgaria and Romania*, pp. 152–153.

112. Buchan, *Bulgaria and Romania*, p. 153n1; *The Times*, 5 April 1920, p. 7, and 6 April 1920, p. 9. The higher "Broad" Socialist vote in 1919 doubtless reflected the fact that at that time they controlled the Ministry of the Interior, with its traditional potential for distorting the electoral process; the 1920 returns would reflect their true position more accurately.

113. Buchan, *Bulgaria and Romania*, p. 153; Schablin, "Otchet Bolgarskoi," p. 3417.

114. Hristov and Vasilev, *Dimitur Blagoev*, pp. 93–94.

115. Arabadzhiev, *Borbata na BKP*, pp. 30–31.

116. Ibid., p. 32.

117. Ibid., pp. 96–98.

118. Ibid., pp. 135–136.

119. Ibid., pp. 155–159.

120. Ibid., pp. 34, 161–162.

121. Avramov, *Politicheskata strategiia*, pp. 172–173.

122. Dimitrov, "The Trade Union Movement," p. 124.

123. "Rezoliutsiia II s'ezda Bolgarskoi kommunisticheskoi partii po voprosu o vnutrennem i mezhdunarodnom polozhenii strany i Kommunisticheskoi partii," *Kommunisticheskii Internatsional*, year 2, no. 2, no. 5 (20 December 1920), pp. 3333–3338.

124. *BKP v rezoliutsii*, pp. 85–108; *Istoriia na BKP*, pp. 244–245; Georgiev, *80 godini*, p. 173.

125. Avramov, *Politicheskata strategiia*, pp. 177–178.

126. Blagoyeva, *Dimitrov*, pp. 34–35; *Vasil Kolarov*, p. 35; D. Blagoev, "Au Comité Executif et a toutes les sections de l'Internationale Communiste," *Bulletin communiste*, year 1, no. 25 (19 August 1920), pp. 14–15.

127. *Istoriia na BKP*, p. 246.

128. Filiu Hristov, pp. 72–77, 86–91; and *passim*; A. Nedialkov, *Voennata organizatsiia na BKP 1920–1923, passim*.

129. *BKP v rezoliutsii*, pp. 136–137; Avramov, *Politicheskata strategiia*, pp. 190–191; Georgiev, *80 godini*, pp. 181–182; *Istoriia na BKP*, pp. 181–182; *Istoriia na BKP*, pp. 251–252.

130. *BKP v rezoliutsii*, pp. 140–142.

131. D. Tishev, *Za suiuz mezhdu rabotnitsite i selianite (1917–1923 g.)*, pp. 77–78.

132. Gerschenkron, "Some Aspects of Industrialization," pp. 222–223.

133. Tishev, *Za suiuz*, p. 60.

134. BKP manipulations of statistics on the peasant problem are sometimes difficult to unravel, since an article in the *Rabotnicheski vestnik* of 21 April 1921 implies that in 1908 there were only 495,000 farms, of which 81 percent belonged to "dwarf" and "small" peasants; but it also speaks of 933,000 "properties", of which 87 percent are "dwarf" and "small" (*Rabotnicheski vestnik: izbrani statii i materiali, vol. 2: 1904–1923* [Sofia, 1965], pp. 76–78). Moreover, the author of the article, Trifon Saraliev, puts the "dwarf" holding limit at five acres, thus placing only 16 percent of farms but 45 percent of all "properties" in that category, whereas Blagoev at the Third Party Congress put the limit at 7½ acres. However, both Blagoev and Saraliev derive their data from the same source, Kiril Popov's *Stopanska Bulgariia prez 1911* (Sofia, 1916). Logio, (*Bulgaria*, p. 95), also using Popov's statistics, quotes the figure of 933,000 as denoting landholders. The *Bol'shaia sovetskaia entsiklopediia* (1st ed., vol. 6, p. 722), quoting data from the Bulgarian statistical annual for 1924, gives 703,000 landholders for 1908, of whom 81 percent are "dwarf" and "small"; using the five-acre criterion, it shows 32 percent in the "dwarf" category. It must be remembered that since 1900, the availability of land per capita of the population engaged in agriculture steadily declined, and, consequently, so did the average size of farms (Gerschenkron, "Some Aspects of Industrialization," p. 220–225).

135. Tishev, *Za suiuz*, pp. 66–74.

136. Hristov, *Revoliutsionnata kriza*, p. 408n4. The BKP position was justified by Kabakchiev in "Pered perevorotom v Bolgarii," *Kommunisticheskii Internatsional*, year 5, no. 26/27 (24 August 1923), pp. 7300–7323, and by Kolarov in "Taktika Bolgarskoi," pp. 602–606.

137. "Kommunistichesko dvizhenie," p. 1820. For a current reinterpretation, see Avramov, *Politicheskata strategiia*, pp. 167–168, or *Materiali po istoriia BKP*, pp. 195–196.

138. Hr. Kabakchiev, "Bourgeois Reaction in Bulgaria," *Inprecorr*, vol. 3, no. 31(13) (5 April 1923), pp. 252–253.

139. E. Arnoldi, "The Political Situation in the Balkans," *Inprecorr*, vol. 3, no. 43(25) (14 June 1923), p. 414.

140. Avramov, *Politicheskata strategiia*, pp. 192–193.

141. Iotov, *Tsentrizmut*, p. 323; V. Kolarov, "Kommunisticheskaia partiia i politicheskoe polozhenie Bolgarii," *Kommunisticheskii Internatsional*, year 3, no. 17 (June 1921), pp. 4343–4344.

142. Iotov, *Tsentrizmut*, pp. 334–335.

143. Ibid., p. 351; Kolarov, "Taktika Bolgarskoi," p. 606.
144. Iotov, *Tsentrizmut,* pp. 355–373; Kolarov, "Kommunisticheskaia partiia," *loc. cit.*
145. Iotov, *Tsentrizmut,* pp. 390–398; Kolarov, "Taktika Bolgarskoi," pp. 606–607; Avramov, *Politicheskata strategiia,* p. 157.
146. Iotov, *Tsentrizmut,* pp. 388–389; *Georgi Dimitrov — biografiia,* pp. 142–144; Dimitrov, "The Trade Union Movement," p. 124; Avramov, *Politicheskata strategiia,* p. 158; *Istoriia na BKP,* p. 248.
147. Iotov, *Tsentrizmut,* pp. 404–408; Avramov, *Politicheskata strategiia,* pp. 157–158; Arabadziev, *Borbata na BKP,* p. 37; Kolarov, "Kommunisticheskaia partiia," *loc. cit.*
148. Schablin, "Otchet Bolgarskoi," p. 3417; "The Situation in the Communist Party," p. 533.
149. A detailed outline of the party organization was given by Kolarov in "Kommunisticheskaia partiia," pp. 4337–4343, and a briefer one by Schablin, "Otchet Bolgarskoi," pp. 3417–3422.
150. The "Instruction to the Parliamentary Group of the BKP," showing the methods by which the party controlled its parliamentary deputies, is given in *Kommunisticheskii Internatsional,* year 3, no. 17 (June 1921), pp. 4347–4350.
151. Schablin, "Otchet Bolgarskoi," p. 3417.
152. "The Situation in the Communist Party," p. 533.
153. Kabakchiev, "Die wirtschaftliche Krisis," p. 342.
154. Schablin, "Otchet Bolgarskoi," p. 3417; Kolarov, "Kommunisticheskaia partiia," *loc. cit.*; "The Situation in the Communist Party," p. 533; *Materiali po istoriia BKP,* p. 198.
155. J. Swire, *Bulgarian Conspiracy* (London, 1939), p. 145; M. Apostolski, et al., *Istorija na Makedonskiot narod* (Skopje, 1969), vol. 3, pp. 176–181.
156. Todorov, *Balkan Firebrand,* p. 179. In 1919 the total income of the BKP had been 2.22 million *leva*; of the labor union federation, 2.04 million; and of the *Robotnicheski vestnik,* 329 thousand *leva* (Schablin, "Otchet Bolgarskoi," pp. 3417–3419). At the 1919 rate of exchange of approximately 20.6 *leva* to the dollar, this was equivalent to $108,000, $99,000, and $16,000, respectively. The party agitation and propaganda budget was 185 thousand *leva* ($9,000). In 1921, the income of the labor union federation was about the sme, 2.05 million *leva* (Dimitrov, "The Trade Union Movement," p. 124), but because of the precipitous drop of the *leva,* this was now worth only about $20,000. The figures for the party income are not available, but it is reasonable to assume a comparable decline in its dollar value, somewhat mitigated by a 20 percent increase in membership, and therefore in dues. In view of the rising volume of party publications, and the rising price of largely imported paper, the tale of Soviet subsidies is credible. In 1921–22, 20 million *leva* would have roughly equaled $150,000.
157. *Istorii na BKP,* p. 247; Kolarov, "Kommunisticheskaia partiia," *loc. cit.* See also *Obshtinskata politika na BKP 1891–1944* (Sofia, 1974), pp. 102–313, *passim.*

158. Kolarov, "Kommunisticheskaia partiia," p. 4346; *Georgi Dimitrov —biografia*, p. 145.

159. *The Times*, 27 May 1921, p. 10; *Istoriia na BKP*, p. 256; Avramov, *Politicheskata strategiia*, p. 186.

160. *Vasil Kolarov*, pp. 36–37.

161. *Istoriia na BKP*, pp. 257–258; V. Kolarov, "Die Hilfe der bulgarischen Arbeiterschaft für die Hungernden in Sowjetrussland," *Inprecorr*, vol. 1, no. 43 (31 December 1921), pp. 377–378; Nikolov, *Deinostta na BKP*, pp. 122–150.

162. W. Münzenberg, "Relief for Russia," *Inprecorr*, vol. 2, no. 32/33 (5 May 1922), p. 259.

163. Nikolov, *Deinostta na BKP*, pp. 157–159; G. I. Cherniaevski and D. Daskalov, *Borbata na BKP protiv Vrangelistkiia zagovor* (Sofia, 1964), pp. 20–26; A. B-off (Bashmakov), *Memoire sur le mouvement communiste en Bulgarie durant les années 1921 et 1922* (Belgrade, 1923?), pp. 23–25; 82–85.

164. *The Times*, 22 September 1921, p. 9; Cherniaevski and Daskalov, *Borbata na BKP*, p. 26.

165. *The Times*, 3 December 1921, p. 9; Cherniaevski and Daskalov, *Borbata na BKP*, pp. 35–37.

166. Cherniaevski and Daskalov, *Borbata na BKP*, pp. 39–67; B-off, *Memoire*, pp. 28–29.

167. "Rezoliutsii Balkanskoi sotsialisticheskoi konferentsii," *Kommunisticheskii Internatsional*, year 2, no. 12 (20 July 1920), pp. 2215–2218.

168. "Soveshchanie Balkanskoi kommunisticheskoi federatsii," *Kommunisticheskii Internatsional*, year 3, no. 17 (June 1921), pp. 4333–4336.

169. "Proekt ustava Balkanskoi kommunsticheskoi federatsii," ibid., pp. 4335–4338.

170. Kolarov, "Kommunisticheskaia partiia," pp. 4344–4346.

171. Ibid.; *Georgi Dimitrov — biografiia*, pp. 140–141.

List of Contributors

Banac, Ivo — Associate Professor of History, Yale University
Fowkes, Frank Benjamin Michael — Senior Lecturer, Polytechnic Institute of North London, England
Karchmar, Lucien — Associate Professor of History, Queens University, Canada
Király, Béla K. — Professor Emeritus, Director Brooklyn College Program on Society in Change
Pastor, Peter — Professor of History, Montclair State College
Szafar, Tadeusz — Visiting Scholar, Russian Research Center, Harvard University

BROOKLYN COLLEGE STUDIES ON SOCIETY IN CHANGE
Distributed by Columbia University Press (except No. 5)
Editor-in-Chief: Béla K. Király

No. 1
Tolerance and Movements of Religious Dissent in Eastern Europe.
Edited by B. K. Király, 1975. Second Printing, 1977.

No. 2
The Habsburg Empire in World War I. Edited by R. A. Kann, B. K.
Király, P. S. Fichtner, 1976. Second Printing, 1978.

No. 3
*The Mutual Effects of the Islamic and Judeo-Christian Worlds: The East
European Pattern.* Edited by A. Ascher, T. Halasi-Kun, B. K. Király,
1979.

No. 4
Before Watergate: Problems of Corruption in American Society. Edited
by A. S. Eisenstadt, A. Hoogenboom, H. L. Trefousse, 1978.

No. 5
East Central European Perceptions of Early America. Edited by B. K.
Király and G. Barany. Lisse, The Netherlands: Peter de Ridder Press,
1977. Distributed by Humanities Press, Atlantic Highlands, N.J.

No. 6
The Hungarian Revolution of 1956 in Retrospect. Edited by B. K.
Király and P. Jónás, 1978. Second Printing, 1980.

No. 7
Brooklyn U.S.A.: Fourth Largest City in America. Edited by R. S.
Miller, 1979.

No. 8
János Decsy. *Prime Minister Gyula Andrássy's Influence on Habsburg Foreign Policy during the Franco-German War of 1870–1871,*
1979.

No. 9
Robert F. Horowitz. *The Great Impeacher: A Political Biography of
James M. Ashley,* 1979.

* * *

Nos. 10–19
Subseries: War and Society in East Central Europe (see Nos. 30–40
also)

No. 10 — Vol. I
Special Topics and Generalizations on the Eighteenth and Nineteenth Centuries. Edited by B. K. Király and G. E. Rothenberg, 1979.

No. 11 — Vol. II
East Central European Society and War in the Pre-Revolutionary Eighteenth Century. Edited by G. E. Rothenberg, B. K. Király, and P. Sugar, 1982.

No. 12 — Vol. III
From Hunyadi to Rákóczi: War and Society in Late Medieval and Early Modern Hungary. Edited by J. M. Bak and B. K. Király, 1982.

No. 13 — Vol. IV
East Central European Society and War in the Era of Revolutions, 1775–1856, edited by B. K. Király, forthcoming.

No. 14 — Vol. V
Essays on World War I: Origins and Prisoners of War. Edited by P. Pastor and S. R. Williamson, Jr., 1982.

No. 15 — Vol. VI
Essays on World War I: Total War and Peacemaking, A Case Study on Trianon, Edited by B. K. Király, P. Pastor, and I. Sanders, 1983.

No. 16 — Vol. VII
Thomas M. Barker. *Army, Aristocracy, Monarchy: Essays on War, Society, and Government in Austria, 1618–1780,* 1982.

No. 17 — Vol. VIII
The First Serbian Uprising, 1804–1813. Edited by Wayne S. Vucinich, 1983.

No. 18 — Vol. IX
Kálmán Janics. *Czechoslovak Policy and the Hungarian Minority, 1945–1948,* 1982.

No. 19 — Vol. X
At the Brink of War and Peace: The Tito–Stalin Split in Historic Perspective. Edited by Wayne S. Vucinich, 1983.

*   *   *

No. 20
Inflation Through the Ages: Economic, Social, Psychological, and Historical Aspects. Edited by N. Schmukler and E. Marcus, 1982.

No. 21
Germany and America: Essays on Problems of International Relations and Immigration. Edited by H. L. Trefousse, 1980.

No. 22
Murray M. Horowitz. *Brooklyn College: The First Half Century*, 1982.

No. 23
Jason Berger. *A New Deal for the World: Eleanor Roosevelt and American Foreign Policy*, 1981.

No. 24
The Legacy of Jewish Migration: 1881 and Its Impact. Edited by D. Berger, 1982.

No. 25
Pierre Oberling. *The Road to Bellapais: Cypriot Exodus to Northern Cyprus*, 1982.

No. 26
New Hungarian Peasants: An East Central European Experiment with Collectivization. Edited by Marida Hollós and Béla Maday, 1983.

No. 27
Germans in America: Aspects of German-American Relations in the 19th Century. Edited by E. Allen McCormick, 1983.

No. 28
Linda and Marsha Frey. *A Question of Empire: Leopold I and the War of the Spanish Succession, 1701–1705*, 1983.

* * *

Nos. 30–40
Subseries: War and Society in East Central Europe (continued; see Nos. 10–19 also)

No. 30 — Vol. XI
The First War Between Socialist States: The Hungarian Revolution of 1956 and Its Impact. Edited by Béla K. Király, Barbara Lotze, and Nándor Dreisziger, 1983.

No. 31 — Vol. XII
István I. Mocsy. *The Effects of World War I: The Uprooted: Hungarian Refugees and Their Impact on Hungarian Domestic Politics: 1918–1921*, 1983.

No. 32 — Vol. XIII
The Effects of World War I: The Class War after the Great War: The Rise of Communist Parties in East Central Europe, 1918–1921. Edited by Ivo Banac, 1983.

No. 33 — Vol. XIV
The Crucial Decade: East Central European Society and National Defense: 1859–1870. Edited by Béla K. Király, forthcoming.

No. 34 — Vol. XV
The Political Dimensions of War in Romanian History. Edited by Ilie Ceausescu, 1983.

No. 35 — Vol. XVI
East Central European Classics of Military Thought: Rákóczi and Kosciuszko. Edited by B. K. Király, E. Halicz, and J. Decsy, forthcoming.

3 1543 50115 6758

335.430947
E27o

832589

DATE DUE

AG 17 '84			

WITHDRAWN

Cressman Library
Cedar Crest College
Allentown, Pa. 18104

DEMCO

3 1543 50115 6758

335.430947
E27o

832589

DATE DUE

AG 17 '84			

WITHDRAWN

Cressman Library
Cedar Crest College
Allentown, Pa. 18104

DEMCO